The
Clear and Simple
Thesaurus
Dictionary

Revised!
Fully Updated!

by Harriet Wittels and Joan Greisman

Grosset & Dunlap

How to Use *The Clear and Simple Thesaurus Dictionary*:

Entry word. All entry words are listed in alphabetical order.

Definition. Sometimes a word can have more than one definition.

Part of speech. The common parts of speech are: verb, noun, pronoun, adjective, adverb, conjunction, and interjection.

Sample sentence

aid 1. *noun* help, relief, assistance, service, support *People have generously given aid to those who lost their homes in the flood.* 2. *verb* help, assist, support, serve *Mountain rescuers, aided by dogs, found the climbers alive.* hinder

Sometimes a word can be used as a different part of speech.

If a word has an antonym (an opposite meaning), it will appear in gray type.

Cover Design: Traci Levine   Interior Design: Susan LiCalsi Design

GROSSET & DUNLAP
Published by the Penguin Group
Penguin Group (USA) Inc., 375 Hudson Street, New York, New York 10014, U.S.A.
Penguin Group (Canada), 90 Eglinton Avenue East, Suite 700, Toronto, Ontario, Canada M4P 2Y3
(a division of Pearson Penguin Canada Inc.)
Penguin Books Ltd, 80 Strand, London WC2R 0RL, England
Penguin Ireland, 25 St Stephen's Green, Dublin 2, Ireland (a division of Penguin Books Ltd)
Penguin Group (Australia), 250 Camberwell Road, Camberwell, Victoria 3124, Australia
(a division of Pearson Australia Group Pty Ltd)
Penguin Books India Pvt Ltd, 11 Community Centre, Panchsheel Park, New Delhi - 110 017, India
Penguin Group (NZ), Cnr Airborne and Rosedale Roads, Albany, Auckland 1310, New Zealand
(a division of Pearson New Zealand Ltd)
Penguin Books (South Africa) (Pty) Ltd, 24 Sturdee Avenue, Rosebank, Johannesburg 2196, South Africa
Penguin Books Ltd, Registered Offices: 80 Strand, London WC2R 0RL, England

Library of Congress Cataloging-in-Publication Data

Wittels, Harriet.
The clear and simple thesaurus dictionary / by Harriet Wittels and Joan Greisman.—Rev., Fully updated.
p.cm.
ISBN 0-448-44309-0 (pbk.)
1. English language—Synonyms and antonyms—Dictionaries, Juvenile. I. Greisman, Joan. II. Title.
PE1591.W67 2006
423'.1—dc22
2005036313
10 9 8 7 6 5 4 3 2 1

A

a *adjective and indefinite article* one, any *I'd like a book about soccer.*

abandon *verb* 1. desert, forsake, leave *Eddie abandoned his friends when they needed him most.* (*Slang*—turn one's back on, wash one's hands of, pull out on) 2. cancel, discontinue, leave undone *She had to abandon her plans for a vacation.* 3. give up, evacuate, withdraw from *Thousands had to abandon their homes during the flood.* keep, fulfill, stay with

abandoned *adjective* deserted, empty *The abandoned house was torn down to make way for a playground.*

abashed *adjective* ashamed, embarrassed, confused, bewildered, humiliated, mortified, disconcerted *You needn't feel abashed—it was just a mistake.*

abate *verb* reduce, lessen, end, stop, decrease *The rain shows no sign of abating.* increase

abbey *noun* convent, monastery *We toured Westminster Abbey while we were in London.*

abbot *noun* monk, friar *The abbot oversaw the building of a new monastery.*

abbreviate *verb* shorten, condense, cut, reduce *"Mister" is usually abbreviated "Mr."* lengthen, increase ABBREVIATION *noun E-mail messages are full of new abbreviations such as "CU."*

abdicate *verb* renounce, give up, resign, relinquish, abandon, quit, surrender *The king plans to abdicate in favor of his son. The leaders have abdicated their responsibility.* retain

abdomen *noun* belly, stomach *Jack was admitted to the hospital with pains in his abdomen.* (*Slang*—tummy) ABDOMINAL *adjective His abdominal injury isn't serious.*

abide *verb* endure, tolerate *I can't abide his bad attitude.*

abide by *verb* accept, obey *Jill promised to abide by her parents' decision.*

ability *noun* power, skill, talent, competence, capacity, capability, aptitude *My mom has the ability to make everyone laugh.* (*Slang*—know-how) inability

abject *adjective* wretched, miserable *Millions of people worldwide live in abject poverty.*

able *adjective* skillful, capable, having power, competent, qualified *He's an able songwriter and musician.* incapable ABLY *adverb The team is ably led by its quarterback.*

abnormal *adjective* irregular, eccentric, odd, unnatural *She was treated for an abnormal heartbeat. Dan refused to explain his abnormal behavior.* normal

aboard *adverb* onboard, on (or into) a ship or train or airplane *He lives aboard his yacht.*

abode *noun* dwelling, residence, home, quarters, housing *Welcome to our humble abode!*

abolish *verb* eliminate, destroy, put an end to, do away with, wipe out *Slavery was abolished by the 13th Amendment to the U.S. Constitution.* retain ABOLITION *noun The group's goal is the abolition of nuclear weapons.*

abominable *adjective* hateful, disgusting, very unpleasant, dreadful, awful, horrible *The crimes he committed were abominable. This is abominable weather for flying.* pleasant

abound *verb* be plentiful, be well supplied, be filled, teem, overflow *The national park abounds with wildlife, including bears, deer, and fish.* scarce

about 1. *preposition* concerning, of *The story is about a young wizard and his friends.* 2. *adverb* nearly, almost, approximately *It's about time for dinner.*

about to *preposition* ready to, on the point of *We're about to leave—are you coming?*

above 1. *adverb* overhead, up, aloft *The clouds above darkened.* 2. *preposition* higher than, over *Your games are on the shelf above the TV.* 3. more than, greater than *The school's enrollment will be above 600 in a couple of years.* below

abreast 1. *adverb* alongside, side by side, beside *The path is too narrow for us to walk four abreast.* 2. *adjective* informed, up-to-date *Jennifer likes to keep abreast of the newest fashions.*

abridge *verb* make shorter, abbreviate, condense, contract, reduce, cut, compress *I've read only an abridged version of her autobiography.* lengthen, increase

abroad *adverb* overseas, away, outside one's country *Sandy's mom goes abroad on business.*

abrupt *adjective* 1. sudden, hasty *The car in front of us came to an abrupt halt.* 2. rude, short, curt *He sometimes seems abrupt and unfriendly.*

abscess *noun* sore, inflammation, wound *The abscess in my tooth really hurts.*

absence *noun* 1. nonappearance, truancy, the state of being away *After an absence of three weeks, he's back in the game.* 2. lack, deficiency, want, nonexistence *Darkness is the absence of light.* presence

absent *adjective* 1. away, gone, missing *Jane is absent today with the flu.* 2. lacking, deficient *Real feeling is absent in the author's work.* present ABSENTEE noun and adjective *She was an absentee from the awards show this year. The absentee votes haven't been counted yet.*

absolute *adjective* complete, perfect, thorough, entire, total, essential, positive, supreme *Egyptian pharaohs had absolute power over the people.* partial ABSOLUTELY adverb *Are you sure this is absolutely necessary?*

absorb *verb* 1. take in, soak up, suck up *The field's black soil absorbed the sun's heat.* 2. engross, fascinate, engage *Janet was so absorbed in the book that she forgot the time.* ABSORBENT noun *Cotton is a very absorbent material.* ABSORPTION noun *She's studying the ozone's absorption of ultraviolet light.*

absorbing *adjective* fascinating, interesting, engrossing, engaging *Gardening can be an absorbing hobby.*

abstain *verb* refrain, give up, do without *Yasmin's family abstains from food and drink between sunrise and sunset during the holy month.* pursue

abstract *adjective* 1. not concrete, apart from any object or real thing *Softness is abstract, but a kitten's fur is real.* concrete 2. difficult, hard to understand *Any explanation of how a computer works is too abstract for me.* clear

absurd *adjective* foolish, ridiculous, not true, unbelievable, impossible, ludicrous *He told us an absurd story about seeing an elephant in his backyard.* meaningful, sensible ABSURDITY noun *Danny realized the absurdity of his own superstitions.* ABSURDLY adverb *She wore absurdly old-fashioned ruffled blouses.*

abundance *noun* great, plenty, large amount, great quantity, profusion (*Slang*—gobs, tons) *We grew an abundance of vegetables in our garden.*

abundant *adjective* plentiful, ample, enough, sufficient *The farmers had abundant rainfall this season.* insufficient, not enough

abuse *verb* 1. mistreat, hurt, harm, injure *We have laws that punish people who abuse animals.* appreciate, take care of 2. misuse, take advantage of *The official abused his power for personal gain.*

academy *noun* school, college, educational institution *She plans to attend the naval academy.*

accelerate *verb* hasten, speed up, quicken, hurry (*Slang*—floor it, step on it) *The car behind us accelerated to pass. The company has made changes that should accelerate its growth.* slow down, delay ACCELERATION noun *This car's acceleration is impressive.*

ACCELERATOR noun *I put a new graphics accelerator in my computer for playing video games.*

accent *noun* 1. emphasis, stress on syllables of a word, tone, inflection *The accent in the noun "produce" is on the first syllable, but in the verb, the accent is on the second syllable.* 2. pronunciation, way of speaking *He speaks with a New England accent.*

accept *verb* 1. take what is offered, consent to, agree to *Mrs. Daniels won't accept late homework. She accepted my apology.* 2. welcome, approve of *I was immediately accepted by her friends.* 3. believe, take as true (*Slang*—buy, swallow) *Dad wouldn't accept my excuse.* reject, deny, dissent ACCEPTANCE noun *The plan hasn't met with much acceptance.*

acceptable *adjective* satisfactory, adequate, suitable, appropriate, tolerable *There's no acceptable explanation for her absence.*

access *noun* entry, way of approach *No one has access to this computer without a password.* ACCESSIBLE adjective *The beach is accessible by a narrow path.*

accessory *noun* addition, extra, supplement *The store sells fashion accessories such as hats, gloves, and scarves.* 2. assistant, accomplice, partner *Doris was charged with being an accessory to the crime.*

accident *noun* 1. mishap, unfortunate event *We were late because of an accident on the freeway.* 2. chance, unplanned event (*Slang*—fluke) *What a lucky accident that we saw you today!*

accidental *adjective* unplanned, unintentional, chance *I'm sorry I broke the dish—it was accidental.* ACCIDENTALLY adverb *Carol accidentally erased the file from the disk.*

acclaim *verb* applaud, approve, hail, praise *The movie was acclaimed worldwide and won many awards.* disapprove, reject

accommodate *verb* 1. hold, have room for *The new airplane will accommodate 555 passengers.* 2. help, assist, serve, oblige *The day-care center accommodates working parents.*

accommodations *noun* housing, lodging, place to stay *The price includes airfare and hotel accommodations.*

accomplice *noun* partner in crime (*Slang*—sidekick) *Both he and his accomplice are in jail.*

accomplish *verb* do, carry out, finish, complete, fulfill, perform, achieve, realize *We accomplished a lot in a short time.* neglect

accomplishment *noun* achievement, attainment, success, triumph *You can be proud* *of your accomplishments.*

accord *noun* agreement, conformity, harmony *The nations were in accord that peace is the goal.* disagreement ACCORDINGLY adverb *When you behave like an adult, you will be treated accordingly.*

according to *preposition* 1. as said by, on the authority of *According to the weather report, it's going to snow.* 2. in agreement with, conforming to, relative to, in line with *The pay varies according to the work you do.*

account *noun* 1. story, description, tale, statement *She's written an account of her travels in Asia.* 2. list, sum, record *Keep an account of your expenses, and we'll pay you back.*

account for *verb* explain, justify, answer for *We have to account for our absences from school. The charity accounts for all the money it spends.*

accumulate *verb* collect, store up, increase, assemble, gather, amass *Dust had accumulated on all the furniture. She's accumulated a large credit-card debt.* ACCUMULATION noun *He straightened up the accumulation of papers on his desk.*

accuracy *noun* correctness, precision, exactness *The golfer drove the ball with amazing accuracy.*

accurate *adjective* correct, exactly right, perfect, okay, all right *David keeps accurate records of what he's spent.* wrong

accuse *verb* blame, charge, impeach, indict, denounce *The army accused him of disobeying orders. Are you accusing me of lying?* absolve ACCUSATION noun *The police are investigating the accusations.*

accustom *verb* get used to, familiarize, adjust, adapt, condition *She blinked and tried to accustom her eyes to the bright light.*

accustomed to *adjective* used to, in the habit of *Jerry was spoiled and had become accustomed to having his own way.*

ache 1. *verb* hurt, throb, sting, smart *My stomach aches from eating too much.* 2. *noun* pain, a throbbing, a smarting, twinge *After resting, I found that the ache in my ankle had gone away.*

achieve *verb* accomplish, carry out, do, finish, complete, fulfill, perform, realize *We must work together to achieve our goals.* fail

achievement *noun* accomplishment, attainment, success, triumph *It is a remarkable achievement to receive a scholarship.*

acknowledge *verb* 1. admit, recognize, concede, grant, accept *Kim acknowledged that she had made a bad choice.* deny 2. greet, salute, notice, hail *Andy acknowledged us with a wave.* ignore 3. show appreciation for, show gratitude for, thank for *After we raked his leaves, Mr. Thompson acknowledged our help by serving us big bowls of ice cream.*

acknowledged *adjective* recognized, known, accepted, agreed *He's the acknowledged expert in his field.*

acknowledgment *noun* 1. recognition, acceptance, approval, agreement *There was a general acknowledgment that we'd made a mistake* 2. greeting, salute, notice *She gave a nod of acknowledgment as she passed.* 3. thanks, gratitude, appreciation *We sent her flowers in acknowledgment of a job well done.*

acquaintance *noun* friend, associate, contact *An old acquaintance and I had coffee together today.*

acquainted *adjective* familiar, associated *I recognize her name, but I'm not acquainted with her.*

acquire *verb* gain, obtain, get as one's own, secure, earn, attain (*Slang*—get hold of) *Students are expected to acquire an understanding of basic math.* lose ACQUISITION *noun The museum has added several acquisitions to its art collection.*

acquit *verb* declare not guilty, absolve, forgive, cleanse, discharge, pardon, excuse *The jury acquitted her of all charges.* blame

acrid *adjective* sharp, bitter, stinging, nasty, biting, harsh *Clouds of acrid smoke poured from the chimney.* sweet, pleasant

acrobat *noun* gymnast, tumbler *Clowns, acrobats, and magicians performed in the street.*

act 1. *verb* do, behave *I'm sorry I acted so stupidly.* 2. perform, entertain, play a part *Jane's going to act in the school play.* 3. *noun* law, statute *The Civil Rights Act was passed in 1964.*

action *noun* 1. behavior, thing done, performance, way of working *The lifeguard's quick action saved the little boy from drowning.* 2. battle *My brother was wounded in action.*

active *adjective* lively, energetic, vivacious, dynamic, animated, spirited (*Slang*—peppy) *We have four active puppies.* lazy 2. working, committed, involved *She plays an active part in her community.* idle

activity *noun* 1. movement, energy, action, liveliness *There's a lot of excitement and activity during the holidays.* 2. interest, hobby, pastime *Sailing is my favorite activity.*

actor *noun* stage player, performer, entertainer *She's a fine actor who's appeared onstage and in movies.*

actual *adjective* real, factual, true, genuine, concrete, authentic *Please don't guess—I need to know the actual number.* nonexistent

actually *adverb* really, in fact *Yes, it actually happened—he didn't make it up.*

acute *adjective* sharp, keen, sensitive *Cats have acute hearing.* dull

adapt *verb* make fit, make suitable, modify, change, alter, vary, adjust, conform *Some people are slow to adapt to new situations. My dad adapted an old barn for use as a workshop.* ADAPTABLE *adjective Wolves are very adaptable animals that can live almost anywhere.* ADAPTATION *noun The movie is an adaptation of an old folktale.*

add *verb* 1. total, tally *Add the cost of all these items.* 2. unite, join, put together, combine *Add the eggs and milk, and stir until smooth.*

addition *noun* 1. supplement, extra *This encyclopedia is a great addition to our library.* 2. annex, room, attachment, extension *We just built an addition on our house.*

additional *adjective* extra, supplementary, added *This keyboard has additional keys for the Internet.*

address 1. *verb* deal with, apply oneself to *We need to address the problems of homeless people.* 2. *noun* speech, talk, lecture *The president's address was broadcast on television.* 3. home, residence, place where mail is delivered *What's your e-mail address?*

adept *adjective* skillful, expert *Donna is an adept auto mechanic. He's adept at writing software.* unskillful

adequate *adjective* sufficient, enough, satisfactory, ample, plenty *Do you have adequate clothing for the cold weather?* inadequate, insufficient

adhere *verb* 1. cling, stick, hold *You need to get paint that will adhere to metal.* 2. follow, stick to, observe, obey *Deborah adheres to a daily exercise routine. The factory adheres to strict safety standards.*

adhesive *noun* glue, paste *Let the adhesive dry for an hour.*

adjacent *adjective* near, adjoining, next to, touching, bordering, neighboring *A house is being built on the lot adjacent to ours.*

adjoin *verb* be next to, be close to, be side by side with, be in contact with, connect to *The girls' hotel room adjoins their parents' room.*

adjourn *verb* postpone, end, put off until a later time, discontinue, suspend, recess *The meeting has been adjourned until tomorrow.*

adjust *verb* arrange, set just right, adapt, make fit, make suitable, modify, change, alter, vary *You can adjust the brightness on your computer monitor.*

adjustment *noun* change, alteration, modification, adaptation *My bicycle seat needs some adjustment.*

administer *verb* 1. manage, execute, preside over *Mr. Michaels administers the state school system.* 2. apply, give, contribute, dispense *The courts administer the law.*

admirable *adjective* praiseworthy, excellent, very good, commendable, deserving *My teacher said I did an admirable job on my book report.* unfavorable, objectionable

admiration *noun* respect, appreciation, esteem, regard *I have great admiration for her courage.*

admire *verb* respect, appreciate, approve, like, regard highly *He admires his father.*

admit *verb* 1. confess, acknowledge, concede (*Slang*—own up, come clean) *I admit that I was wrong.* deny 2. allow to enter, receive *She's been admitted to medical school.*

admonish *verb* warn, caution, criticize, scold *Dad admonished us for staying out late without calling.* praise

adopt *verb* 1. approve, choose, assume, accept, take on *The city has adopted a no-smoking policy.* reject 2. give a home to, accept as one's own. *My parents adopted my little brother when he was a baby.* ADOPTION noun *The government is recommending adoption of the new constitution.*

adorable *adjective* lovable, sweet, endearing, attractive, lovely *The puppies are so adorable.* ugly

adore *verb* love and respect, worship, idolize, cherish, admire, revere *Mom and Dad adore each other.* hate ADORATION noun *He gazed at her with adoration.*

adorn *verb* beautify, decorate, ornament, garnish, glamorize *The tables were adorned with white tablecloths and fresh flowers.*

adroit *adjective* smart, clever, adept, skillful, expert, apt, proficient *He is adroit at handling customer's complaints.* unskillful

adult *adjective* full-grown, grown-up, mature, developed, of age *They have three adult sons.* immature, juvenile

advance 1. *verb* go forward, move ahead, proceed, progress *The traffic advanced only a few yards at a time. Joanie advanced two grades in one year.* 2. improve, increase, develop, expand *Our knowledge of space has advanced greatly in recent years.* 3. *noun* improvement, advancement, development, innovation *Advances in medical technology are saving lives.*

advantage *noun* benefit, upper hand, leverage, gain (*Slang*—edge) *You have the advantage of a lot of experience.* disadvantage

advantageous *adjective* helpful, useful, favorable, beneficial *It would be advantageous to you to study French before you go to France.*

adventure *noun* unusual experience, undertaking, event, happening, occurrence, exploit *Our hot-air balloon ride was a real adventure.* ADVENTURER noun *Spanish adventurers came to America in search of gold.*

adventurous *adjective* bold, fearless, brave, courageous *Some of the adventurous tourists try mountain climbing.* cautious

adversary *noun* enemy, opponent, rival *Our team will face its old adversary, Washington High School, in its next game.*

adverse *adjective* 1. unfavorable, harmful *A poor diet had an adverse effect on her health.* favorable, helpful 2. unfriendly, hostile *Our ideas attracted some adverse criticism.* friendly

adversity *noun* trouble, hardship, distress, misfortune *Early settlers faced a lot of adversity.* prosperity

advertise *verb* announce, notify publicly, call attention to, broadcast (*Slang*—plug) *We saw a nice car advertised in the newspaper today.* conceal, hush ADVERTISEMENT noun *We answered an advertisement for some puppies for sale.*

advice *noun* plan, suggestion, recommendation, instruction, direction, tip *Could you give me some advice on what computer to buy?*

advisable *adjective* wise, sensible, prudent *It is advisable to plan ahead.*

advise *verb* suggest, guide, recommend, counsel, instruct *I advise you to see a lawyer.*

advocate *verb* recommend publicly, speak in favor of, defend, support *The new government advocates equal rights for all people.* oppose

affair *noun* occasion, occurrence, event, happening, matter, concern, business, party, festivity *The fireworks display is an annual affair.*

affect *verb* 1. influence, change, modify, alter *The choices we make today will affect our futures.* 2. move, touch, stir the feelings of, upset, distress *I was affected deeply by her death.*

affection *noun* friendly feeling, admiration, love and respect, fondness *We were greeted with warmth and affection.* dislike

affectionate *adjective* loving, caring, friendly, warm *Gloria has a very affectionate nature.*

affirm *verb* assert, confirm, ratify, state, pronounce, declare, validate, endorse, certify *The government affirmed its commitment to peace.* veto, deny

affluent *adjective* wealthy, abundant, plentiful, ample, rich, bountiful, well-off, well-to-do *The more affluent families have summer homes on the lake.* poor

afford *verb* have the means *Mom says we can't afford a new car.*

afraid *adjective* frightened, fearful, scared (*Slang*—chicken) *He's very afraid of heights.* courageous

after 1. *preposition* following, next, subsequently *I'll meet you after class. We leave the day after tomorrow.* before 2. in search of, in pursuit of *The police are after the person who robbed the bank.* 3. *adverb* behind *You're first in line, and Jake comes after.* 4. *conjunction* as soon as, when, following a time that *We'll go to a movie after we've had dinner.*

again *adverb* another time, once more, anew, afresh, repeatedly *Can you come by again tomorrow? The baby is crying again.*

against 1. *preposition* in opposition to, versus *The majority voted against the proposal.* with 2. in the opposite direction to *The waves beat against the shore.* 3. on, in contact with *Lean the ladder against the wall.*

age 1. *noun* time of life, period in history *She could read by the age of three. The ice age ended about 10,000 years ago.* 2. *verb* grow older, mature, ripen *He doesn't seem to have aged at all.*

aged *adjective* old, elderly, mature, senior, ancient, advanced in years. *She was an aged woman—at least ninety.*

agency *noun* operation, office, organization, bureau *Your state's consumer protection agency helps protect against fraud.*

agent *noun* 1. representative, manager, negotiator, broker, go-between *I know a real-*

estate agent who can help you sell your home. 2. cause, means, driving force, instrument *Modern technology is an agent of change.*

aggravate *verb* 1. annoy, irritate, provoke, exasperate, infuriate (*Slang—*miff, peeve, rile) *Your humming is beginning to aggravate me.* pacify 2. make worse, intensify, exaggerate, heighten *Tony aggravated an old shoulder injury in today's game.*

aggression *noun* attack, assault, offense, invasion *The country's aggression led to war.* defense AGGRESSOR noun *The nation denied that it was the aggressor.*

aggressive *adjective* 1. hostile, belligerent, offensive, militant, combative *Female animals can become aggressive when protecting their young.* peaceful 2. forceful, assertive, determined, insistent *The group was dominated by a few outspoken and aggressive members.*

aghast *adjective* astonished, surprised, amazed, astounded, shocked, thunderstruck, awed, flabbergasted, horrified *We were aghast at the destruction caused by the tornado.*

agile *adjective* nimble, fast, alert, quick, spry, athletic *Our cat is an agile tree climber.* clumsy, slow AGILITY noun *He has the agility of a gymnast.*

agitate *verb* 1. disturb, incite, instigate, excite, stir up, inflame, provoke *The wasps were agitated and began to sting.* 2. move, stir up, shake, stir, churn *A sudden wind over the lake agitated the water's surface.* calm AGITATION noun *He paced the room in agitation.*

agony *noun* suffering, pain, grief, distress, anguish, torture, torment, heartache, woe *June's sprained ankle was causing her a lot of agony.* peace

agree *verb* 1. consent, assent, accept, say yes *David agreed to play ball tomorrow.* 2. concur, coincide, be in agreement *We don't always agree, but we respect each other's opinions.* disagree

agreeable *adjective* 1. pleasant, enjoyable, comfortable *We spent an agreeable evening with friends.* unpleasant 2. to one's liking, suitable, acceptable *We worked out a plan that is agreeable to everyone.* unacceptable 3. friendly, pleasant, likable *Charles is a most agreeable man.* disagreeable

agreement *noun* 1. pact, contract, understanding, bargain, treaty, alliance, deal *He had only a one-year agreement to play for the team. The two sides are trying to reach an agreement.* 2. accord, harmony, concurrence *He nodded his head in agreement.* disagreement

agriculture *noun* farming, cultivation, husbandry *Agriculture is very important to our economy.* AGRICULTURAL adjective *We live in a rural, agricultural community.*

ahead *adverb* in front, before, forward, in advance, leading, winning *Their team was ahead 21-14 at halftime. Go ahead and I'll follow. You have a difficult task ahead of you.* behind

aid 1. *noun* help, relief, assistance, service, support *People have generously given aid to those who lost their homes in the flood.* 2. *verb* help, assist, support, serve *Mountain rescuers, aided by dogs, found the climbers alive.* hinder

ail *verb* 1. trouble, bother, perturb, disturb *You seem unhappy—what's ailing you?* 2. be ill, suffer, feel awful, feel sick *Grandmother has been ailing for some time.*

ailment *noun* sickness, illness, disease, disorder *He's home from the hospital, recovering from his ailments.*

aim 1. *verb* point, direct, target *Aim just above the bull's-eye. Our advertising is aimed at teenagers.* 2. try, intend, seek, aspire, endeavor *Our teacher always aims to make learning fun.* 3. *noun* purpose, intention, objective, goal, end, target *Her aim is to provide us with a good education.*

air 1. *noun* atmosphere, space, sky *The startled bird flew quickly into the air.* 2. manner, quality *Claude has an air of mystery about him.* 3. *verb* express, announce, make known, proclaim *My parents allow me to air my problems.* 4. ventilate, freshen *The cottage needs airing after being closed all winter.*

airy *adjective* 1. light, breezy, roomy, spacious *The dining room was large and airy, with windows overlooking the garden.* gloomy, dark, stuffy 2. lighthearted, merry, carefree, cheerful, happy *He gave an airy wave as he left.* grave, serious

aisle *noun* passage, passageway, corridor, lane, opening, walkway *She pushed her cart down the frozen-food aisle.*

ajar *adjective* open, gaping *The door was ajar, so we peeked in.* closed

alarm 1. *verb* startle, arouse, frighten, shock, jar, jolt, agitate, disturb, unnerve *We became alarmed when he didn't answer his phone.* calm 2. *noun* signal, call, warning, summons *Someone's car alarm is going off in the parking lot.*

alcoholic *adjective* intoxicating, inebriating, fermented *She never drinks alcoholic beverages.* ALCOHOL noun *This restaurant serves alcohol.*

alert 1. *adjective* observant *The deer became still and alert as we approached. An alert police officer recognized the car's license number.* dull 2. *noun* warning, notification, alarm, signal *A severe weather alert is in effect for the entire island.*

alibi *noun* excuse, story *The police are checking the man's alibi for the night of the crime.*

alien *adjective* foreign, different, strange, unfamiliar *Everything in her new home seemed alien to her.*

allegiance *noun* loyalty, faithfulness, devotion, fidelity *He pledged his allegiance to his country.*

alley *noun* narrow backstreet, path, passageway, lane, opening *They walked down a narrow alley onto the main street.*

alliance *noun* agreement, pact, contract, understanding, bargain, treaty *Local groups formed an alliance to raise money for a community center.*

allied *adjective* joined, united, combined *The general is commander of the allied forces.*

allot *verb* distribute, share, divide, assign, apportion, allocate, budget (*Slang*—give out, deal out, dole out, mete out, hand out, dish out, shell out, fork out) *The teacher allotted each student five minutes for an oral book report.*

allow *verb* permit, approve, allot, give, let have *We're allowed only an hour of television a day.* forbid

allowance *noun* allotment, portion, fee, grant, ration, budget *Salespeople get travel allowances. Most children get an allowance from their parents.*

almost *adverb* nearly, close to, just about *Almost nothing is known about his family. We've lived here almost ten years.*

alone 1. *adverb* without help, unaided, on one's own, solo *He brought up his children alone.* 2. *adjective and adverb* solitary, isolated, unaccompanied *She's been alone since her husband died.* accompanied

aloof *adjective* away, apart, distant, remote, unsociable, reserved, standoffish, cool *George is a little aloof and doesn't warm up to others easily.* friendly

aloud *adverb* out loud, audibly, verbally *We took turns reading the story aloud.*

also *adverb* too, in addition, as well, besides *I like football, but I like basketball also.*

alter *verb* make different, change, vary, modify, revise *Word-processing software makes it easy to alter documents.* maintain ALTERATION *noun The clothes didn't need any alterations to make them fit.*

alternate *verb* take turns, switch, interchange, spell *Maria alternated easily between English and Spanish.*

alternative *noun* choice, substitute, replacement, possibility, option *We should first consider the alternatives. She had no alternative but to do as she was told.*

altogether *adverb* completely, wholly, entirely, thoroughly, totally *Henry was altogether too excited to sleep.* partly

always *adverb* forever, all the time, eternally, permanently (*Slang*—for good, for keeps) *We will always be friends.* never

amass *verb* accumulate, collect, store up, increase, assemble, gather *He amassed a fortune of over $100 million.*

amateur *noun* nonprofessional *Only amateurs are permitted to play on college teams.* professional

amaze *verb* surprise, astonish, astound *Dad is amazed by how much we kids know about computers.*

amazement *noun* surprise, wonder, shock, astonishment *We watched in amazement as the airplane made a perfect landing on the highway.*

ambition *noun* goal, aim, objective, hope, desire, longing *His ambition is to return to college and earn his degree.*

ambitious *adjective* 1. aspiring, determined, motivated *The ambitious young man was quickly promoted in his job.* 2. bold, impressive, elaborate, complicated, challenging *The city has ambitious plans to renovate the downtown area.*

amble *verb* stroll, saunter *We ambled through the village, stopping occasionally to look in the shops.* rush

ambush 1. *noun* surprise attack *The soldiers were captured in an ambush.* 2. *verb* to suddenly attack *She was ambushed by a snowball on her way to school.*

amend *verb* change, correct, improve, revise, alter *The club members voted to amend the rules.* AMENDMENT *noun The first ten amendments to the U.S. Constitution are called the Bill of Rights.*

amiable *adjective* friendly, good-natured, pleasant, agreeable *Grandpa has a gentle, amiable nature.*

ammunition *noun* shot, bullets, bombs, shells, missiles (*Slang*—ammo) *Guns and ammunition were seized at a weapons factory.*

among *preposition* amid, between, surrounded by, in with *We rested in a clearing among* *the trees. The kingdom was divided among the three brothers.*

amount *noun* sum, quantity, value, measure, price *What is the amount I owe you?*

amount to *verb* total, add up to, equal *The phone bill amounts to $30.*

ample *adjective* abundant, enough, sufficient, plenty, adequate *You have ample time to prepare for the test. The house has ample closet space.* insufficient

amuse *verb* entertain, divert, delight, tickle, interest, fascinate *Uncle John amused my little sister by making silly faces.*

amusement *noun* entertainment, enjoyment, fun, pleasure, delight *His eyes twinkled with amusement. The movies are a source of amusement for the whole family.*

amusing *adjective* entertaining, pleasing, charming, delightful *I don't know how Anne comes up with such amusing jokes.*

analyze *verb* examine, study, consider, investigate, explore *The scientists used a computer to analyze the data.*

ancestor *noun* forebear, predecessor, forefather, foremother *My ancestors came from Ireland in the 1800s.*

anchor 1. *verb* fasten, secure, fix, attach *The tent is anchored securely to the ground.* 2. *noun* newscaster, journalist, announcer *She's the anchor on the evening news.*

ancient *adjective* old, aged, antique, archaic *The ancient city of Troy is located in modern-day Turkey.* young, new, modern

anecdote *noun* story, tale, yarn, account, narrative, joke *We love hearing Aunt Marge's anecdotes about her travels.*

angelic *adjective* lovely, beautiful, innocent, kind *Babies have such angelic faces.*

anger 1. *noun* wrath, ire, rage, fury, annoyance, irritation *The drivers of the cars in the accident shouted in anger at each other.* 2. *verb* infuriate, enrage, rile, annoy, irritate *Parents were angered by the school board's decision to close the neighborhood school.*

angry *adjective* annoyed, irritated, mad, furious, enraged *The players were angry about the umpire's call.* ANGRILY *adverb The bees buzzed angrily when we disturbed their hive.*

anguish *noun* agony, suffering, pain, grief, distress, torment, heartache *He felt great anguish at seeing the people living in poverty.* peace

animal *noun* creature, beast *We visited a farm that had lots of animals.*

~~~~~~

animated *adjective* lively, gay, vigorous, spry, active, vivacious *We heard animated conversation and laughter coming from the party next door.* inactive

animation *noun* cartoon, moving picture, video image, simulation *Animation can be done on your home computer with graphics software.*

animosity *noun* hatred, dislike, ill will, bitterness *He felt a great deal of animosity toward the company that fired him.* love, goodwill

annex 1. *verb* add, attach, join, unite with *Texas was annexed to the United States in 1845.* 2. *noun* something joined, addition, wing, extension *The school board voted to build an annex to the middle school.*

announce *verb* make known, proclaim, report, broadcast, declare, state, notify, tell *My sister announced that she is getting married.* ANNOUNCEMENT *noun They made an announcement that the flight will be delayed an hour.* ANNOUNCER *noun He was once a football player, but now he's a sports announcer.*

annoy *verb* tease, vex, disturb, irritate, make angry *That TV program really annoys me; please change the channel. Stop annoying your brother!* please, calm

answer 1. *verb* reply, respond, acknowledge *Did you answer Jane's e-mail?* 2. *noun* reply, response, acknowledgment *I didn't hear your answer to my question.* 3. solution, remedy, key, resolution *Scientists are trying to find an answer to the energy crisis.*

antagonize *verb* make an enemy of, arouse hostility in, provoke, alienate *Caroline always manages to antagonize people with her constant criticism.* soothe

anticipate *verb* expect, await, hope for, foresee *We're anticipating having a great summer.* ANTICIPATION *noun Schools are closing early today in anticipation of the snowstorm.*

antics *noun* capers, pranks, funny gestures, practical jokes, tricks (*Slang*— shenanigans) *We all enjoyed the clown's antics.*

antique *adjective* ancient, old, aged, archaic *My older brother restores antique cars.* new

anxiety *noun* worry, nervousness, concern, fear *Dad says we caused him a lot of anxiety when we were late.* calm

anxious *adjective* 1. uneasy, concerned, fearful, troubled, bothered, perturbed, agitated, worried *I felt really anxious about my exams.* relaxed 2. eager, desirous, keen *I'm anxious to see her face when she opens her present.* ANXIOUSLY *adverb Joyce is anxiously awaiting her test scores.*

apartment *noun* flat, suite, dormitory *The family lives in an apartment above their store.*

apathy *noun* indifference, unconcern, lethargy *Voter apathy resulted in few people voting in the last election.* enthusiasm, feeling, interest

apologize *verb* beg pardon, ask forgiveness, express regret, offer an excuse *I apologize for being late.* APOLOGETIC adjective *Diane was very apologetic about missing her appointment.*

apology *noun* request for forgiveness, expression of regret, explanation *You were very rude to Mitch; he deserves an apology.*

appall *verb* horrify, shock, dismay, terrify, stun *We were appalled by the violence.*

apparatus *noun* equipment, gear, gadget, device, mechanism, contraption *Antique machines and apparatuses are displayed at the museum.*

apparel *noun* clothing, dress, garments, garb, attire *The store sells formal apparel.*

apparent *adjective* plain, obvious, evident, clear, noticeable *It's apparent that you're tired—rest awhile. Barry had no apparent injuries.* hidden, mysterious APPARENTLY adverb *No one has answered the bell—apparently they're not home.*

appeal 1. *verb* ask earnestly, beg, plead, urge, implore, entreat *The governor appealed for help for the earthquake victims.* 2. attract, interest, please, fascinate, tempt *Winter sports don't appeal to him at all.* 3. *noun* fascination, allure, charm *The excitement of a big city has great appeal for me.* 4. plea, request, call, entreaty *Residents of the neighborhood made an appeal for volunteers to help clean up the park.*

appear *verb* 1. seem, look, look like *What appeared to be a UFO may have been a meteorite.* 2. come into view, emerge, materialize *The sun appeared briefly from behind the clouds.* disappear

appearance *noun* 1. arrival, entrance, coming into sight, presence *The appearance of tulips and daffodils is a sign of spring.* 2. look, aspect, demeanor, air *His sparkling eyes and white beard gave him the appearance of Santa Claus.*

appease *verb* calm, satisfy, pacify *We appeased Mom by promising to clean our rooms.* irritate

appendix *noun* addition, supplement *See Appendix B for more details.*

appetite *noun* hunger, desire, craving, taste *I really have an appetite for pizza tonight.*

applaud *verb* approve, praise, cheer, hail, acclaim, clap (*Slang*—root for) *The* *audience applauded the performance enthusiastically. We applaud your efforts to do better in class.* disapprove, reject

applause *noun* clapping, approval, praise, cheers *Let's hear a nice round of applause for a job well done.*

appliance *noun* tool, machine, device, instrument, implement, utensil *The store sells household furniture and appliances.*

application *noun* 1. request, petition, appeal, bid *My brother has submitted applications to several colleges.* 2. use, purpose, function, relevance *Chemistry is a science that has many practical applications.* 3. software, program *You can download lots of games and multimedia applications from the Internet.*

apply *verb* 1. request, ask, petition *Tom applied for a summer job as a lifeguard.* 2. put on, rub on, spread over *The first coat of paint has to dry before we apply the second.* 3. relate, pertain, fit, concern *I don't see how this rule applies to us.* 4. use, employ, utilize, direct *Apply as much pressure as you can.* APPLICANT *noun The company has thirty applicants for the same job.*

appoint *verb* elect, choose, name, vote for, assign, nominate *She's been appointed the committee's chairperson.*

appointment *noun* 1. meeting, date, engagement *Your dentist appointment is at 10:00.* 2. job, position, assignment, post *He accepted an appointment as a member of the board.*

appreciate *verb* 1. be thankful for, be grateful for, welcome, value, enjoy, think highly of *We appreciate your advice. I really appreciated having Jenny here for the weekend.* 2. understand, realize, be aware of, comprehend *I appreciate your problem, but I don't know what I can do to help.* APPRECIATIVE *adjective You're the most appreciative audience we've performed for.*

appreciation *noun* 1. thanks, gratitude, gratefulness, thankfulness *Janice received a certificate of appreciation for her volunteer work.* 2. understanding, awareness, realization, grasp, comprehension *The students have a new appreciation for the value of education.*

apprehend *verb* arrest, capture, seize *Police apprehended a suspect in the robbery.*

apprehensive *adjective* afraid, worried, anxious, uneasy, concerned, fearful, troubled, bothered, agitated, perturbed *I'd be apprehensive about skydiving if I were you.* relaxed

apprentice *noun* beginner, learner, novice, amateur *Benjamin Franklin began working* *at age twelve as an apprentice in his brother's print shop.* experienced, expert, master

approach 1. *verb* come near, advance, come toward *The cat silently approached the mouse. The deadline for turning in your papers is approaching.* retreat 2. handle, deal with, consider, tackle *We need to approach the problem in a new way.* 3. *noun* method, procedure, way of handling, style, slant, tactic *Different teaching approaches should be considered.*

appropriate 1. *adjective* suitable, proper, fitting *The movie is not appropriate for young children.* inappropriate 2. *verb* share, divide, distribute, budget, give out, deal out, hand out (*Slang*—shell out, fork out) *Money is being appropriated for the purchase of land for a national park.* APPROPRIATION noun *Community colleges will receive an increase in appropriations next year.*

approval *noun* 1. praise, admiration, appreciation *Joseph received gratitude and approval for his kind act.* disapproval 2. permission, consent, agreement, authorization, support *The proposal is likely to win the approval of Congress.*

approve *verb* 1. like, think well of, admire, accept, be pleased with *Mom and Dad say they approve of the job I'm doing in school this year.* disapprove, frown on 2. permit, agree to, accept, ratify, endorse, okay *The city council has approved the new recycling program.*

approximate *adjective* close, rough, estimated *What's the approximate time you expect to arrive?* exact

approximately *adverb* nearly, almost, about, around *Approximately 250 people attended the event.*

arbitrary *adjective* unreasonable, chance, unsupported, personal *Judges are not supposed to make arbitrary decisions.* fair, reasonable

arbitrate *verb* settle, negotiate, referee, decide *Mom refused to arbitrate my sister's and my argument—she said we had to settle it ourselves.*

architecture *noun* building, structure, construction *Classical architecture began in Greece with the construction of temples and public buildings.*

area *noun* 1. size, expanse, range, surface, space *The area of our house is 1,800 square feet.* 2. district, neighborhood, section, territory, region *The city along with the surrounding area has a population of 3,000,000.* 3. subject, field, topic, sphere *An area in which you could improve is mathematics.*

argue *verb* 1. reason, persuade, claim, discuss, plead *The environmental organization argued for stronger laws against pollution.* 2. disagree, fight, quarrel, dispute, bicker

~~~~~~

(*Slang*—hassle) *Stop arguing with your brother or you'll go to your room!* agree, get along

argument *noun* 1. disagreement, fight, quarrel, dispute, squabble *An argument began over whether or not the ball was out of bounds.* 2. reason, grounds, case *We heard several convincing arguments both for and against the plan.*

arid *adjective* dry, waterless *Some plants in arid climates have adapted by developing long roots that get water from deep underground.* wet, fertile

arise *verb* happen, come about, occur, appear *I will speak to her about the problem as soon as the opportunity arises.*

aristocrat *noun* nobleman, noblewoman, gentleman, gentlewoman, lord, lady *They were aristocrats, incredibly wealthy, and related to the king.*

arm 1. *noun* limb *Grandma held out her arms for a hug.* 2. *verb* equip, supply, fortify, empower *Armed with maps and a compass, we set off on our hike. The aircraft is armed with the latest weapons.*

armistice *noun* peace, truce, treaty, agreement, pact, contract, understanding, concord, alliance, deal *The armistice that ended World War I was signed on November 11, 1918.*

arms *noun* weapons, guns, weaponry, firearms, armaments *The museum has a display of arms from the Revolutionary War.*

army *noun* 1. armed forces, troops, soldiers, military *Hannibal is most famous for leading his army and war elephants across the Alps.* 2. crowd, throng, legion *An army of supporters gathered to hear the candidate's speech.*

aroma *noun* fragrance, odor, perfume, scent *What's that wonderful aroma coming from the kitchen?* AROMATIC *adjective Sage, thyme, and mint are a few aromatic herbs.*

around 1. *preposition* near, close to, about *It's around noon.* 2. *preposition and adverb* all over, throughout, about, here and there *Please don't leave your clothes lying around your room. We looked around to see where the noise was coming from.*

arouse *verb* stir, excite, awaken, move, provoke, kindle, stimulate *Producing hydrogen as a fuel from water has aroused much scientific interest.*

arrange *verb* 1. put in order, place, lay out, classify, catalog, systematize *The books are arranged alphabetically by author.* 2. plan, organize, set up, schedule *Jesse and I arranged to meet at 8:00 for coffee.* cancel

arrangement *noun* 1. layout, display, order, grouping *Students and staff eat together* *around a U-shaped arrangement of tables.* 2. plan, procedure, preparation *Have you made your travel arrangements yet?*

arrest 1. *verb* seize, catch, apprehend, capture, take prisoner *The police arrested the man and charged him with burglary.* release 2. *noun* capture, apprehension *No arrests have been made yet for the crime.*

arrival *noun* appearance, coming, entrance, approach *They just announced the arrival of Dad's flight. We're awaiting the arrival of spring.* departure

arrive *verb* come, reach, get to, appear (*Slang*—show up, turn up) *A package for you just arrived in the mail.* leave

arrogant *adjective* too proud, haughty, insolent, conceited, self-important, stuck-up *Her fame had made her arrogant.* humble, modest ARROGANCE noun *His arrogance made him unable to accept criticism.*

art *noun* 1. drawing, painting, sculpture, design, work, composition, masterpiece *I plan to study art and music in college. Uncle Joe collects modern art.* 2. skill, knack, craft, technique *She's studying the art of filmmaking. He understands the art of compromise.*

artery *noun* 1. blood vessel *The arteries carry blood to all parts of the body.* 2. main road, channel *Traffic on a major artery into the city is backed up for miles.*

article *noun* 1. composition, story, essay, report *The teacher has asked me to write an article for the school newspaper.* 2. object, thing, item *The charity is asking us to donate articles of clothing for children.*

artificial *adjective* false, pretended, substitute, not genuine, unreal, fake, synthetic, imitation, counterfeit *Those artificial flowers look real to me.* natural, real, authentic

ascend *verb* go up, rise, climb, mount *The elevator ascended slowly to the tenth floor.* descend

ascent *noun* climb, rise, scaling, going up *This was the first ascent of the mountain by British climbers. She made a remarkable ascent from junior executive to president of the company in three years.* descent

ashamed *adjective* embarrassed, humiliated, abashed, mortified *Janet was ashamed for having lied. I was ashamed to admit I had forgotten their names.* proud

ask *verb* 1. question, find out, inquire *Sue asked the new student where he was from. Ask Margaret how old she is.* 2. invite, have over, request *Mom asked Judy to stay for dinner.* 3. demand, expect *We thought they were asking more for the car than it is worth.*

asleep *adjective* 1. sleeping, dozing, napping *The cat and dog are curled up together asleep.* awake 2. numb, with no feeling *My foot's asleep.*

aspect *noun* 1. view, viewpoint, side, position *There are several important aspects to consider before making a decision.* 2. look, appearance, feature, quality *The sky has a gray, stormy aspect.*

aspiration *noun* goal, objective, ambition, hope, desire *Rachel has aspirations to be a jet pilot.*

aspire *verb* seek, desire, be ambitious, aim, strive *The small territory aspired to independence.*

assassin *noun* murderer, killer *Government leaders are often the targets of assassins.*

assassinate *verb* murder, kill *Four presidents of the United States have been assassinated.*

assassination *noun* murder, killing *President Ronald Reagan was shot and wounded in an attempted assassination.*

assault 1. *noun* attack, offensive, onslaught, charge, raid *The platoon leader led the assault on the enemy.* 2. *verb* attack, strike, charge *An army of knights and foot soldiers assaulted the castle. The man was charged with assaulting a police officer.*

assemble *verb* 1. meet, gather together, congregate, rally, collect, accumulate *Protestors assembled in the street. The gallery has assembled a large collection of modern art.* scatter, disperse 2. put together, construct, build, fit together *Can you help me assemble this model airplane?* take apart

assembly *noun* 1. gathering, meeting, get-together, congregation, rally *The principal announced that there will be a special school assembly at 10:00.* 2. construction, putting together *The bookcase came in a flat pack and requires assembly.* taking apart, breaking down, dismantling

assert *verb* declare, state, insist on, affirm, pronounce *The citizens asserted the right to rule themselves.* ASSERTION *noun His assertion that he had done nothing wrong turned out to be untrue.*

asset *noun* 1. valuable things, property, funds, wealth, accounts, resources, goods, capital *Their assets, which include a house, boat, and car, are worth about $300,000.* 2. advantage, strength, quality, resource, plus *Jeff has proved to be a tremendous asset to the team.*

assign *verb* 1. give out, allocate, distribute, allot (Slang—hand out) *Mom and Dad* assign each of us chores to do around the house. 2. appoint, choose, name, designate, delegate *The older kids are assigned to take care of the younger ones.*

assignment *noun* job, task, duty, responsibility *Your homework assignment is to read the next chapter.*

assist *verb* help, aid, support, lend a hand *My sister likes to assist Mom with the cooking.*

assistance *noun* help, aid, support *We asked for assistance changing our flat tire.*

assistant *noun* helper, supporter, aide, subordinate, deputy *My older sister works as a teacher's assistant at our school.*

associate 1. *verb* connect, relate, identify, link *I associate summer with vacation, swimming, and camping* 2. socialize, spend time, mix, mingle *We tend to associate with people who have the same interests as we do.* 3. *noun* partner, coworker, colleague *He's an associate in my father's law office.*

association *noun* organization, society, alliance, group, club *As a member of our library association, Dad is helping to raise money for a new library.*

assorted *adjective* various, different, mixed *I rummaged through the drawer of assorted nuts, bolts, and miscellaneous parts.*

assortment *noun* variety, range, mixture, collection *The room was cluttered with an assortment of furniture.*

assume *verb* 1. suppose, take for granted, presume, suspect, understand, believe, think *We all assumed that Darcy was telling the truth.* 2. take on, accept, undertake, adopt *He assumes full responsibility for the decisions he makes.*

assumption *noun* belief, theory, guess, idea *Our assumptions about people who are different from us are not always correct.*

assurance *noun* promise, guarantee, pledge *I received assurances from the salesperson that the software would work with my computer.*

assure *verb* convince, make certain, promise, guarantee, pledge *The doctor assured me that my broken leg would heal just fine.*

astonish *verb* surprise, astound, amaze *The Grand Canyon has always astonished visitors. My parents were astonished by my straight As.*

astonishment *noun* surprise, amazement, wonder, shock *Imagine our astonishment when we looked outside and saw a tornado in the distance.*

asylum *noun* refuge, shelter, sanctuary, safety *A large number of people are seeking asylum from repressive governments.*

athlete *noun* sports person, player, contestant, team member *More than 400 athletes competed in the Olympics.*

athletic *adjective* active, agile, fit, in good shape, strong *Mom and Dad are pretty athletic; they swim and work out whenever they can.*

attach *verb* fasten, join, connect, affix, add, put together, unite *The directions say to attach the legs to the base with screws.* detach

attached *adjective* close, fond, devoted *We became attached to the kittens the minute we saw them.*

attachment *noun* 1. affection, fondness, warmth, love, bond *The brothers have a strong attachment to each other.* 2. accessory, add-on, addition, extra, supplement *Mary Jo included an attachment to her e-mail.*

attack 1. *noun* raid, siege, bombardment, assault, offense, onslaught, charge, drive, push *The troops launched a surprise attack on the enemy.* 2. *verb* assault, raid, strike *Pirates regularly attacked merchant ships along the coast of North America.* 3. criticize, disagree with, condemn, denounce *The candidate attacked her opponent's plan for cutting the budget.*

attain *verb* reach, gain, accomplish, fulfill, achieve, realize *She has attained her goal of winning the state speech contest. My dad is receiving an award for attaining excellence in his profession.*

attempt 1. *verb* try, endeavor, make an effort (*Slang*—take a shot at, have a go at) *The team is attempting to win its fourth game in a row.* 2. *noun* effort, try, endeavor, (*Slang*—shot, go) *The climbers made an unsuccessful attempt to reach the mountain's summit.*

attend *verb* 1. be present, visit, go to *We've been invited to attend my cousin Emily's wedding.* be absent 2. serve, help, work for, administer to, care for *Teachers attend to the educational needs of their students. Doctors and nurses attend to the sick.*

attendance *noun* 1. presence, appearance *I had perfect attendance at school this year.* 2. number present, turnout, crowd, audience *The concert attendance was around 800.*

attendant *noun* helper, assistant, aide, guide *The flight attendants are coming around with drinks.*

attention *noun* 1. notice, concentration, awareness, thought *The speaker wasn't interesting enough to hold my attention. You need to pay attention to the details. The movement* *in the tall grass caught my attention.* inattention 2. care, courtesy, consideration, concern, kindness, devotion *I always receive a lot of attention from my grandparents.* neglect

attentive *adjective* 1. paying attention, alert, intent, concentrating, focused *The speaker had an attentive audience.* 2. considerate, courteous, polite, thoughtful *Our waiter was very friendly and attentive.*

attire *noun* clothes, dress, clothing, garments, apparel *The couple was wearing formal evening attire.*

attitude *noun* viewpoint, standpoint, position, opinion, state of mind, mood *Mike's cooperative attitude makes him easy to work with.*

attract *verb* pull, interest, draw, fascinate, allure, charm, tempt, captivate, infatuate *The museum attracts millions of visitors every year. The scandal is attracting a great deal of attention.*

attraction *noun* draw, charm, pull, allure, fascination *The main tourist attraction is a huge indoor water park.*

attractive *adjective* pleasing, winning, charming, desirable, beautiful *Everyone in Ned's family is very attractive. The seaside is an attractive vacation destination.* unattractive

attribute 1. *verb* assign, ascribe, give, place, apply *The ninety-seven-year-old woman attributed her long life to good diet and exercise.* 2. *noun* characteristic, quality, trait, nature, feature *Mark's sense of humor is his best attribute.*

audible *adjective* can be heard, distinct, clear, plain *The cat's purr was soft but audible.* inaudible

authentic *adjective* real, reliable, genuine, legitimate, actual, factual, true *The restaurant is known for its authentic Italian cooking. You need to show an authentic ID card to pass through security.* false, artificial, counterfeit

author *noun* writer, creator, novelist, poet, columnist *The book is based on the author's own life.*

authority *noun* 1. power, right, influence, ability *Police officers have the authority to enforce the law.* 2. expert, specialist, professional *Anna has a reputation as an authority on Chinese art.*

authorize *verb* give power to, legalize, enable, assign, allow, permit, give permission *You're not authorized to use the computer without a password.*

autograph 1. *verb* sign, endorse *The author autographed my book.* 2. *noun* signature *My dad has a baseball with team members' autographs on it.*

automatic *adjective* self-acting, self-working, self-operating, mechanical *This digital camera has fully automatic settings.* manual **AUTOMATICALLY** adverb *The lights go on automatically when someone enters the room.*

available *adjective* ready, at hand, obtainable, offered, to be had *A new version of the software is available.* unoffered, unobtainable

average 1. *adjective* usual, ordinary, passable, fair *Dolores's grades are about average.* unusual, extraordinary 2. middle, medium, mean *The average number of days missed by students in our school is nine.* extreme 3. *noun* mean, norm, standard *The rainfall amount this year has been below the average.*

avid *adjective* eager, greedy *My sister Peggy is an avid reader of mystery novels.*

avoid *verb* keep away from, shun, evade, snub *We took the back roads in order to avoid heavy traffic.* seek

award 1. *noun* prize, grant, gift, trophy, reward, medal *The movie was nominated for three awards.* 2. *verb* give, present, bestow, grant *The Canadian skaters were awarded a gold medal.*

aware *adjective* knowing, realizing, conscious, cognizant, knowledgeable, mindful, alert *I wasn't aware of how late it is—I have to leave.*

awe *noun* wonder, amazement, astonishment, surprise, respect *The pyramids, built of stones weighing up to forty tons, inspire awe in visitors.*

awful *adjective* unpleasant, terrible, horrible, dreadful, wretched *We had an awful camping trip—it stormed all weekend.* pleasant, wonderful

awfully *adverb* extremely, very, terribly, terrifically *It's awfully hot in here. Do you want to hear an awfully funny story?*

awkward *adjective* 1. clumsy, ungraceful, uncoordinated, ungainly *Penguins are awkward on land but are excellent swimmers.* graceful 2. cumbersome, bulky, unwieldy *This cooler full of food is awkward to carry.* 3. embarrassed, uncomfortable *I feel awkward speaking in front of a crowd.* comfortable

B

babble 1. *noun* chatter, prattle, gabble *Cheerful babble filled the crowded room.* 2. murmur, gurgle *The brook's babble lulled us to sleep in our tents.* 3. *verb* chatter, jabber, gab, prattle *Don't mind us, we're just babbling on about our children.*

baby *noun* infant, newborn, child *The tiny baby in the photo is my little brother.*

back 1. *noun* rear, reverse, farther part *The index is at the back of the book. The only seats available are in the back of the plane. Turn it over and look at the back.* 2. *adjective and adverb* behind, rear, earlier *I read the story in a back issue of the magazine. Please step back.* 3. *verb* support, help, encourage, favor, advocate *The community backs our team whether the team is winning or losing.*

background *noun* 1. experience, knowledge, training, practice, upbringing *Andrea has a background in languages and works as a translator.* 2. distance, rear, setting, surroundings *I'll take a photo of you with the hills in the background. The painting is of red flowers on a white background.* foreground

bad *adjective* 1. awful, poor, terrible, dreadful, lousy, inferior, abysmal *That movie was really bad!* good, great, wonderful 2. unpleasant, disagreeable, nasty, foul *Margaret is certainly in a bad mood today.* pleasant 3. naughty, mischievous, disobedient, unruly *Ellen was punished for her bad behavior.* good 4. unhealthy, harmful, dangerous, damaging *Smoking is bad for your health.* good 5. serious, severe *We had a bad thunderstorm last night.* slight, mild 6. sorry, regretful, apologetic, ashamed, guilty *I feel bad about getting into an argument with my sister.*

badger *verb* tease, annoy, torment, bother, pester, harass, bait (*Slang*—bug, pick on, ride) *Will you please stop badgering me with questions.*

baffle *verb* puzzle, perplex, confound, mystify, bewilder, stump *I'm baffled by these complicated instructions.*

bag *noun* sack, container *Do you want a paper bag or plastic?*

baggage *noun* luggage, suitcase, bags *The airline lost our baggage.*

bait 1. *verb* badger, question, tease, annoy, torment, bother, pester, harass (*Slang*— pick on, ride) *A group of troublemakers began baiting the speaker.* 2. *noun* lure, attraction, inducement, temptation *Small varieties of fish are sometimes used as bait to catch large fish.*

balance *noun* 1. steadiness, stability, equilibrium *Dana slipped on the ice and lost her* *balance. We try to keep a balance between work and play.* 2. remainder, rest, surplus, residue, difference *I'll be home for the balance of the week. We paid off the balance on our credit card.* 3. *verb* steady, stabilize, maintain equilibrium *Can you balance a book on your head?*

bald *adjective* hairless, bare, simple, open, nude, uncovered *Mom says I was bald when I was born. Forest fires have left the hills bald.* hairy, covered

balk *verb* be unwilling, be stubborn, be obstinate, refuse, stop *My horse balked when we came to the fence. I balk at eating liver.* be willing

ballot *noun* vote, choice, poll *Seventy percent of voters turned out to cast their ballots.*

balmy *adjective* mild, soft, gentle, pleasant *After a hot summer day, the balmy evening breeze felt great.*

ban 1. *verb* prohibit, forbid, outlaw, bar, block, obstruct, exclude, shut out *Smoking is banned in restaurants.* allow 2. *noun* prohibition, restriction, embargo *There's a ban against pets in our apartment building.*

band 1. *noun* group, gang, crowd, crew, troop *The movie is a Western about a band of outlaws.* 2. musical group, ensemble, orchestra, combo *She's the lead singer in a rock band.* 3. *verb* join, assemble, unite, gather *The children have banded together to raise money for a new animal shelter.*

bandit *noun* outlaw, robber, thief, crook, gangster *A masked bandit held up the stagecoach.*

bang 1. *noun* loud noise, explosion, crash, boom, slam *We heard a loud bang just as we saw lightning strike the tree.* 2. *verb* strike, knock, beat, hit, pound *Bang on the door a little harder; I don't think they heard you.*

banish *verb* exile, expel, force away, drive away, deport, outlaw *Napoleon was banished to the island of Elba in 1814. Mom banishes us from the kitchen while she's getting dinner.* BANISHMENT *noun Banishment was often used by kings and queens as a way of getting rid of their enemies.*

bank 1. *noun* shore, barrier, slope *We fished along the bank of the stream.* 2. pile, heap, mound *Let's dig a tunnel through the bank of snow.* 3. reserve, store, collection, stock *The blood bank is asking people to donate blood.* 4. *verb* deposit, save money, have an account *We bank at the First Federal Bank downtown.* 5. lean, slope, tilt *The plane banked as we came in for a landing.*

banquet *noun* feast, formal dinner, affair *There will be a banquet at the hotel after the wedding.*

bar 1. *verb* block, obstruct, exclude, shut out, forbid, ban, prohibit *People under the age of eighteen are barred from buying cigarettes.* allow 2. *noun* pole, rod, stick *Many zoos no longer keep their animals in cages with bars.* 3. saloon, tavern, pub, nightclub, lounge *The waiter asked if we'd like anything to drink from the bar.* 4. obstruction, barrier, restriction, obstacle *Gail doesn't see her physical disability as a bar to achieving her goals.*

bare 1. *adjective* naked, nude, bald, open, uncovered *If you're going outside, put sunscreen on your bare shoulders.* covered 2. vacant, empty, unfurnished *The room was bare except for one chair.* 3. *verb* expose, reveal, uncover, show, display *The dog in the doorway bared its teeth.* hide

barely *adverb* scarcely, hardly, just *We barely got home before it started to rain.*

bargain 1. *noun* good deal, good buy, discount (*Slang*—steal) *I got a real bargain on this video game.* 2. agreement, contract, pact, arrangement *Dad and I have a bargain: If I help him clean the garage, he'll give me money for a movie.* 3. *verb* make a deal, negotiate, haggle, barter *My brother bargained for a CD player at a yard sale and got it for $3.*

barren *adjective* unproductive, infertile, sterile, bare *A rain forest becomes a barren wasteland when the trees are destroyed.* fertile, productive

barricade *noun* obstruction, barrier, fortification *The fallen trees formed a barricade across the road.*

barrier *noun* barricade, obstruction, fortification, obstacle, hindrance *Not being able to speak the language can be a barrier to traveling in a foreign country. Beavers build dams as barriers across streams to make ponds.*

barter *verb* trade, deal, exchange, swap *Many cities and towns in North America were founded as fur-trading centers, where Europeans bartered with Native Americans for furs.*

base 1. *verb* found, establish, build *The movie is based on a true story.* 2. *noun* bottom, foundation, support, stand *The base of the lamp is made of brass.* 3. station, headquarters *Danny's father is being transferred to a naval base in California.*

bashful *adjective* awkward, uneasy, shy, timid, coy *The bashful boy hid behind his father.* aggressive

basic *adjective* essential, fundamental, underlying, primary, key, most important *Loyalty is a basic ingredient in a friendship.*

bathe *verb* 1. wash, shower, soak, take a bath, give a bath to *Mom bathes my baby brother before putting him to bed.* 2. drench, cover, saturate, flood *The snow-covered hills were bathed in moonlight.*

batter *verb* beat, pound, smash, thrash *The waves battered the shore.*

battle 1. *noun* struggle, fight, combat, war, contest, conflict *The Battle of Gettysburg is probably the most famous battle of the Civil War.* peace 2. *verb* fight, struggle with, wrestle with, contend with *Firefighters have been battling the flames all day.*

bawl *verb* shout, cry, wail, weep, sob, howl *My little sister began bawling when she fell and scraped her knees.*

beach *noun* shore, coast, waterfront, seaside *Jane won the contest at the beach for the best sand castle.*

beacon *noun* watchtower, signal, alarm, flare *Ships are guided in the fog by the lighthouse beacon.*

beam 1. *verb* shine, glow, gleam, radiate *The sun beamed through breaks in the clouds.* 2. smile, grin *Everyone in the photograph was beaming.* 3. *noun* ray, glow, stream of light, shaft of light *A laser beam can harm your eyes if you look directly into it.* 4. girder, timber, rafter, bar *Birds have built nests in the beams of the old barn.*

bear *verb* 1. endure, tolerate, put up with, suffer *I cannot bear to see my little sister hurt.* 2. carry, support, hold, take on, shoulder *Each hiker was bearing a heavy backpack. Mom and Dad bear responsibility for our family.* 3. produce, yield *The raspberry bushes begin bearing fruit in early July.*

bearing *noun* 1. influence, relation, connection, impact, effect *The amount of exercise we get has a direct bearing on our health.* 2. manner, air, attitude, demeanor *She has the graceful bearing of a ballet dancer.*

bearings *noun* direction, way, course *We had trouble finding our bearings in the dark.*

beast *noun* animal, creature *A farmer found the bones of a dinosaur, a frightening beast that looked like Tyrannosaurus rex.*

beat 1. *verb* strike, hit, punch, pound *The child beat her new toy drum.* 2. mix, stir, blend *Beat the eggs and sugar, then add the flour.* 3. defeat, outdo, triumph over *Our team beat the opponents, 14-7.* 4. surpass, top. *You can't beat summer vacation.* 5. *noun* accent in music, rhythm *The audience clapped their hands to the beat.*

beautiful *adjective* 1. pretty, handsome, attractive, lovely, good-looking *The woman in the photograph is beautiful.* 2. pleasant, lovely, splendid, delightful, wonderful, fair, fine *What a beautiful day! The snowcapped mountains are very beautiful.* unattractive, unpleasant

beauty *noun* attractiveness, loveliness, splendor *We admired the beauty of the oil painting.* unattractiveness, ugliness

beckon *verb* gesture, motion, invite, signal *The teacher beckoned to me to come to the front of the classroom.*

become *verb* 1. turn into, turn out to be, develop into, come to be *The weather is becoming warmer. That puppy is going to become a very large dog.* 2. suit, flatter, look good on *That outfit becomes you.*

becoming *adjective* flattering, attractive, appropriate, suitable *Her new hairstyle is very becoming.* unattractive, unbecoming, inappropriate

before 1. *adverb* earlier, previously, already, formerly, in the past *I was here before you.* after 2. *preposition* in front of, in the presence of *The man stood before the judge.*

beg *verb* ask, beseech, appeal, plead, implore, entreat *I begged my parents to let me stay up another hour.*

begin *verb* start, commence, initiate, embark on *Let's begin by opening our books to the first page. James begins his new job on Monday.* end, finish, stop

beginning *noun* start, first part, commencement, opening *I always look forward to the beginning of spring.* end

behave *verb* 1. act, conduct oneself *George's little sister was scolded for behaving badly. The sailboat behaves well in a high wind.* 2. be good, act properly, stay out of mischief *I promise to behave.* misbehave

behavior *noun* conduct, action, acts, manner *Dad says he expects our behavior to be respectful.*

behind 1. *preposition* in back of, at the back of *We keep our garbage cans behind the house.* 2. *adverb* following, farther back, at the rear, last *The smaller children came trailing behind.* ahead

behold *verb* see, look at, observe, notice *The first flowers of spring are a joy to behold.*

belated *adjective* late, overdue, delayed *Dana wished me a belated happy birthday.*

belief *noun* conviction, judgment, view, opinion *Galileo went to prison for his belief that the earth revolved around the sun.*

believe *verb* trust, accept as true, accept as real, think, imagine (*Slang*—swallow) *I believe what Jerry tells me. People once believed that the world was flat.*

belly *noun* abdomen, stomach (*Slang*—tummy) *The dog rolled over to have its belly scratched.*

belong *verb* 1. fit in, be part of, be appropriate *We want to make the new student feel he belongs.* 2. have as a place *The crayons belong in the box.* 3. be a member of, be associated with *My mom reads a lot and belongs to a book club.* 4. be the property of, be owned by *Every summer we visit the farm that belongs to my grandparents.*

belongings *noun* possessions, property, things, gear (*Slang*—stuff) *We hauled my sister's belongings in a trailer to her college apartment.*

below 1. *preposition* under, underneath, beneath, lower than *The sun sank below the horizon.* above 2. *adverb* under, underneath, beneath, lower *The office you want is on the floor below.* above

bend 1. *verb* curve, turn, twist, bow *The tree branches bent under the weight of the snow.* 2. stoop, lean over *Dad bent to hear what I was saying.* 3. *noun* curve, turn, twist *Our house is just past the bend in the road.*

beneath *preposition* under, underneath, below, lower than *The stairs beneath him creaked.* above, over

beneficial *adjective* favorable, helpful, profitable, useful, advantageous *Exercise is beneficial to your health.* harmful

benefit 1. *noun* help, advantage, asset, value *Trained firefighters are a benefit to the community.* 2. *verb* help, aid, be good for *More rain would benefit the farmers.*

bent *adjective* determined, set *Karen is bent on becoming an Olympic skater.*

beside *preposition* next to, alongside, by, adjacent to *Stand here beside me while Dad takes a picture.*

besides *adverb* moreover, also, too, in addition, as well *I don't want to go to a movie today; besides, I have homework to do.*

best 1. *adjective* finest, greatest, top choice *Jody is the best player on the team.* worst 2. *adverb* most, to the greatest extent *The student best able to spell will compete in the spelling bee.* worst

bet 1. *noun* wager, gamble, challenge *I made a bet with my brother that I could beat him at the video game.* 2. *verb* wager, gamble, challenge *Dad and I bet Mom we could make a better pizza than she could.*

betray *verb* mislead, deceive, trick (*Slang*—double-cross) *I know my friends would* *never betray me.*

better 1. *adjective* superior, preferable, improved, more valuable *Your drawing is better than mine.* worse 2. *adverb* to a greater degree, in a more acceptable way *These shoes fit better than the other pair.* worse 3. *verb* improve, surpass, advance, top *Diane is trying to better her piano-playing skills with practice.*

between *preposition* 1. in the middle of, among, amid *The river flowed between steep banks. We shared the food between us.* 2. connecting, joining, linking *The highway between here and Chicago is under construction.*

beware *verb* be careful, guard against, take care, look out, watch out (*Slang*—keep one's eyes peeled, watch one's step) *The sign at the gate warned to beware of the dog.*

bewilder *verb* confuse, baffle, puzzle, perplex, confound, mystify (*Slang*—stump) *Grown-ups are far more bewildered by computers than children are.* clarify

beyond *preposition* 1. on the farther side of, past, behind *Carl lives just beyond those hills.* 2. later than, past, after *My parents let me stay up beyond my bedtime.*

bias 1. *noun* prejudice, tendency, leaning, preference *Judges must not let any bias influence their decisions.* 2. *verb* prejudice, influence, sway. *Don't let Jane's opinions bias your decision.*

bid 1. *verb* offer, propose, submit *I bid $10 for the table but lost to someone who bid $10.50.* 2. *noun* offer, proposal, amount *We accepted a bid of $75,000 for our house.*

big *adjective* 1. large, huge, immense, gigantic *I ate a big plate of spaghetti.* little, small 2. important, great, significant, major, serious *Deciding on a career is a big decision.* insignificant 3. grown-up, adult, mature *My big brother is away at college.* little

bill 1. *noun* invoice, statement, check *We just got the bill for our cell phone calls.* 2. *verb* charge, invoice, debit *The restaurant billed us for drinks we didn't order.* 3. advertise, announce, publicize *The movie is billed as one of the year's best.*

bind *verb* 1. tie, fasten, wrap, secure *I will bind the package with clear plastic tape.* 2. oblige, require *The contract binds me to the agreement.*

birth *noun* 1. childbirth, delivery *Mom says I weighed seven pounds at birth.* death 2. beginning, origin, start, dawn *We celebrate the birth of the United States on July* 4. end 3. family, descent, origin *Kings and queens are of noble birth.*

bit *noun* 1. small amount, piece, fragment, trace, morsel, scrap *Bits of paper were blowing around in the wind. May I have a tiny bit of your ice cream?*

bite 1. *verb* cut with the teeth, nibble, gnaw, nip, chomp *I bit into the apple. Don't worry—our dog won't bite you.* 2. *noun* mouthful, taste, nibble, piece *Danny took a huge bite of the chocolate bar.* 3. sting, wound, puncture *Spider bites can be very painful.*

biting *adjective* 1. cold, frigid, icy, piercing *It's below zero, with a biting wind; dress warmly.* warm, hot 2. sharp, cutting, sneering, sarcastic, acid *Kim's biting remarks hurt Anne's feelings.* kind, sympathetic

bitter *adjective* 1. sour, acid, harsh, sharp, unpleasant *The skins of oranges taste bitter.* 2. resentful, angry, upset, cheated *Mr. Peterson felt bitter about being fired from his job.* 3. hostile, vicious, antagonistic *The bitter enemies have finally agreed to peace talks.*

blade *noun* cutting part, knife-edge *This blade needs sharpening.*

blame 1. *verb* accuse, hold responsible, hold accountable *The driver blamed icy roads for the accident.* absolve 2. criticize, find fault with, reproach *You can't blame the fans for being unhappy with the poor way the team played.* 3. *noun* responsibility, guilt, fault *I won't take the blame for something I didn't do.*

blank *adjective* empty, void, vacant, bare *That blank wall should have pictures hung on it.*

blast 1. *noun* loud noise, boom, roar, bang *The blast from the factory whistle could be heard all over town.* 2. gust, draft, rush *A blast of cold air hit us when we opened the door.* 3. *verb* blow up, explode, demolish, detonate *Workers blasted a tunnel through the mountain for the new road.*

blaze 1. *noun* fire, flames *The firefighters put out the blaze before it destroyed the cabin.* 2. glow, glare *It's too hot in the blaze of the afternoon sun.* 3. *verb* burn, be on fire, flare *A warm fire blazed in the fireplace.* 4. shine, glow, illuminate *Lights blazed throughout the house.*

bleak *adjective* bare, chilly, cold, dreary, dismal *Today's a bleak, rainy November day.* cheerful

bleed *verb* to lose blood *Donna's knees were bleeding from her fall.*

blemish 1. *noun* defect, imperfection, flaw, stain, scar *The old landfill is a blemish on the landscape. His reputation as an honest man is without blemish.* 2. *verb* spoil, ruin, damage, mar *The hail has bruised and blemished the fruit.*

blend 1. *verb* mix, combine, join, stir, beat *Blend the butter and sugar until the mixture is smooth.* separate 2. *noun* mixture, combination *Green is a blend of blue and yellow.*

blight *noun* 1. disease, decay, plague, affliction *Blight destroyed the potato crop in*

Ireland in 1845.

blind 1. *adjective* sightless, visionless *Braille is a system of reading and writing for people who are blind.* 2. without thought, without judgment, uncritical *Jackie sometimes has blind trust in the wrong people.* 3. hidden, concealed, unseen, out of sight *Drivers who don't slow down for that blind curve can cause accidents.* 4. *noun* window shade, shutter *Close the blind a little; the sun is in my eyes.*

bliss *noun* happiness, joy, delight, glee, elation *Mom says that soaking in a warm bubble bath is pure bliss.*

blissful *adjective* happy, joyful, delightful *We spent a blissful Saturday afternoon at the lake.*

block 1. *verb* obstruct, hinder, stop, bar, hold back *An avalanche blocked traffic on the mountain road.* 2. *noun* solid, mass, chunk, lump *The pyramids are built of blocks of stone.*

blood *noun* 1. body fluid *Blood leaves the heart by way of the arteries and returns by way of the veins.* 2. family, birth, descent, parentage *We're related by blood.*

bloom 1. *noun* flower, bud, blossom *Lilacs have very fragrant blooms.* 2. *verb* flower, bud, blossom *The daffodils are the first flowers to bloom in our garden.*

blossom 1. *noun* flower, bud, bloom *The apple blossoms are white with a little pink.* 2. *verb* flower, bud, bloom *Fruit trees blossom in the spring.* 3. develop, grow, flourish *Sandy's and my friendship blossomed very quickly.*

blow 1. *verb* move, drive, carry, sweep *The wind blew the cap from his head.* 2. breathe out, puff, exhale *Jackie blew on the hot soup to cool it.* 3. *noun* hit, knock, punch, whack, rap *A blow to the head can cause brain damage.* 4. disappointment, upset, setback, misfortune *Tonight's loss was a blow to the team's hopes for a championship.* boost

blowout *noun* flat tire, flat, puncture *We had a blowout on the highway and discovered our spare tire was flat, too.*

blow up *verb* 1. explode, destroy, blast *A warehouse full of fireworks blew up.* 2. inflate, fill up, expand *We blew up balloons to use as party decorations.* deflate 3. become very angry, explode, lose one's temper, become furious *Kate blew up when I was an hour late.* 4. make larger, enlarge, expand, magnify *Mom said the photo I took is good enough to blow up and hang on the wall.*

bluff 1. *verb* deceive, trick, mislead *You won't bluff your teacher into believing you studied if you fail the test.* 2. *noun* trick, deception, fake, pretense *He acted as if he had good cards, but it was a bluff.* 3. steep bank, cliff, hill *The Mississippi River flows between scenic bluffs.*

blunder 1. *noun* mistake, error, slip (*Slang*—goof, bungle) *A series of players' blunders caused the team to lose.* 2. *verb* make a mistake *I really blundered by calling the principal by the wrong name.* 3. stumble, stagger, flounder *We blundered around in the dark trying to find candles when the lights went out.*

blunt *adjective* 1. dull, not sharpened *Small children are given blunt scissors so they don't cut themselves.* sharp 2. outspoken, candid, frank, straightforward, direct *When I asked Mother if she liked my outfit, her answer was a blunt "No!"*

blur 1. *verb* cloud, obscure, make fuzzy, dim *The fog blurred the oncoming car's headlights. Tears blurred her vision.* 2. *noun* something indistinct, haze, cloudiness *Without my glasses, everything in the distance is a blur.*

board 1. *verb* get on, enter, embark *We had to wait two hours before boarding our airplane.* 2. *noun* wood, lumber, plank, timber, beam *We used old boards from a barn to build a tree house.* 3. food, meals *My sister is working to pay for her room and board at college.* 4. committee, cabinet, council *The school board meets every month.*

boast *verb* brag, gloat, pat oneself on the back *Carla boasted about getting all As on her report card.*

body *noun* 1. figure, build, physique, frame *I exercise to keep my body healthy.* 2. group, collection, throng, crowd *The student body and the teachers attended an assembly.* 3. mass, area, quantity *The Pacific Ocean is the largest body of water in the world.*

boil *verb* cook, bubble *When the water is boiling, add the spaghetti.*

boisterous *adjective* noisy, lively, unrestrained, active, rowdy, disorderly *Dad said we are too boisterous and should go outside to play.* serene

bold *adjective* 1. brave, courageous, fearless, daring, adventurous *Bold explorers set out to reach the North Pole.* 2. bright, vivid, showy, striking *I like bold colors such as red, orange, and yellow.*

bolt 1. *noun* fastener, bar, rod, pin, lock, latch *You need to tighten the nuts and bolts to keep the chair from wobbling.* 2. run, dart, dash *The startled rabbit made a bolt for it.* 3. *verb* fasten, bar, lock, latch *Bolt the door before you go to bed.* 4. run, flee, break away, make a run for it, break away, dart, dash *The horse bolted as soon as Jerry opened the barn.*

bonus *noun* extra, reward, premium, benefit, plus *I get a bonus to my allowance when I do extra chores.*

boom 1. *noun* loud noise, roar, rumble, bang *Deafening booms followed the fireworks.* 2. growth increase, gain, expansion *The U.S. has seen a boom in the game of soccer.*

3. *verb* roar, rumble, bang *Thunder boomed in the distance.* 4. grow, increase, expand, prosper, flourish *Business is booming.*

boost 1. *verb* lift, push, shove, thrust, hoist *Joyce boosted Sharon over the fence.* 2. encourage, raise, lift, improve *The team's win today boosted their hopes for the play-offs.* 3. *noun* lift, push, thrust, hoist, shove *Give me a boost so I can reach the tree branch.*

boot 1. *noun* type of foot covering *He wore fancy leather cowboy boots.* 2. *verb* kick *He booted the ball into the stands.*

booty *noun* plunder, prize, loot, stolen goods *The captain of the pirate ship shared the booty with his crew.*

bore *verb* make weary, tire, fatigue *Listening to the adults' conversation bored me and I fell asleep.*

born *adjective* brought forth, produced, hatched *We saw newly born lambs and chicks when we visited the farm.*

borrow *verb* ask for a loan, take temporarily *I borrowed $1 from Mom and told her I'd pay her back out of my allowance.* lend

boss *noun* supervisor, manager, chief, director *Dad's boss just promoted him.*

boss around *verb* order around, direct, control, bully, push around *My big brother sometimes thinks he can boss me around.*

bother 1. *verb* annoy, pester, disturb (*Slang*—bug) *Quit bothering me—I'm studying!* 2. *noun* worry, fuss, trouble, problem, nuisance (*Slang*—hassle) *It's no bother at all having Freddie over for dinner—he always helps with the dishes.*

bottom *noun* 1. base, foundation, lowest part *We rested at the bottom of the hill before climbing to the top.* top 2. underside, underneath *The price is on a label on the bottom.*

bounce 1. *verb* spring back, rebound *The ball bounced once before Ted caught it.* 2. jump, leap, spring *My little sister likes to bounce up and down on the bed.* 3. *noun* springiness, elasticity *This tennis ball has lost its bounce.*

bound 1. *verb* leap, jump, spring, hop *The deer bounded into the woods.* 2. border, adjoin, be next to, touch *The United States is bounded on the north by Canada and on the south by Mexico.* 3. *adjective* obligated, obliged, required, compelled *I feel bound to stand up for my friend.* 4. certain, sure, destined, very likely *Sarah is bound to do well on the test—she studied hard.* 5. *noun* jump, leap, spring, hop *The rabbit disappeared into the brush in a single bound.*

boundary *noun* limit, border, division, barrier *The Rio Grande forms part of the boundary between the United States and Mexico.*

boundless *adjective* unlimited, endless, infinite *The universe is boundless. Carol seems to have boundless energy.* limited

bounds *noun* limits, boundaries, limitations, confines *Our dog does not go beyond the bounds of our yard. My parents have set reasonable bounds for me.*

bow 1. *verb* bend, stoop, kneel, curtsy, salute *All the knights bowed to King Arthur.* 2. give in, yield, surrender, submit *I bowed to my parents' wishes.* 3. *noun* nod, curtsy, salute *The lead actor took a bow at the end of the play.*

box 1. *noun* container, carton, package, crate, case *We packed our old toys in cardboard boxes to give to a charity.* 2. square, rectangle *Put a check mark in the box.* 3. *verb* pack, package, crate *Wrap the dishes in paper before you box them.*

boy *noun* young man, youth, fellow *The boy next door is my age.*

brace 1. *verb* support, strengthen, reinforce, buttress, hold up *The roof is braced to hold the heavy snow.* 2. prepare, make ready *We braced ourselves for the scolding we expected to get.* 3. *noun* support, prop, buttress, reinforcement *We used three poles as braces for the wall.*

brag *verb* boast, pat oneself on the back, crow *Grandparents like to brag about their grandchildren.*

brake *verb* stop, slow down, decelerate *Dad braked the car quickly when a ball rolled into the street.* accelerate

branch 1. *verb* divide, split, fork, separate, diverge *When the road branches, go to the left.* 2. *noun* limb, bough, twig *Do you see the bird sitting on the top branch of the tree?* 3. division, department, office *Dad manages a branch of First National Bank.*

brand *noun* 1. mark, burn, label, tag *The brand on the cattle wandering through our yard shows they belong to our neighbor.* 2. kind, sort, type *What brand of toothpaste should I buy?*

brave 1. *adjective* courageous, bold, valiant, gallant, heroic *Firefighters are brave men and women.* cowardly 2. *verb* face, bear, endure, suffer *Early settlers in North America braved cold winters and hunger.*

bravery *noun* courage, heroism, boldness, gallantry *My grandfather was awarded a medal for bravery in battle.*

break 1. *verb* smash, fracture, shatter, rupture, crack, burst *Tammy broke her arm when she fell off her bike. If you put too much air in the balloons, they'll break.* heal, mend 2. disobey, violate, defy, disregard *It's breaking the law to drive faster than the speed limit. My friend Janet has never broken her promise.* uphold, obey 3. exceed, beat, surpass, top *Danny broke the school record in the high jump.* 4. end, stop, interrupt *It's hard to break a habit.* 5. *noun* interruption, pause, interval, rest *Dr. Johnson takes a lunch break and doesn't see patients between 12:00 and 1:00.* 6. chance, opportunity, good luck *Joe's pass interception was a real break for the team.*

breed 1. *verb* raise, bring up, rear, cultivate, grow *We got our puppy from a man who breeds black Labs.* 2. cause, create, bring about, produce *Carelessness breeds mistakes.* 3. *noun* type, variety, kind, strain, sort *Persians are a breed of cat with long hair.*

breezy *adjective* 1. brisk, blustery, windy *Today is cool and breezy.* 2. cheerful, carefree, jolly, lighthearted *David has a pleasant, breezy manner.*

brew *verb* cook, prepare, ferment *I can smell the coffee brewing.*

bribe *verb* buy off, pay off *He's in jail for trying to bribe a police officer.*

bridle *noun* harness, halter *We put the bridle on the horse's head.*

brief 1. *adjective* short, concise, succinct *I got a brief e-mail from Tanya today; she says she's fine.* long, lengthy 2. short, momentary, quick, short-lived, temporary, fleeting *I got a brief glimpse of the deer before it disappeared into the woods.* 3. *verb* inform, tell, instruct, update, fill in *A government official briefed reporters on what took place during the meeting.*

bright *adjective* 1. shining, clear, vivid, glowing *Bright pink is Doris's favorite color.* 2. smart, alert, intelligent, clever *Kevin is a very bright student. Mary came up with some bright ideas for gifts for everyone.* 3. pleasant, cheerful, lively *She greeted us with a bright smile.* dull

brilliant *adjective* 1. sparkling, bright, shining, clear, vivid, dazzling *We walked out of the dark building into brilliant sunlight.* 2. talented, able, skillful, exceptional, accomplished *She's a brilliant violinist.* 3. magnificent, wonderful, splendid *We congratulated the actor on his brilliant performance.*

brisk *adjective* 1. cool, fresh, invigorating, refreshing *There is a brisk breeze off the lake.* warm 2. energetic, lively, quick, active, vigorous *Let's take a brisk walk after breakfast.* relaxed

brittle *adjective* fragile, crisp, breakable, frail, delicate *Very old newspapers become yellowed and brittle.*

broad *adjective* wide, large, expansive, extensive, sweeping *The encyclopedia has information on a broad range of subjects.* narrow, limited, restricted

broadcast 1. *verb* show, televise, telecast, air, transmit *The game will be broadcast on TV.* 2. publicize, publish, circulate, make known, report, spread, distribute, announce *Rumors about him were being broadcast all over town.* 3. *noun* program, show, transmission, telecast *The first commercial television broadcast was on July 1, 1941.*

broken *adjective* 1. smashed, fractured, shattered, cracked *Be careful of the broken glass.* 2. not operating, defective, faulty, out-of-order, damaged *I took my broken watch to be repaired.* working, operating

browse *verb* read, scan, skim, glance through *I browsed through the magazines at the dentist's office.*

bruise *verb* injure, hurt, wound, damage, harm, discolor *Sally bruised her knee when she tripped and fell. The apples were bruised during shipping.* heal

brush 1. *verb* clean, rub, polish, scrub, sweep, smooth, remove, groom *Mother brushed the tangles from my hair. Brush your teeth before you go to bed.* 2. touch, stroke, caress, scrap, contact *The cat brushed against her leg.* 3. *noun* bushes, shrubs, undergrowth *The rabbit disappeared into the brush.*

brutal *adjective* cruel, barbaric, savage, ruthless, vicious, inhuman *The country is ruled by a brutal dictatorship.* humane

buck *verb* jump, leap, spring, vault *The horse bucked, but the cowboy hung on.*

buckle 1. *noun* clasp, fastener, clip, hook, catch *The country singer's belt has a big silver buckle.* 2. *verb* fasten, hook, clasp, clip, secure *Be sure to buckle your seat belt.* 3. bend, fold, sag, collapse, cave in *The roof buckled under the weight of the snow.*

bud 1. *verb* bloom, flower, blossom, grow, open, develop, flourish *It's spring, and the lilacs are budding.* 2. *noun* sprout, blossom, shoot *The buds on the pussy willow are soft like fur.*

buddy *noun* friend, pal, companion, partner, comrade, chum *My buddies and I are going to the park to play basketball.*

budge *verb* move, stir, shift, dislodge, push, shove *The piano was too heavy to budge. We tried to bargain on the price, but the salesclerk wouldn't budge.*

budget 1. *noun* allowance, allotment, ration *The family's weekly budget for food is $150.* 2. *verb* plan, allow, ration, schedule *We need to budget for a new and faster computer.*

buff *verb* polish, rub, shine, wax, burnish *My brother waxes and buffs his car every chance he gets.*

build 1. *verb* construct, make, create, assemble, manufacture *Dad helped us build a tree house. Robots will help build an international space station.* 2. *noun* figure, body, physique, shape, frame *Gordon is tall, has a heavy build, and is very strong.*

bulky *adjective* large, awkward, cumbersome *We dragged the bulky bags of trash to the curb.*

bulletin *noun* message, circular, news, statement, flash, newsletter *A weather bulletin on TV alerted us to the tornado.*

bully *verb* tease, pester, annoy, badger, torment, bother, harass *Don't let your older sister bully you.*

bump 1. *verb* hit, knock, strike, collide with, shake *I bumped the table and knocked over the glass of milk.* 2. jolt, bounce, jerk, jar *We bumped along the old dirt road.* 3. *noun* thump, crash, bang, thud *We heard a bump when the dog jumped off the bed.* 4. swelling, lump, bulge *I have a bump on my head where I fell and hit it.*

bunch 1. *noun* group, set, batch, cluster, collection *We picked a bunch of grapes. A bunch of us walk home from school together every day.* 2. *verb* cluster, collect, gather, huddle, group *The cows were bunched together in the pasture.*

bundle *noun* parcel, package, packet *This bundle of newspapers should be recycled.*

bungle *verb* botch, make a mess of, mess up, spoil *I really bungled my first attempt at sewing.*

burden 1. *noun* load, weight, cargo, freight *A camel can carry a burden of 400 pounds.* 2. problem, worry, difficulty, hardship, strain, stress *Just paying the rent is a burden to many elderly people.* 3. *verb* weigh down, trouble, load down, bother *Teachers shouldn't be burdened with disciplinary problems.*

burglar *noun* robber, thief, intruder, crook *The police caught a burglar trying to break into our neighbor's house.*

burglary *noun* theft, robbery, crime, breaking and entering *A man was arrested for the burglary of a convenience store.*

burn 1. *verb* blaze, be on fire, flame, glow, smolder *Be sure you don't leave the campfire burning.* 2. set on fire, ignite, set ablaze, light *He burned the old letters.* 3. scorch, singe, char *Don't burn the toast.* 4. *noun* injury, blister, scald, scorch *I got a burn on my shoulders from the sun.*

burrow 1. *verb* dig, tunnel, excavate *A groundhog burrowed under our porch.* 2. snuggle, nestle, hide *I burrowed under the blankets and fell asleep.* 3. search, hunt, rummage *She burrowed through the junk in the drawer for her keys.* 4. *noun* hole, den, tunnel, hiding place *Foxes live in underground burrows.*

burst 1. *verb* break open, explode, blow up, split, rupture *The pipes froze and burst. Dan burst the balloon with a pin.* 2. *noun* sudden release, rush, surge, eruption, outbreak *In a burst of speed, she crossed the finish line in first place.*

bury *verb* 1. inter, lay to rest, entomb *We buried the dead bird.* 2. cover, conceal, hide *Mayan ruins were found buried in the jungle.* uncover, expose

business *noun* 1. work, occupation, profession, job, career *My dad travels a lot in his business.* 2. company, corporation, firm, enterprise, organization *George is starting a software-development business.* 3. trade, sales, marketing, commerce, dealings *Northern resorts do most of their business during the summer.* 4. concern, affair, interest, problem, responsibility *I told Diane that my grade on the test was my business, not hers.*

bustle *noun* fuss, activity, flurry, ado, action, stir, commotion, excitement, hubbub, to-do *We like the noise and bustle of a big city.* calm

busy *adjective* 1. working, active, occupied, engaged, on the go *The family is busy with school, work, sports, and weekend activities.* idle, inactive 2. full of activity, hectic, eventful, demanding *Mom has a busy schedule today.*

but 1. *conjunction* however, nevertheless *We thought we might miss our flight, but we made it on time.* 2. *preposition* except, other than, excluding *Everyone is present but Janet.* 3. *adverb* only, just, merely, simply *We have but one chance to succeed.*

button 1. *noun* fastener, clasp *The top button on my shirt is missing.* 2. knob, switch *Click the left mouse button twice.* 3. *verb* fasten, clasp, hook, close *Button your jacket—it's cold.* unbutton, open

buy 1. *verb* purchase, get, acquire, pay for *Dad says I have to buy CDs with my own money.* sell 2. *noun* bargain, good deal *I got a real buy on a digital camera.*

by *preposition* 1. near, beside, at, next to *Dana's house is the one by the high school.* 2. before, sooner than, no later than *We'll be there by 7:00.*

C

cab *noun* taxi, taxicab *We called a cab to take us to the airport.*

cabin *noun* small house, cottage, bungalow, hut, lodge *We stayed in a cabin in the woods during vacation.*

cable *noun* 1. telegram, message, telegraph, wire, telecommunications system *Most news is transmitted by satellite now, rather than by cable.* 2. wire, rope, cord, line, chain *The cables that hold suspension bridges are made of thousands of steel wires bound tightly together.*

cafeteria *noun* restaurant, café, snack bar, diner *The school cafeteria served pizza for lunch today.*

cage 1. *noun* pen, coop, enclosure *The gerbils' cage has a wheel for them to exercise on.* 2. *verb* confine, enclose, pen, fence in *The zoo no longer cages animals but lets them roam outdoors in natural habitats.*

calculate *verb* compute, figure, estimate, reckon, analyze *Becky calculated the cost of her purchases. Ben calculated the chances of his winning the competition.*

call 1. *verb* shout, yell, cry out *Daphne called out from the next room.* 2. telephone, phone, dial, ring *Sharon called to say she'd be late.* 3. summon, command, order, bid, fetch *The dog comes when you call him.* 4. name, label, designate, dub *Alexander was the first king to be called "the Great."* 5. *noun* shout, yell, cry *The lifeguard quickly responded to the swimmer's call for help.* 6. request, plea, appeal *The organization has made a call for volunteers.*

calm 1. *adjective* quiet, still, peaceful, serene, tranquil, cool, relaxed *My mom manages to stay calm during any family crisis.* excited, agitated 2. *verb* relax, soothe, quiet, pacify *I calmed my crying brother with hugs and kisses. His reassurances calmed our fears.* excite

camouflage 1. *noun* disguise, protective coloring, mimicry, cover, screen, mask *Camouflage conceals an animal from its predators.* 2. *verb* conceal, disguise, hide, mask *A chameleon is able to camouflage itself by changing color to match its surroundings.*

campaign 1. *noun* crusade, drive, cause, movement *The senior class started a campaign in order to raise money for medical supplies to help the victims of the recent earthquake.* 2. *verb* crusade, push, strive, fight, battle *People around the world continue to campaign for civil* *rights. The mayor has decided to campaign for reelection.*

can 1. *noun* container, tin, receptacle *When you're at the store, buy a couple of cans of beans.* 2. *verb* preserve, tin, bottle *I helped pick and can the tomatoes from our garden.*

canal *noun* waterway, channel *Ship canals make it possible to transport goods more quickly from one part of the world to another.*

cancel *verb* stop, call off, set aside, do away with *The game was canceled because of rain. I canceled an appointment with my dentist.*

candid *adjective* sincere, blunt, outspoken, frank, straightforward, direct *My friend Sandra knows she won't hurt my feelings by being candid with me.*

candidate *noun* applicant, nominee, runner, contestant, contender *I haven't decided which candidate for class president I'll vote for.*

cap *noun* cover, top, crown, lid *Joey always leaves the cap off the toothpaste.*

capability *noun* ability, power, fitness, capacity, skill, talent, competency, efficiency *Maria has the capability to do well at anything she tries. This software has fax and e-mail capabilities.* inability

capable *adjective* able, competent, skilled, talented, efficient *Our team is capable of winning the title. Leon is a capable student.*

capacity *noun* 1. size, volume, content, space, room *The auditorium has the capacity to seat 300.* 2. ability, capability, talent, skill *Darlene has a remarkable capacity for making people feel at ease.* 3. position, function, duty, role *In her capacity as guidance counselor, Mrs. Santini helps students with their problems.*

capital *noun* 1. money, funds, stock, assets, cash, wealth, savings *You need to raise capital in order to start a business.* 2. government seat, headquarters *Washington, D.C., is the capital of the United States.* 3. large letter *A proper name should be written with a capital.*

capsize *verb* upset, overturn, overthrow, tip over *The canoe capsized when we tried to get in it.*

caption *noun* title, heading, headline, subtitle, description *The caption next to each picture tells what it is.*

captivate *verb* charm, fascinate, delight, bewitch *The audience was captivated by the children's singing.*

capture 1. *verb* arrest, seize, apprehend, catch, take *The object of the game is to capture the other player's towers.* 2. *noun* arrest, seizure, apprehension *A reward was offered for the capture of the bank robbers.*

car *noun* automobile, vehicle, auto *Dad forgot where he parked the car at the mall.*

care *noun* 1. thought, worry, anxiety, stress, concern *He behaves as if he hasn't a care in the world.* neglect 2. attention, caution, carefulness, thought, heed *She drove with care through the fresh snow.* 3. protection, charge, supervision, keeping, custody *Great-Grandmother is in the care of a full-time nurse.*

career *noun* profession, occupation, vocation, calling, trade *I'm thinking of a career as a veterinarian.*

care for *verb* 1. love, like, have affection for, be fond of *You can see that Grandpa and Grandma care deeply for each other.* 2. take care of, attend to, look after, watch over *I promised Dad I'd care for a puppy if we got one.* 3. want, desire, like to have *Would you care for something to drink?*

carefree *adjective* happy, gay, lighthearted, breezy, lively, jolly, spry, energetic, spirited, active *Tomorrow we return to school after a carefree summer vacation.* unhappy

careful *adjective* 1. prudent, vigilant, wary *Be careful crossing Main Street. We were careful not to tell Raul about his surprise party. Our family is careful about money.* careless, reckless 2. thorough, conscientious, precise, accurate *Ellen takes careful notes in class.* careless **CAREFULLY** adverb *I copied down the phone number very carefully. We walked carefully down the steep path.*

careless *adjective* 1. reckless, irresponsible, thoughtless, negligent, unthinking *A careless driver didn't stop for the red light.* 2. sloppy, messy, slovenly, negligent *I try not to be careless about my appearance.* careful

cargo *noun* load, freight, shipment *We waited while cargo and baggage were loaded onto the plane.*

carnival *noun* fair, festival, celebration *Our town celebrates the 4th of July with a carnival and fireworks display.*

carol *noun* song, hymn, ballad *Christians sing carols at Christmas.*

carpet *noun* 1. rug, mat, floor covering *I help clean sometimes by vacuuming the carpet.* 2. covering, layer, mass *The woods has a carpet of leaves in the fall and a carpet of flowers in the spring.*

carriage *noun* vehicle, conveyance, buggy *Cinderella's horse-drawn carriage turned into a pumpkin at midnight.*

carry *verb* 1. transport, convey, move, bring, take *David carried the groceries out to the car.* 2. bear, support, sustain *The rafters carry the weight of the roof. We carry responsibility for our own actions.* 3. stock, offer for sale, furnish, supply, provide *The grocery store where we shop carries organic food.*

carve *verb* 1. cut, slice *Grandpa carved the Thanksgiving turkey.* 2. sculpt, cut, whittle, form, shape *Uncle Louis carves birds out of wood and sells them at a crafts show.*

case *noun* 1. container, box, crate, carton *The teacher ordered a case of dictionaries for our class.* 2. instance, example, event, situation, circumstance *The principal is looking into several cases of cheating at our school.* 3. lawsuit, legal action *The case will be decided by a jury.*

cash *noun* money, currency, bills, coins *Will this purchase be cash or credit card?*

cast 1. *verb* throw, fling, pitch, toss *We stood on the shore casting stones into the water.* 2. mold, form, shape *Many ancient Greek and Roman statues were cast in bronze.* 3. produce, form, create, send out, throw off *The late-afternoon sun cast long shadows.* 4. *noun* throw, pitch, toss, fling *On my first cast, my fishing line snagged on a branch.* 5. company, performers, actors, troupe, players *The entire cast took a bow at the end of the play.*

castle *noun* fort, fortress, stronghold, citadel, palace, château *Castles were originally built to defend communities against invaders.*

casual *adjective* 1. informal, relaxed, leisure *We changed into casual clothes for the picnic.* 2. unplanned, chance, unexpected, accidental *Antonio and I became close friends after a casual meeting at a party.* planned, scheduled

casualty *noun* victim, wounded person, injured person, dead person, fatality *Reducing the number of highway casualties is a priority.*

catalog 1. *noun* list, record, file, index, directory *Most libraries now have computerized catalogs of their books.* 2. *verb* list, classify, record, sort, index, arrange *Doris cataloged her rock collection.*

catastrophe *noun* calamity, misfortune, tragedy, disaster *The quick cleanup of the oil spill prevented an environmental catastrophe.*

catch 1. *verb* take, arrest, seize, apprehend, capture *The police were able to catch the thief before he left the scene.* 2. grab, grasp, seize, receive, intercept *Mitch caught the pass* *and ran down the field for a touchdown.* 3. become infected with, get, come down with, contract *Nearly everyone at school caught the flu.* 4. discover, surprise, find, notice *Mom caught me trying to hide her birthday present.* 5. *noun* grab, snatch *Connie made a great one-handed catch.* 6. fastener, latch, hook, clasp *Dad put a stronger catch on the gate so the horse doesn't escape.* 7. problem, snag, difficulty, drawback, hitch *This sounds too good to be true—what's the catch?*

catchy *adjective* attractive, memorable, appealing, popular *That's a catchy tune.*

category *noun* group, division, class, type, classification *The book won first prize in the children's category.*

cause 1. *noun* reason, basis, grounds, source, origin *Investigators are trying to determine the cause of the fire. There is no cause for alarm.* 2. interest, mission, purpose, goal *My father supports women's rights causes.* 3. *verb* make happen, begin, bring about, produce *High winds and hail caused damage to the crops.*

caution 1. *verb* warn, advise, alert, admonish, remind *Parents need to caution their children against speaking to strangers.* 2. *noun* care, attention, vigilance, watchfulness, wariness *Drivers are urged to proceed with caution in highway construction zones.*

cautious *adjective* attentive, watchful, wary, careful, vigilant *I am always cautious when I walk past a house with a large dog in the yard.* reckless

cave *noun* cavern, grotto, tunnel *Karen and I explored a cave in the side of a hill.*

cavity *noun* hole, pit, crater, hollow, opening, void *The birds nest in cavities in cliffs, rocks, and walls.*

cease *verb* stop, end, halt, quit, discontinue *The rain ceased after three days.* continue

celebrate *verb* 1. honor, observe, commemorate *Our family celebrated my great-grandmother's ninetieth birthday.* 2. enjoy oneself, have fun, make merry, revel, party *The TV program showed college students celebrating during spring break.*

celebrity *noun* famous person, star, superstar, notable personality *Anna got the autographs of a couple of celebrities when she visited Hollywood.*

cell *noun* small room, chamber, cubicle, lockup *The prison cell measured ten feet by ten feet.*

cement 1. *noun* concrete, mortar *The truck came today with the cement for the foundation of our new house.* 2. adhesive, glue, paste, bonding material *We use rubber cement for our classroom art projects.* 3. *verb* join, fasten, bond, stick, glue *This handle can be cemented back onto the cup.*

cemetery *noun* graveyard, burial ground *Grandpa goes to the cemetery to visit Grandma's grave every month.*

center 1. *noun* middle, heart, core, nucleus, interior *Chocolates with cherries in the center are my favorites.* 2. building, facility, complex *Last night we saw a play at the performing-arts center.* 3. *verb* focus, concentrate *The scientist's research centers on finding a cure for cancer.*

central *adjective* main, chief, principal, leading *Frankenstein is the central character in a novel by Mary Shelley.* unimportant 2. middle, inner, interior, mid *Mexico City is located in central Mexico.* outer

ceremony *noun* observance, service, rite, ritual, celebration *Last night we went to my sister's high school graduation ceremony.*

certain *adjective* 1. sure, positive, definite, confident, convinced *I am certain that Glenda can be trusted with our secret.* uncertain 2. particular, specific, precise, special *Certain requirements must be met before you can be admitted to the advanced class.*

certainly *adverb* positively, surely, without doubt, definitely *That certainly was a good meal.*

certify *verb* guarantee, testify, vouch for, affirm, confirm *The fire safety inspector certified that the school is safe.*

chain 1. *noun* series, string, sequence, course, succession *The police officer explained the chain of events that led to the arrest of the suspect.* 2. group, string, franchise, company *My uncle Tony owns a chain of restaurants.* 3. *verb* fasten, secure, tie, hold, restrain *It's against the law to chain your bicycle to trees in our town.*

chair 1. *noun* seat, bench, armchair, rocker *We didn't have enough chairs for our guests, so I sat on the floor.* 2. *verb* lead, direct, preside over *Mrs. Paske will chair tonight's meeting.*

chairperson *noun* presiding officer, chairman, chairwoman, chair, director, head, leader *Ruth's mother is chairperson of the mayor's campaign for reelection.*

challenge 1. *noun* dare, invitation, call, bidding, summons *I accepted my sister's challenge to beat her at chess.* 2. difficulty, test, problem, trial, task *I find math word problems a challenge.* 3. *verb* dare, invite, summon *Anne challenged Carol to a race.* 4. question, dispute, object to, disagree with *The defendant's lawyer challenged the judge's decision.*

champion 1. *noun* winner, victor, best, conqueror *The champion was awarded a trophy in a ceremony following the game.* loser 2. defender, upholder, protector, advocate

Dr. Martin Luther King, Jr., was a champion of civil rights. 3. *verb* support, defend, fight for, advocate *John Muir championed conservation and the creation of national parks.* CHAMPIONSHIP noun *Our school has won its third softball championship.*

chance 1. *noun* opportunity, occasion, opening *If you get a chance, please stop at the store for milk.* 2. possibility, probability, likelihood, prospect *The weather forecast says there's a chance of rain tonight.* 3. luck, fate, fortune, accident *Chance has led to the discovery of the dinosaur fossils.* 4. risk, gamble, hazard *We took no chances during the tornado warning and went to the basement.* 5. *verb* happen, occur, come about, take place *I was passing by when I chanced to see Juan in the yard, so I stopped to say hello.* 6. try, attempt, risk, gamble, hazard *You might be able to drive home safely in this blizzard, but why chance it?*

change 1. *verb* alter, vary, modify, transform, make different *Carlene changed her appearance by dyeing her hair red. Dennis changed his plans for the weekend.* 2. exchange, switch, replace, substitute *Let's change seats—I can't see the movie.* 3. *noun* alteration, modification, transformation, difference *The survey shows a change in public opinion.* 4. coins, cash *Do you have any change for the snack machine?*

channel *noun* 1. waterway, straight, passageway, corridor, artery *The main channel of the river is marked with buoys.* 2. TV station *If you don't like the program, change the channel.*

chaos *noun* confusion, disorder, unruliness, commotion, turmoil *There was total chaos when the winning team's fans rushed onto the field to celebrate.* order

chap *verb* crack, break, split, become rough *My lips chap in the cold weather.*

chapter *noun* 1. section, part, division, portion *Open your books to the third chapter.* 2. branch, group, division *My mom volunteers for the local chapter of the American Red Cross.*

character *noun* 1. nature, personality, temperament, quality, trait, makeup *His charm and amusing character make him very likable.* 2. honor, integrity, honesty, moral strength *A person with character knows the difference between right and wrong.* 3. person, actor, performer, player *The main character in the book is a private detective.* 4. letter, sign, symbol *Several thousand characters are used in the modern Chinese alphabet.*

characteristic 1. *adjective* typical, distinguishing, distinctive, individual, specific *Lemons have their own characteristic flavor. A tropical oceanic climate is characteristic of the islands of Hawaii.* 2. *noun* quality, feature, attribute, trait *I think Michael's sense of humor is his best characteristic.*

charge 1. *verb* bill, ask as a price, expect, require *The company charges extra for shipping if you want to receive your order the next day.* 2. record for payment later, bill, debit *Charge this to my account, please.* 3. rush, attack, storm, assault *The brigade charged the fort.* 4. accuse, indict, impeach, blame *The police charged the man with receiving stolen property.* 5. *noun* price, cost, amount, rate *What's the charge for a room with a king-size bed?* 6. accusation, complaint, allegation, indictment *The charge against her was dropped when someone else confessed.* 7. attack, assault, rush *The Confederate cavalry charged up the hill.* 8. responsibility, care, custody, protection, guardianship *The new nanny announced that while the children were in her charge, they must always say "please" and "thank you."*

charitable *adjective* generous, kindly, giving, bighearted *Mr. Hershey was a charitable man who left his fortune to a school for orphans.* selfish

charity *noun* 1. financial help, donations, contributions, gifts, relief, aid *The organization has asked for food and clothing for families who depend on charity to survive.* 2. aid agency, charitable foundation *Gifts to charities are tax-deductible.*

charm 1. *noun* appeal, allure, attractiveness, attraction *We stayed in the country at a bed-and-breakfast with loads of charm.* 2. *verb* please, delight, fascinate, captivate, enchant *We were charmed by our host's warm greeting.*

charming *adjective* pleasing, delightful, fascinating, appealing, enchanting, alluring *We visited many charming villages on our trip to Ireland. Eleanor and David are a charming couple.* obnoxious

charter *verb* hire, lease, rent *Our class chartered a bus for a field trip to a historic fort.*

chase 1. *verb* run after, pursue, follow, hunt, tail, trail, track *Our cat chases mice.* 2. drive away, send away *A mockingbird will chase anyone or anything that gets too close to its nest.* 3. *noun* pursuit, hunt *The police caught the escaped prisoners after a short chase.*

chat 1. *verb* talk, converse, gossip *The player signed autographs and chatted briefly with his fans.* 2. *noun* talk, conversation, discussion, gossip *Let's meet for coffee and a chat.*

chatter 1. *verb* jabber, babble, rattle on, chat *The children chattered away in the backseat.* 2. *noun* talk, babble, chitchat *The students' chatter in the back of the room disturbed the class.*

cheap *adjective* 1. inexpensive, low-priced, reasonable, low-cost, economical, bargain-priced *The food at this restaurant is cheap and really good.* expensive 2. poor quality, inferior, shoddy, shabby (*Slang*—tacky, trashy) *The company makes cheap toys that break after a week's use.* good quality, superior

cheat *verb* defraud, swindle, deceive, mislead, trick, dupe, con *A friend of my parents was cheated out of $10,000 in an Internet fraud.*

check 1. *verb* stop, control, halt, curb, contain, suppress, restrain *He checked himself before he said something he might regret.* 2. examine, inspect, look at, investigate, study *Inspectors checked our passports at the gate.* 3. *noun* examination, inspection, investigation, study *Make a check of all the doors to see that they're locked.* 4. control, constraint, restraint, hindrance, deterrent *Mom says we need a budget as a check on our spending.* 5. bill, tab, invoice *We left a tip for the waiter when we paid our check.*

checkup *noun* examination, physical *I went to the doctor for a checkup before going to camp.*

cheer 1. *verb* shout, yell, applaud, hail, root for *The crowd cheered the team as it came onto the field.* 2. raise one's spirits, hearten, brighten, perk up, enliven *It cheers nursing home residents to see their families. Mom and Dad were really cheered up by my good report card.* 3. *noun* shout, yell, applause *The band was greeted with loud cheers from the audience.* 4. happiness, cheerfulness, joy, delight, pleasure *Sitting around a campfire roasting marshmallows brought cheer to the campers.*

cheerful *adjective* 1. happy, glad, joyful, lighthearted, merry *Vicky's cheerful attitude makes her fun to be around. Kelly greeted us with a friendly "Hello" and a cheerful grin.* 2. bright, sunny, pleasant *The room is painted a cheerful yellow.*

cherish *verb* adore, hold dear, treasure, prize, love, care for *We cherish our families most of all.*

chest *noun* 1. box, crate, case, trunk, container *My dad keeps his tools in a chest in the garage.* 2. upper body, ribs, breast, thorax *We watched an old Tarzan movie in which he yells and beats his chest.*

chew *verb* bite, grind, nibble, munch *Our dog loves to chew on rawhide bones.*

chief 1. *noun* leader, head, director, boss, ruler *Most tribal chiefs are democratically elected officials.* 2. *adjective* principal, leading, main, most important, primary *The chief reason for Grandma and Grandpa's move to Florida was its warm weather.*

chiefly *adverb* mainly, mostly, above all, especially *Thomas Edison is known chiefly for his invention of the electric lightbulb, even though he patented over 1,000 other inventions.*

child *noun* 1. youngster, baby, tot, juvenile, youth, young boy or girl, kid *There was no television when Grandma was a child.* 2. offspring, son, daughter, descendant *Parents enjoy reading some of the same books their children enjoy.*

chill 1. *noun* coldness, coolness, iciness, bite, nip *There was a chill in the air that felt like autumn.* warmth 2. *verb* make cold, cool, refrigerate, freeze *The fruit smoothie should be chilled. The cold wind chilled us to the bone.* heated, warmed

chilly *adjective* cold, cool, brisk, nippy, wintry *It's much too chilly to go outside without a jacket.* warm

chime *verb* ring, jingle, peal *The clock on the steeple chimed every hour.*

chip 1. *verb* break, crack, damage, nick *I chipped a plate when I was washing it.* 2. *noun* fragment, piece, bit, flake *Wood chips used around plants in your yard keep weeds from coming up.*

chip in *verb* contribute, help, participate, take part *If we all chip in, we can get the housework done and go to a movie. Everyone chipped in to buy a birthday present for our teacher.*

chisel *verb* cut, carve, shape, sculpt *The ancient Egyptians chiseled their hieroglyphic writing into stone.*

chivalrous *adjective* courteous, gallant, polite, noble *Knights of the Middle Ages were taught to be chivalrous.*

choice 1. *noun* selection, pick, option, alternative, preference *I have to make a choice between a bicycle and a bat and glove for my birthday. The restaurant offers a choice of specials.* 2. *adjective* best, excellent, fine, prime, first-rate *The farmers' market has a large selection of choice fruits and vegetables.*

choke *verb* 1. smother, suffocate, strangle, muffle *The Heimlich maneuver can save the life of someone who is choking on food.* 2. block, clog, plug, obstruct *The storm-water drains in the street are choked with leaves.*

chop 1. *verb* cut, slice, dice, cube *I helped Dad chop the onions and carrots for the stew.* 2. fell, hew, hack, split *My sister and I chopped wood for the fireplace.* 3. *noun* blow, punch, stroke *A legend tells of Paul Bunyan, who could cut down a tree with a single chop of his ax.*

chore *noun* task, job, work, assignment, duty, function *Before I leave for school, I have three chores: to feed the cats, make my bed, and take out the garbage.*

chorus *noun* choir, singing group, vocal group *Janice is the best singer in the school chorus.*

chronic *adjective* constant, persistent, long-lasting, continuing *Physical therapy can help people with chronic back pain.*

chronicle *noun* history, story, account, journal, narrative *The book* South *is a chronicle by Sir Ernest Shackleton of his attempt to reach the South Pole.*

chubby *adjective* plump, round, stout, fat, pudgy, stocky, chunky *My baby brother has chubby cheeks and curly, dark hair.* skinny

chuck *verb* 1. tap, pat, tickle *Uncle Henry chucked the baby under the chin.* 2. throw, toss, pitch, fling, cast *We chucked our empty cans into the container labeled "recycle."*

chuckle 1. *verb* laugh, giggle, snicker, titter, chortle *Dad chuckled to himself as he read the joke e-mail.* 2. *noun* laugh, giggle, snicker *I get a real chuckle out of slapstick comedy.*

chum *noun* friend, mate, buddy, pal, companion, partner, comrade *Mom and Dad are looking forward to seeing all their old school chums at their college reunion.*

chunk *noun* lump, wad, bulk, mass, hunk *Farah offered me a huge chunk of chocolate candy.*

church *noun* place of worship, chapel, cathedral, temple *I sing in the youth choir at our church.*

circle 1. *noun* ring, disk, loop, sphere *Arrange the chairs in a circle.* 2. group, set, crowd, clique *The popular professor has a wide circle of friends both inside and outside the university.* 3. *verb* surround, enclose, ring *I circled my answers on the test. A ring of trees circled the building.* 4. move around, go around, revolve, orbit *Communication satellites circle the earth at the same speed as the earth's rotation.*

circulate *verb* 1. spread, distribute, pass around, go around, broadcast *A rumor is circulating around town that our school is closing.* 2. flow, move, travel, whirl *The ceiling fan helps circulate the warm air throughout the room.*

circumstance *noun* condition, situation, state of affairs *Under the same circumstances, I would do just as you did.*

citizen *noun* inhabitant, occupant, resident *Over 600,000 people become U.S. citizens each year.*

city *noun* metropolis, municipality, urban area, town *Carolyn has always lived on a farm and has never visited a big city.*

civil *adjective* 1. public, civic, municipal, community *In the United States our civil liberties are guaranteed by the Constitution.* 2. polite, courteous, cordial, pleasant *I try to be civil to people, no matter how rude they are.* uncivil

civilization *noun* culture, society *The Mayan civilization was one of the most advanced in Mexico and Central America.*

clad *adjective* clothed, dressed, attired *The painting showed knights clad in armor riding horses.*

claim 1. *noun* right, demand, title, interest *During the gold rush, miners staked a claim to an area of ground.* 2. *verb* say, declare, assert, maintain, argue *The umpire claimed that the runner didn't touch home plate and was out.* 3. take, demand, require, call for *Homework is claiming too much of my time.*

clamor 1. *verb* demand, call, cry out *Fans are clamoring for tickets to the rock group's concert.* 2. *noun* commotion, noise, uproar, din, racket *We couldn't hear the speech above the clamor of the protesters.*

clamp *verb* fasten, clasp, brace *You need to clamp the parts together while the glue dries.*

clan *noun* group, crowd, clique, tribe, folk, family *The Burchard clan gets together every summer for a family reunion.*

clap 1. *verb* applaud *The audience clapped loudly until the group came back for an encore.* 2. pat, slap, tap, strike *Everyone clapped Bobby on the back after he hit a home run.* 3. *noun* sudden loud noise, crack, crash *The lightning was followed immediately by a clap of thunder.*

clarify *verb* explain, refine, make clear, simplify *I asked the teacher to clarify the last question on the test.* confuse

clash 1. *verb* disagree, come into conflict, quarrel, argue, fight *My parents and I clashed over my bedtime.* agree 2. *noun* crash, clatter, clang, bang *The music ended with a clash of the cymbals.* 3. *noun* disagreement, conflict, quarrel, argument, fight *There were daily clashes between the soldiers along the border between the enemy countries.*

clasp 1. *noun* fastener, hook, clip, catch *I lost my bracelet when the clasp broke.* 2. *verb* grasp, hold, clutch *He leaned back in his chair, clasped his hands behind his head, and fell asleep.*

class 1. *noun* category, division, classification, group, type, kind, sort *Insects are the largest class of organisms in the world.* 2. course, subject, lesson, session, seminar *The computer class meets in this room.* 3. *verb* categorize, classify, arrange, sort, group *You must be classed as an amateur in order to compete in the race.*

classify *verb* organize, group, categorize, sort, arrange, rank *The companies in this list are classified by zip code.*

clean 1. *adjective* spotless, sanitary, unsoiled, washed, fresh, pure, uncontaminated *Be sure your hands are clean before you eat. I showered and changed into clean clothes.* dirty

2. *verb* wash, cleanse, scrub, scour, wipe, launder *Cats clean their fur with their tongues. I helped Mom clean the kitchen while Dad cleaned and vacuumed the living room.* dirty

clear 1. *adjective* transparent, sheer, see-through, translucent *The water was so clear we could see schools of fish 20 feet down.* opaque 2. bright, sunny, cloudless, fair *It was clear this morning but clouded up in the afternoon.* *cloudy* 3. easily understood, plain, evident, obvious, apparent *It is clear from the evidence that he is lying. The witness gave a clear account of the accident.* unclear 4. *verb* tidy, clean, straighten, empty *If you clear the table, I'll wash the dishes.* 5. brighten, become sunny *The weather cleared after a brief thundershower.* 6. absolve, acquit, pardon, free, let go, release, discharge, excuse *The accused was cleared of the robbery charges when the police could find no evidence.*

clever *adjective* skillful, cunning, bright, smart, alert, intelligent *Lydia is the cleverest student in class and always the first to raise her hand. It was very clever of you to get the solution to that puzzle.* dull

client *noun* customer, prospect, patron *Mr. Sanchez is an excellent lawyer with many clients.*

cliff *noun* bluff, rock face, precipice, promontory *Native Americans lived in spectacular dwellings built into the cliffs of the southwestern United States.*

climate *noun* weather, temperature, environment, atmospheric conditions *Florida's climate is warm and humid.*

climax *noun* high point, culmination, peak *The game came to an exciting climax when the quarterback threw a pass for the winning touchdown.*

climb 1. *verb* mount, ascend, rise, go up *The kitten climbed to the top of the tree. The plane climbed to a cruising altitude of 32,000 feet.* descend 2. increase, rise, escalate *Gas prices climbed to their highest level in years.* descend 3. *noun* ascent *The view from the top of the hill is worth the climb.* descent

cling *verb* hold, grip, adhere, stick *Static electricity makes the clothes from the dryer cling to each other.*

clip *verb* 1. cut, trim, snip, shear, prune *The hedges next to the house need clipping. I clipped an ad for a bicycle from the newspaper and showed it to Dad.* 2. fasten, attach, hold, staple *Clip all the pages together in order.*

cloak 1. *noun* cape, shawl, wrap, robe, mantle *Little Red Riding Hood wore a red cloak and hood.* 2. cover, screen, veil, blind, shroud *The spies operated under a cloak of secrecy.* 3. *verb* hide, conceal, cover, obscure, camouflage, protect *The campfire died and the campsite became cloaked in darkness.*

clog *verb* block, obstruct, choke, stop up, congest, jam *The highway was clogged with weekend traffic.*

close¹ 1. *verb* shut, fasten, lock, seal, secure, bolt *Please close the door. I kept closing my eyes and dozing off.* open 2. end, conclude, finish, wind up, wrap up *The speaker closed by asking for questions from the audience.* 3. *noun* end, conclusion, finish, cessation, windup, wrap-up *Your work must be turned in by the close of the school day.*

close² 1. *adjective* near, nearby, adjacent, neighboring *Our houses are close together.* distant 2. approaching, imminent, at hand *The deadline for making your reservations is close.* distant 3. intimate, familiar, friendly, inseparable *The twins are really close. Dana and I are close friends.* distant 4. careful, thorough, strict, rigorous, firm. *Pay close attention.* 5. nearly equal, evenly matched *We finally won after a very close game.* 6. *adverb* near, nearby *Come closer so I can hear you better.*

clothe *verb* dress, cover, wrap, attire *The children were clothed in snowsuits, scarves, and mittens.*

cloudy *adjective* dark, overcast, gloomy, gray, sunless, hazy *Tuesday will be cloudy with a chance of rain.* sunny, clear

clown 1. *verb* fool, play, joke, act silly *Quit clowning around and start your homework.* 2. *noun* comedian, comic, jester, joker, prankster *The circus clowns entertained the children by juggling and doing silly stunts.*

club 1. *verb* hit, beat, strike, bat, knock, slug, bash (*Slang*—clobber) *The puppets in the show clubbed each other with rubber bats.* 2. *noun* bat, stick, staff, nightstick, cudgel *Clubs are sometimes used by police to control riots.* 3. organization, association, society, group, league *Our school science club won second place for its experiment in a state competition.* 4. meeting place, facility, center *Mom and Dad go to the health club twice a week to work out.*

clue *noun* hint, evidence, sign, lead, tip, information *Witnesses provided clues that led to the suspect's arrest. Can you help me with this crossword-puzzle clue?*

clump *noun* cluster, bunch, group, mass *Clumps of trees and bushes covered the hillside.*

clumsy *adjective* awkward, ungraceful, ungainly, cumbersome, uncoordinated *The cast on Jeanne's broken leg made her very clumsy. I made a clumsy attempt to catch the fly ball.*

cluster 1. *noun* bunch, group, set, batch, clump *Clusters of grapes hung from the vines.* 2. *verb* collect, assemble, gather, congregate, huddle *Everyone clustered around the star for her autograph.*

clutch *verb* cling, hold, grasp, grip, seize, hang on to *I clutched the railing to keep from falling down the stairs.*

clutter *noun* disorder, mess, litter, untidiness, confusion *I had to clean up the clutter in my room before I could go out.*

coach 1. *verb* train, teach, tutor, instruct *My older sister coaches swimmers during the summer.* 2. *noun* trainer, teacher, instructor, tutor *The tennis coach told me I need to work on my serve.* 3. carriage, stagecoach *Many early travelers in the United States traveled by coach and steamboat.*

coarse *adjective* rough, scratchy, abrasive, grainy *The beach near here is made up of pebbles and coarse sand. Coarse cloth such as burlap is used for making sacks.* fine, smooth

coast 1. *verb* slide, glide, slip, drift, cruise, ride *We coasted down the hill on our bicycles.* 2. *noun* seacoast, coastline, seashore, seaside, shore, shoreline, waterfront *Many ships have been wrecked off the coast of North Carolina.* COASTAL adjective *Manatees live in the warm coastal waters of Florida.*

coat *noun* 1. jacket, overcoat, topcoat, raincoat, parka, sport coat *Put on a coat and mittens—it's cold today.* 2. layer, covering, film, glaze, coating *The walls in my room need a fresh coat of paint.* 3. fur, hair, wool *The cat sat in the sun washing its coat.* 4. *verb* cover, spread, smear *The furniture was coated with dust.*

coax *verb* persuade, influence, urge, induce, prevail upon *I tried to coax a smile out of the little boy. We coaxed Mom and Dad into letting us sleep in a tent in the backyard.*

code *noun* 1. laws, rules, set of regulations, policy, system *Our school has a dress code that the students must follow.* 2. secret writing, cipher *The spy sent her message in code.*

coil 1. *verb* loop, twist, curl, wind, twine *The rope was coiled neatly on the boat's deck.* 2. *noun* loop, twist, ring, spiral *Gina wore a bracelet of gold coils.*

coin 1. *verb* invent, make up, devise, originate *William Shakespeare likely coined the word "fashionable."* 2. *noun* money, change, coinage *This vending machine only takes coins.*

coincide *verb* agree, correspond, match, concur, accord *We scheduled our vacation to coincide with the children's spring break.*

coincidence *noun* chance, luck, accident, fate *By coincidence we met a family from our hometown in a restaurant in Italy.*

cold 1. *adjective* chilly, cool, freezing, icy, frigid, bitter *A cup of hot chocolate is really good on a cold day.* warm, hot 2. unfriendly, unfeeling, distant, aloof, uncaring *Carrie's*

~~~~~~

been cold to me ever since we argued. caring, friendly 3. *noun* flu, virus, illness, sickness, runny nose *Our teacher is home in bed with a cold.* 4. chill, chilliness, coldness, iciness, wintriness *I had to stand in the cold while waiting for the bus. Bundle up against the cold before you go outside.* warmth

collapse 1. *verb* cave in, give way, buckle, crumple, fall in, fall down *The roof collapsed under the heavy snow.* 2. fail, break down, end, fall through *The peace talks collapsed after a week.* 3. *noun* cave-in, giving way, crumpling *The earthquake caused the collapse of many buildings.* 4. failure, breakdown, end, disintegration *The collapse of the Roman Empire occurred in the fifth century.*

collar 1. *verb* catch, corner, grab, seize, arrest (*Slang*—nab) *A police officer collared a shoplifter who was leaving the store.* 2. *noun* neckband *The collar on this shirt feels like it's choking me.*

colleague *noun* associate, coworker, partner, associate, assistant, teammate, comrade *Dad took me with him to his office yesterday and introduced me to his colleagues.*

collect *verb* 1. assemble, gather, accumulate, pile up, amass, assemble, stockpile *There's a lot of old stuff collecting in our attic. A crowd collected to watch the street performers.* 2. raise, obtain, acquire, secure *Our club collects annual dues of $5.00.*

collection *noun* accumulation, assortment, stockpile, supply, mass *The library has a large collection of books.*

collide *verb* crash, hit, bump, ram, smash, run into *Dad swerved to avoid colliding with a deer that was crossing the road.*

collision *noun* crash, accident, impact, smash *No one was hurt in the collision at the corner of Main and Washington.*

colony *noun* society, group *A coral reef is a colony of tiny living animals.*

color 1. *noun* hue, shade, tint, dye, pigment, tinge *The colors in a rainbow are red, orange, yellow, green, blue, indigo, and violet.* 2. *verb* tint, dye, stain, paint, tinge *Mom colored the frosting on my birthday cake pink.*

colorful *adjective* 1. bright, vivid, vibrant, rich, multicolored *The dancers at the festival wore colorful traditional costumes.* colorless, drab 2. interesting, exciting, imaginative, vivid, lively *Aunt Helen gave a colorful and detailed account of her trip.* dull, boring, colorless

column *noun* 1. pillar, cylinder, post, support *Thirty-eight columns surround the Lincoln Memorial in Washington, D.C.* 2. article, feature, editorial, paragraph *Did you have a* *chance to read the sports column in the newspaper today?*

combat 1. *noun* battle, struggle, fight, contest, conflict, war *Both sides agreed to a pause in combat to give the peace talks a chance.* 2. *verb* fight, oppose, contest, battle, struggle against *The city is looking for new ways to combat homelessness.*

combination *noun* mixture, blend, composite, grouping *The word "blog" is a combination of the words "Web" and "log."*

combine *verb* join, unite, mix, connect, couple, blend, fuse *My parents says it's not always easy combining work and parenthood. Combine the ingredients in a small bowl and stir vigorously.* separate

come *verb* 1. arrive, appear, show up, turn up *My cousin came to spend the weekend. The school bus comes early every morning.* 2. approach, move toward, go to *People with tickets for the 1:30 flight were asked to come to the front of the line.* 3. occur, happen, take place, come about, fall *Tornadoes usually come in spring.* 4. reach, extend, stretch *The drapes come to the floor.* 5. be available, be offered, be sold *The cell phones come in six fashionable colors.* 6. originate, hail from, arise, derive *The word "language" comes from a Latin word that originally meant "tongue." My father's family came from Poland.*

comedian *noun* comic, wit, humorist, clown, joker *The best comedians make it look easy to be funny.*

comedy *noun* humor, wit, funniness, joking, clowning *Slapstick is my favorite type of comedy.*

comfort 1. *verb* console, reassure, soothe, cheer, gladden *Dad comforted my crying brother after my brother lost his teddy bear.* 2. *noun* relief, reassurance, support, help, aid, cheer *Letters from home bring comfort to soldiers who are away.* 3. ease, luxury, relief, well-being *We relaxed in comfort in our air-conditioned hotel room after a day in the hot sun.*

comfortable *adjective* 1. cozy, snug, secure (*Slang*—comfy) *I fell asleep on the comfortable sofa in the living room.* uncomfortable 2. relaxed, at ease, calm, tranquil, unbothered *I don't feel comfortable speaking in public.* uneasy, uncomfortable, bothered 3. pleasant, luxurious, affluent *My grandparents are trying to save enough money to have a comfortable lifestyle when they retire.*

comical *adjective* amusing, funny, humorous, hilarious, silly, ridiculous *My sister looked comical wearing round glasses with a huge false nose and mustache.* tragic

command 1. *verb* bid, order, direct, instruct, demand *The king and queen commanded Christopher Columbus to discover and conquer new lands.* 2. lead, head, be in charge of,

manage, control, supervise *A fleet admiral in the U.S. Navy commands a group of ships.*
3. *noun* order, decree, demand, instruction, direction, bidding *Our dog is trained
to obey when we give him commands.* 4. leadership, authority, management, control,
power, supervision *The captain knows the name of every person under his command.*

commemorate *verb* honor, celebrate, observe, salute, pay tribute to *Each year we
have a holiday to commemorate the life of Dr. Martin Luther King, Jr.*

commence *verb* begin, start, open, launch, initiate *Construction on the highway
is scheduled to commence in the spring. The government announced that it was ready to
commence peace talks.*

commend *verb* praise, compliment, approve, applaud, speak highly of *The soccer
coach was commended for teaching team members good sportsmanship.* criticize, disapprove

comment 1. *verb* remark, note, observe, mention, say, express *Our guests commented
on what a good cook my mom is.* 2. *noun* remark, note, statement, observation, opinion
People always make comments about how much alike my sister and I are.

commerce *noun* trade, business, dealings, buying, selling *Commerce today is dependent
on computer technology.*

commit *verb* 1. promise, pledge, vow, obligate, bind *It's easy to commit yourself to
too many activities and not have enough time for your homework. An anonymous donor has
committed $1,000,000 to the new arts center.* 2. do, perform, carry out *He admitted to
having committed the crime.* 3. entrust, hand over, confine, assign, institutionalize
She committed herself to the hospital for treatment for an eating disorder.

committee *noun* council, group, delegation, board, team *The members of the
committee voted to accept the proposal.*

common *adjective* 1. public, general, shared, joint, mutual, collective, communal
*My friend Carlos and I share a common interest in tennis. It is for the common good that
we need to clean up the environment.* private 2. usual, familiar, ordinary, everyday,
unexceptional, normal, average, routine *The doctor said that all I had was a common
cold. An eclipse of the moon is a fairly common occurrence.* unusual, uncommon
COMMONLY adverb *Jonathan David Samson, Jr., is more commonly known as "Dave."*

commotion *noun* disturbance, tumult, confusion, action, stir, fuss, excitement,
hubbub, to-do *A great deal of commotion surrounded the arrival of the famous movie star.
He heard the commotion in the forest, and a bear came plunging out of the trees.* calm, order

communicate *verb* 1. inform, tell, enlighten, report, convey *Babies communicate their* *needs by crying.* 2. talk, speak, converse, keep in touch *Cousin Jason communicates with me by e-mail.*

community *noun* 1. neighborhood, area, district, town, city, locality *For our rural community to attract business and industry, it needs good educational and health-care services.* 2. society, association, group, body *Acupuncture is gaining acceptance in the medical community.*

commute *verb* travel, go, shuttle *Dad commutes 20 miles round-trip to the city each day.*

compact 1. *adjective* dense, solid, firm, condensed, compressed *Shape the bread dough into a compact ball; then cover it and let it rise.* 2. small, little, tiny, miniature, trim, neatly arranged *My brother found a two-room apartment with a compact kitchen.* 3. *verb* compress, pack, condense, squeeze, press together *It's easier to walk on a beach with sand that has been compacted than on one with soft sand.* 4. *noun* agreement, contract, pact, treaty, bargain, understanding, deal *World leaders have signed a compact to promote peace, human rights, and environmental sustainability.*

companion *noun* partner, buddy, friend, pal, comrade, chum *The twins have been companions throughout their lives. Dad's afraid to fly, so Mom's traveling companion is her sister.*

company *noun* 1. business, firm, enterprise, corporation *Ted is getting a summer job with a landscaping company.* 2. guests, visitors, callers *We're having company for the weekend and need to shop for food.* 3. companionship, friendship, fellowship *We enjoyed the company of family and friends at last night's party.*

compare *verb* 1. evaluate, contrast, assess, balance, weigh, judge *We compared the features of the two cameras before we decided which brand to buy.* 2. equal, rival, approach, compete, measure up *Store-bought vegetables cannot compare with those picked fresh from the garden.*

comparison *noun* 1. contrast, evaluation, assessment, analysis, appraisal *A comparison of the price per can of the six-pack and the twelve-pack shows that the twelve-pack is a better value.* 2. likeness, similarity, resemblance *There's no comparison between the earliest personal computers and those of today.*

compassion *noun* sympathy, concern, kindness, care, consideration, understanding *The charity's volunteers show compassion for those who are less fortunate.* harshness, severity COMPASSIONATE adjective *The compassionate doctor offers free treatment to people too poor to pay.*

compatible *adjective* in agreement, in harmony, like-minded, well-suited *My tent mate at camp and I are very compatible.* incompatible

compel *verb* force, make, require, pressure, oblige *The troops suffered heavy losses and were compelled to retreat.*

compensate *verb* 1. pay, reward *Our neighbors always compensate me well for mowing their lawns.* 2. balance, make up for, even up, counteract, offset *It's important to drink water to compensate for fluid loss when running a race.*

compete *verb* contend, participate, take part, enter *A student from our school will compete in the national spelling bee finals this year.*

competent *adjective* able, effective, capable, qualified, fit, skilled, proficient, adept *A competent doctor won't be upset if you get a second opinion from another doctor.* incompetent

competition *noun* 1. rivalry, opposition, conflict, struggle *She overcame fierce competition to win the tennis championship.* 2. contest, game, match, meet *Jane won third place in the poetry-writing competition.*

compile *verb* gather, collect, assemble, accumulate, bring together *I compiled a list of the books I'd like to read.*

complain *verb* grumble, find fault, criticize, object, protest, gripe *Dad complained to the waiter that the food was cold. Customers are complaining about long lines at the checkout counter.*

complaint *noun* criticism, protest, grievance, objection *Mom filed a complaint with the manufacturer after the dishwasher broke a second time.*

complete 1. *verb* finish, conclude, accomplish, fulfill, end, wind up, finalize, wrap up *As soon as you've completed your chores, you may go out with your friends.* start, begin 2. *adjective* whole, entire, total. *A complete set of baseball cards once sold for $800,000.* incomplete 3. thorough, perfect, absolute *Dana's birthday party came as a complete surprise to her.* COMPLETELY *adverb Connie looks completely different with her hair cut short.*

complex 1. *adjective* difficult, hard, complicated, involved, puzzling, perplexing *The instructions for assembling the furniture were too complex for me to follow.* simple, easy 2. intricate, elaborate, compound *The International Space Station is a complex structure the size of two football fields.* simple 3. *noun* development, structure, center, facility *Great-Grandpa is moving into the new elderly housing complex.*

complicate *verb* confuse, muddle, snarl, make difficult, make involved *A snowstorm complicated travel this weekend.* simplify

complicated *adjective* difficult, involved, complex, intricate *My sister helps me understand complicated math problems.* easy, simple

compliment 1. *noun* praise, approval, admiration, acclaim, flattery *Juan received many compliments on his art project.* 2. *verb* praise, admire, commend, speak highly of *Mom complimented me on the breakfast I made for her on Mother's Day.*

comply with *verb* obey, abide by, consent to, submit to, conform to, follow, respect *You must comply with the regulations or pay a penalty.* disobey

compose *verb* 1. make up, make, form, constitute, comprise *Rocks are composed of one or more minerals.* 2. create, write, produce, devise, author *My music teacher helped me compose a piece of music on my guitar.* 3. calm, quiet, soothe, still, settle *She took a deep breath and tried to compose herself before giving her speech.*

composition *noun* piece of writing, paper, essay, document *The teacher had us write a composition about our favorite vacation.*

compound 1. *noun* mixture, mix, blend, combination *Water is a compound made up of hydrogen and oxygen.* 2. *verb* mix, blend, combine, unite, put together *Fifty years ago pharmacists compounded most medicines themselves.*

comprehend *verb* understand, realize, know, grasp, follow, perceive *It is difficult to comprehend that light from the nearest star, other than the sun, takes 4.3 years to reach Earth.*

comprehensive *adjective* complete, full, inclusive, broad, extensive, thorough *The tourist bureau provides a comprehensive guide to the city's museums.* limited, incomplete

compress *verb* squeeze, press, reduce, condense, concentrate, crush *Recycling machines compress shredded paper into large bales.* expand, spread

comprise *verb* include, contain, incorporate, encompass *The Hawaiian Island chain comprises over 100 volcanoes, of which only three are active.* exclude

compromise 1. *verb* settle, yield, concede, adjust, meet halfway *We both wanted the last piece of pie, but we compromised and cut it in half.* 2. *noun* understanding, settlement, deal, bargain, arrangement, middle ground *When Mom wanted to eat out and Dad wanted to stay home, they reached a compromise by ordering takeout.*

compulsory *adjective* required, necessary, mandatory, obligatory *Education for children is compulsory in this country.* optional

compute *verb* calculate, count, figure, estimate, reckon, work out *I computed the number of lawns I'd have to mow to earn enough for my own TV.*

comrade *noun* buddy, friend, pal, companion, partner, chum *Winning the Olympic gold medal is something he and his team comrades will never forget.*

conceal *verb* hide, cover, cloak, veil, camouflage *Clouds concealed the moon and stars. Marian tried hard to conceal her anger.* disclose

concede *verb* 1. admit, allow, grant, acknowledge, confess *I conceded that I was wrong. The candidate conceded defeat in the election.* deny, refuse 2. yield, surrender, give up, hand over, forfeit *Jim conceded the golf match after 15 holes.*

conceited *adjective* arrogant, vain, self-important, proud, superior, haughty, boastful, cocky *Charles was conceited enough to think that every girl he met fell in love with him.* modest

conceive *verb* imagine, picture, envision, think up, dream up *The Wright brothers conceived, designed, and built the first practical airplane.*

concentrate *verb* 1. think about, focus, contemplate, be absorbed in *Sharon was concentrating on the chess game and didn't see me enter the room.* 2. collect, gather, come together, center, converge *The population of Australia is concentrated along the eastern and southeastern coasts.* CONCENTRATION *noun The problem required my full concentration.*

concept *noun* thought, notion, idea, theory *The concept of cell phones began in 1947, but it took thirty-seven years for cell phone service to become available in the United States.*

concern 1. *verb* interest, affect, involve, relate to, pertain to *Tonight we will discuss issues that concern the entire community.* 2. worry, bother, trouble, disturb, upset *Parents are concerned about their kids' online activities.* 3. *noun* interest, business, affair, matter, involvement *My dad's salary is none of your concern.* 4. anxiety, worry, distress, apprehension *There is concern among environmental groups over the rain forests.*

concert *noun* music, recital, show, performance *The children's orchestra is giving a concert in the auditorium tonight.*

concise *adjective* brief, short, succinct, condensed *Definitions in a dictionary should be clear and concise.* lengthy

conclude *verb* 1. close, end, finish, stop, terminate, complete, wind up *The Olympic closing ceremony concludes with the extinguishing of the flame. We concluded the meeting at 9:00 and went home.* begin 2. decide, determine, reckon, deduce, assume, suppose *From the damage done to our garden, we concluded that a raccoon had got in while we were away.*

conclusion *noun* 1. close, end, ending, finish, termination, finale *Mom and Dad let me stay up late to watch the conclusion of the movie.* 2. decision, opinion, judgment, deduction, assumption *After examining the evidence, the police came to the conclusion that they had the wrong man.*

concrete *adjective* real, solid, substantial, tangible *There are lots of stories about people seeing ghosts but no concrete evidence that they exist.* abstract, flimsy

concur *verb* agree, assent, consent, go along with, accept *I concur with Jody's opinion that that was the worst movie we've ever seen.* disagree

condemn *verb* 1. criticize, disapprove of, denounce, attack *The organization condemns the use of animals in scientific experiments.* 2. doom, convict, sentence *In the nineteenth century, many British convicts were condemned to exile in Australia.*

condense *verb* 1. shorten, compress, abbreviate, abridge *She condensed her paper from five pages to two.* expand, lengthen 2. concentrate, reduce, thicken *Cook over low heat until the sauce starts to condense.*

condition 1. *noun* form, shape, order, state, fitness *Riding a bike to work every day keeps Dad in good condition. The roof on our house is in poor condition and needs to be replaced.* 2. illness, disease, ailment, disorder, problem *Grandpa takes medication for his heart condition.* 3. qualification, restriction, requirement, provision *Students must maintain a 3.5 grade point average as a condition of membership in the honor society.* 4. *verb* adapt, accustom, train, habituate *Some pets never become conditioned to car travel.*

conduct 1. *verb* lead, take, guide, show, accompany, escort, steer *The usher conducted us to our seats.* 2. manage, direct, control, supervise, operate *Melanie conducts a real-estate business out of her home.* 3. behave, act, acquit *The player conducted himself in an unsportsmanlike manner.* 4. *noun* behavior, actions, manner, demeanor, deportment *The soldier was awarded a medal for gallant conduct and bravery.*

confer *verb* 1. consult, discuss, talk over, converse *The president conferred with his cabinet before making a decision.* 2. award, grant, bestow, present *Knighthood is conferred as a reward for public service.*

conference *noun* meeting, talk, consultation, discussion, conversation *There's no school today because there are parent-teacher conferences.*

confess *verb* admit, acknowledge, disclose, reveal, own up (*Slang*—come clean) *My sister confessed to having broken the vase. The police got the suspect to confess.* deny

confide *verb* 1. disclose, reveal, confess, tell *Geraldine confided that she was afraid to fly.*

2. show trust, unburden oneself, reveal all *My brother and I always confide in each other.*

confidence *noun* 1. self-assurance, self-reliance, assurance, poise, self-possession *Winning three tournaments restored his confidence.* 2. trust, faith, belief, conviction, certainty, assurance *I have complete confidence in Danny's honesty.* 3. secret, confidentiality, intimacy *You can tell Will anything—he never reveals a confidence.*

confident *adjective* certain, sure, convinced, positive, assured *I am confident that computer technology will continue to change.* unsure

confidential *adjective* secret, unpublishable, private, classified, restricted, off-the-record *All financial information will remain strictly confidential. A confidential document was leaked to the press.*

confine *verb* 1. enclose, surround, contain, keep in, coop up, imprison *A parrot should not be confined in a small cage.* free, release 2. limit, restrict *Please confine your questions to today's topic.*

confirm *verb* verify, support, validate, corroborate, endorse, back up *The government confirmed the news reports.*

confiscate *verb* seize, take, remove, take away *The police will confiscate the thief's counterfeit money and arrest him.*

conflict 1. *verb* clash, oppose, disagree, differ, vary *The opinions of parents and their children often conflict. The testimony of the witness conflicted with the evidence.* agree 2. *noun* war, battle, fight, combat, struggle *World War II was a global conflict that started in 1937 and ended in 1945.* peace 3. *noun* disagreement, argument, feud, quarrel, clash *The conflict between the workers and the company was over wages.* agreement

conform to *verb* comply with, agree with, submit to, obey, observe, follow, coincide with *All new buildings must conform to the building codes.*

confront *verb* challenge, face, meet, stand up to, defy, encounter *When the thief was confronted by police, he surrendered.*

confuse *verb* 1. bewilder, puzzle, baffle, perplex, mystify *Miranda's directions to her house confused me, so I had to ask someone for help.* 2. mix up, mistake, muddle, jumble *I always confuse one twin with the other.*

confusion *noun* 1. bewilderment, uncertainty, perplexity, misunderstanding *Have your baggage clearly labeled to avoid confusion.* 2. disorder, chaos, bustle, commotion, turmoil *The crowded convention hall was in a state of confusion.*

congested *adjective* overcrowded, clogged, packed, jammed *The freeways are congested with traffic during rush hour.* empty

congratulate *verb* compliment, commend, praise, acknowledge, cheer, applaud *My friends congratulated me on winning the science project competition.*

congratulations *plural noun* greetings, good wishes, best wishes, compliments *We offered our congratulations to the couple on their twenty-fifth wedding anniversary.*

congregate *verb* crowd, gather, meet, assemble *Everyone congregated around the star to get his autograph.* disperse, scatter

connect *verb* 1. join, unite, combine, link, attach, fasten *Connect the printer cable to the printer and then to the computer.* disconnect, separate 2. relate, associate, link, identify, equate *I always connect that brand name with high-quality products.*

connection *noun* 1. attachment, coupling, joint, junction *Check to see that the connection hasn't come loose.* 2. association, relationship, link, bond, tie *He maintains a close connection with the community. I see no connection between the two events.*

conquer *verb* overtake, vanquish, defeat, crush, win, triumph over *Alexander the Great conquered most of the known world by the age of twenty-nine.*

conscientious *adjective* exacting, particular, faithful, scrupulous *Dad says his employees are dependable and conscientious workers.* neglectful

conscious *adjective* 1. aware, mindful, knowledgeable, cognizant *I suddenly became conscious of the time and realized I was late for my appointment.* 2. deliberate, intentional, calculated, purposeful, determined *I was bored and had to make a conscious effort to stop myself from yawning.*

consecutive *adjective* following, successive, continuous *It's been raining for five consecutive days.* interrupted

consent 1. *verb* agree, assent, comply, approve, give in, permit *My parents consented to my flying alone to Chicago to visit my cousin.* refuse 2. *noun* agreement, assent, approval, permission *We need a parent's consent before we can go on a field trip.*

consequence *noun* result, effect, outcome, upshot, aftermath *I was grounded for a week as a consequence of my misbehavior. Depletion of the ozone layer may have serious health and environmental consequences.*

conservation *noun* preservation, protection, management, safeguarding *Wind and solar power can contribute to energy conservation.*

conservative *adjective* conventional, traditional, moderate, conformist *Mom dresses in conservative suits for work but wears blue jeans at home.*

conserve *verb* preserve, save, keep, guard, protect, maintain *We're asked to conserve power on hot summer days by turning down air conditioners.*

consider *verb* 1. think about, study, ponder, reflect on, contemplate, deliberate (*Slang*—mull over) *Carefully consider your response before answering the question.* 2. think of, regard, judge, believe, look upon, deem *I consider my friendship with Allan to be very important.* 3. take into account, account for, allow for, bear in mind *Granddad and Grandma are very active, if you consider their age.*

considerable *adjective* sizable, substantial, significant, extensive, appreciable, great *There's a considerable difference in price between the two cameras. Valerie is in considerable pain from her broken arm.*

considerate *adjective* thoughtful, mindful of others, kind, sympathetic *Loren is always considerate of other people's feelings.* inconsiderate, thoughtless

consideration *noun* 1. thought, reflection, attention, analysis, study, deliberation *Choosing a career requires careful consideration.* 2. thoughtfulness, concern, kindness, compassion, sympathy, respect *My parents expect me to be polite and show consideration for others.* 3. factor, issue, concern, aspect, point *Climate was the most important consideration in Grandma's decision to retire in Florida.*

considering *preposition* taking into account, keeping in mind, in view of *I'm not very tired, considering how late it is.*

consist *verb* comprise, include, contain, be made up *The talent show consisted of six acts, including singing, playing musical instruments, and juggling.*

consistency *noun* texture, firmness *The recipe says that the batter should have the consistency of thick cream.*

console *verb* comfort, cheer, soothe, calm *I finally consoled my crying sister by giving her a teddy bear.*

consolidate *verb* unite, combine, join, merge *Carey consolidated all his debts and has only one monthly payment.*

conspicuous *adjective* noticeable, distinct, clear, obvious, prominent, outstanding *The rose-breasted grosbeak is a bird with a black head and back and a conspicuous red breast.* inconspicuous

conspiracy *noun* plot, scheme, plan, intrigue *In the movie, a small-time thief becomes involved in a conspiracy to rob the palace treasury.*

constant *adjective* 1. uniform, even, regular, steady, stable, unchanging, fixed *Cruise control helps to maintain a constant driving speed.* 2. continuous, uninterrupted, unceasing, endless, perpetual, nonstop *Children need constant attention while they are playing near water.*

constantly *adverb* always, continually, continuously, regularly, persistently, endlessly *Mom is constantly having to tell my sister to clean up her room.* seldom, scarcely

construct *verb* manufacture, form, build, make, create, fabricate *My friends and I constructed a tree house out of some lumber our neighbor gave us.*

consult *verb* 1. confer, discuss, talk over, deliberate *Mom and Dad consult with each other before allowing me to watch some TV programs.* 2. look in, refer to, check *You can consult a dictionary to find a word's meaning.*

consume *verb* 1. eat, drink, devour, swallow, down (*Slang*—put away, guzzle) *Americans consume billions of hot dogs during the summer months.* 2. destroy, demolish, wipe out, devour, burn up *Last year major fires consumed homes and destroyed millions of acres of forest.* 3. waste, use up, exhaust, squander *A rapidly accelerating car consumes more gas than one that speeds up slowly.*

contact 1. *verb* get in touch with, communicate with, reach, connect to *If you need me, you can contact me on my cell phone.* 2. *noun* touch, exposure, union, proximity *To keep from getting the flu, avoid contact with surfaces that may be contaminated and wash your hands frequently.* 3. communication, touch, connection, correspondence *The control tower is in contact with the airplane. My friends from camp and I have stayed in contact over the winter.*

contagious *adjective* catching, infectious, communicable, transmittable, spreadable *We received vaccinations for contagious diseases before we started school.*

contain *verb* 1. hold, include, consist of, carry, incorporate *Dad's wallet contains pictures of his family. Encyclopedias contain lots of valuable information.* exclude 2. control, restrain, curb, limit, suppress, hold back *The kids could hardly contain their excitement when they found out they would each have their own room in the new house.*

contaminate *verb* pollute, foul, spoil, soil, taint, dirty, corrupt *The floodwater contaminated the well.* purify

contemplate *verb* 1. consider, think, study, ponder on *My best friend's family is* *contemplating moving to the country. I lay on the grass contemplating the stars.* 2. plan, intend, expect *I am contemplating going to the movies tonight.*

contempt *noun* scorn, disdain, dislike, disrespect, disapproval, disgust, hatred *I feel nothing but contempt for the bullies who pick on smaller children.*

contend *verb* 1. fight, struggle, battle, wrestle, combat, face *The scientists in Antarctica must contend with the cold year-round.* 2. compete, vie, run, challenge, strive, contest *The two teams are contending for the gold medal in women's softball.* 3. argue, assert, allege, claim, maintain, hold *The lawyer contended that his client was innocent.*

content 1. *adjective* satisfied, pleased, happy, comfortable, contented *My little brother is content to play for hours in the sandbox with his cars.* dissatisfied 2. *verb* satisfy, please, gratify, gladden, make happy *It was cold and rainy, so I contented myself with a cup of hot chocolate and a good mystery story.* 3. *noun* satisfaction, pleasure, happiness, comfort, gratification *The grandfather smiled with content as he watched his grandchildren playing.*

contest 1. *noun* competition, game, tournament, meet, match, challenge *The prize in the contest is a trip for two to the Bahamas.* 2. battle, struggle, fight, conflict *The contest between the candidates is heating up.* 3. *verb* challenge, question, oppose, dispute, argue, contend, debate *Parents contested the school board's decision to close the neighborhood school.*

continual *adjective* repeated, frequent, constant, persistent, regular, steady *We played the first half of the game in a continual downpour.*

continue *verb* 1. last, endure, go on, keep on, persist, remain, live on *I expect our friendship to continue forever.* discontinue, stop 2. resume, restart, renew, carry on with, return to *The government plans to continue talks with the rebels next week.* discontinue, end

continuous *adjective* uninterrupted, endless, nonstop, constant, unbroken *There was a continuous line of traffic leaving the city for the weekend.*

contract 1. *noun* agreement, pact, understanding, bargain, treaty, alliance, deal *My parents have signed a contract with the sellers to buy a house. The actor was sued for breaking his contract to star in the movie.* 2. *verb* agree, promise, arrange, commit, pledge *He has contracted to play with the team for another three years.* 3. catch, get, develop, come down with, become infected with *Many people died in the nineteenth century after contracting yellow fever.* 4. shorten, tighten, tense, narrow, shrink *The muscles of the heart contract and relax automatically.* 5. abbreviate, condense, reduce, shorten, abridge *"Does not" can be contracted to "doesn't."*

contradict *verb* deny, oppose, dispute, challenge, disagree with *Galileo contradicted the theory that the earth is stationary and that the sun, stars, and planets revolve around it.*

contrary *adjective* 1. opposed, opposite, different, clashing, conflicting, counter *Contrary to popular belief, bats do not attack humans but benefit us by consuming huge numbers of insects.* compatible, agreeing 2. stubborn, obstinate, headstrong, rebellious, difficult, disobedient *My parents say I was a contrary child and refused to go to bed when it was time.* agreeable

contrast 1. *verb* compare, distinguish, differentiate, put side by side *The news broadcast contrasted scenes of the city before and after the earthquake.* 2. *noun* difference, dissimilarity, distinction, comparison *There is a marked contrast between the weather in southern Florida and that in northern Minnesota. My sister is fair-haired in contrast to me.*

contribute *verb* grant, endow, present, furnish, supply *Everyone in the class contributed at least a dollar to the charity. My dad contributes blood twice a year.* 2. influence, help, cause, support, lead to, promote *Exercise contributes to good health.*

contribution *noun* 1. gift, donation, grant, present, offering, payment *The local food bank is asking for contributions to help feed homeless and hungry people.*

contrive *verb* invent, scheme, plan, plot, devise, conspire *In 1774 the British parliament offered a reward to anyone who contrived a way to determine a ship's longitude at sea.*

control 1. *verb* direct, manage, conduct, command, supervise, govern, rule, run *The city treasurer controls the financial affairs of the city.* 2. restrain, check, contain, curb, suppress *Some people find it hard to control their craving for chocolate.* 3. *noun* charge, authority, management, supervision, rule, power, direction *Britain was under the control of Rome from the first to the fifth century.* 4. restraint, check, limitation, constraint, regulation *Environmentalists are asking for stricter controls on pollution.*

controversy *noun* dispute, argument, quarrel, disagreement, debate *There is considerable controversy surrounding the effects of global warming.*

convene *verb* gather, meet, assemble, congregate, collect, rally *The First Continental Congress convened in Philadelphia on September 5, 1774, to talk about self-government.* disperse

convenience *noun* benefit, advantage, accessibility, use, enjoyment *The library has installed computers for the public's convenience.*

convenient *adjective* handy, suitable, beneficial, helpful, useful, advantageous *My brother's cell phone was very convenient when he locked himself out of his car.* inconvenient

convention *noun* conference, meeting, assembly, gathering, congress *Our teachers are at a state convention, so we have no school today.*

conventional *adjective* customary, usual, traditional, accepted, established *Conventional behavior requires that you say "please" and "thank you."* unusual

conversation *noun* discussion, talk, chat, dialogue, conference, exchange *Our family had a conversation at the dinner table about where we'd each like to spend our vacation.*

converse *verb* talk, speak, discuss, communicate *Gloria and I had to converse in whispers so Betty wouldn't overhear us planning her surprise party.*

convert *verb* change, transform, modify, adapt, alter, turn *We spent the night in a Victorian mansion that had been converted into a bed-and-breakfast.*

convey *verb* 1. carry, transport, take, move, transfer *Irrigation water is conveyed through ditches from the river to the farm.* 2. communicate, express, relate, tell, reveal, disclose, make known *Some people have difficulty conveying their thoughts and emotions.*

convict 1. *verb* condemn, sentence, find guilty, judge guilty *The jury convicted the defendants of attempting to bribe a public official.* acquit 2. *noun* prisoner, criminal, lawbreaker, offender, felon *The escaped convicts were recaptured by police.*

convince *verb* persuade, assure, promise, guarantee, satisfy, prove to, sway *The candidate must convince voters that she can do a better job than her opponent.*

cook *verb* prepare, make, fix, boil, bake, broil, fry, heat, steam, roast *Mom cooked my favorite dinner: spaghetti and meatballs.*

cool 1. *adjective* chilly, fresh, chill, nippy, cold, frigid, icy *The weather this summer is unusually cool. A swim in the cool lake is refreshing on a hot day.* warm, heated 2. calm, unexcited, composed, collected, unflappable, unruffled, unemotional *The platoon leader remained cool throughout the battle.* excited 3. unfriendly, distant, aloof, reserved, detached *Conrad has been cool toward me ever since our argument.* friendly 4. *verb* chill, refrigerate, freeze, make cold, become cold *The air-conditioning cooled the apartment. Put the soda in the refrigerator to cool.* 5. *noun* self-control, composure, calmness *Denise was very angry but never lost her cool.*

cooperate *verb* work together, collaborate, unite, join forces *When the players cooperate, the team is unbeatable.*

cooperation *noun* collaboration, teamwork, participation, coordination, support, help, aid *We can accomplish a lot more through cooperation than we can alone.*

cooperative *adjective* helpful, supportive, willing, obliging *Aunt Jasmine is so cooperative when she visits us, offering to help in any way she can.*

coordinate *verb* unite, adapt, harmonize, synchronize, bring together, match *The nations are coordinating their efforts to bring about peace. Choose a color for the chair that coordinates with the sofa. Learning to swim involves coordinating arm and leg movements.*

cope with *verb* manage, handle, deal with, struggle with, put up with, face, contend with *Mom and Dad say that even with both of them working, they have trouble coping with all the bills.*

copy 1. *verb* duplicate, reproduce, photocopy, recreate *It is illegal to copy software except as a backup for yourself. She copied the document for her file.* 2. imitate, mimic, follow, echo, mirror, repeat *Her drawings copied the style of her favorite cartoonist.* 3. *noun* duplicate, reproduction, photocopy, re-creation, carbon, facsimile, imitation *The teacher handed out copies of the instructions. The statue was a good copy of the original.* original 4. issue, example, publication, version *I ordered two copies of the book. Pick up a copy of the newspaper on your way home.*

cord *noun* string, twine, rope, cable, line *She tied the boat to the dock with heavy nylon cord.*

cordial *adjective* sincere, hearty, warm, friendly, hospitable *The president received a cordial welcome during his visit.* unfriendly

core 1. *noun* center, middle, kernel *You need to cut out the tough core of a pineapple.* 2. essence, heart, substance, nucleus, basis, crux *Poverty lies at the core of some countries' problems.* 3. *adjective* important, essential, central, principal, main *Our teacher focuses on the core subjects of mathematics, English, and science.*

corner 1. *noun* angle, bend, edge *That's me in the lower right-hand corner of the picture.* 2. intersection, junction, fork *The grocery store is at the corner of Tenth Avenue and Center Street.* 3. *verb* trap, block, confine, restrict, pin down *The cat had the mouse cornered.*

corporation *noun* industry, company, business, firm, enterprise *Uncle George's corporation manufactures microchips for computers.*

correct 1. *verb* revise, alter, improve, fix *The spell-checker in the word-processing software automatically corrects my spelling.* 2. *adjective* accurate, right, exact, precise *Do you have the correct time?* 3. proper, suitable, appropriate, acceptable, accepted, fitting, right *The correct thing to do is write a thank-you note. The ambassador's manner is always formal and correct.*

correction *noun* revision, alteration, change, adjustment, amendment, improvement *The teacher made corrections to my essay.*

correspond *verb* 1. write, communicate, keep in touch *My cousin Bonnie and I correspond regularly by e-mail.* 2. agree, match, conform, fit, concur *The statements of the two witnesses don't correspond.*

corridor *noun* hallway, passageway, aisle, passage *Go down the corridor, turn right, and you'll find Mr. Rodriguez's office on the left.*

corrode *verb* deteriorate, eat away, rot, rust *Salt put on icy highways corrodes metal and causes cars to rust.*

corrupt 1. *adjective* dishonest, crooked, shady, untrustworthy, wicked, evil *The country was ruled by a brutal and corrupt government.* 2. *verb* warp, ruin, degrade, contaminate, taint *Television violence is sometimes blamed for corrupting youth.*

cost *noun* 1. price, charge, rate, fee, amount *When the cost of oil goes up, we pay more to heat our house.* 2. sacrifice, loss, damage, hurt, expense, suffering *She was determined to win no matter what the cost.*

costume *noun* outfit, attire, clothing, clothes, uniform, ensemble *My little sister wore a pumpkin costume for Halloween.*

council *noun* conference, assembly, committee, group, delegation, governing body *The city council meets once a month.*

counsel 1. *verb* advise, recommend, instruct, guide *Our school has a psychologist who counsels students who have problems.* 2. *noun* advice, guidance, direction, suggestions, recommendations, information *My parents are wise and give me good counsel.*

count 1. *verb* add up, total, calculate, tally, compute *The votes are still being counted.* 2. matter, be important, make a difference, signify *What really counts is that you're home safely.* 3. rely, depend, trust, have faith *You can count on my help.* 4. *noun* calculation, tally, sum, amount *When we finished the count, we found that we were one short.*

counter 1. *noun* table, desk, work surface *You can get tickets at the counter at the front door.* 2. *verb* oppose, dispute, answer, argue against, rebut *Danny countered my suggestion with a better one.* 3. *adjective* and *adverb* opposite, contrary, contradictory *The defendant's testimony ran counter to the evidence.*

counterfeit 1. *verb* fake, forge, reproduce, copy, imitate *It's a crime to counterfeit money.* 2. *adjective* fake, forged, copied, bogus, imitation, phony *The police seized thousands of chips used to make counterfeit video games.* 3. *noun* fake, copy, forgery, reproduction, imitation *She claimed she didn't know the twenty-dollar bills were counterfeits.*

countless *adjective* many, endless, unlimited, innumerable *Her favorite jeans are tattered from countless washings.* limited

country *noun* 1. nation, state, republic, kingdom, realm *Australia is both a country and a continent.* 2. region, territory, land, district, area *My parents went camping in Alaska's wild country.* 3. rural area, countryside, wilderness, farmland *Jeremy's family sold its farm in the country and moved to the city.*

couple 1. *noun* pair, twosome, duo, two, team *The couple at the next table were both talking on their cell phones. I had a couple of friends over to watch the game on TV.* 2. *verb* join, connect, attach, fasten, unite, bind *Two semitrailers were coupled together behind the truck tractor. His sense of humor coupled with his intelligence makes him good company.*

courage *noun* bravery, boldness, valor, gallantry, heroism, fearlessness, nerve *It takes courage to become a firefighter or a police officer.* cowardice

courageous *adjective* brave, bold, heroic, fearless, daring, valiant, gallant *She received the Nobel Peace Prize for her courageous struggle against the brutal government.*

course 1. *noun* class, lesson, program, lecture series, seminar *Don teaches an introductory course in computers at the technical college.* 2. sequence, order, advance, development, direction *Name three presidents who you think changed the course of events in the United States.* 3. direction, path, route, track, heading, bearing *The oil tanker was a mile off course when it hit a rock.* 4. *verb* flow, run, rush, pour, stream *Tears coursed down his cheeks.*

court *noun* 1. law court, tribunal, chambers *The defendant and her lawyer will appear in court at ten o'clock.* 2. playing area, arena *The new athletic club has a pool and tennis courts.*

courteous *adjective* polite, civil, gracious, obliging, respectful *Salesclerks must be courteous to customers at all times.* rude

courtesy *noun* politeness, good manners, consideration, civility *It's common courtesy to say "please" and "thank you."* rudeness

cover 1. *verb* coat, blanket, hide, bury, overlay, layer *The furniture was covered with dust.* 2. protect, shelter, wrap *I covered the baby with a blanket.* 3. include, deal with, comprise, contain, involve *The book covers the childhood and youth of John Muir. My grandparents' farm covers 360 acres.* exclude 4. travel, cross, traverse, pass over, pass through *We covered nearly 600 miles the first day of our trip.* 5. *noun* shelter, protection, refuge, sanctuary, concealment *Everyone ran for cover when it began to pour.* 6. covering, wrapping, jacket, top, lid *Mom sewed new covers for the sofa pillows.*

covert *adjective* secret, hidden, disguised, covered, veiled, concealed *The spies used covert listening devices to listen to the enemy.* open

coward *noun* sissy, weakling (*Slang*—chicken, wimp) *Your fear of roller coasters doesn't make you a coward.* hero, brave person

cozy *adjective* comfortable, snug, warm, relaxed, pleasant, safe, secure *The campers were cozy, all curled up in their sleeping bags.* uncomfortable

crack 1. *noun* bang, crash, boom, report, pop, snap *The crack of the thunder came immediately after the lightning.* 2. opening, gap, slit *The cat slipped out through the crack of the door we had left ajar.* 3. break, fracture, flaw, fissure *The cracks in the walls of the old building need repair.* 4. *verb* snap, pop, bang, boom, explode *A hunting rifle cracked nearby. Stop cracking your knuckles!*

cradle 1. *verb* support, hold, carry, nestle *Janice cradled the purring kitten in her arms.* 2. *noun* crib, bed, bassinet *Dad rocked my baby sister in her cradle.*

craft *noun* 1. skill, ability, talent, technique *The person who carved these statues was a master of the craft.* 2. job, profession, occupation, trade *Furniture making is a craft that requires great skill.* 3. boat, vessel, ship, plane, aircraft, spacecraft *We returned to shore as soon as we heard there were small-craft warnings.*

cram *verb* stuff, fill, load, pack, squeeze, force, jam *I tried to cram everything for the trip into one suitcase.*

cramp 1. *verb* confine, box in, limit, restrict *Our family is cramped for space with only two bedrooms and one bath.* 2. *noun* pain, ache, spasm, contraction, twinge *Lauren had a muscle cramp in her leg and couldn't finish the marathon.*

cranky *adjective* cross, irritable, bad-tempered *The baby gets cranky and cries when he's hungry.* good-humored

crash 1. *verb* smash, hit, bump, collide *Everything on the shelves crashed to the floor during the earthquake. The waves crashed against the rocks.* 2. *noun* bang, boom, clang, din *There was a loud crash from the kitchen when Gerald dropped a kettle.* 3. collision, accident, smash, wreck *No one was hurt in last night's crash on the interstate highway.*

crate *noun* box, container, packing case *We packed my sister's things in a crate and shipped them overseas to her.*

crave *verb* want, desire, wish for, long for *My parents want me to eat healthy food, but sometimes I crave a candy bar.*

crawl 1. *verb* creep, inch, wriggle, slither *We crawled through a narrow tunnel to reach the cave's large room.* 2. *noun* creep, slow pace *Holiday traffic slowed to a crawl.*

crazy *adjective* 1. absurd, foolish, silly, irrational, mad *You'd be crazy to take Bernie up on his dare.* sensible 2. enthusiastic, excited, passionate, wild, fanatical *Jacob is crazy about snowboarding. I'm not crazy about your latest scheme.*

crease 1. *verb* wrinkle, crinkle, pucker, gather, furrow *When Jenna concentrates, her brow creases.* 2. *noun* fold, pleat, ridge, line, tuck *Dad's pants have sharp creases down the legs.*

create *verb* 1. make, form, invent, originate, manufacture *How do I create a new folder on my computer's desktop? The new factory in town will create jobs for around 100 people.* 2. cause, produce, bring about *The rock star's arrival created quite a commotion.*

creation *noun* 1. formation, origination, development, production, invention design *The transistor led to the creation of the integrated circuit and the microprocessor.* 2. achievement, work, product, masterpiece *Spiderwebs are extraordinary creations.*

creative *adjective* inventive, imaginative, innovative, original, resourceful, productive *She has a creative mind full of new ideas. The college offers courses in many creative skills, including painting, photography, architecture, and design.* unimaginative

creature *noun* animal, beast, entity, organism *Many people believe there is such a creature as the Loch Ness Monster.*

credit *noun* praise, acclaim, approval, acknowledgment, recognition, tribute *You deserve a lot of credit for standing up to that bully.*

creed *noun* doctrine, principle, belief, rule, teaching *The company's creed is to provide superior quality and service.*

creek *noun* stream, brook, channel, rivulet *Deer and birds come to drink at the creek flowing through our property.*

creep *verb* crawl, inch, sneak, steal, tiptoe, slip *I crept downstairs when everyone was sleeping. The cat crept up on the mouse.*

crest *noun* peak, ridge, summit, top, crown *The crest of the wave broke over the sand. The view from the crest of the hill was spectacular.*

crevice *noun* crack, fissure, gap, rift, cleft *There were ferns and moss growing from the crevices in the rock wall.*

crew *noun* staff, force, team, group *Reporters and a camera crew covered the news story.*

crime *noun* 1. offense, illegal act, wrong, violation, illegality, misdeed *Shoplifting is a crime. Two gang members were arrested for committing the crime.* 2. shame, outrage, wrong *It's a crime that families in our community go hungry.*

criminal 1. *noun* lawbreaker, offender, felon, delinquent, crook *The system is designed to punish criminals for their crimes.* 2. *adjective* unlawful, illegal, wrong, dishonest *Graffiti can be considered a criminal act.*

cripple *verb* damage, weaken, disable, injure *A power blackout crippled the Northeast.*

crisis *noun* emergency, disaster, catastrophe, predicament, trouble, difficulty *Renewable energy sources may help to avoid an energy crisis.*

crisp *adjective* 1. fresh, sharp, clear, bracing *The air is cool and crisp.* 2. crunchy, brittle, hard *I really enjoy a crisp, tart apple.*

critical *adjective* 1. disapproving, faultfinding, judgmental, disparaging *The coach was critical of the team's poor performance.* approving 2. crucial, decisive, urgent, pressing *It is critical that we protect the habitat of endangered plants and animals.* unimportant

criticize *verb* find fault with, condemn, disapprove of, judge *You shouldn't criticize him unless you know all the facts. She was criticized for having failed to do her job.*

crook *noun* criminal, gangster, lawbreaker, thief, swindler, cheat *Be careful of crooks on the Internet who offer get-rich-quick schemes.*

crop 1. *noun* harvest, yield, production, growth *The farmers can expect a good corn crop this year.* 2. *verb* cut, clip, trim, shear *I had Mom crop my hair really short for summer.*

cross 1. *verb* go across, pass over, travel over *Be sure you have a "walk" signal before you cross Center Street. If you travel from New York to Los Angeles, you cross three time zones.* 2. intersect, meet, join, converge *Meet me where the path and the road cross.* 3. *noun* hybrid, mix, mixture, blend, combination *My dog is a cross between a collie and a yellow Lab.* 4. *adjective* annoyed, angry, mad, upset, irritated, bad-tempered *The neighbors got cross with us for playing loud music.* good-humored

crouch *verb* stoop, squat, bend, hunch *Mom crouched down to talk to the little boy.*

crowd 1. *noun* group, mass, throng, mob, gathering *A crowd of 100,000 showed up for the festival.* 2. *verb* gather, congregate, cluster, flock, swarm *The schoolchildren crowded* *around the dinosaur exhibit.* 3. push, shove, pack, squeeze *People kept trying to crowd into the bus.*

crown 1. *noun* head ornament, tiara, wreath *The children made crowns of dandelions.* 2. *verb* made king or queen, invest, install, induct *Kings and queens of Britain have been crowned at Westminster Abbey since 1066.*

crucial *adjective* important, critical, decisive, central *Alonzo played a crucial role in Saturday's 14-10 victory.* unimportant

crude *adjective* 1. primitive, rough, makeshift, basic, simple *We made a crude table and two chairs out of shipping crates for our playhouse.* refined 2. rude, impolite, tasteless, offensive *My parents do not tolerate crude language.*

cruel *adjective* mean, heartless, brutal, ruthless *I could never be cruel to an animal.* kind

cruise 1. *noun* boat trip, voyage, sail *My aunt and uncle took a cruise to the Bahamas last winter.* 2. *verb* sail, voyage, travel, boat, navigate *The Petrulis family is cruising the Greek Isles on a sailboat.*

crumble *verb* break up, disintegrate, fall apart, crush *Good gardening soil should crumble when you squeeze it.*

crumple *verb* 1. crush, crinkle, wrinkle, crease, ripple *The fender of our car crumpled in the collision. She crumpled the paper into a ball.* 2. collapse, buckle, fall, give way, topple *Edie crumpled, exhausted, to the ground after the marathon.*

crusade *noun* cause, movement, drive, campaign *We are asking everyone to join the crusade against cancer.*

crush *verb* 1. squeeze, mash, press, squash, trample *The grapes are crushed to extract the juice for wine.* 2. subdue, quell, suppress, put down, overcome, destroy, defeat, stamp out *The rulers crushed the rebellion.*

cry 1. *verb* sob, weep, bawl, shed tears, wail *I'm sorry—please don't cry.* 2. call, shout, yell, call out, bellow, scream, howl *Dad cried out for help as the grocery bags broke.* 3. *noun* exclamation, yell, shout, scream *Catlin gave a cry of delight when she saw the birthday cake and all the gifts.*

cuddle *verb* snuggle, nestle, fondle *We all like to cuddle our kittens.*

cue *noun* hint, signal, clue, sign, suggestion *I'll scratch my right ear as a cue for us to leave.*

culprit *noun* person responsible, guilty party, offender, wrongdoer *I'm looking for the culprit who borrowed my favorite sweater.*

cultivate *verb* 1. till, farm, plow, work, grow, raise, plant *The farmers begin cultivating their fields in the spring.* 2. pursue, foster, promote, develop, encourage *You need to cultivate good study habits if you are going to succeed in college.*

culture *noun* civilization, society, way of life, traditions, customs *Ancient Greek culture is famous for its art, architecture, and literature.*

cunning *adjective* shrewd, ingenious *The Great Train Robbery was a cunning scheme to rob two safes of gold bullion aboard a train.*

curb *verb* check, control, restrain *I ate enough to curb my hunger but was still looking forward to dinner.*

cure 1. *noun* remedy, treatment, antidote, medicine, therapy *Will scientists ever find a cure for cancer?* 2. *verb* heal, remedy, treat, make well, alleviate *The antibiotics will cure your strep throat.*

curious *adjective* 1. strange, odd, unusual, weird, peculiar *Raccoons have a curious habit of washing their food before they eat it.* 2. inquisitive, interested (*Slang—*nosy) *Aren't you curious about your grade?* CURIOSITY *noun Children's natural curiosity helps them to learn.*

currency *noun* money, cash, legal tender *Not all members of the European Union have adopted the euro as their currency.*

current 1. *noun* flow, stream, tide *The current carried the canoe rapidly downstream.* 2. *adjective* present, existing, present-day, contemporary, latest, modern *What is your current address? We discuss current events in social studies class.*

curse 1. *noun* hex, spell, jinx *The evil fairy's curse put Sleeping Beauty into a deep sleep.* 2. evil, affliction, trouble, burden, plague *My aunt the nutritionist claims that fast food is the curse of modern society.* 3. *verb* condemn, denounce *My uncle curses whichever political party is in power.*

curve 1. *noun* bend, turn, twist, arc *As we rounded the curve, we saw the castle.* 2. *verb* bend, wind, turn, arc, arch, curl, twist *The road curved around the mountain.*

cushion 1. *verb* soften, support, cradle, lessen, moderate, dampen, deaden *The deep snow cushioned my fall.* 2. *noun* pillow, pad, bolster, mat *The kids lay on cushions on the floor, watching the game on TV.*

custody *noun* care, guardianship, charge, supervision, control *Dody's parents have had joint custody of her since their divorce.*

custom *noun* tradition, use, habit, practice, way, manner *Understanding different cultures and customs helps to eliminate prejudice.*

customary *adjective* usual, normal, routine, regular, ordinary, accustomed *My customary bedtime is 9:30.*

cut 1. *verb* carve, slice, chop, dice, sever *Please cut me a slice of pizza.* 2. clip, trim, snip, prune, crop, mow *I like to use the riding mower to cut the grass.* 3. wound, gash, nick, slash *Be careful you don't cut yourself with that razor blade.* 4. reduce, decrease, restrict, limit, curtail *Mom claims that we need to cut our spending.* 5. stop, discontinue, halt, disconnect *Electrical power was cut when poles were snapped off by the tornado.* 6. *noun* wound, gash, nick, scratch, incision *That cut will heal in a few days.* 7. reduction, decrease, cutback, drop *Employees were asked to take a cut in salary to save the company from bankruptcy.*

cute *adjective* smart, cunning, attractive, charming, appealing, adorable *The girls in my class think the new boy is cute. Doris has on a really cute outfit today.* dull

cycle *noun* series, sequence, period, course, round, rotation, phase *The washing machine is in the rinse cycle. A tadpole is one stage in the life cycle of a frog.*

D

dab 1. *verb* pat, smear, daub, blot, wipe, touch *Dad dabbed lotion on my sunburned shoulders.* 2. *noun* touch, spot, drop, dash, bit, daub, speck *I'd like just a dab of cream in my coffee.*

dabble *verb* putter, tinker, toy, fiddle, experiment, try one's hand *My older sister likes to dabble with car engines on weekends. Cousin Andrew dabbled at painting for a while but gave it up.*

daily 1. *adverb* every day, regularly, once a day, day after day, day by day *Janet goes daily to the gym to work out.* 2. *adjective* everyday, routine, regular, common *I have a job delivering the daily newspaper each day before school. Doctors recommend daily exercise.*

dainty *adjective* 1. delicate, fine, exquisite, elegant, pretty, graceful *The bride carried a bouquet of dainty pink roses.* clumsy 2. choosy, fussy, particular, finicky *My friend Carol is a dainty eater who will eat only certain foods.*

damage 1. *noun* harm, injury, hurt, destruction, ruin, loss *The drought is causing damage to the corn crop.* 2. *verb* harm, hurt, injure, ruin, impair, spoil, wreck *The rumors of scandal are likely to damage the reputation of the candidate.* repair, help

damp *adjective* 1. moist, wet, soggy, clammy *The wood was too damp to get a campfire going.* dry 2. humid, rainy, foggy, muggy, drizzly *It's too damp and miserable a day to be outside.* dry

dampen *verb* 1. moisten, wet, sprinkle *Dampen the clothes before you iron them.* dry 2. discourage, diminish, curb, check, stifle, depress *Even the bad weather failed to dampen the enthusiasm of the crowd that celebrated the team's victory.*

dance 1. *verb* sway, twirl, move to music *It takes a lot of training to dance onstage in a ballet. Men and women in traditional dress danced to the songs of folk musicians.* 2. prance, skip, hop, jump, leap, wiggle, cavort *The children danced with delight at the clowns' performance.* 3. *noun* ball, prom, formal, hop *My sister is looking for a dress to wear to the dance on Saturday night.*

danger *noun* hazard, jeopardy, risk, peril *My parents have warned me of the danger of swimming alone. We were in danger of running out of gas on the highway.* safety

dangerous *adjective* unsafe, hazardous, risky, perilous, chancy *Icy roads are very dangerous. Mom and Dad don't want me to participate in dangerous sports.* safe

dangle *verb* hang, swing, sway, suspend, droop, sag *Karen sat on the edge of the pool and dangled her feet in the water.*

dare 1. *verb* challenge, defy, provoke, goad, taunt *My best friend dared me to ask his cute sister for a date.* 2. venture, risk, brave, face, have the courage, have the nerve *Daniel Boone dared to cross the Allegheny Mountains and find out what lay beyond.* 3. *noun* challenge, provocation, taunt *I accepted Alicia's dare to jump across the stream and landed in the water.*

daring 1. *adjective* bold, brave, courageous, adventurous, fearless *The circus performers thrilled the audience with their daring trapeze act.* 2. *noun* bravery, courage, heroism, boldness, nerve, fearlessness *The firefighters' daring saved the family.*

dark 1. *adjective* gloomy, dismal, dreary, murky, dim, shady, shadowy, unlit *I love scary stories that begin, "It was a dark and gloomy night."* 2. black, brown, brunette, dusky *Callie has dark hair and green eyes.* 3. *noun* evening, night, dusk, nighttime, nightfall, twilight *Dark comes early in the winter.* 4. darkness, gloom, dimness, murk, blackness *I groped around in the dark, trying to find a light switch.* light

darken *verb* grow dark, dim, grow dim, blacken, cloud over *The sky darkened as the storm approached.* lighten, brighten

darling 1. *noun* beloved, dear, precious, pet, sweetie *Good night, darling; sleep well.* 2. *adjective* adored, cherished, beloved, loved, precious, treasured *Grandma began her letter, "My darling grandson."* 3. adorable, sweet, cute, charming, lovely, enchanting, precious *What darling puppies!*

dart *verb* dash, bolt, sprint, race, rush, scamper, scurry, scoot *A rabbit darted across the road in front of us.*

dash 1. *verb* rush, hurry, race, hasten, run, scurry, bolt *Mom had to dash off to work for an early appointment.* 2. throw, fling, hurl, sling, smash, slam *The violent storm dashed the ship against the rocks.* 3. ruin, destroy, shatter, crush, frustrate, spoil *The team's hopes for a gold medal were dashed when it was beaten in the third round.* 4. *noun* run, rush, bolt, sprint *The race ended with a dash to the finish line.* 5. trace, splash, drop, pinch, touch *Add a dash of hot pepper sauce.*

data *noun* information, facts, statistics, records, numbers, figures *Computer hard disks hold a lot of data.*

date *noun* 1. day, week, month, year, time *What is the date of your birth? July 4, 1776, is the date that the Declaration of Independence was signed.* 2. appointment, meeting, get-together, engagement, rendezvous *Dad has a lunch date with a client.* 3. boyfriend, girlfriend, companion, escort, partner *My sister won't tell me who her date is for the prom.*

dawdle *verb* linger, waste time, delay, loiter, dally *Don't dawdle on your way to school. I dawdled over my homework and got to bed late.* rush

dawn *noun* 1. daybreak, daylight, sunrise, sunup *I get up at the crack of dawn to deliver the newspapers.* dusk 2. beginning, start, birth, commencement, arrival, emergence, appearance, origin *The launching of Sputnik in 1957 brought the dawn of the space age.* end

day *noun* 1. daytime, daylight, daylight hours *Days are longer in summer than in winter.* night 2. time, era, period, generation, age *Great-Grandpa says that in his day, kids who lived in the country had to walk long distances to a one-room schoolhouse.*

daze 1. *verb* stun, confuse, shock, bewilder, befuddle *Being awakened by the alarm at five o'clock in the morning left me dazed and wondering where I was.* 2. *noun* state of confusion, haze, stupor *She was in a daze after falling from her horse.*

dazzle 1. *verb* amaze, astonish, impress, overwhelm, fascinate *Visitors to the museum are dazzled by the large number of exhibits.* bore 2. *noun* brightness, brilliance, glare *Visitors to the city are sometimes overwhelmed by the dazzle of the lights.*

dead 1. *adjective* lifeless, deceased, departed, late, passed on *The cat brought home a dead mouse.* live, alive 2. not working, inoperative, useless, ineffective, inactive *The phone line is dead.* 3. complete, absolute, total, utter *The teacher demands dead silence in study hall.* 4. *adverb* completely, absolutely, entirely, totally, utterly *My parents are dead serious when they say they want me home before 9:30.* 5. directly, straight, exactly, precisely *A large rock lay dead ahead of our canoe.*

deadly *adjective* fatal, lethal, poisonous, toxic, dangerous, harmful, destructive *The venom of some snakes is deadly.*

deal 1. *verb* concern, have to do with, be about, involve, discuss, treat, consider *Astronomy deals with the study of the universe. The book deals with the life of President John F. Kennedy.* 2. distribute, hand out, give out, allocate, dispense, allot, apportion, administer, deliver *The relief agency dealt out food and water to the flood victims.* 3. handle, manage, cope, see to, take care of *The guidance counselor deals with students' problems.* 4. trade, do business, buy, sell *The grocery store where my mother shops deals in organic foods.* 5. *noun* bargain, arrangement, agreement, understanding, contract, transaction *My brother made a really good deal with my uncle for his used car.*

dear 1. *adjective* beloved, adored, loved, darling, cherished, precious *The letter began, "My dear wife."* 2. *noun* lovable person, darling, sweetheart, pet, love *Grandpa is a dear.*

debate 1. *noun* discussion, argument, dispute, disagreement *The debate between the presidential candidates will be televised Wednesday.* 2. *verb* discuss, argue, dispute, consider, deliberate *The school board debated the issue of funding for the new school.*

debris *noun* wreckage, rubble, fragments, rubbish, litter, trash *Debris from the lost ship washed up on the beach. My Scout troop is cleaning up debris along the roadside.*

debt *noun* money owed, bill, balance due, account, obligation *My brother got a loan to pay for college, and after graduation he will have to pay off the debt.*

decay 1. *verb* rot, spoil, decompose, corrode, disintegrate *Bacteria cause garden compost to decay.* flourish, bloom 2. *noun* decline, collapse, deterioration, degeneration *The once-beautiful old building is in a state of decay.* 3. rot, decomposition, corrosion *The dentist found no tooth decay on my last visit.*

deceased. *adjective* dead, late, departed *The deceased millionaire left no will.* living

deceive *verb* mislead, betray, trick, lie to, double-cross, fool, dupe *Alchemists deceived people by promising to turn their base metals into gold.*

decent *adjective* 1. proper, appropriate, suitable, fitting, respectable, polite *The decent thing to do is to offer to pay for the window you broke.* improper 2. adequate, good enough, fair, satisfactory *We had a decent meal at the restaurant, but I prefer home cooking.* inadequate 3. kind, courteous, helpful, considerate, obliging, well-mannered *Grandma says my sister's boyfriend seems like a decent young man.*

decide *verb* 1. make a decision, settle on, conclude, determine *Mom and Dad decided we'd wait until next year to get a new car. I can't decide between blue or green.* 2. rule, resolve, judge, decree, settle *The judge will decide the case.*

decipher *verb* solve, explain, decode, interpret, work out, crack *The Rosetta stone helped scientists decipher ancient Egyptian hieroglyphics.*

decision *noun* 1. choice, conclusion, determination, resolution *The coach hasn't made a decision yet as to who will be on the team.* 2. judgment, ruling, verdict, findings *The judge's decision was overruled by a higher court.*

decisive *adjective* 1. determined, resolute, firm, positive, forceful *The company needs a decisive leader to take over as its president.* 2. conclusive, deciding, final, crucial, critical, definitive *The basketball team's 25-point win was a decisive victory.*

declare *verb* 1. state, assert, say, affirm, claim, maintain *He declared that once he had his mind made up, nothing could make him change it.* 2. announce, proclaim, pronounce, make known *The colonies declared their independence in 1776.*

decline 1. *verb* refuse, reject, turn down, pass up *Janet declined my invitation to go skating. The police declined to comment on the investigation.* accept 2. weaken, lessen, wane, worsen, deteriorate *Some historians say the Roman Empire began to decline in the third century.* strengthen 3. *noun* lessening, decrease, downturn, waning, slump, dwindling, falling off, deterioration *Sales of big, gas-guzzling cars have declined since the price of gas has gone up.*

decorate *verb* adorn, trim, beautify, ornament, fix up (*Slang*—doll up) *Our class decorated the gym for the party.*

decrease 1. *verb* reduce, cut, lessen, lower, diminish, drop, curtail *The organization's goal is to decrease the amount of waste produced and increase recycling. The rate of inflation decreased this quarter.* increase 2. *noun* reduction, cut, drop, decline, loss, downturn *We've seen steady decreases in the cost of computers.* increase

decree 1. *noun* order, command, act, law, rule, proclamation, mandate *The king issued a decree against the practice of witchcraft.* 2. *verb* order, command, dictate, direct, pronounce, proclaim *The emperor decreed that a holiday be set aside to celebrate his reign.*

dedicate *verb* devote, commit, give over, pledge, offer *Nelson Mandela dedicated his life to the struggle for racial equality in South Africa.*

deduct *verb* subtract, remove, withdraw, take away, take off, discount *Deduct 30 percent from the original price.* add

deed *noun* act, action, feat, exploit, achievement, accomplishment *The captain's heroic deed saved the lives of his soldiers.*

deep *adjective* 1. extending far down, bottomless, cavernous, yawning *My little brother is forbidden to play at the deep end of the pool.* 2. profound, extreme, great, intense *Our Spanish teacher, Mr. Herrera, has a deep understanding of the Hispanic culture.* 3. absorbed, engrossed, preoccupied, immersed, lost *I startled my sister, who was deep in thought.* 4. obscure, hidden, secret, mysterious, unclear, unfathomable *The universe is still a deep mystery to most.*

deface *verb* mar, blemish, disfigure, deform, damage *Graffiti defaced the walls of the subway station.* improve

defeat 1. *verb* beat, conquer, overcome, vanquish, win a victory over, triumph over, crush, rout *Chief Crazy Horse joined forces with Chief Sitting Bull and defeated General George Custer at Little Bighorn.* 2. *noun* loss, reverse, beating, overthrow, rout, trouncing *The women's tennis team suffered its first defeat of the season Friday.*

defect *noun* flaw, fault, blemish, imperfection, weakness, deficiency, failing *I got my jacket at a discount because of a small defect in the lining.* perfection

defective *adjective* imperfect, flawed, deficient, malfunctioning, broken, out of order *The store will repair or replace defective items at no charge.* perfect

defend *verb* 1. protect, safeguard, shield, secure, shelter, fortify *The castle's wide moat, drawbridge, and high walls defended it against attack.* attack 2. support, uphold, stand up for, champion, endorse, back *The people vowed to defend their liberties. The doctor used the results of her scientific research to defend her claim of a cure.* attack

defense *noun* protection, shield, guard, security, safeguard *A healthy diet is a defense against disease.*

defenseless *adjective* helpless, unprotected, vulnerable, powerless *Computer users without antivirus software are defenseless against e-mail viruses.* protected

defer *verb* postpone, put off, delay, suspend, reschedule *The committee deferred its decision until the next meeting.*

defiance *noun* disobedience, opposition, resistance, rebellion, insubordination, insolence *I know I'll be grounded for my defiance if I refuse to do as I'm told.* obedience

deficiency *noun* lack, shortage, absence, want *A vitamin C deficiency is the primary cause of scurvy.* sufficiency

define *verb* explain, describe, characterize, interpret, clarify *Dictionaries define words. His paintings are defined by bright colors and bold strokes.*

definite *adjective* precise, specific, exact, clear, clear-cut, explicit, particular *In order to be seen at a definite time with little or no waiting, it is recommended that you make an appointment.* indefinite

definition *noun* meaning, explanation, description, interpretation, clarification, sense *If you don't know a word's meaning, you can find its definition in the dictionary.*

deform *verb* disfigure, misshape, mar, spoil, damage, injure *Tight shoes can cramp and deform the toes.* improve, beautify

defy *verb* 1. disobey, resist, ignore, disregard *Some residents defied orders and refused to leave their homes during the hurricane.* obey 2. challenge, dare *I defy you to name all fifty states.* 3. withstand, frustrate, foil *Ghosts defy all rational explanation.*

degrade *verb* disgrace, debase, cheapen, discredit, shame, humiliate *I would never degrade myself by cheating.*

degree *noun* 1. stage, step, level *Rock climbing, gymnastics, kayaking, and dancing are all wonderful fitness activities requiring varying degrees of skill.* 2. amount, extent, proportion, measure *My sister has a high degree of confidence that she will be accepted at the university.*

dejected *adjective* discouraged, depressed, disappointed, unhappy, sad *Dejected travelers had to spend the night in the airport after their flight was canceled.* cheerful, happy

delay 1. *verb* postpone, put off, defer, shelve *The software release was delayed six months in order to solve security problems* 2. detain, impede, slow down, obstruct *We got delayed in traffic, and I was late for my dentist appointment.* 3. *noun* postponement, interruption, halt, stoppage *Flight delays caused us to miss our connection in Chicago.*

delegate 1. *noun* representative, agent, ambassador, deputy, emissary *In 1945 delegates from fifty countries wrote the charter that created the United Nations.* 2. *verb* assign, give, allocate, pass on, allot, entrust *Mom and Dad have delegated to my sister the task of setting the table and the task of washing the dishes to me.*

deliberate 1. *adjective* intentional, calculated, purposeful, premeditated *Malicious hackers make deliberate attempts to destroy computer systems.* accidental, unintentional 2. careful, thoughtful, cautious, regular, measured *The countries claim they are taking deliberate steps toward achieving peace.* hasty 3. *verb* consider, discuss, evaluate, review *The jury deliberated three days before reaching a verdict.*

delicate *adjective* 1. fine, dainty, nice, elegant, exquisite, pleasing, attractive *The table was decorated with vases of delicate yellow roses.* 2. fragile, flimsy, breakable, brittle, insubstantial, frail, weak *Wrap all the delicate china carefully before you pack it to be moved.* 3. awkward, difficult, tricky, sensitive, touchy, complicated *I found myself in a delicate situation when my best friends asked me to settle their disagreement.*

delicious *adjective* tasty, appetizing, delectable, scrumptious, yummy *Mmm, this meal is delicious.*

delight 1. *noun* joy, pleasure, happiness, enjoyment, gladness *Great-Grandpa takes delight in telling me how things were when he was young.* displeasure 2. *verb* please, cheer, amuse, gladden, gratify, thrill *Nothing delights my uncle more than playing pranks on us kids.* depress, sadden

delightful *adjective* pleasant, lovely, charming, appealing, pleasing *Mom says she had a delightful visit with her college roommate, whom she hadn't seen in fifteen years.*

deliver *verb* 1. carry, transport, distribute, convey *The mail carrier delivers our mail in the afternoon.* 2. supply, provide, furnish, produce, dispense *The company failed to deliver the high-quality service we expected.* 3. communicate, speak, say, give, express, announce, recite *The president will deliver a speech to the nation tonight.* 4. set free, free, release, liberate, save, rescue *The hostages were delivered from the enemy in a hostage exchange.* 5. deal, administer, give, inflict, strike *In karate, the object is to deliver a blow that will stop an attacker.*

demand 1. *verb* call for, request, insist on, urge, order *Citizens are demanding tougher auto safety standards.* 2. require, need, want, call for, necessitate *Computer graphics demand a lot of computer memory.* 3. *noun* requirement, need, necessity, market *Oil producers will have to increase production to meet the demand.* 4. request, plea, pressure, insistence, claim *The company gave in to the employees' demands for higher pay.*

demolish *verb* destroy, wreck, ruin, dismantle, tear down, level *Bulldozers demolished the old buildings to make way for condominiums.* restore

demon *noun* devil, evil spirit, fiend, monster, villain *Trick-or-treaters dressed as demons and ghosts knocked on the door.*

demonstrate *verb* 1. display, show, illustrate, clarify *The salesperson demonstrated the vacuum cleaner by vacuuming up a pile of dirt he had dumped on the carpet.* 2. march, protest, rally, picket *Environmentalists demonstrated against the cutting of tropical forests.*

demonstration *noun* 1. *A flower-arranging demonstration will be held Saturday at ten in the morning.* 2. protest, march, rally, meeting, picket, sit-in *Thousands participated in a peaceful demonstration against the government.*

demote *verb* downgrade, reduce, lower, relegate, degrade (*Slang*—bust) *The army deserter was demoted from corporal to private.* promote

den *noun* lair, hole, hollow, cave, shelter *Groundhogs, also called woodchucks, live in dens that are two to four feet underground.*

denote *verb* indicate, mean, signify, mark, show, imply, express *A round yellow road sign with a black X denotes a railroad crossing.*

denounce *verb* condemn, accuse, charge, indict, blame, censure, reproach *In 1692, in Salem, Massachusetts, over twenty women and men were denounced as witches.* commend

dense *adjective* thick, solid, close, compact, compressed, crowded, packed *Dense fog rolled in from the ocean. A dense crowd gathered around the stage entrance to get a glimpse of the rock group.* thin, empty

dent 1. *noun* hollow, nick, pit, cavity, depression *The movers put a dent in our table.* 2. *verb* hit, bump, bang, nick, damage *The car was barely dented in the accident.*

deny *verb* 1. dispute, contradict, refute, disagree, protest *The accused man denied his guilt.* 2. refuse, reject, veto, dismiss, turn down *I couldn't deny the stray cat some food. My parents denied my request for an advance on my allowance.*

depart *verb* leave, go away, exit, pull out, head off *Hurry—your bus is about to depart.* arrive

department *noun* section, division, branch, agency, bureau, area *The job of the fire department is to save lives and property from being damaged or destroyed by fire. Professor Nakamura is head of the biology department at the university.*

departure *noun* leaving, going away, setting off, taking off, exit, withdrawal *You have to be on the plane at least twenty minutes before departure.*

dependable *adjective* reliable, trustworthy, responsible, faithful, steady *Our old car is* *no longer dependable. Dad says his new employee is conscientious and dependable.* unreliable, untrustworthy

depend on *verb* 1. rely on, trust in, count on, have confidence in *You can always depend on Candace to be on time.* 2. rest on, be contingent on, be determined by, be subject to *Whether we go camping this weekend depends on the weather.*

depict *verb* portray, show, picture, represent, illustrate, describe, characterize *The photograph depicts four generations of the family.*

deposit 1. *verb* leave, put down, put, lay, place *The waves deposited debris on the beach. Deposit the package by the back door.* 2. *noun* money, cash, asset, sum, savings *I have $250 in deposits in my savings account.* 3. down payment, security, pledge, stake *Mom and Dad are saving money for a deposit on a new house.* 4. accumulation, layer, sediment, lode, vein, seam *The first deposit of coal in America is said to have been discovered in what is now Illinois in 1680.*

depress *verb* 1. sadden, discourage, dishearten, deject *It depresses me sometimes to think that my brother will soon be leaving home for college.* cheer 2. press, push, lower *Depress all three keys at the same time to reboot the computer.* raise

depression *noun* 1. despair, gloominess, melancholy, misery, dejection, despondency, sadness, unhappiness *Someone who is out of work can suffer from depression.* 2. economic decline, slump, downturn, recession, crash *The stock market crash in 1929 led to a depression that affected economies worldwide.* 3. hollow, hole, dent, indentation, cavity *Depressions left in the earth when a glacier recedes are called "kettles."*

deprive *verb* deny, refuse, rob, strip, dispossess *People in prison are deprived of their freedom.*

deputy *noun* agent, assistant, representative, delegate *The sheriff has two deputies to help him enforce the law.*

derive *verb* get, obtain, receive, gain, acquire *Grandma says she derives great pleasure from her grandchildren's visits.*

descend *verb* 1. drop, fall, plummet, plunge, come down, go down, sink *Skydivers descended from thousands of feet and landed on the playing field.* ascend 2. issue, derive, originate, spring *Many of our presidents are descended from British royalty.*

descendant *noun* successor, child, offspring, progeny, issue *My friend Anna is a descendant of the first settlers in the area.*

descent *noun* 1. ancestry, parentage, lineage, origin *The Kamehameha Schools in*

Hawaii were set up to educate children of Hawaiian descent. 2. drop, fall, plunge, decline *We watched the climbers' descent down the rock face.* ascent

describe *verb* tell, report, relate, depict, portray, characterize, define, picture, represent *The brothers describe their travels among the islands of Indonesia.*

description *noun* portrayal, depiction, characterization, picture, report, account, statement *The police officer asked for a description of the robber.*

desert 1. *verb* abandon, give up, leave, forsake *Many families were forced to desert their homes and move to higher ground during the flood.* 2. *noun* arid land with little vegetation *Someday I would love to visit the desert.*

deserve *verb* merit, be worthy of, have a right to, be entitled to *Children deserve a good education.*

design 1. *noun* plan, blueprint, pattern, sketch, drawing, diagram *Mom says I should come up with a design for a robot that will do her housework.* 2. *verb* create, plan, originate, fashion, devise *I can design my own website with the software I downloaded.*

designate *verb* 1. show, indicate, point out, specify *Signs designate which are bike trails and which are hiking trails.* 2. name, nominate, appoint *Mr. Lorenzo has been designated by the mayor as chairman of the commission.*

desirable *adjective* attractive, agreeable, pleasing, pleasant, nice, sought after *We're lucky to live in a city that ranks among the top ten most desirable cities in the U.S.*

desire 1. *noun* wish, want, inclination, longing, yearning, eagerness *Applicants for the scholarship must have a desire to make a meaningful contribution to society.* 2. *verb* wish for, want, long for, yearn for *Grandpa and Grandma are finally taking the cruise they have always desired.*

despair 1. *noun* hopelessness, discouragement, dismay, desperation, dismay *To our utter despair, we realized the rowboat was sinking.* 2. *verb* give up hope, lose hope, lose heart, resign oneself *I despaired of ever finding our lost cat just as he came home.*

desperate *adjective* 1. frantic, anxious, worried *My parents were becoming desperate when I was late.* 2. reckless *The prisoners were caught in a desperate attempt to escape.*

despise *verb* hate, loathe, disdain, scorn *The common people despised the emperor for his extravagance.*

destination *noun* journey's end, stopping place, last stop, end, goal *The pilot announced that we would reach our destination in about forty minutes.*

destroy *verb* demolish, ruin, wreck, devastate, obliterate, spoil, wipe out, ravage *There were 2,500 acres of forest destroyed in the fire.*

destruction *noun* obliteration, ruin, devastation, demolition, annihilation *The town is being rebuilt after its destruction by a tornado.*

detach *verb* separate, unfasten, disconnect *I lost my house key when it became detached from my key chain.* join, attach

detail 1. *noun* part, portion, aspect, point, particular, item *My sister told me every detail of the plot and spoiled the movie for me.* 2. *verb* itemize, elaborate, specify, list, describe, tell fully *The instructor detailed the steps to take in an emergency.*

detain *verb* 1. delay, hold up, slow up, keep, hinder, impede *We were detained by rush-hour traffic and were late for an appointment.* 2. hold, arrest, confine, restrain, capture *The police detained the man for questioning.*

detect *verb* discover, notice, spot, recognize, perceive *We detected an odor of gas and immediately left the building.*

deter *verb* stop, discourage, hinder, hold back, scare off, impede, restrain *Warnings of the danger of falling off the edge of the earth did not deter explorers who believed the earth was round.*

determine *verb* 1. decide *Tonight's game will determine which team goes on to the finals.* 2. discover *Officials say an investigation will determine what led to the accident.*

determined *adjective* intent, resolved, firm, resolute, sure *I am determined to not make the same mistake twice. He had a determined look on his face.* hesitant, doubtful

detest *verb* hate, dislike, loathe, abhor, despise *I detest spinach.*

detour *noun* alternate route, bypass, indirect route, deviation, diversion *We had to take a detour to get to Grandma's because the bridge is being repaired.*

devastate *verb* destroy, demolish, ravage, ruin, wreck *The forests devastated by the Mount St. Helens eruption in 1980 have been replanted.*

develop *verb* 1. grow, mature, flourish, expand, advance, progress *The plants in our garden are beginning to develop. As computer technology developed, typewriters became nearly obsolete.* 2. acquire, form, get, obtain, pick up, establish *My teacher says I need to develop better study habits.*

development *noun* creation, invention, originating, establishment, growth, evolution *The development of integrated circuits led to the development of small electronic* *devices. Tourism is important to the economic development of our town.*

device *noun* 1. gadget, implement, instrument, apparatus, tool, contrivance *A mouse is a device that allows you to move a cursor around a screen and select items on the screen with the click of a button.* 2. plan, scheme, trick, plot, gimmick, ploy, maneuver, way *We need a device to get Claudia out of the house while we prepare for her surprise party.*

devise *verb* invent, contrive, create, fashion, concoct, conceive, plan *Environmentalist John Muir devised an alarm-clock bed that dumped him out on his feet every morning.*

devote *verb* dedicate, give, apply, offer, commit, pledge, surrender *Mother Teresa devoted her life to caring for the poorest people of the world.*

devoted *adjective* loyal, faithful, true, steadfast, dedicated, committed *Annie and Joey are devoted friends.*

devotion *noun* love, admiration, affection, caring, fondness, dedication, loyalty *Grandma and Grandpa's devotion to each other is apparent.* indifference, disloyalty

devour *verb* eat, consume, swallow, gulp, wolf down, gobble *After hiking all morning, we devoured every bit of the lunch Dad fixed.*

devout *adjective* religious, pious, dedicated, devoted, sincere *My friend Akram is a devout Muslim.* indifferent

diagnose *verb* identify, analyze, detect, establish, interpret, deduce *The doctor diagnosed my little brother as having an allergy to peanuts. My older sister is good at diagnosing problems with car engines.*

diagnosis *noun* identification, analysis, interpretation, judgment, opinion, finding *The doctor's diagnosis was strep throat, so I'm taking antibiotics.*

diagram 1. *noun* drawing, sketch, design, illustration, picture, outline, representation *A diagram at the back of the book shows you how to wire the plug.* 2. *verb* draw, sketch, depict, design, illustrate, outline, represent *The coach diagrammed the first-quarter plays on the chalkboard.*

dial 1. *noun* knob, handle, control, button *The dial on the front controls the volume.* 2. *verb* phone, call, telephone *Dial her number—she should be home.*

dialogue *noun* conversation, talk, speech, discussion *The first feature-length movie with both sound and dialogue was* The Jazz Singer.

diary *noun* journal, account, chronicle, record, memo *Aunt Helen keeps a diary of her travels.*

dice *verb* cut, cube, chop *The recipe says to finely dice the carrots.*

dictate *verb* 1. speak, say, read aloud *The lawyer dictated a letter to her secretary.* 2. order, direct, decree, prescribe, impose *The commander dictated the terms of the enemy's surrender.*

die *verb* 1. perish, expire, pass away, pass on *Some of our garden plants died when we were on vacation because of the dry weather.* live 2. fade *The sound of the jet died in the distance.*

differ *verb* 1. be different, be unlike, vary, diverge *Laws differ from state to state.* 2. disagree, conflict, clash, dissent, be at odds *We differ about what to get Dad for his birthday: I say golf balls, and Sarah says a tie.*

difference *noun* 1. contrast, dissimilarity, variation *The only difference between the twins is that one is left-handed and the other is right-handed.* 2. remainder, balance, rest *I have only $5, and the bill is $7. Will you pay the difference?* 3. disagreement, argument, dispute, misunderstanding, quarrel *The union and the company have finally settled their differences.*

different *adjective* 1. contrasting, dissimilar, varying, unlike *Mom and I have different opinions about what I can wear to school.* 2. distinct, separate, individual, unique, diverse *I'm looking for something different to wear for Halloween. Aiko and Celine come from very different cultures but are best friends.*

difficult *adjective* 1. hard, demanding, challenging, rough, tough, arduous, strenuous *Finding cures for some diseases is a difficult task.* easy 2. stubborn, obstinate, unmanageable *Jason is difficult and always expects to have his own way.*

difficulty *noun* problem, trouble, hardship, obstacle, struggle, snag *Uncle George says his company is experiencing financial difficulties. We had no difficulty at all finding your house.*

dig *verb* 1. excavate, scoop, burrow, tunnel, shovel *The Panama Canal was dug across the Isthmus of Panama between 1904 and 1914.* 2. search, delve, probe, investigate, look *I dug through several books before I found what I needed for my report.*

digest assimilate, process, absorb, break down *The human body uses enzymes to digest food.*

dignified *adjective* noble, stately, majestic, grand, imposing, distinguished *The ambassador had a dignified manner.* undignified

dignity *noun* 1. self-respect, pride, self-esteem, confidence, composure *The candidate maintained her dignity despite the crowd's noisy jeering.* 2. formality, grandeur, majesty, stateliness, decorum *The queen's manner was one of graciousness and dignity.*

dilapidated *adjective* run-down, shabby, ramshackle, decrepit, broken-down *My* *aunt and uncle bought a dilapidated old house and completely remodeled it.*

diligent *adjective* hardworking, industrious, energetic, conscientious *If I'm diligent, I can improve my grades.*

dilute *verb* weaken, thin, cut, water down, mix *Mom lets me drink a little coffee diluted with milk.* strengthen

dim 1. *adjective* faint, weak, pale, feeble *I couldn't read in the dim light.* bright 2. blurry, indistinct, vague, darkish *I could make out only dim shapes in the dense fog.* distinct
3. *verb* turn down, lower, darken, reduce *The theater dimmed its lights a couple of times to signal the end of intermission.* turn up

dimension *noun* measurement, size, proportion, extent, expanse *I need enough paint for a room with the following dimensions: 12 feet by 16 feet, with a height of 8 feet.*

diminish *verb* decrease, lessen, reduce, weaken, abate, lower, ebb, fade away *The wind diminished, and we had to motor back to port in our sailboat.* increase

din *noun* noise, racket, clamor, uproar, tumult *The din from the party next door kept us awake most of the night.* quiet

dine *verb* eat, feast, consume food, feed *No one wanted to cook tonight, so we're dining at a restaurant.*

dingy *adjective* dirty, dull, drab, grimy, dark, gloomy *Mom suggested we replace the dingy curtains covering my bedroom window.*

dip 1. *verb* dunk, sink, plunge, immerse, duck, submerge *I dipped my toes in the icy lake and decided not to swim.* 2. descend, sink, go down, set, disappear *The sun dipped below the horizon.* 3. *noun* soak, swim, plunge, bathe *We all went for a dip in the lake to cool off.*
4. decline, fall, slump *A local manufacturer says a dip in their profits may result in their having to let workers go.* 5. hollow, depression, slope *Slow down for the dip in the road.*

diplomatic *adjective* careful, discreet, tactful, judicious, polite *I gave a diplomatic answer to avoid hurting my friend's feelings.*

direct 1. *verb* guide, show, point, lead, steer *Can you direct me to the nearest bus stop?*
2. aim, point, target, focus *The TV show is directed specifically at preschool children.*
3. command, order, instruct, dictate, tell *The police officer directed the traffic to stop while the ducks and ducklings crossed the road.* 4. manage, administer, control, supervise, govern *Jason's mother directs emergency services at the hospital.* 5. *adjective* straight, shortest, unswerving, through, express *The interstate highway is the direct route, but the back roads are more scenic.*

direction *noun* 1. control, management, supervision, guidance, leadership, administration *The middle-school orchestra, under the direction of Ms. Johannsen, will perform in the auditorium at seven o'clock.* 2. way, course, route, path, road *Which direction did they go?*

directions *noun* instructions, guidelines, rules, regulations, commands, orders *Be sure to follow the directions at the start of the test.*

directly *adverb* 1. straight, right, nonstop, unswervingly *Come directly home after school.* 2. exactly, precisely *The building you're looking for is directly across the street.* 3. immediately, quickly, promptly, without delay, soon, shortly *I have to leave directly after the meeting in order to get home by nine o'clock.*

dirt *noun* 1. earth, soil *A truck delivered a load of dirt for our new lawn.* 2. grime, mud, soil, filth, grease, dust *The clothes Dad wears in his workshop get covered in dirt.*

dirty *adjective* 1. soiled, unclean, filthy, grimy, grubby, greasy *Change your good clothes before you get them dirty.* clean 2. nasty, unfair, mean, low *Putting a rubber spider on Susie's chair was a dirty trick.*

disable *verb* put out of order, make useless, make ineffective, make inoperable *We disabled the buzzer on the clothes dryer so it wouldn't wake the baby.* enable

disadvantage *noun* drawback, handicap, liability, inconvenience *My sister thinks the biggest disadvantage to living in the country is that there are no malls.* advantage, plus

disagree *verb* differ, quarrel, argue, conflict, dispute, oppose *The crowd booed the umpire when they disagreed with his call.* agree

disagreeable *adjective* 1. unpleasant, offensive, displeasing, nasty, distasteful, obnoxious, repulsive *Nonsmokers find cigarette smoke disagreeable.* agreeable 2. irritable, cross, bad-tempered, unfriendly *It puts my brother in a disagreeable mood to have an argument with his girlfriend.* agreeable

disagreement *noun* 1. conflict, opposition, disharmony, dissension *The film critics are in disagreement over whether or not the movie is worth seeing.* 2. argument, quarrel, fight, dispute, misunderstanding *When my sister and I have a disagreement, our parents make us take a time-out.*

disappear *verb* 1. vanish, fade away, recede from view, evaporate, withdraw *The moon disappeared behind a cloud. Our cat disappeared one evening and didn't return for two days.* 2. die out, cease to exist, end, perish, become extinct *The passenger pigeon disappeared in 1914, when the last bird of the species died in captivity.*

disappoint *verb* let down, displease, depress, upset, fail *I hate to disappoint you, but I ate the last piece of pie.*

disappointment *noun* 1. displeasure, dissatisfaction, discontent, sadness, regret *My parents expressed disappointment in my poor grades.* 2. letdown, failure, disaster, fiasco *The first movie was great, but the sequel was a disappointment.*

disapprove *verb* dislike, object to, frown on, be against, criticize *My parents disapprove of my watching violent TV shows.* approve

disaster *noun* catastrophe, tragedy, calamity, misfortune, mishap, accident *The sinking of the* Titanic *on April 15, 1912, was one of the greatest disasters in history.*

disbelief *noun* doubt, incredulity, lack of belief, distrust, discredit *Our reaction to the rumor that our teacher was resigning was one of shock and disbelief.*

discard *verb* reject, throw away, get rid of, dispose of, scrap, cast off (*Slang*—junk) *Don't discard those old newspapers—recycle them.*

discharge 1. *verb* unload, empty, dump, let out, disembark *The ship discharges its cargo at the dock.* 2. release, dismiss, send away, fire, terminate, remove, expel, let go *Stephanie was discharged from her job for poor performance.* 3. eject, give off, send out, pour forth, leak, ooze *The chimney discharged a plume of black smoke.* 4. *noun* release, liberation, dismissal, removal, termination, expulsion *Aunt Helen received an honorable discharge from the army.*

disciple *noun* follower, believer, devotee, student, pupil *The old Buddhist master had many disciples.*

discipline 1. *noun* self-control, strictness, orderliness, training, exercise, practice, drill *It takes discipline to learn to play a musical instrument well.* 2. correction, punishment, reprimand, penalty *Mom doesn't believe that spanking is an effective form of discipline.* 3. *verb* drill, instruct, train, exercise, prepare *The sergeant disciplined his men and women to be good soldiers.* 4. correct, punish, penalize, chastise *I had to discipline the dog for barking at night.*

disclose *verb* reveal, tell, make known, expose, uncover, show *The newspaper reporter refused to disclose the source of his information.* hide, conceal

discomfort *noun* pain, ache, distress, irritation, annoyance, unpleasantness, misery, suffering *Wet tents and sleeping bags caused the campers a lot of discomfort.*

discount *noun* deduction, reduction, markdown, price cut, rebate *The theater offers a student discount.*

~~~~~~

discourage *verb* 1. deter, prevent, keep from, stop, dissuade, hinder *The city hopes its new commuter rail system will discourage people from driving cars into the city.* encourage 2. dishearten, dispirit, daunt, deject, depress, intimidate *Getting turned down for the role did not discourage the actor, and he went on to become famous.* encourage

discover *verb* 1. find, locate, come across, turn up, uncover, spot *Despite many searches, Amelia Earhart's plane has not been discovered.* 2. reveal, learn, realize, determine, ascertain *We were surprised to discover that our friend had been lying.*

discovery *noun* finding, location, uncovering, detection, identification *In August 1848 the* New York Herald *printed news of the discovery of gold in California. The discovery of penicillin revolutionized the way doctors treat patients with infections.*

discriminate *verb* 1. show prejudice, be biased, be intolerant *It is illegal for an employer to discriminate against someone because of his or her race.* 2. distinguish, separate, tell the difference, differentiate *People who are color-blind cannot discriminate between red and green.*

discuss *verb* debate, talk over, consider, confer, deliberate *World leaders are meeting next week to discuss environmental issues.*

discussion *noun* debate, talk, conversation, dialogue, discourse, consideration *After some discussion, we finally agreed on which movie to rent.*

disease *noun* illness, sickness, ailment, malady, disorder, affliction *Diseases that once killed people can now be prevented.* health

disgrace 1. *noun* shame, dishonor, humiliation *She was sent home from college in disgrace after having cheated on her final exams.* 2. stain, blemish, blot, scandal, embarrassment *Racism is a disgrace to society.* 3. *verb* shame, dishonor, discredit, humiliate, embarrass, stain, tarnish *The players disgraced their team by taking bribes.*

disguise 1. *noun* costume, camouflage, cover, mask, concealment *Warren wore a wig and glasses as a disguise.* 2. *verb* conceal, hide, cover, camouflage, misrepresent *I tried to disguise a yawn by covering my mouth and looking interested.*

disgust 1. *noun* distaste, aversion, loathing, revulsion, nausea *She wrinkled her nose in disgust at the bad smell.* 2. *verb* sicken, offend, repel, revolt, nauseate *Dad says the unsportsmanlike behavior of some athletes disgusts him.*

dish *noun* container, receptacle, bowl, plate, platter, saucer *We each had a dish of ice cream for dessert.*

dishearten *verb* discourage, depress, sadden, deject *Don't let that low grade dishearten you.* cheer

dishonest *adjective* lying, deceitful, untruthful, fraudulent, misleading, deceptive, corrupt, crooked *Shoplifting is stealing and it's dishonest.* honest

disintegrate *verb* break up, fall apart, fragment, break down, crumble, decay, decompose *The papers stored in boxes in the attic disintegrated into dust when we touched them.*

dislike 1. *verb* hate, detest, despise, loathe, disapprove, frown on *Grandma and Grandpa dislike cold weather and snow, so they retired to Florida.* 2. *noun* hatred, loathing, distaste, revulsion, aversion *People's fear and dislike of snakes is often based on a lack of knowledge about the reptile.*

dismal *adjective* gloomy, dreary, bleak, dull, cheerless, miserable *The day started out to be dark and dismal, but the sun came out in the afternoon.* bright, cheerful

dismay 1. *verb* bewilder, disturb, upset, unsettle, unnerve, alarm, frighten *We were dismayed at the amount of damage the tornado had done.* 2. *noun* shock, alarm, distress, bewilderment, anxiety, fright *My best friend is moving to another town, much to my dismay.*

dismiss *verb* 1. excuse, disband, release, allow to go *Classes were dismissed early today because of the snowstorm.* 2. discharge, expel, give notice, let go, fire *Dad had to dismiss an employee today for not doing her job.* hire, enlist

disobedient *adjective* badly behaved, defiant, rebellious, unruly, contrary, naughty *You have to teach a disobedient puppy early on what behavior is not allowed.* obedient

disobey *verb* disregard, break, ignore, defy, resist, overstep, violate *If you continue to disobey the rules, you will be punished.* obey

disorder *noun* 1. chaos, disarray, mess, clutter, disorganization, confusion, muddle, jumble *I can't go out until I clean up the disorder in my room.* order 2. ailment, condition, disease, illness, malady, sickness, syndrome *My younger sister is being treated for attention deficit disorder.*

disorderly *adjective* 1. messy, untidy, chaotic, cluttered, disorganized *Our garage is such a disorderly mess, we can't get the car inside.* orderly 2. unruly, rowdy, uncontrollable, unmanageable, disobedient, undisciplined *The disorderly students were sent to the principal's office.* orderly

dispel *verb* drive away, banish, dismiss, eliminate, disperse, scatter *Grandma dispelled her fear of computers by taking a class in how to use them.* attract

dispense *verb* distribute, give out, deal out, issue, allot *The pharmacy dispenses medicine only by a doctor's prescription.*

disperse *verb* scatter, break up, disband, dissipate, dissolve *The crowd dispersed when it started to rain.*

display 1. *verb* demonstrate, illustrate, exhibit, show, reveal, present *Nicole displayed a real talent for acting as the lead in the school play. Leonardo da Vinci's work of art, the* Mona Lisa, *is displayed at the Louvre in Paris.* conceal 2. *noun* show, spectacle, exhibition, presentation, demonstration *We always enjoy the Fourth of July fireworks display.*

dispose of *verb* throw away, throw out, discard, get rid of, dispense with, dump, scrap *Dispose of your plastic bottles in the bin labeled "Recyclables."* keep

disposition *noun* nature, temperament, character, inclination *His calm disposition makes him a patient father.*

dispute 1. *verb* argue, quarrel, disagree, clash, squabble, fight *School board members disputed over the location of the new school.* agree 2. challenge, question, contest, deny, resist, oppose *Each country disputed the other's claim to the territory.* 3. *noun* argument, debate, disagreement, conflict, clash, row, fight *Mom ended my brother's and my dispute by sending us to our rooms.* agreement

disrupt *verb* disturb, upset, interrupt, interfere with, obstruct, impede, confuse, mess up *The accident on the freeway disrupted traffic for more than an hour.*

dissent 1. *verb* disagree, differ, take exception *Three of the judges dissented from the opinion of the other four.* agree 2. *noun* opposition, disagreement, dissension, rebellion *Dissent was not permitted by the dictator.* assent, agreement, consent

dissolve *verb* 1. melt, liquefy, soften, mix *To make bread, you first dissolve the yeast in warm water.* 2. end, discontinue, break up, disband, terminate *The partners dissolved their partnership after a quarrel.*

distance *noun* space, stretch, gap, span, expanse, length, width, depth *The distance between New York and Los Angeles is approximately 2,800 miles. Measure the distance from here to that post.*

distant *adjective* far, remote, far-off, far-flung, outlying *The Hubble Space Telescope sent photographs of distant galaxies back to earth.*

distinct *adjective* 1. definite, clear, obvious, noticeable, marked, apparent *I see a distinct resemblance between you and your mother.* indefinite, unclear 2. different, dissimilar, separate, diverse *The upper Midwest has four distinct seasons.* similar

distinguish *verb* 1. set apart, differentiate, separate, tell apart, tell the difference

His red hair distinguishes him from his brother. It's not easy to distinguish between fact and fiction in the book. 2. identify, recognize, make out, see, perceive, observe *I couldn't distinguish his face in the darkness.* 3. honor, win acclaim for, glorify, dignify *She has distinguished herself with her service to the community.*

distinguished *adjective* important, great, outstanding, noted, celebrated, honored *The distinguished artist has paintings on display in many galleries.*

distort *verb* 1. twist, misrepresent, falsify, alter, change *The politicians accused one another of distorting the facts.* 2. deform, bend, contort, misshape *The ripples in the pond distorted my reflection.*

distract *verb* divert, sidetrack, turn aside, deflect, interrupt *Dad turned the TV off so it wouldn't distract me from my homework.*

distress 1. *noun* pain, suffering, agony, misery, anguish, worry, concern, anxiety *Gloria's sprained ankle caused her a lot of distress.* 2. danger, peril, trouble, difficulty, need *The coast guard rescued the crew of a boat in distress.* 3. *verb* upset, trouble, disturb, bother, worry, torment *It distresses me to think that some people mistreat animals.*

distribute *verb* 1. give out, hand out, issue, dispense, allot, allocate, supply, deliver *The volunteers distributed food to the refugees.* 2. scatter, disperse, spread *Your weight should be distributed evenly on both legs and your back should be straight.*

district *noun* area, region, zone, neighborhood, section, territory, locality, place *The downtown district has expanded to include new hotels, restaurants, and shops.*

disturb *verb* 1. bother, irritate, annoy, interrupt, distract *I entered the room quietly so as not to disturb my sleeping sister.* 2. trouble, concern, upset, distress, worry, perturb, alarm *It disturbed me to hear of your accident.* 3. disarrange, disorganize, mess up, move, shift, touch, remove *Be careful not to disturb anything on my desk.*

disturbance *noun* 1. disruption, interruption, distraction, interference, intrusion *Mom resents any disturbance when she's working.* 2. commotion, uproar, turmoil, tumult, riot *The arrival of the rock group caused quite a disturbance at the airport.*

dive 1. *verb* plunge, descend, drop, plummet, jump, leap *The eagle dove and caught a fish in its talons.* 2. *noun* plunge, descent, drop, jump, leap *Her graceful dive won second place in the competition.*

diverse *adjective* varied, mixed, diversified, assorted, distinct *U.S. society is culturally and ethnically diverse.* same

divert *verb* 1. redirect, reroute, switch, deflect, turn aside *A snowstorm caused flights* *to be diverted to other airports or to be canceled.* 2. amuse, entertain, delight, interest, absorb, engross, tickle *The clown's antics diverted the children.*

divide *verb* 1. separate, split, cut, break up, branch, diverge, part *The teacher divided the class into two groups. When the road divides, take the left fork.* 2. share, distribute, divide up, allocate, allot, apportion, split *We divided the four apples among us.*

divine *adjective* holy, sacred, spiritual, saintly, heavenly *Most religions believe in a divine being or beings.*

division *noun* 1. separation, splitting, partition *Most dictionaries show the division of words into syllables.* 2. part, branch, department, section, sector *Dad's company has divisions in two other cities.* 3. boundary, dividing line, border, divide *The Mississippi River is often thought of as the division between the eastern and western United States.*

divorce 1. *verb* divide, split up, break up, part *Jody's parents divorced last year.* 2. *noun* separation, split, breakup, parting *Since the divorce, Jody lives with her mother and visits her father every other weekend.*

dizzy *adjective* giddy, unsteady, light-headed, faint, woozy *Heights make me dizzy.*

do *verb* 1. perform, accomplish, carry out *I can usually do my homework in two hours.* 2. behave, act, conduct oneself *Our parents expect us to do as they have raised us to do.* 3. be responsible for, prepare *When we go camping, Dad does the cooking and I do the dishes.* 4. create *My friend Barbara does drawings of cartoon characters.* 5. figure out *Computers can do complex mathematical calculations in seconds.* 6. progress, manage, fare, get along *How are you doing today?*

docile *adjective* gentle, tame, mild, obedient, manageable, controllable *Our big black Lab is a docile and affectionate dog.*

dock *noun* pier, quay, mooring, anchorage, wharf *We tied our boat to the dock.*

doctor *noun* physician, surgeon, medical practitioner, healer *The doctor said that I just have a bad cold.*

doctrine *noun* belief, teaching, creed, principle, tenet *I'm interested in learning about the doctrines of other religions.*

document *noun* official paper, paper, record, writing, text, instrument, certificate *The U.S. Constitution is a document that contains the laws, principles, and procedures of the government and guarantees certain rights to the people.*

dodge *verb* 1. move, duck, dart, sidestep, swerve *I managed to dodge behind a tree just* *as my sister threw the snowball.* 2. avoid, evade, fend off, elude *The official dodged the reporter's awkward question.*

domain *noun* realm, province, property, territory, region *According to legend, Camelot was the domain of King Arthur.*

domestic *adjective* 1. household, family, home, residential *We share domestic duties such as cooking and cleaning at our house.* 2. tame, trained, pet, docile, not wild *Cats, dogs, horses, cows, sheep, and pigs are all domestic animals.*

dominant *adjective* 1. main, chief, principal, leading *The car is the dominant mode of transportation in the United States.* 2. ruling, controlling, commanding, most influential *The dominant male lion in a pack always gets to eat first.*

dominate *verb* control, rule, command, lead, govern *My sister's volleyball team dominated the league, winning thirty-three straight matches.*

donate *verb* give, contribute, grant, bestow, provide *Our supermarket donates food to the needy.*

donation *noun* gift, contribution, grant, present, offering *Caitlin's donation of a kidney to her brother saved his life.*

done *adjective* finished, completed, ended, concluded, over, wound up, through with *My chores are done. Are you done with your homework?* unfinished

donor *noun* contributor, donator, giver, grantor *An anonymous donor established a scholarship fund to assist disadvantaged students.*

doom 1. *noun* ruin, misfortune, catastrophe, destruction, disaster *Many people predicted doom on January 1, 2000, when computers having dates with two-digit years were expected to crash.* 2. *verb* fate, destine, condemn *The princess was doomed to die but was rescued by the gallant knight.*

door *noun* entrance, access, entry, path, way *A quality education opens the door to success.*

dosage *noun* amount, quantity, portion, measure *Strictly follow the dosage prescribed by your doctor.*

double 1. *adverb* twice, twice as much *The construction workers were paid double for overtime.* 2. *verb* increase twofold, multiply by two *Double two to get four. Their investment has doubled.*

doubt 1. *verb* misbelieve, distrust, suspect, question, challenge, dispute *My science teacher doubts the existence of flying saucers.* believe 2. *noun* distrust, misgiving, reservation, suspicion, uncertainty *My mom has doubts about my flying alone to visit my cousins.*

doubtful *adjective* uncertain, unclear, questionable, unlikely, improbable *It is doubtful that the quarterback's injury has healed enough for him to play today.* certain

down 1. *adverb* downward, to a lower place, below, beneath *This elevator is going down.* up 2. *preposition* along, through *The principal's office is two doors down the hall.* 3. *verb* knock down, fell, tackle, bring down, defeat, overcome *The high winds downed trees and power lines.* 4. drink, consume, gulp, swallow, guzzle, chug *I just had time to down a glass of juice before dashing off to school.*

downfall *noun* failure, ruin, end, undoing *Napoleon's downfall was his defeat at the Battle of Waterloo.*

downpour *noun* rainstorm, cloudburst *A heavy downpour prevented the ball game from continuing.*

downright *adverb* totally, completely, utterly, absolutely, positively *Driving in a blizzard is downright dangerous.*

doze *verb* nap, drowse, snooze, sleep *My cat likes to doze at the foot of my bed.*

drab *adjective* dull, colorless, dingy, plain, cheerless, gloomy, unattractive, uninteresting *Mom and Dad said I can paint the drab walls in my room any color I want.* bright, interesting

draft 1. *noun* wind, breeze, air, current *I feel a draft; did someone leave a window open?* 2. rough copy, outline, sketch, summary, plan, version *The teacher helped me improve the first draft of my story.* 3. *verb* outline, plan, sketch, prepare, draw up *The U.S. Constitution was drafted in Philadelphia in the summer of 1787.*

drag *verb* 1. pull, haul, draw, tug, tow, heave, trail *My sister dragged her suitcase up the stairs.* 2. creep, crawl, move slowly, linger on, lag *The boring movie seemed to drag on forever.*

drain *verb* 1. dry, empty, draw off, let out, discharge *Florida's Everglades were drained for farmland.* 2. use up, exhaust, consume, deplete, sap, empty *The ten-mile bike ride drained all my energy.*

dramatic *adjective* exciting, sensational, spectacular, thrilling, impressive *To see the Grand Canyon is to see nature at its most dramatic.*

drastic *adjective* extreme, severe, radical, tough, harsh, strong *Grandpa made drastic* *changes in his lifestyle and diet after he had a heart attack.*

draw 1. *verb* sketch, illustrate, portray, picture, design *Darrell is good at drawing caricatures of people's faces.* 2. pull, drag, haul, tow, tug *Draw up a chair and join us.* 3. pull out, remove, extract, produce *The knight drew his sword.* 4. attract, lure, interest, invite, capture *Kevin tried to draw my attention by waving frantically.* 5. come, move, go *The dinner party drew to a close at 10:00.* 6. *noun* tie, stalemate, deadlock, standoff, dead heat *The game ended in a 14-14 draw and had to go into overtime.*

drawback *noun* disadvantage, shortcoming, flaw, problem, obstacle, catch, defect, difficulty *The only drawback to our house is that there is no dishwasher, and I have to do the dishes.* advantage

dread 1. *noun* fear, fright, terror, apprehension, horror *The thought of coming face-to-face with a grizzly bear fills me with dread.* 2. *verb* fear, be afraid of, be terrified by, be anxious about, be worried about *I dreaded being on the water in a boat until I learned to swim.*

dreadful *adjective* bad, terrible, awful, unpleasant, horrible, vile, wretched, detestable, ghastly *The camping trip was dreadful—it rained the whole time. The Komodo dragon is a dreadful-looking lizard that grows to ten feet and has a poisonous bite.*

dream 1. *noun* goal, ambition, vision, hope, aspiration, desire, wish *Mom's dream is to return to school to get a master's degree.* 2. *verb* imagine, consider, conceive, think *I'd never dream of harming an animal.*

dreary *adjective* gloomy, dull, dismal, bleak, depressing, cheerless *When I complained about having to spend the cold, dreary day inside, Mom put me to work cleaning my room.* pleasant

drench *verb* soak, wet, saturate, flood *Danny drenched me with the garden hose.*

dress 1. *noun* gown, frock *I've never seen my sister wear a dress—she's always in jeans.* 2. apparel, garments, clothing, clothes, attire, wear, garb *The invitation says the dance requires formal dress.* 3. *verb* clothe, attire, outfit, put on clothes *My little brother is learning to dress himself and accidentally put his shoes on the wrong feet.*

drift 1. *verb* float, glide, coast, flow *Leaves drifted down the river with the current.* 2. wander, roam, stray, meander *Please watch your sister so she doesn't drift off and get lost in the crowd.* 3. accumulate, pile up, gather, collect *The wind causes sand to drift and form dunes.* 4. *noun* pile, heap, bank, mass, accumulation *The snow lay in deep drifts.*

drill 1. *noun* practice, exercise, preparation, training, instruction *Fire drills make* *you familiar with the procedures for exiting a building safely.* 2. *verb* bore, pierce, puncture, penetrate *The first successful oil well in the United States was drilled in 1859 in Pennsylvania and was 69½ feet deep.* 3. train, coach, instruct, rehearse *The band director drilled the marching band on the field every afternoon.*

drink 1. *verb* swallow, guzzle, gulp, sip *You need to drink extra water when you are exercising.* 2. *noun* beverage, liquid refreshment *Water is the best drink to quench your thirst.* 3. swallow, sip, taste, glass, cup *May I have a drink of juice?*

drive 1. *verb* operate, control, handle, steer, run *Dad says I'll be old enough next summer to drive the lawn tractor.* 2. take, chauffeur, transport *Dad drove Sam and me to the movie.* 3. force, move, push, propel, thrust *The storm drove the boat onto the shore.* 4. pound, hit, knock, strike *We used a rock to drive in the tent stakes.* 5. *noun* ride, trip, outing, journey, excursion *Last summer we took a drive along the California coast.* 6. effort, campaign, crusade, movement, cause *The Red Cross is asking everyone to donate blood at the community blood drive.* 7. ambition, determination, energy, initiative *Dad says the young woman he hired has a lot of drive to succeed.*

drizzle *noun* light rain, shower, sprinkle, mist *Heavy rain was predicted, but we had nothing more than a drizzle.*

droop *verb* hang down, sag, wilt, bend, bow, slump *Put the flowers in water before they begin to droop. Her eyelids drooped, and soon she was sound asleep.*

drop 1. *verb* fall, descend, plunge, sink, dive *The temperature dropped, and it began to snow.* rise 2. abandon, discontinue, give up, end, stop, cease, forgo *I'd like to drop violin lessons and take guitar lessons instead.* 3. omit, leave out, eliminate, remove *Drop the "e" in "hide" before adding "ing."* 4. *noun* descent, fall, plunge, slope *The mountain path ended in a sudden drop.* 5. decline, reduction, decrease, cut, lowering *A drop in the price of computers will enable me to buy a new one.* 6. droplet, bead, globule, bubble *Drops of dew on the spiderweb looked like tiny jewels.*

drown *verb* 1. drench, submerge, soak, cover, douse, swamp, inundate, flood *Heavy rain drowned farmers' crops. Dad drowns his baked potato in butter.* 2. stifle, deaden, overwhelm, overpower, mask, hide, obscure *Static drowned out her voice on the cell phone.*

drowsy *adjective* sleepy, tired, weary, heavy-eyed *I always get drowsy when I ride in a car.* awake, alert

drug *noun* 1. medicine, medication, cure, remedy, pharmaceutical *My brother takes a drug for his asthma.* 2. narcotic, illegal substance, stimulant, depressant (*Slang*—dope) *A man was arrested yesterday for trying to sell drugs near the school.*

drum *verb* beat, tap, strike, rap *Stop drumming on the table with your fingers.*

drunk *adjective* intoxicated, inebriated, tipsy, drunken *Driving while drunk is irresponsible and dangerous.* sober

dry *adjective* waterless, arid, parched, thirsty *Cacti can live in the dry desert because they have the ability to store and conserve water.*

dual *adjective* twofold, double, duplicate, twin *This motorcycle has dual exhausts.*

duck *verb* 1. bend, stoop, crouch, bow, drop, lower *I ducked to avoid hitting my head on the low branch.* 2. dunk, plunge, submerge, sink, immerse, dip *The kids were ducking each other in the pool.* 3. avoid, dodge, sidestep, evade, escape *The politician had become good at ducking reporters' questions. The thief ducked the police by turning down an alley.*

due 1. *adjective* proper, fitting, appropriate, correct, sufficient, adequate *Treat your teacher with due respect.* 2. owed, owing, payable *The bill is due at the end of the month.* paid 3. scheduled, expected, anticipated *The essays are due tomorrow. The school bus is due in a few minutes.* 4. *adverb* directly, straight, exactly, precisely *The road goes due north out of town.*

duel *noun* fight, contest, struggle, battle *The outlaw challenged the sheriff to a duel.*

dull 1. *adjective* blunt, not sharp, unsharpened *This knife has a dull edge.* 2. boring, uninteresting, tedious, unexciting, monotonous, tiresome, dry *I'd much rather read a book than watch this dull TV show.* interesting, exciting 3. gloomy, gray, dismal, dreary, cloudy, overcast *The sky was dull with a foreboding hint of rain.* 4. *verb* blunt, dim, lessen, decrease, reduce, diminish *The afternoon snacks dulled the children's appetites.*

dumb *adjective* silly, foolish, stupid, unintelligent *My little sister loves dumb "knock-knock" jokes.* clever

dummy *noun* 1. doll, figure, puppet, marionette, mannequin *A ventriloquist makes it look as if the dummy is talking.* 2. imitation, copy, reproduction, fake *The weapons on display aren't real—they're only dummies.*

dump 1. *verb* empty, unload, discharge, deposit, pour out *The truck dumped a load of gravel for the driveway.* 2. get rid of, throw away, discard, dispose of, scrap *Someone dumped a bag of garbage on the roadside.* 3. *noun* landfill, junkyard, trash pile, rubbish heap, scrap heap *We need to take the trash to the dump.*

duplicate 1. *noun* copy, reproduction, facsimile, replica, photocopy, carbon copy *We made a duplicate of the key for our door in case we lose the original.* 2. *verb* copy, reproduce, replicate, repeat *Scientists duplicate the conditions of space for astronauts to train in.*

~~~~~~

durable *adjective* sturdy, strong, enduring, long-lasting, sound *Mountain climbers need durable gear. Negotiators are moving toward a durable peace.*

dusk *noun* sundown, sunset, nightfall, twilight, evening *Dusk comes early in the winter.*

dust 1. *verb* clean, wipe off, brush *I dusted the furniture and vacuumed the floor.* 2. sprinkle, scatter, cover *Dust the brownies with powdered sugar.* 3. *noun* dirt, soot, fine powder *The old newspapers had turned to dust. The furniture was thick with dust.*

duty *noun* 1. task, job, work, function, assignment, responsibility, obligation *It's a soldier's duty to serve his or her country.* 2. tariff, tax, toll, levy, fee *When you return home from overseas, you may have to pay a duty on your purchases.*

dwell *verb* live, reside, inhabit, abide *Neolithic people dwelled in simple huts made of mud or stone.*

dwindle *verb* shrink, decrease, diminish, lessen, decline, ebb, fade, drop off *The population of whooping cranes dwindled to fifteen migrating birds, but the number is gradually increasing.*

dye 1. *noun* color, coloring, stain, tint, pigment *Natural blue dye is often made from the indigo plant, native to southeastern Asia.* 2. *verb* color, tint, stain *My sister dyed her hair pink, but luckily the color wasn't permanent.*

dynamic *adjective* active, energetic, forceful, strong, lively, intense, animated, spirited *The actor gave a dynamic performance as the lead in Shakespeare's* Richard II.

E

eager *adjective* enthusiastic, anxious, keen, avid, ready, willing, impatient *The children were eager to finish their meal and get outside to play. My parents were pleased that the teacher called me an "eager learner."* indifferent, apathetic, unenthusiastic

early 1. *adjective* initial, beginning, first, opening *The early morning is my favorite time of day.* 2. *adverb* ahead of time, beforehand, in advance, prematurely *You should arrive at the theater early to get a good seat.*

earn *verb* 1. get, obtain, receive, make, collect, secure *I earned forty-five dollars last week by shoveling sidewalks.* 2. deserve, merit, win, be worthy of *Mr. Rodriguez's business* *skills and integrity have earned him the respect of the local business community.*

earth *noun* 1. world, planet, globe *The continents make up 29 percent of the earth's surface.* 2. ground, dirt, soil, land, sod *Decomposed organic material gives earth its dark brown color.*

ease 1. *verb* soothe, comfort, relax, lighten, relieve, lessen, reduce *The neighbors' friendliness helped ease our anxiety over moving to a new city. Mom gave me an aspirin to ease the pain of my sprained ankle.* 2. *noun* comfort, contentment, security, peace, enjoyment, relaxation *Mom and Dad said they enjoyed a life of ease on their Caribbean cruise.* 3. effortlessness, easiness, facility, simplicity *I chose this camera for its ease of use. Doris won the tennis match with ease.*

easy *adjective* 1. simple, effortless, uncomplicated, straightforward *Gin rummy is an easy card game to learn. Computers are supposed to make our lives easier.* 2. comfortable, carefree, luxurious, leisurely *My pets have an easy life.* 3. pleasant, natural, casual, informal *Colin has an easy charm that makes him especially likable.* 4. lenient, undemanding, moderate, unexacting, tolerant *The police officer was easy on us for having a taillight out, and just gave us a warning.*

eat *verb* dine, consume, devour, swallow, chew, feed, feast *We eat our lunch in the school cafeteria. Have you eaten yet?*

eat away *verb* corrode, rust, erode, wear away, rot, decay, destroy *Road salt slowly eats away the sheet metal of your car.*

ebb *verb* 1. recede, flow back, retreat, withdraw, subside *The tide ebbed and left the boat stranded on the shore.* 2. decline, lessen, decrease, diminish, fade *The popularity of the group's music has never ebbed, and it is still played on radio stations.*

eccentric *adjective* unusual, peculiar, odd, irregular *The artist Vincent van Gogh was regarded by some as eccentric and by others as mad.*

echo 1. *noun* reverberation, reflection, rebound, ricochet, ringing *The empty room produced an echo when we talked.* 2. *verb* reverberate, reflect, rebound, ricochet, ring *Our voices echoed around the cave.*

eclipse *verb* 1. hide, conceal, cover, obscure, cast a shadow over, darken, shade *The moon is eclipsed when the earth passes between the sun and the moon.* 2. overshadow, outshine, surpass, exceed, outdo *The runner's record time has totally eclipsed the previous record.*

economical *adjective* 1. thrifty, frugal, prudent, careful, sparing, cautious *An* *economical shopper waits until something's on sale before buying it.* 2. inexpensive, cheap, reasonable, low-priced *Small cars are more economical to drive because they use less gas.*

ecstatic *adjective* thrilled, elated, delighted, happy, joyful *Aunt Margaret was ecstatic when she learned she'd won a trip to Hawaii.*

edge 1. *noun* border, fringe, boundary, rim, side, margin, limit *Early sailors thought the earth was flat and that if they sailed too far from shore, they would fall off the edge.*
2. advantage, head start, upper hand *Her height gives her the edge on the basketball court.*
3. *verb* ease, inch, creep, move, pick one's way, steal *He edged his way out of the crowd.*
4. border, bound, surround, trim, decorate *The linen tablecloth was edged with lace.*

edit *verb* check, revise, amend, rewrite, modify, alter *Word-processing software makes it easy for me to edit my class papers.*

educate *verb* teach, instruct, train, tutor, coach, enlighten *A teacher's job is to educate his or her students.*

education *noun* knowledge, learning, schooling, training, enlightenment, instruction *Education can prepare you for a rewarding career.*

eerie *adjective* strange, weird, spooky, scary, unnerving *The shadows in the pale moonlight made the forest eerie at night.*

effect 1. *noun* result, outcome, consequence, product *Poor health can be the effect of a poor diet.* 2. influence, impact, impression *The bad weather had little effect on the crowds celebrating the team's win.* 3. *verb* cause, bring about, produce, create, make, accomplish, achieve *Computers have effected many changes in the way we work.*

effective *adjective* 1. efficient, useful, productive, successful, valuable *The new vaccine is highly effective in preventing the disease.* ineffective 2. in effect, operational, operative, in force, active *The dress codes are effective immediately.*

efficient *adjective* effective, productive, competent, organized *Our school secretary is very efficient and doesn't waste time.*

effort *noun* 1. exertion, energy, work, labor, strain, struggle, strength *We put a lot of time and effort into remodeling our old house.* 2. attempt, try, endeavor *The negotiators claim they are making a genuine effort to reach an agreement.*

eject *verb* 1. release, emit, spout, discharge, spew *The volcano continues to eject ash and steam.* 2. remove, drive out, expel, throw out, force out *The security guard ejected the intruder from the building.*

elaborate 1. *adjective* complex, detailed, complicated, intricate, involved *The actors wore elaborate eighteenth-century costumes. Dad is making elaborate plans to celebrate Mom's fortieth birthday.* 2. *verb* expand, detail, enlarge, explain, add to *The police refused to elaborate on the arrest.*

elastic *adjective* stretchy, stretchable, springy, flexible *She uses an elastic band to hold her ponytail.*

elated *adjective* overjoyed, delighted, jubilant, thrilled, excited, ecstatic *The divers were elated at having discovered the sunken treasure ship.*

elder 1. *adjective* older, senior *She has two elder brothers.* 2. *noun* senior citizen, senior *Society should respect and care for its elders.*

elderly *adjective* aged, aging, mature, of advanced years, senior, old *Meals on Wheels is an organization that delivers hot meals to elderly people in their homes.*

elect *verb* 1. vote for, cast a ballot for, appoint, designate, pick, name, nominate *We elect a president every four years.* 2. choose, decide, opt, determine *We elected to order a pizza rather than cook.*

elegant *adjective* stylish, sophisticated, exquisite, beautiful, fine, graceful *Cinderella wore an elegant white gown to the ball.*

element *noun* component, part, factor, feature, ingredient, constituent *The book is fiction but contains historic elements. There is an element of truth in what you say.*

elementary *adjective* basic, fundamental, beginning, introductory, simple *I know some elementary French, but not enough to understand the French exchange student.* advanced

elevate *verb* lift, raise, boost, hoist *The doctor told me to elevate my sprained ankle.* lower

eligible *adjective* qualified, fit, entitled, worthy, suitable *My sister will be sixteen next week and will be eligible for a driver's license.* ineligible

eliminate *verb* remove, discard, reject, exclude, get rid of, dispose of *I had to eliminate milk, eggs, and nuts from my diet because I'm allergic to them.* include

elude *verb* avoid, evade, dodge, duck, escape, lose *In the movie the hero eluded the bad guys by getting on a bus just as it pulled away from the curb.*

emancipate *verb* free, release, liberate, deliver, rescue, save *England passed an act in 1833 that emancipated its slaves thirty-two years before slavery was abolished in the United States.*

embark on *verb* begin, start, commence, undertake, attempt *Aunt Eleanor has finished medical school and is embarking on a career as a doctor.*

embarrass *verb* fluster, confuse, make uncomfortable, disconcert, humiliate, shame, mortify *Dad was embarrassed at having to tell the waiter that he forgot his wallet.*

emblem *noun* symbol, sign, insignia, logo, badge, token *The dove is the emblem of peace.*

embrace 1. *verb* hug, grasp, clasp, enfold, hold, clutch *Dad embraced Mom, my sister, and me when he returned from his business trip.* 2. adopt, accept, take up, welcome *The immigrants embraced the customs of their new homeland.* 3. include, contain, comprise, cover, encompass, incorporate *The countryside embraces lush farmland and many pretty villages.* 4. *noun* hug, squeeze, hold, cuddle *I gave Grandma a warm embrace.*

emerge *verb* appear, come out, come into view, come into sight, surface *The sun emerged from behind a cloud. More facts are emerging from the investigation.* hide

emergency *noun* crisis, accident, danger, difficulty, trouble *The babysitter has the number where we can be reached in an emergency. We take a first-aid kit when we go camping, in case of an emergency.*

emigrate *verb* move away, move, relocate, migrate *The Hmong living in the United States emigrated here from Laos.*

eminent *adjective* prominent, distinguished, famous, outstanding, great *Eminent physicist Albert Einstein won the Nobel Prize for physics in 1921.* unknown

emit *verb* give off, discharge, send out, release, radiate *The sun emits energy in the form of heat and light.*

emotion *noun* feeling, sentiment, sensitivity, passion, excitement *I got caught up in the emotion of the sad story.*

emphasis *noun* stress, importance, significance, weight, attention, priority *My teacher puts a lot of emphasis on reading skills.*

emphasize *verb* stress, highlight, accentuate, call attention to *Our doctor emphasizes the importance of a healthy diet.* diminish

employ *verb* 1. hire, engage, retain, enlist, contract, take on *The resorts in tourist areas employ college students for the summer.* 2. use, utilize, make use of, put to use, apply *The Mississippi riverboat employed a steam engine to turn its paddle wheel.*

employee *noun* worker, laborer, staff person, assistant, wage earner *Uncle George has* *more than twenty employees working for his company.*

employer *noun* boss, manager, owner, director, company, business, firm *The largest employer in town is planning to hire more people.*

empty 1. *adjective* vacant, unfilled, blank, bare, unoccupied, hollow *We drove around and around looking for an empty parking space.* full 2. meaningless, useless, trivial, idle, aimless, hollow *Don't make empty promises you can't keep.* 3. *verb* drain, pour out, use up, clear, clear out, vacate, evacuate *She emptied the last of the milk on her cereal. The school emptied quickly after the last class.* fill

enable *verb* allow, permit, make possible, empower, qualify, authorize *Scholarships enable students who could otherwise not afford college tuition to go to college.* prevent

enchant *verb* 1. bewitch, cast a spell on *In the fairy tale "Sleeping Beauty" the witch enchants the princess.* 2. delight, charm, fascinate, captivate, enthrall *The children were enchanted by the animals at the petting zoo.*

enclose *verb* 1. surround, shut in, seal off, wall in, encircle *The swimming pool is enclosed by a fence to keep anyone from falling in.* 2. include, insert, put in, add *My grandparents enclosed a check with my birthday card.*

encore *noun* repeat, curtain call, repetition, reprise *The audience cheered until the band came back for an encore.*

encounter 1. *noun* meeting, contact, confrontation *The hiker told a story of his encounter with a bear in the forest.* 2. *verb* meet, come across, experience, face, confront *I encountered difficulties trying to download a file from the Internet.*

encourage *verb* 1. urge, prompt, invite, inspire, motivate *The teacher encouraged us to ask questions if we didn't understand something.* discourage 2. assist, help, foster, promote, advance, boost *Art activities encourage the imagination.* discourage

end 1. *noun* finish, conclusion, close, ending, finale, windup *Our assignment is due at the end of the week. I stayed up late so I could watch the end of the movie.* beginning 2. edge, limit, border, boundary, extremity, tip *Our house is at the end of the road. Sharpen the end of the stick to use as a tent stake.* 3. purpose, goal, objective, aim, intention *He wants to achieve his ends by honest means.* 4. *verb* finish, conclude, close, stop, complete, cease, halt, wind up *The game ended with a victory for the opposing team.* begin

endanger *verb* put in danger, risk, imperil, jeopardize *An oil spill along the coast could endanger the wildlife living there.*

endeavor 1. *verb* try, strive, attempt, labor, struggle (*Slang*—have a go at, take a crack at, make a stab at) *Medical science endeavors to cure and treat disease.* 2. *noun* attempt, effort, struggle, striving, undertaking, venture *I asked Mr. Morales to help me in my endeavor to learn to speak Spanish.*

endless *adjective* continuous, uninterrupted, constant, ceaseless, unending, limitless, interminable *We got stuck in an endless stream of traffic this morning. My teacher has endless patience.*

endorse *verb* approve, accept, support, back, okay *Both governments endorsed the proposals contained in the peace plan.* denounce

endure *verb* 1. bear, stand, tolerate, experience, suffer, undergo, withstand *The lost hikers endured freezing temperatures until they were found.* 2. last, continue, remain, stay, persist *Many superstitions endure even though they have no basis in fact.*

enemy *noun* opponent, foe, opposition, adversary *During the U.S. Civil War the North and the South were enemies.*

energetic *adjective* lively, active, vigorous, spirited, dynamic, vital *Mrs. Tanaka at age seventy-three is still energetic; she walks two miles every day.*

energy *noun* strength, vigor, spirit, pep, vitality, stamina, force, power, drive *We woke up full of energy on the first day of vacation.*

enforce *verb* apply, administer, carry out, implement *The job of the police is to enforce the law.*

engage *verb* 1. absorb, engross, interest, fascinate, involve, hold one's attention, occupy *I was so engaged in the adventures of the young wizard and his friends that I read all night long.* 2. employ, hire, appoint, take on, contract for, busy *My parents engaged a carpenter to add a porch to our house.*

engagement *noun* appointment, commitment, date, meeting, arrangement *My parents have a dinner engagement this evening.*

engaging *adjective* attractive, appealing, charming, enchanting, captivating, delightful, lovely *My sister is a beautiful baby with an engaging smile.* unattractive, unappealing

engineer *verb* direct, conduct, manage, control, run, lead, guide *Diana engineered the process of decorating the gym.*

engrave *verb* carve, cut, inscribe, etch *The wedding rings are engraved with their names.*

engross *verb* occupy, absorb, engage, fascinate, enthrall *I was too engrossed in the computer game to hear my mother call me to dinner.*

engrossing *adjective* absorbing, engaging, fascinating, gripping, riveting, enthralling *Aunt Emily gave an engrossing account of her trip to China.*

enhance *verb* improve, increase, heighten, add to, strengthen, intensify, amplify *Trees, shrubs, and flowers enhance the beauty of a lawn.* impair

enjoy *verb* 1. like, appreciate, love, take pleasure in, savor, relish *Mom and I enjoy gardening, and Dad and my sister enjoy golf.* dislike 2. have, possess, own, hold, benefit from *Great-Grandpa is eighty-five years old and still enjoys good health.*

enjoyment *noun* pleasure, amusement, fun, joy, delight, satisfaction *The children ate the birthday cake with obvious enjoyment. I get enjoyment out of building model airplanes.*

enlarge *verb* increase, expand, extend, broaden, magnify *I had the photos enlarged and framed to hang on the wall.* reduce, shrink

enlighten *verb* inform, instruct, educate, teach, illuminate *The TV documentary enlightened us about the causes of global warming.*

enlist *verb* 1. join, enroll, sign up for, enter, volunteer for *My aunt Marjory enlisted in the navy right after college.* 2. recruit, obtain, engage, secure *Dad enlisted our help in planning the tree house.*

enormous *adjective* large, great, vast, tremendous, huge, immense, giant, colossal *Mom caught an enormous salmon while fishing in Alaska.* tiny

enough *adjective* adequate, sufficient, ample, satisfactory *We haven't enough milk for breakfast, so we'll stop at the store.* insufficient

enrage *verb* anger, infuriate, madden, incense, provoke *When the monster in the movie became enraged and out of control, I covered my eyes.*

enrich *verb* improve, better, enhance, develop *Compost enriches the soil. Art and literature enrich our lives.*

enroll *verb* register, join, sign up, enlist *Mimi and Mom have enrolled in a yoga class.*

ensure *verb* assure, make certain guarantees, confirm, certify *Ensure that everyone in the boat is wearing a life jacket.*

enter *verb* 1. come into, go into, pass into, penetrate *Please enter the building using the door on your right.* exit, leave 2. begin, start, join, enroll, enlist, register *My brother is* *entering high school in the fall. I entered a contest to win a laptop computer.* 3. list, record, note, write down, post *I entered my friends' e-mail addresses in the address book on my computer.*

enterprise *noun* project, undertaking, venture, deed, exploit, adventure *Author Jules Verne foresaw the future in his stories of daring enterprise such as* Around the World in Eighty Days *and* 20,000 Leagues Under the Sea.

entertain *verb* amuse, delight, interest, excite, fascinate, engage, occupy *We bring books, cards, and games along to entertain ourselves on long car trips.*

entertainment *noun* amusement, fun, enjoyment, pleasure, diversion, recreation *The resort has a live band for the guests' entertainment.*

enthusiasm *noun* eagerness, excitement, passion, zeal, fire, interest *His enthusiasm for the team remained strong even when it lost.*

enthusiastic *adjective* eager, excited, avid, passionate *My little brother is enthusiastic about starting school.*

entire *adjective* whole, complete, full, total *My parents have lived in the same town their entire lives.*

entirely *adverb* completely, wholly, altogether *She's not entirely wrong.*

entitle *verb* 1. name *She will entitle her book:* Fresh. 2. allow, permit, authorize, sanction, qualify, enable *This ticket entitles you to three carnival rides for the price of two.*

entrance *noun* 1. entry, way in, access, doorway, door, passageway, gate *I'll meet you at the entrance to the theater.* 2. appearance, arrival, entry *The audience applauded when the singer made her entrance.*

entry *noun* 1. admission, access, permission to enter, entrance, admittance *He was refused entry without the proper pass.* 2. entrance, door, doorway, entryway, opening, gate *Deliveries are received at the back entry.* 3. note, record, memo, item, listing *The teacher made an entry in the daily attendance book.*

envelop *verb* wrap, cover, cloak, surround, blanket, engulf *Clouds enveloped the mountaintops.*

envious *adjective* jealous, covetous, desirous, resentful *I'm envious of my sister's musical talent.*

environment *noun* surroundings, setting, atmosphere, vicinity, locality *Most cacti grow in warm, sunny, dry environments.*

envy 1. *noun* jealousy, greed, resentment *I was sure my friends looked at me with envy when they saw my new bike.* 2. *verb* be jealous of, covet, begrudge, resent *I don't envy my friend who has to work on a farm all summer while we swim and play ball.*

episode *noun* 1. occurrence, happening, event, incident *An important episode in American history was the establishment of the Underground Railroad to help slaves escape to freedom.* 2. installment, chapter, part, section, show *We'll find out who stole the diamond on the final episode of the TV series.*

equal 1. *adjective* identical, equivalent, the same, comparable *The twins are of equal height.* 2. *noun* match, peer, equivalent, counterpart *She has no equal in tennis. He treats all his employees as equals.* 3. *verb* amount to, make, correspond to, be equivalent to *Five times six equals thirty. His time in the race equaled the record.*

equip *verb* provide, furnish, supply, fit, outfit, prepare, stock *General Washington's army was poorly trained and equipped.*

equipment *noun* apparatus, paraphernalia, gear, supplies, tools, things, materials *My brother likes to play on the playground equipment in the park. Our hardware store will rent us the equipment we need to spray-paint our house.*

equivalent 1. *adjective* equal, the same, identical, alike, like, similar *A yard is roughly equivalent to a meter in length.* 2. *noun* equal, counterpart, match, like, double *A European count is the equivalent of a British earl.*

era *noun* epoch, period, age, time *My great-grandparents still enjoy dancing to the music of the big-band era.*

erase *verb* remove, rub out, wipe out, blot out, delete, cancel, obliterate *Be sure to back everything up before you erase your hard drive.*

erect 1. *adjective* straight, upright, vertical *The soldier had erect posture.* 2. *verb* build, construct, put up, raise, set up, assemble *We erected a flagpole in our backyard. Neighbors used to get together at a barn raising to erect a barn.*

erode *verb* wear away, wear down, eat away, corrode *Wind and water destroy farmland by eroding the topsoil.*

errand *noun* task, job, chore, assignment, mission *Stephanie is out running errands for her boss.*

erratic *adjective* irregular, changeable, unpredictable, variable, inconsistent, uncertain *His pitching was erratic, and he was replaced by a relief pitcher in the sixth inning.*

error *noun* mistake, blunder, slipup, slip, inaccuracy, fault *I had one spelling error in my book report.*

erupt *verb* explode, blow up, burst, break out *Cheers erupted from the crowd as the winner crossed the finish line. Kilauea, in Hawaii, is the world's most active volcano and has been erupting continuously since 1983.*

escape 1. *verb* get away, run away, break out, flee *The parakeet escaped from its cage and was flying around the room.* 2. evade, elude, dodge, get by, avoid, get out of *The team narrowly escaped defeat. I remember his face, but his name escapes me.* 3. *noun* getaway, flight, departure, breakout *The prisoners had no means of escape.*

escort 1. *verb* guide, accompany, conduct, lead, usher, attend *The tugboat escorted the ship to port.* 2. *noun* attendant, companion, guide, bodyguard *The rock star's limousine had a police escort as it traveled from the airport.*

especially *adverb* particularly, principally, chiefly, mainly, mostly, primarily *I was very hungry, so dinner tasted especially good tonight.*

essay *noun* composition, paper, article, thesis, theme, report *The teacher asked us to write an essay on what we would do to help improve the environment.*

essence *noun* most important part, basis, core, heart, substance, essential part *The essence of beauty comes from within.*

essential *adjective* necessary, fundamental, needed, vital, required, basic *Light is essential to the growth of plants.*

establish *verb* 1. create, set up, found, institute, begin, launch *The Founding Fathers established a government with three branches: the executive, legislative, and judicial.* 2. confirm, determine, prove, show, verify *The lawyer established that the defendant was in another city when the crime was committed.*

establishment *noun* 1. creation, formation, founding, start *The club voted for the establishment of a committee to nominate new officers.* 2. business, institution, organization, enterprise, firm *The dry-cleaning establishment is located on Eighteenth Street.*

esteem 1. *noun* regard, respect, admiration, honor, approval, reverence *Other actors held him in high esteem.* 2. *verb* appreciate, admire, honor, approve, revere, value *Nobel Prize winners Marie Curie and her husband were esteemed for their study of radioactivity.*

estimate 1. *verb* calculate, figure, judge, guess *I estimate we will arrive at our destination in about an hour.* 2. *noun* approximation, calculation, guess, evaluation, guesstimate *Be sure you get an estimate of the cost before you have the mechanics repair the car.*

eternal *adjective* endless, perpetual, permanent, everlasting, constant, continual, ceaseless *Geoff and I have sworn eternal friendship and loyalty to each other.* temporary

etiquette *noun* manners, courtesy, politeness, custom *Etiquette requires that you thank someone who gives you a gift.*

evacuate *verb* leave, abandon, vacate, exit, get out, empty, quit *Everyone evacuated the building when the fire alarm sounded.* enter

evade *verb* avoid, escape, dodge, duck, sidestep *I evaded Mom's question about what time we got to bed at last night's sleepover by changing the subject.*

evaluate *verb* assess, weigh, appraise, judge, calculate, measure, determine *Report cards are intended to evaluate our achievement.*

evaporate *verb* disappear, vanish, disperse, dissipate, vaporize *Sea salt is made by evaporating seawater. My New Year's resolution evaporated the first time Mom made a chocolate cake.*

even 1. *adjective* equal, identical, the same, like *They divided the money into even shares.* 2. level, flat, smooth, straight, uniform *Dad sanded the wood floor until it had an even surface.* uneven 3. steady, regular, constant, consistent, unchanging, uniform *The drummer kept an even drumbeat.* irregular 4. *adverb* still, yet, more so *It's supposed to get even hotter tomorrow.* 5. *verb* balance, make equal, level, make uniform *Michigan evened the score at 14-14.*

evening *noun* nightfall, sunset, sundown, dusk, twilight *Did you see the news on TV last evening?*

event *noun* 1. occurrence, happening, incident, episode, experience, occasion *An important event in the last century was the first moon landing.* 2. competition, contest, game, tournament *Time trials are being held for the 50-meter freestyle event.*

eventually *adverb* finally, ultimately, in time, in the end *We'll finish cleaning the garage eventually.*

ever *adverb* 1. always, forever, continuously, at all times, eternally *They lived happily ever after.* 2. at any time, on any occasion *Have you ever seen a more beautiful sunset?*

everlasting *adjective* endless, ceaseless, unending, continual, constant, eternal, perpetual *Our hope is for everlasting peace.* temporary

every *adjective* each, all *Read every word of the instructions before you begin.*

everyday *adjective* ordinary, normal, common, average, usual *There's no need to dress up—your everyday clothes are fine.*

evidence *noun* facts, proof, grounds, data, information *The police had all the evidence they needed to arrest the man for robbery.*

evident *adjective* clear, plain, apparent, obvious, clear-cut *It's evident from the empty cookie jar why you're not hungry.* unclear

evil 1. *adjective* bad, wicked, wrong, immoral, sinful, harmful *The evil witch cast a spell over the prince and turned him into a frog.* good 2. *noun* wickedness, bad, wrong, sin, immorality, vice *Crime and poverty are evils of society.* good

evolve *verb* develop, grow, change *As animals evolve, some develop coloring that helps to protect them from their enemies.*

exact *adjective* precise, accurate, correct, faithful *Do you have the exact bus fare? This is an exact copy of the original.*

exactly *adverb* precisely, just, in every respect, absolutely *I found exactly what I wanted, and it was on sale. You are exactly on time.*

exaggerate *verb* overstate, stretch, overdo, magnify, enlarge *I exaggerated when I said I got bit by a million mosquitoes.*

examination *noun* 1. checkup, inspection, observation, check, going-over, exam *Dad goes in tomorrow for his annual physical examination.* 2. test, exam, final, quiz *Your examination will cover everything we've studied this quarter.*

examine *verb* 1. check, inspect, observe, study, analyze *The doctor examined my eyes and said I had 20/20 vision.* 2. question, test, quiz, interrogate, query *The police officer examined the witnesses to the accident.*

example *noun* sample, instance, case, specimen, illustration, model *Giant pandas and snow leopards are two examples of endangered species.*

exasperate *verb* irritate, annoy, bother, disturb, aggravate, frustrate *My little sister's constant questions were beginning to exasperate me.*

excavate *verb* dig, dig up, unearth, uncover, burrow, hollow *While excavating the subway tunnels under Mexico City, workers discovered several archaeological sites.*

exceed *verb* surpass, pass, better, outdo, beat, top *The book's popularity has grown so* *much that sales have more than exceeded the publisher's original expectations.*

excel *verb* stand out, shine, dominate, outdo, exceed *Becky excels at gymnastics, and she would like to compete in the Olympics someday.*

excellence *noun* distinction, greatness, brilliance, superiority, merit, quality *Tanya's excellence in sports and academics has won her a scholarship to the university.*

excellent *adjective* outstanding, exceptional, brilliant, superb, splendid, first-rate *Grandma always serves us an excellent meal when we visit.* poor

except *preposition* excluding, omitting, besides, aside from, leaving out *I ate everything except the spinach.* including

exceptional *adjective* unusual, extraordinary, remarkable, notable *The cool weather this late in the summer is exceptional.* ordinary

excess 1. *adjective* extra, too much, surplus, additional *Passengers have to pay fifty dollars for each item of excess baggage loaded on an airplane.* 2. *noun* surplus, oversupply, remaining, spare *We caught so many fish, we had to give away the excess.*

excessive *adjective* extreme, immoderate, too much, extravagant, lavish, undue, unnecessary *Excessive rainfall caused the stream to flood.*

exchange 1. *verb* swap, trade, switch, change, substitute, barter *The store said Dad can exchange the gift I bought him if he doesn't like it.* 2. *noun* swap, trade, switch, replacement, substitution *The two sides agreed to an exchange of prisoners of war.*

excite *verb* arouse, stir, stimulate, enliven, thrill, provoke *Don't excite your brother too much just before bedtime. I was excited by the chance to see my favorite major-league team play ball.* calm, compose

exciting *adjective* thrilling, stirring, stimulating, exhilarating, rousing, breathtaking, sensational *The most exciting part of our visit to Washington, D.C., was seeing the Air and Space Museum.* dull, boring, uninteresting

exclaim *verb* cry out, call out, shout, yell *"Wow! I didn't know you were so handsome!" my sister exclaimed when she saw me dressed in a suit.*

exclude *verb* bar, shut out, keep out, forbid, prohibit, reject *Dad says we can't exclude girls from our club.* include

excursion *noun* trip, journey, outing, tour *Mom is taking us on a shopping excursion for school clothes.*

excuse 1. *verb* forgive, overlook, pardon, let off the hook *Please excuse my anger yesterday—I was tired and irritable.* 2. release, exempt, free, relieve *I'm excused from gym class until my broken arm heals.* 3. *noun* explanation, reason, grounds, alibi, story *My only excuse for being late is that I overslept.*

execute *verb* 1. accomplish, perform, do, carry out, complete, achieve, put into effect *She executed a perfect cartwheel.* 2. put to death, kill, murder *King Henry VIII of England had his second wife, Anne Boleyn, executed for treason.*

executive 1. *noun* administrator, manager, director, officer, official *Jon is the top executive in his office.* 2. *adjective* directing, managing, administrative *An executive committee makes the decisions for the organization.*

exempt *verb* free, excuse, release, except, let off *The state exempts food that we buy at stores from sales tax.*

exercise 1. *noun* physical activity, workout, training, drill, practice *Walking is an excellent form of exercise for all ages.* 2. application, use, practice, implementation, employment *Crossing a busy street requires the exercise of caution.* 3. *verb* apply, use, implement, employ, exert *I find it hard to exercise self-control when Dad bakes brownies.* 4. work out, train, drill, practice *When I exercise strenuously, I need to drink more water.*

exert *verb* use, apply, employ, exercise, utilize, wield *I had to exert a lot of pressure on my suitcase in order to close it.*

exhaust *verb* 1. use up, consume, finish, drain, spend *The expedition exhausted its food supply and had to turn back.* 2. tire, fatigue, wear out, weary *Moving into a new house exhausted us.*

exhaustion *noun* fatigue, tiredness, weakness, weariness *The stranded climbers were suffering from exhaustion when they were rescued.*

exhibit 1. *noun* show, display, demonstration, presentation *We went to see an exhibit of art at the children's museum.* 2. *verb* show, display, demonstrate, reveal *Both boys exhibit musical talent.*

exhilarate *verb* excite, thrill, enliven, invigorate, stimulate, refresh *The early morning swim in the lake exhilarated us.*

exile 1. *verb* banish, expel, deport, oust, send away *Napoleon was overthrown in 1814 and exiled to the island of Elba.* 2. *noun* banishment, expulsion, deportation, ostracism *Napoleon spent less than ten months in exile on Elba, at which time he escaped.*

exist *verb* live, survive, dwell, endure, last, continue *Dinosaurs haven't existed on earth* *for more than sixty million years. Mom says I can't exist on ice cream alone.*

existence *noun* 1. life, survival, being *Our existence depends on a healthy environment.* 2. reality, fact, actuality, occurrence *Do you believe in the existence of ghosts?*

exotic *adjective* unusual, different, unfamiliar, novel, strange, foreign *You'll find exotic birds, reptiles, and plants living along the Amazon River in South America.*

expand *verb* enlarge, grow, swell, increase, get larger, extend *Water expands when it freezes. We have expanded our house by adding on a bedroom.*

expect *verb* anticipate, look for, count on, depend on, await *We expect you to be home by 9:00.*

expedition *noun* 1. trip, journey, trek, tour, excursion *Our neighbors are going on an expedition to the Himalayas.* 2. group, party, team, crew, troop, company *The first archaeological expedition in search of Troy was led by Heinrich Schliemann.*

expel *verb* dismiss, throw out, eject, oust, banish *Any student who steals will be expelled.*

expense *noun* cost, price, amount, charge *My brother is working to help pay the expense of college tuition.*

expensive *adjective* costly, high-priced, exorbitant *A new car is too expensive, so we bought a used one.*

experience 1. *noun* event, adventure, occurrence, happening, incident, episode *The experience of going to school in another country is one I will never forget.* 2. knowledge, skill, practice, know-how, background, learning *Aunt Sharon has ten years' experience as a nurse.* 3. *verb* have, encounter, undergo, meet *Did you experience any difficulty finding our house?*

experiment 1. *noun* test, trial, investigation, examination, research *Marconi's experiments with transmitting electrical signals led to the invention of the radio.* 2. *verb* test, try out, investigate, examine, research *I experimented with mixing the primary colors red, yellow, and blue and got black.*

experimental *adjective* test, trial, pilot, investigational, early, new *Before Neil Armstrong became an astronaut, he was a test pilot who flew experimental aircraft.*

expert 1. *noun* authority, specialist, professional, master *A geologist is an expert in the structure of the earth.* 2. *adjective* skilled, skillful, proficient, professional, knowledgeable *This fine old cabinet shows expert craftsmanship.* incompetent

expire *verb* 1. end, cease, finish, lapse, run out *You need to renew your driver's license before it expires.* 2. die, perish, pass away, depart *The soldier expired on the battlefield despite all that the medic tried to do for him.*

explain *verb* 1. describe, illustrate, demonstrate, show, clarify *Our science teacher explained the formation of raindrops.* 2. justify, account for, defend *Can you explain yesterday's absence?*

explanation *noun* 1. reason, justification, account, excuse *I hope you can give an explanation for your bad behavior.* 2. description *The art teacher gave us an explanation of abstract expressionism.*

explode *verb* blow up, detonate, burst, go off, blast, discharge *Thousands of fireworks exploded on the Fourth of July and lit up the sky.*

exploit 1. *noun* feat, adventure, deed, stunt, achievement *I love to read about the exploits of King Arthur and his knights.* 2. *verb* use unfairly, take advantage of, manipulate, abuse, misuse *The unscrupulous company exploited the natural resources of the country.*

explore *verb* 1. discover, travel, survey, tour, scout *More missions to send robots to explore Mars are scheduled.* 2. examine, investigate, search, study, research, look into *We're exploring destinations for our next family vacation.*

explosion *noun* 1. blast, detonation, discharge, bang, boom *The loud explosion of a firecracker frightened our cat.* 2. increase, flood, outbreak, upsurge *There has been an explosion of interest in organic food.*

expose *verb* 1. subject, lay open, lay bare *We put on sunscreen before being exposed to the hot sun.* 2. reveal, disclose, show, display, uncover *The newspapers exposed the scandal.*

express 1. *verb* declare, state, say, indicate, speak, proclaim *The candidate expressed her thanks to her supporters.* 2. *adjective* fast, quick, rapid, speedy, swift *We sent the package by express mail.* 3. definite, specific, sole, particular, exact *The donation is for the express purpose of feeding needy children.*

expression *noun* 1. look, appearance, aspect, air *You should have seen the expression on his face when we surprised him.* 2. indication, sign, demonstration, statement, declaration *She sent flowers as an expression of appreciation.* 3. phrase, saying, idiom, term, proverb *Does anyone know the origin of the expression "once in a blue moon"?*

exquisite *adjective* beautiful, delicate, lovely, wonderful, attractive, elegant *Dad gave Mom an exquisite diamond ring when they got engaged.*

extend *verb* 1. expand, lengthen, enlarge, increase, widen, open *The telescoping pole on the window washer can be extended to sixteen feet.* 2. reach, stretch, run, spread *The Louisiana Purchase extended from the Mississippi River to the Rocky Mountains.* 3. offer, give, present *Mom extended an invitation to dinner to my friends.*

extensive *adjective* big, large, huge, vast, wide, broad *The hurricane caused extensive damage. Uncle Bill has an extensive collection of antique cars.*

exterior 1. *adjective* outside, outer, external, outdoor *The exterior walls of our house are insulated to save energy.* interior 2. *noun* outside, surface, covering *The building's exterior is made of brick.*

exterminate *verb* destroy, get rid of, eliminate, kill, dispose of, annihilate *We exterminated the termites that were infesting our porch and replaced the damaged wood.*

external *adjective* outside, outer, outward, exterior, surface *A turtle's shell is an external skeleton made of bone.* internal

extinct *adjective* wiped out, gone, obsolete, deceased, vanished, lost, nonexistent *The passenger pigeon, once one of the most abundant species on earth, is now extinct.* living

extinguish *verb* 1. put out, smother, quench, douse *Be sure to extinguish your campfire before you leave.* 2. eliminate, destroy, crush, end, wipe out, abolish, suppress *The team's loss extinguished any hope of our winning the tournament.*

extra 1. *adjective* additional, surplus, spare, supplementary, more *We need to save extra money for emergencies.* 2. *adverb* especially, very, exceptionally, unusually *I studied extra hard for the test.* 3. *noun* accessory, addition, option, add-on, supplement, bonus *Mr. Schneider has a new car with many extras, including a GPS navigation system and a DVD player in the backseat.*

extract 1. *verb* remove, take out, pull out, withdraw *The dentist extracted one of my sister's wisdom teeth.* 2. *noun* essence, juice, concentrate, solution *You can make your own vanilla extract for flavoring by soaking a vanilla bean in alcohol.*

extraordinary *adjective* remarkable, exceptional, outstanding, amazing, special, unusual, uncommon, rare *Kareem Abdul-Jabbar's extraordinary height and skills enabled him to be a top basketball player.* ordinary

extravagant *adjective* extreme, excessive, unreasonable, immoderate, wasteful, lavish *The star's extravagant spending on Rolls-Royces and Mediterranean villas finally bankrupted him.* reasonable, frugal

extreme *adjective* 1. great, intense, excessive, tremendous, intense, severe *Extreme* *cold at the South Pole made the rescue of a sick worker dangerous.* moderate 2. farthest, outermost, remotest, most distant *The Hubble Space Telescope discovered a new planet-like object orbiting the sun at the extreme edge of our solar system.* nearest

eye 1. *verb* look, watch, observe, regard, view, inspect, stare *The stray dog eyed my sandwich greedily.* 2. *noun* one of the two organs on your face that you use to see with *One of Sue's eyes is blue, and her other eye is brown.*

eyesight *noun* vision, sight *My brother wears contact lenses to correct his eyesight.*

F

fable *noun* legend, story, tale, allegory, myth, yarn *The fable about the tortoise and the hare teaches us that "slow and steady wins the race."*

fabric *noun* cloth, textile, material *My Halloween costume is made of orange and black fabric.*

fabulous *adjective* amazing, unbelievable, fantastic, remarkable, extraordinary, surprising *Sixteenth-century explorers searched South America for El Dorado, a fabulous city of gold.*

face 1. *noun* countenance, look, expression, appearance *You should have seen Gene's face when he bit into the lemon.* 2. front, surface, outside, exterior *Can you name the four presidents whose images are carved into the face of Mount Rushmore?* 3. *verb* confront, oppose, challenge, meet, encounter, brave *The team faces its toughest opponent in today's game.* avoid 4. look toward, point toward, overlook, front on *Muslims face Mecca, the birthplace of the prophet Muhammad, during their daily prayers.*

facility *noun* 1. ease, effortlessness, lack of difficulty *Calvin is able to learn languages with great facility.* 2. aptitude, ability, skill, talent, knack *The writer has a remarkable facility for storytelling.* 3. system, resource, equipment, convenience, amenity *The athletic facility includes a pool, racquetball courts, and a jogging track.*

fact *noun* 1. detail, point, item, particular, factor, piece of information, data *I need more facts on which to base my decision.* 2. truth, reality, actuality, certainty *The book is a mix of fact and fiction.* lie

factor *noun* consideration, influence, aspect, component, issue, cause, element, part, basis *The high price was a big factor in Dad's decision to not buy the new car.*

factory *noun* plant, works, workshop, mill *A factory in our town makes picnic tables out of recycled plastic.*

faculty *noun* 1. teachers, staff, professors, instructors *The college is hiring faculty and staff for the next school year.* 2. talent, gift, ability, capacity, aptitude *Dad has a great faculty for remembering names.*

fad *noun* fashion, style, craze, rage *Bell-bottom pants were a fad in the 1970s.*

fade *verb* 1. dim, pale, lose color, dull, bleach, wash out *Bright colors could fade if you wash them in hot water.* 2. weaken, decline, diminish, dwindle, grow faint, wane *The sound of the small airplane faded in the distance.*

fail *verb* 1. be unsuccessful, fall through, fall short, miss the mark, flop, flunk *His attempt to set an Olympic record failed.* succeed 2. neglect, miss, omit, forget *She failed to call to say she'd be late. You never fail to amaze me!* 3. weaken, fade, decline, diminish, dwindle, wane *Our neighbor moved to a nursing home when his health began to fail.* strengthen

failure *noun* 1. lack of success, defeat, breakdown, malfunction *A computer virus led to the system's failure. The rebels were blamed for the failure of the peace talks.* success 2. disappointment, letdown, fiasco, blunder, botch, flop *The picnic was a failure because of the rain.* success

faint 1. *adjective* weak, soft, indistinct, vague, feeble, unclear, slight *I heard a faint "meow" coming from the top of a tree. The faint scent of wood smoke lingered in the campground.* clear, strong 2. light-headed, dizzy, giddy, weak *I felt a little faint after the roller-coaster ride.* 3. *verb* pass out, lose consciousness, collapse, black out, swoon *Several people in the crowd fainted from the heat.*

fair 1. *adjective* just, impartial, unbiased, objective, open-minded, reasonable, square *Everyone has the right to a fair trial.* unjust, unfair 2. light, pale, white, blond, flaxen *As a baby, she had fair hair.* dark 3. clear, sunny, bright, pleasant, mild, favorable *The forecast is for fair weather.* cloudy 4. average, mediocre, adequate, tolerable, passable, decent *You need more than a fair understanding of arithmetic before you study algebra.* outstanding 5. beautiful, lovely, attractive, good-looking *The knight rescued the fair princess from the dragon.* 6. *noun* festival, exhibition, show, bazaar, exposition, market *At the county fair, you can take carnival rides, eat hot dogs, listen to music, and see prizewinning farm animals.*

faith *noun* 1. trust, belief, confidence, reliance, hope *My parents say they have faith in my ability to make good decisions.* 2. teaching, creed, belief, religion *We respect the right of people of all faiths to worship as they please.*

faithful *adjective* loyal, devoted, dependable, trustworthy, steadfast, true *A crowd of faithful fans welcomed the team home after their loss.* unfaithful

fake 1. *adjective* false, imitation, counterfeit, artificial, make-believe, mock, fraudulent, phony *Fake plants made of plastic decorated the office.* real, authentic
2. *verb* imitate, feign, pretend, copy, reproduce, falsify, counterfeit *I faked an interest in the conversation to be polite.* 3. *noun* imitation, copy, counterfeit, forgery, phony, fraud *The painting turned out to be a fake.*

fall 1. *verb* drop, descend, plunge, tumble, plummet *Snow began falling during the night. The boy stumbled and fell.* ascend 2. surrender, submit, yield, give in *The cities of Babylon and Persia fell to Alexander the Great's army.* 3. decrease, diminish, grow less, lower, subside, fade, ebb *The river level fell because of the drought. The girls' voices fell to a whisper as we approached them.* 4. happen, occur, take place, come *My birthday falls on a Sunday this year.* 5. *noun* drop, plunge, descent, tumble *My little sister took a fall and scraped her knees.* 6. decrease, decline, cut, reduction *We plan to wait for a fall in the price of LCD TVs before we buy one.* 7. downfall, ruin, collapse, failure, descent, decline *Rome's fall was in A.D. 476.*

false *adjective* 1. untrue, incorrect, inaccurate, fabricated, erroneous, invalid, wrong, lying *The accused gave a false account of her whereabouts when the crime was committed.* true 2. fake, artificial, mock, imitation, counterfeit *The man wore a false beard as a disguise. She entered the country using a false passport.* real, authentic

fame *noun* celebrity, renown, reputation, recognition, glory, popularity, notoriety *Leonardo da Vinci gained fame as an artist and scientist.*

familiar *adjective* 1. common, customary, everyday, usual, accustomed, well-known *Frogs and toads are familiar examples of amphibians.* unfamiliar 2. close, friendly, personal, intimate *The members of the soccer team are on familiar terms with one another.* 3. acquainted, aware of, informed in, versed in, knowledgeable about *I'm not familiar with that book.* unfamiliar

family *noun* 1. household, kin, relative, relations, folk *The whole family gets together for Thanksgiving dinner.* 2. group, category, kind, line, class, order *Members of the cat family include big cats like lions and small cats like my pet, Max.*

famine *noun* food shortage, hunger, starvation, deprivation *The United Nations is* *sending food to parts of Africa, where drought has caused a famine.* plenty, sufficiency

famished *adjective* hungry, ravenous, starved *What's for lunch? I'm famished.*

fan *noun* admirer, follower, devotee, enthusiast (*Slang*—groupie) *Fans poured onto the football field following the victory.*

fancy 1. *adjective* elaborate, ornate, decorative, intricate, showy, fussy, frilly *My sister prefers jeans to fancy dresses.* plain 2. *noun* notion, idea, whim, impulse *Uncle Karl has sudden fancies to travel to exotic places.* 3. fondness, liking, love, longing, yearning, wish *Marianne has a fancy to own a horse.* dislike

fantastic *adjective* 1. wonderful, marvelous, terrific, superb, fabulous *The view from the hilltop is fantastic.* 2. odd, strange, weird, bizarre, incredible, unreal *The book* Gulliver's Travels *describes an Englishman's voyage to fantastic lands such as Lilliput, where people are six inches tall.* ordinary, usual

fantasy *noun* vision, dream, illusion, fancy, imagination *Traveling into space or to the bottom of the ocean were once fantasies but now are realities.*

far 1. *adverb* considerably, a great deal, much, significantly *I liked the first movie in the series far more than I did this one.* 2. *adjective* distant, remote, faraway, outlying, far-off *I hope someday to visit far places.* near, nearby

fare 1. *noun* charge, cost, price, fee *What is the bus fare to Boston?* 2. *verb* manage, get along, do, make out, progress, thrive, prosper *How do you think you fared on your test?*

farewell 1. *interjection* good-bye, so long, good day, see you later *Farewell! Call when you get back!* 2. *noun* good-bye, departure, exit, leaving, parting, taking leave *Farewells can be sad.*

farm 1. *noun* ranch, plantation, spread, homestead *My cousin lives on a dairy farm in Wisconsin.* 2. *verb* cultivate, grow, plant, raise, ranch, harvest *His parents farm for a living.*

far-reaching *adjective* broad, wide, extensive, sweeping, widespread *Global climate changes could have far-reaching effects.* limited

fascinate *verb* interest, excite, enthrall, thrill, delight, intrigue, attract, captivate, enchant, charm *Magic tricks fascinate me.* bore

fashion 1. *noun* style, manner, mode, way, method, approach, system *Everyone left the building in an orderly fashion during the fire drill.* 2. trend, craze, fad, style *Jeans with holes in the knees are the latest fashion.* 3. *verb* make, build, construct, fabricate, create, shape, mold *At summer camp we fashioned jewelry out of wire and colorful glass beads.*

fast 1. *adjective* quick, speedy, swift, rapid *The horse took off at a fast gallop.* slow
2. secure, fastened, fixed, tight *I kept a fast hold on my little brother's hand.* 3. steadfast, faithful, loyal, devoted, lasting *Dad and his college roommate have remained fast friends.*
4. *adverb* quickly, speedily, rapidly, hastily, hurriedly *I had to run fast in order to catch the bus.*

fasten *verb* attach, secure, tie, lock, close, bind, connect, buckle, button, zip *She fastened her ponytail with a rubber band. Be sure to fasten your seat belt. The shelf is fastened to the wall with special brackets.*

fat 1. *noun* oil, grease, lard, shortening *Fried foods contain a lot of fat.* 2. *adjective* overweight, heavy, obese, plump, stout, chubby *Mom says I was fat as a baby.* thin

fatal *adjective* deadly, lethal, terminal, mortal *Snake bites from venomous snakes are seldom fatal if you get immediate medical assistance.*

fate *noun* fortune, destiny, luck, chance *In Shakespeare's play* Romeo and Juliet, *fate brings the lovers together and also ends their lives.*

father *noun* 1. male parent, dad, daddy, pop, pa *My father was thirty-two years old when I was born.* 2. founder, originator, initiator, leader, elder *George Washington is known as the father of our country.*

fatigue 1. *noun* exhaustion, tiredness, weariness *Her fatigue is due to a lack of sleep.*
2. *verb* exhaust, tire, wear out *My brother said the stress of exam week fatigued him and he plans to sleep for a month.*

fault *noun* 1. responsibility, accountability, burden, cause for blame *It's my fault we're late—I lost track of the time.* 2. defect, flaw, shortcoming, weakness *My sister has her faults, but I love her, anyway.* 3. mistake, error, inaccuracy, blunder *The seller made a fault in calculating the sales tax.*

favor 1. *noun* kindness, service, good deed, courtesy *Can you do me a favor and drive me to school?* 2. approval, acceptance, support, esteem, backing *The young quarterback is gaining favor with the fans.* 3. *verb* prefer, like better, support, approve, choose, back *Which candidate for class president do you favor?* 4. resemble, look like *My brother favors my father; both have dark hair and blue eyes.* 5. oblige, accommodate, reward, satisfy, gratify *The band favored us with two encores.*

favorable *adjective* good, beneficial, promising, encouraging, helpful, conducive *The wind is favorable for sailing.* unfavorable

favorite 1. *adjective* preferred, favored, ideal, chosen, most liked, prized *What's your favorite ice-cream flavor?* 2. *noun* preference, first choice, pick, darling *I can't decide which of the movies is my favorite.*

fear 1. *noun* fright, dread, anxiety, terror, panic, apprehension *To get over her fear of computers, Grandma took a class in how to use them.* 2. *verb* be afraid of, be scared of, be fearful of, dread *Our cat fears the neighbor's big dog.*

fearless *adjective* bold, brave, courageous, unafraid, daring, valiant, heroic, audacious *Superman and Batman are fearless superheroes of comics and movies.*

feast 1. *noun* banquet, dinner, meal, spread *Family members gather on the eve of the Chinese New Year for a feast of food items that signify good wishes.* 2. *verb* dine, eat, feed, banquet, partake, indulge, devour *At the picnic we feasted on hot dogs, hamburgers, potato salad, and chocolate cake.*

feat *noun* deed, act, exploit, performance, achievement *The trapeze artists and tightrope walkers performed feats of daring.*

feature 1. *noun* characteristic, trait, attribute, quality, element *New cars have high-tech features such as navigational systems and DVD players in the backseats.* 2. *verb* highlight, emphasize, promote, headline, spotlight, star *The music festival features top country bands and singers.*

fee *noun* charge, dues, toll, fare, cost *Book fees for grades 5–12 are around $250.*

feeble *adjective* weak, faint, dim, failing, frail *We had only the feeble light of a candle when the power went out.* strong

feed 1. *verb* nourish, supply, sustain, support, maintain *Dad grilled enough hamburgers to feed an army!* 2. eat, consume, devour, live, exist *Sharks normally feed on anything from tiny crustaceans to other sharks, but not on people.* 3. *noun* food, fodder, forage *My rabbit's feed is a mixture of vegetables, fruits, and seeds.*

feel 1. *verb* touch, handle, finger, stroke *Feel my kitten's fur.* 2. sense, experience, know, be aware of, undergo, suffer, endure *I didn't feel much pain when the nurse gave me the shot.* 3. think, believe, consider, suspect, be of the opinion, understand, know *I feel we should leave—it's getting late.* 4. *noun* touch, sensation, feeling *I like the feel of the cool evening breeze.*

fence 1. *noun* barrier, enclosure, wall *There's a fence between our backyard and the alley.* 2. *verb* enclose, surround, encircle, pen, confine *We fenced our garden to keep the deer and raccoons out.*

ferocious *adjective* fierce, savage, vicious, brutal, cruel, ruthless *The beast in the forest was so ferocious that he had eaten all the dragons that once lived there.* gentle, tame

ferry 1. *noun* boat, ferryboat *The ferry carries passengers and cars across Lake Michigan in two and a half hours.* 2. *verb* carry, transport, haul, cart *Log rafts ferried the explorers' supplies across the river.*

fertile *adjective* productive, fruitful, bountiful, rich, lush *Much of the land that was fertile prairie is being used for agriculture.* unproductive, barren

festival *noun* celebration, holiday, event, commemoration, party *An arts festival is held every year so that local artists can show their work.*

festive *adjective* merry, joyful, joyous, celebratory, gala *In Mexico, the breaking of a piñata is part of almost every festive occasion.*

fetch *verb* bring, go get, retrieve, carry *My dog loves to fetch a ball thrown into the lake.*

feud *noun* quarrel, dispute, fight, conflict, squabble *The war was the result of a tribal feud.*

fever *noun* temperature, flush, infection, illness, sickness *She had a fever of 102 degrees.*

few *adjective* not many, very little, scarce, rare, limited, uncommon *Few people are billionaires.* many

fib 1. *noun* lie, falsehood, untruth, story, tale *Dad claims parents usually know when their kids tell a fib.* truth 2. *verb* lie, deceive, misrepresent, exaggerate *I'm not fibbing when I tell you I got an A+ on the test.*

fiction *noun* fantasy, invention, untruth, legend, myth, fable, story, tale *I can't tell if what he says is fact or fiction because he exaggerates so much.* fact

fidget *verb* squirm, twitch, wiggle, wriggle, fuss *Rusty was bored with the adults' conversation and began to fidget.*

field *noun* 1. meadow, clearing, pasture, grassland, tract, plot *The deer were browsing in the farmer's field.* 2. playing field, athletic field, arena, stadium, ballpark *The team was on the field doing push-ups.* 3. subject, area, domain, sphere, realm, profession, occupation, trade *Jack is a teacher in the field of special education.*

fierce *adjective* 1. aggressive, ferocious, vicious, savage, dangerous *When we think of fierce animals, we think of lions, tigers, bears, and sharks.* kind, gentle 2. intense, violent, strong, powerful, raging *A fierce hurricane with winds up to 135 miles an hour hit the coast.*

fiesta *noun* celebration, festival, feast, party, event, holiday *The seventh-grade class* *held a huge fiesta on September 16 to celebrate Mexican Independence Day.*

fight 1. *noun* battle, brawl, combat, skirmish *The bully got a bloody nose in a fight with a bigger boy who stood up to him.* 2. argument, disagreement, dispute, quarrel, row *My sisters got into a fight over who messed up their room and should clean it.* 3. *verb* battle, combat, oppose, contend, wage war *Americans fought against the British in the Revolutionary War.* 4. argue, dispute, quarrel, bicker, squabble, feud *The two families have been fighting for years.*

figure 1. *noun* number, numeral, digit, symbol, character *Add up the figures in column one.* 2. price, charge, cost, amount *We put a figure of $3,000 on our car, but will take $2,500 if someone offers it.* 3. shape, form, outline, silhouette *I can see a figure of a woman standing in the doorway.* 4. picture, drawing, diagram, illustration, design, pattern, chart, sketch *Figure 20 illustrates the population increase over the past ten years.* 5. person, celebrity, dignitary, individual, personage, personality, character *She's an influential figure in the community.* 6. *verb* think, suppose, guess, imagine *I figure we should leave home about 11:00 to arrive on time.*

figure out *verb* calculate, solve, compute, discover, work out, decipher *I was able to figure out what was wrong with the computer. Can you figure out what 5 percent tax is on $5?*

file 1. *noun* record, report, information, data *The dentist checked my file to see when I last had my teeth cleaned.* 2. line, column, row, string *A file of soldiers marched by.* 3. *verb* organize, arrange, categorize, classify, sort, group, catalog, store *The birth records are filed by date.* 4. apply, register, submit, enter *No charges have been filed yet against the suspect.* 5. march, parade, troop, walk *The audience filed out of the theater into the pouring rain.* 6. smooth, grind, sand, scrape *My sister filed her nails, then painted each a different color.*

fill *verb* 1. load, pack, stuff, cram, jam *I filled my backpack with books and snacks, then left for school.* empty 2. plug, fill in, seal, stop up, block *The dentist filled my cavity.* 3. supply, provide, furnish, stock *The pharmacist filled the doctor's prescription.* 4. occupy, hold, perform the duties *Mrs. Sanchez is filling the position of vice principal until someone new can be hired.*

film 1. *noun* movie, motion picture, picture *We watched an old film starring Humphrey Bogart on TV last night.* 2. layer, coat, coating, covering, blanket *A film of dust covered the furniture.* 3. *verb* photograph, take a picture, record, shoot *The photographer filmed Kate's wedding.*

filter 1. *noun* sieve, strainer, screen, mesh *Our mechanic says to change the oil filter when we change the oil in our car.* 2. *verb* strain, screen, sift, clean, cleanse, purify *Your nose* *warms, moistens, and filters air before it enters your lungs.* 3. seep, flow, trickle, ooze, leak, percolate *In a rain forest, very little light filters through the leaves of the tallest trees.*

filthy *adjective* dirty, grubby, grimy, muddy, messy, soiled *The children's clothes were filthy after playing in the mud.* clean

final *adjective* 1. last, ending, closing, concluding *The final score in today's game was 17-14.* beginning, opening 2. conclusive, definitive, absolute, definite, unalterable *The decision of the judges is final.*

finale *noun* climax, close, conclusion, finish, end *The grand finale of the fireworks display included more than 2,000 explosions.* beginning, opening

finance *verb* sponsor, back, pay for, support, subsidize *An anonymous donor helped to finance the community center.*

find 1. *verb* locate, come across, come upon, recover, retrieve *Our neighbor found our cat locked in his garage. I found the missing sock under my bed.* lose 2. discover, learn, determine, get, obtain, acquire, come up with *I haven't found the solution to my problem yet.* 3. decide, determine, realize, become aware, conclude *I found that it's best to tell the truth.* 4. *noun* discovery, bargain, treasure *The desk I got at the yard sale for seven dollars was a real find.*

fine 1. *adjective* excellent, good, great, splendid, outstanding *He gave a fine performance. It's a fine day for a long walk.* poor 2. tiny, minute, small, thin, delicate *This beach has very fine grains of sand. I strung beads on fine wire to make a bracelet.* coarse 3. *adverb* excellently, well, splendidly *Grandpa was ill but is doing fine now.* 4. *verb* penalize, punish, charge *He was fined for parking in a no-parking zone.*

finish 1. *verb* end, complete, conclude, close, accomplish, finalize *When you've finished reading the book, I'd like to read it.* begin 2. use up, consume, exhaust, empty, drain *Who finished the carton of milk?* 3. *noun* close, end, ending, conclusion, completion (*Slang*—windup) *The magnificent sunset was a perfect finish to the day.* beginning

fire 1. *noun* blaze, flames, burning, combustion, inferno *Every year fires burn thousands of acres of forest.* 2. gunfire, shooting, shots, bombardment, shelling *The troops came under enemy fire.* 3. *verb* ignite, light, kindle, set on fire *Someone had to fire the wood-burning stove to warm an old one-room schoolhouse in the winter.* 4. shoot, discharge, set off *Police officers fire their guns at targets to keep in practice.* 5. dismiss, let go, get rid of, discharge, release (*Slang*—sack) *Nellie was fired from her job for being late three days in a row.* hire

firearm *noun* gun, weapon, rifle, pistol *Uncle Phil is a hunter and owns several firearms.*

firm 1. *adjective* solid, rigid, stiff, dense, compact *The pond's ice should be firm enough for skating soon.* 2. definite, certain, fixed, determined, resolved, set *The prime minister is firm in his commitment to peace.* uncertain 3. secure, strong, steady, tight, fast, safe, stable *The fence posts are firm in the ground. Take a firm grip on my hand.* unsteady 4. *noun* business, company, enterprise, corporation, organization, establishment *There are three law firms in our town.*

first 1. *adjective* earliest, initial, opening, original *Neil Armstrong was the first person to set foot on the moon.* 2. *adverb* initially, originally *Where did you and Dad first meet?* 3. *noun* beginning, start, outset *I wasn't sure I liked my teacher at first, but now he's my favorite.*

fit 1. *verb* suit, go with, be right, be proper, conform, correspond, match *The role of Harry in the movie fits him perfectly.* 2. equip, supply, furnish, provide, outfit *Our camper is fitted with a stove, refrigerator, and room for six to sleep.* 3. *adjective* suitable, proper, right, appropriate, correct *Thanks, Mom; the meal was fit for a king.* unfit 4. strong, healthy, well, robust, vigorous *Swimming every day keeps her fit.* unhealthy

fix 1. *verb* mend, repair, correct, renovate, restore, overhaul, patch *We called a repair person to fix our dishwasher.* break, damage 2. fasten, attach, secure, connect, join, anchor *The bathroom tiles are fixed to the wall with adhesive.* 3. settle, establish, arrange, agree on, determine, specify *We fixed the selling price for our house at $130,000.* 4. *noun* jam, predicament, difficulty, plight, dilemma, quandary *I'd have been in a fix if Cynthia hadn't lent me some money to pay for my lunch.*

flag *noun* banner, pennant, standard, ensign *The flags of member nations fly in front of the United Nations building in New York.*

flag down *verb* wave at, signal, hail *A stranded motorist flagged us down to help with a flat tire.*

flame *noun* blaze, fire *The candle's flame flickered and went out.*

flap *verb* flutter, wave, beat, swing, flail *The boat's sails flapped in the wind.*

flash 1. *noun* blaze, flare, burst, glare, gleam, glimmer, flicker *A flash of lightning lit up the sky.* 2. instant, second, moment, jiffy *The dog came in a flash when I called.* 3. *verb* flare, gleam, glint, glimmer, flicker *The driver ahead of us flashed his brake lights and we slowed down.* 4. rush, speed, race, hurry, fly, dash *The runner behind me flashed by me to the finish line.*

flat *adjective* 1. level, even, smooth, horizontal *The land was so flat, we could see all the* *way to the horizon. The house has a flat roof.* uneven 2. unexciting, boring, bland, dull, uninteresting, lifeless *The actor gave a flat performance. This stew needs some spices—it tastes flat.* interesting 3. fixed, set, firm, invariable, uniform *The phone company charges a flat rate of nine cents a minute for long-distance calls.* variable

flatter *verb* compliment, praise (*Slang*—butter up) *By flattering me and telling me how good the sweater looked on me, the salesclerk expected me to buy it.* insult

flavor 1. *noun* taste, tang, essence, relish *The toothpaste has a mint flavor.* 2. *verb* season, spice, give taste *Dad flavored the sauce with salt, pepper, basil, and oregano.*

flaw *noun* blemish, defect, fault, imperfection *I returned the jacket because it had a flaw in the fabric.* perfection

flee *verb* run away, escape, take off, bolt *The thief tried to flee from the police.*

flexible *adjective* 1. bendable, pliable, elastic, springy *A garden hose is flexible.* stiff, inflexible 2. adaptable, variable, adjustable, changeable *Mom works flexible hours at home.* inflexible

flicker 1. *verb* twinkle, glimmer, flash, blink, waver, flutter *The lights flickered and went out.* 2. *noun* flash, blink, twinkle, glimmer *The flicker of light signaled the spy to come ashore.*

flight *noun* 1. flying, soaring, gliding *We watched the eagle's flight as it hunted for fish above the lake.* 2. group, flock, formation *A flight of geese started its migration south.* 3. aviation, flying, air transportation, aeronautics *We saw a TV program about the history of flight.*

flimsy *adjective* fragile, weak, delicate, insubstantial, rickety *The refugees lived in tents and flimsy huts.* strong, sturdy, substantial

flinch *verb* cringe *Betty flinched when the nurse put antiseptic on her scraped knee.*

fling 1. *verb* throw, toss, pitch, cast, heave *The children had fun flinging stones into the pond.* 2. *noun* throw, toss, pitch, heave *Gordon won the javelin throw with the longest fling.*

float *verb* drift, sail, glide, hover *Fallen leaves floated on the lake.* sink

flock 1. *noun* herd, crowd, gathering, group *A flock of geese flew overhead, heading south for the winter.* 2. *verb* gather, collect, assemble, congregate *People flocked to the park for a free concert.*

flood 1. *noun* deluge, overflow, torrent *A broken fire hydrant caused a flood in the street.* 2. *verb* overfill, drench, overflow, deluge, inundate *Sunlight floods my room every morning.*

floor 1. *noun* bottom, base, ground, bed *Many shipwrecks lie on the floor of the sea.* top
2. story, level, deck, tier *Take the elevator to the second floor and turn right.* 3. *verb* knock
down, level, fell *The boxer floored his opponent in the second round.* 4. confuse, puzzle,
baffle, beat, defeat *The final test question floored me.*

flop 1. *verb* drop, fall, sink, slump *I flopped into a chair exhausted.* 2. *noun* failure,
disaster, fiasco *The TV series was a flop and has been canceled.*

flow 1. *verb* run, gush, pour, flood, stream, surge *Blood flowed from the cut.* 2. *noun*
current, stream, course, tide *The flow of traffic increases during rush hour.*

flower 1. *noun* blossom, bloom *I picked some flowers from the garden for our table.*
2. *verb* blossom, bloom, bud *The cherry trees flower in May.*

fluffy *adjective* soft, downy, feathery, woolly, furry *We have a fluffy pet rabbit named Bugs.*

fluid 1. *noun* liquid *Drink lots of fluids when you exercise.* 2. *adjective* liquid, watery, running,
flowing *Fluid lava from a volcano can travel for miles before hardening into rock.* solid

flush *verb* 1. blush, redden, color *Dan flushed when I told him Sarah thinks he's cute.*
2. wash out, cleanse, clean out, rinse, flood *I flushed the sour milk down the drain.*

flutter *verb* beat, flap, flit, wave, move *The flag fluttered in the breeze.*

fly *verb* 1. soar, take flight, wing, glide, sail, hover *Monarch butterflies fly south to
Mexico for the winter.* 2. race, dash, rush, hurry, hasten *We flew down the street after the
bus as it pulled away.*

foam *noun* froth, lather, suds, bubbles *Large waves with foam were beginning to form.*

focus 1. *noun* center, hub, spotlight, core *The triplets are the focus of attention when
Dad takes them out in the stroller.* 2. *verb* concentrate, direct, fix, center *I focused all my
attention on the ball as it sped toward me.*

foe *noun* enemy, adversary, opponent *The evil scientist Lex Luthor is Superman's greatest
foe.* friend

fog 1. *noun* mist, haze, vapor, cloud *The sun burned off the early morning fog.* 2. *verb*
cloud, mist, blur *The windshield fogged over. The steam from my hot shower fogged the
bathroom mirror.*

foggy *adjective* 1. hazy, misty, murky *It's too wet and foggy for us to ride our bikes to school
today.* clear 2. confused, muddled, bewildered, unclear, fuzzy *I have only a foggy idea of
how a computer works.* clear

foil *verb* stop, frustrate, thwart, spoil, ruin *The cartoon superhero foiled the villain's attempt to destroy the earth.*

fold 1. *verb* bend, double over, pleat *Please fold the towels.* 2. clasp, wrap, close, tuck in *The bird landed on a branch and folded its wings.* 3. fail, close, collapse, go out of business *The neighborhood grocery store folded when the supermarket opened.* 4. *noun* crease, pleat, bend *The piece of paper tore in half at the fold.*

follow *verb* 1. come next, come after, succeed, trail *"N" follows "M" in the alphabet. Our new puppy keeps following me wherever I go.* lead, precede 2. obey, observe, heed, abide by, adhere to, respect *Dad is following his doctor's advice to get more exercise.* ignore 3. understand, comprehend, grasp, get, catch on to *I didn't follow the teacher's explanation and asked him to repeat it.*

fond *adjective* loving, affectionate, adoring, devoted, tender, warm *The mother gave her daughter a fond look.*

font *noun* typeface, lettering, type *The teacher wants us to use the Times New Roman font for our reports.*

food *noun* nourishment, nutrition, provisions, edibles (*Slang*—eats, chow, grub) *We packed food in a cooler for our picnic.*

fool 1. *verb* deceive, trick, mislead, con, dupe *The thief fooled the police by disguising himself as a woman.* 2. tease, joke, play tricks on, kid, pretend *My sister was only fooling when she told me she ate all my birthday cake.* 3. *noun* dummy, idiot, blockhead, moron, dope, simpleton *He's a fool to believe he can get something for nothing.*

foolish *adjective* silly, stupid, dumb, ridiculous, absurd, unwise, irrational *It's foolish to cross a busy street without looking both ways.*

foot *noun* base, bottom, lowest part, foundation *We relaxed in the ski lodge at the foot of the mountain.* top

forbid *verb* prohibit, disallow, bar, ban, outlaw *My parents forbid me to be out after dark alone.* allow, permit

force 1. *verb* compel, make, require, obligate, oblige, pressure *You don't have to force my sister to read—she enjoys it.* 2. break, pry, push, shove, drive, thrust, ram *The pirates forced open the lid of the treasure chest.* 3. *noun* power, strength, energy, might *The force of the wind blew the door shut with a bang.* 4. body, unit, team, crew, squad *George Washington had a small, poorly trained force of men to fight the British.*

forceful *adjective* strong, dynamic, energetic, influential, persuasive, effective, convincing *In the latter half of the nineteenth century, suffragists made a forceful plea for a constitutional amendment allowing women to vote.*

forecast 1. *noun* prediction, prophecy, prognosis, projection *The forecast is for rain tonight.* 2. *verb* predict, prophesy, foretell, project *There's no way to forecast the winner of tomorrow's game.*

foreign *adjective* alien, distant, faraway, remote, exotic *Casey has traveled to many foreign countries.*

foremost *adjective* chief, leading, principal, primary, notable, important, top *Marie Curie, who died in 1934, was one of the foremost scientists of her time.*

foresee *verb* anticipate, predict, forecast, foretell, prophesy *We couldn't have foreseen all these problems.*

forest *noun* woods, timberland, woodland, tree plantation *Forests destroyed by fire are being replanted.*

foretell *verb* predict, prophesy, forecast, foresee *In Greek mythology, Cassandra had the ability to foretell the future, but nobody would believe her.*

forever *adverb* always, evermore, eternally, perpetually *Enjoy this beautiful weather—it won't last forever.*

forfeit *verb* lose, sacrifice, give up, surrender *Our team had to forfeit the game when several players didn't show up.*

forge *verb* 1. make, shape, form, create *Blacksmiths forged horseshoes out of iron.* 2. counterfeit, falsify, fake, copy *The police arrested a man for forging travel documents.*

forget *verb* not remember, overlook, lose sight of *Don't forget to lock the door before you go to bed.* remember

forgive *verb* excuse, pardon, let off, absolve *Please forgive me for arriving late.* blame

fork *noun* 1. silverware, utensil, flatware *Which fork do I use to eat my salad?* 2. branch, split, junction *When you come to a fork in the road, go right.*

form 1. *noun* shape, configuration, pattern, design *I cut out paper ornaments in the form of snowflakes.* 2. kind, sort, type, variety, class *Cars are the most popular form of transportation. Ice is the solid form of water.* 3. document, paper, application, sheet *Fill in the order form at the back of the catalog.* 4. *verb* make, create, organize, establish, set up *My brother and his friends have formed a rock band.* 5. appear, develop, take shape, materialize, arise, grow *Ice crystals formed on the tree branches.*

formal *adjective* official, correct, proper, systematic, structured, regular, customary *Parents must give formal permission for their children to go on school trips.* informal

formation *noun* arrangement, configuration, shape, structure, design, layout *The Grand Canyon's spectacular rock formations are hundreds of millions of years old. The planes flew over in formation.*

former *adjective* earlier, past, previous, preceding, prior *Former president Ronald Reagan died at age ninety-three.* latter

forsake *verb* leave, abandon, desert, give up, quit *Benedict Arnold was a traitor who forsook his country.*

fort *noun* fortress, stronghold, fortification, castle, citadel *Alcatraz, before it was a prison, was the first fort on the West Coast of the United States.*

forth *adverb* forward, onward, on, ahead *They set forth on their trip yesterday.* back

fortunate *adjective* lucky, privileged, blessed, well-off, happy *I know I am fortunate to have such a wonderful family.* unfortunate

fortune *noun* 1. luck, chance, fate, destiny *Fortune was against us when our quarterback got injured.* 2. riches, wealth, prosperity, treasure *People rushed to California to seek an easy fortune when gold was discovered.*

forward 1. *adverb* onward, ahead, frontward *Traffic moved forward very slowly.* backward 2. *adjective* front, fore, leading, advance, head *We had a forward cabin on the cruise ship.* 3. bold, aggressive, presumptuous, brazen *Don't be so forward as to invite yourself to the party.* shy 4. *verb* pass on, send, dispatch, redirect *The post office forwards our mail to our new address.*

fossil *noun* remains, trace, vestige, relic *My friend Sam went hunting for dinosaur fossils on his vacation.*

foul *adjective* 1. dirty, nasty, offensive, disgusting, vile, revolting, sickening *Rotten eggs have a foul odor.* pleasant 2. bad, stormy, wet, rainy, blustery, inclement *The foul weather ruined our picnic.* fair, good

found *verb* create, establish, set up, start, organize *The pilgrims founded a colony at Plymouth Rock, Massachusetts, in 1620.*

foundation *noun* 1. basis, fundamentals, groundwork *A solid understanding of chemistry and anatomy is a good foundation for studying nursing.* 2. base, bottom, footing, support *The foundation of our new house was put in today.*

fountain *noun* spring, spout, spray, jet *Children splashed in the fountain in the park.*

fraction *noun* part, portion, division, segment, section *Mom says she accomplished only a fraction of what she had hoped to accomplish today.* whole

fracture 1. *noun* break, crack, rupture, split *Earthquakes and weathering can cause fractures in rocks.* 2. *verb* break, splinter, crack, rupture, split, shatter *Darrell fractured his arm when he fell while skateboarding.*

fragile *adjective* delicate, breakable, flimsy, brittle, frail *Handle that vase carefully—it's very fragile.* strong, sturdy

fragment *noun* piece, part, chip, bit, sliver, portion, section, segment *Only a few fragments of the ancient manuscript survive.* whole

fragrant *adjective* sweet-smelling, perfumed, aromatic, scented *Lilacs are very fragrant flowers.*

frail *adjective* weak, slight, delicate, dainty, fragile *Great-Granddad seems frail since his illness.* strong

frame 1. *noun* framework, structure, support, skeleton *The new building has a frame of steel.* 2. body, build, shape, figure, size, physique *The body builder had a huge frame.* 3. *verb* make, put together, build, construct, erect, shape *The community helped the farmer frame a new barn after the old one burned.* 4. border, edge, bound, trim *Dad framed the picture I painted and hung it in the living room.*

frantic *adjective* frenzied, panicky, agitated, anxious, excited *I was frantic when I couldn't find my report for class.* calm, unexcited

fraud *noun* 1. cheating, trickery, dishonesty, deception, swindle *Criminals keep finding new ways to commit fraud using e-mail and the Internet.* 2. imposter, fake, cheat, phony *Everyone knows the carnival fortune-teller is a fraud.*

fray *verb* unravel, wear, wear out, tatter, shred, come apart *The cuffs on my favorite shirt are fraying.*

free 1. *adjective* complimentary, at no cost, without charge, gratis *When you buy one pair of socks, you get another pair free.* 2. independent, self-governing, liberated, emancipated *We are fortunate to live in a free country.* enslaved, restricted 3. allowed, permitted, able *I'm free to do what I want when I've finished my chores.* restricted 4. *verb* release, let go, liberate, turn loose, emancipate *We freed the bird from the cage as soon as its broken wing healed.* enslave, imprison

freedom *noun* independence, liberty, free will, autonomy, emancipation *The U.S. Constitution protects freedom of speech.* bondage

freeze *verb* 1. chill, ice up, ice over, harden, solidify *The lake freezes in winter.* melt 2. stop, stand still, halt *I froze when I saw the skunk in my path.* move

freight *noun* cargo, load, merchandise, goods *A truck unloading freight blocked the alley.*

frenzy *noun* furor, turmoil, agitation, excitement, commotion *The crowd was in a frenzy when, in the last two seconds of the game, the home team scored the winning touchdown.* calmness, serenity

frequent *adjective* repeated, numerous, recurrent, regular, constant, continual *You can avoid frequent trips to the dentist by brushing and flossing your teeth twice a day.* infrequent

fresh *adjective* 1. not spoiled, not stale, recent, newly harvested *You can buy the freshest fruit and vegetables at a farmers' market.* stale 2. new, different, another, original, innovative, novel *We need to find a fresh approach to the problem.* old 3. healthy, clean, pure, refreshing *Open a window and let in some fresh air.* stale 4. energetic, vigorous, alert, bright, refreshed *I'm feeling nice and fresh after that swim.*

friction *noun* 1. grinding, scraping, chafing, rubbing, abrasion *Friction from my new shoes gave me blisters.* 2. conflict, hostility, tension, antagonism *Friction between the nations brought them close to war.* harmony

friend *noun* companion, comrade, chum, buddy, pal, acquaintance, intimate *Mom and Dad said I could invite my friends over for pizza.* enemy

friendship *noun* companionship, comradeship, fellowship, closeness, intimacy *Some friendships last a lifetime.*

fright *noun* fear, terror, alarm, dread, horror, panic *Heights fill me with fright.*

frighten *verb* scare, terrify, alarm, startle, panic *I'm sorry—I didn't mean to frighten you.*

frigid *adjective* cold, freezing, wintry, nippy, raw, icy, sharp *The temperature today is a frigid 12 degrees below zero.* warm

fringe *noun* border, margin, edge, rim *New subdivisions are being built on the fringe of the city.*

frolic *verb* play, romp, frisk *The puppies frolicked in the wading pool.*

front 1. *noun* beginning, first part, face, head *The table of contents is at the front of the book.* back 2. *adjective* first, foremost, leading *Cory wanted to sit in the front seat of the car.* back

frontier *noun* border, boundary, limit, edge, back country *The Louisiana Purchase extended the western frontier of the United States beyond the Mississippi River.*

frost *noun* ice crystals *The frost formed beautiful patterns on the car windshield during the night.*

frosting *noun* icing, topping, glaze *Mom decorated my birthday cake with red and blue frosting.*

frown 1. *verb* scowl, pout, grimace, look sullen, look displeased *My mother frowned when she saw my filthy clothes.* smile 2. *noun* scowl, pout, grimace *George stared at the test with a frown on his face.* smile

frustrate *verb* 1. foil, thwart, defeat, spoil, ruin *The rain frustrated my plans to mow the lawn.* 2. discourage, upset, annoy, bother, exasperate *Mom says her lack of success finding a job is beginning to frustrate her.*

fry *verb* cook, sauté, deep-fry, stir-fry *I like potatoes fried with onions.*

fuel *noun* source of energy, petroleum, oil, gas, coal, wood *Grandpa's farm tractor uses diesel fuel.*

fugitive *noun* escapee, runaway, deserter, outlaw *Police are searching for a fugitive who escaped yesterday from the prison.*

fulfill *verb* 1. accomplish, achieve, perform, do, carry out, finish, complete *Laila has fulfilled her dream of becoming a teacher.* 2. satisfy, meet, answer, fill, comply with *Kendall has fulfilled all the requirements for admission to the practice of law.*

full 1. *adjective* complete, entire, whole, thorough, comprehensive *Claire gave us a full account of her week at camp.* 2. filled, packed, crammed, crowded, stuffed *The parking lot was full, so we had to park on the street.* empty 3. *adverb* completely, entirely *Fill the bucket full.*

fumble *verb* 1. mishandle, drop, miss *The receiver fumbled the ball, and it was recovered by the opposing team.* 2. stumble, blunder, flounder, grope, feel around *I fumbled around in the dark for my slippers and woke my brother.*

fun *noun* amusement, entertainment, recreation, pleasure, enjoyment, play *We had a lot of fun playing with the dogs in the park.*

function 1. *noun* purpose, role, task, use, job *The heart's function is to pump blood to all parts of the body. My brother's function is to manage and maintain his company's computer network.* 2. event, occasion, gathering, party, celebration, ceremony *We attended a* *function to honor my grandfather for his service to the community.* 3. *verb* serve, be used, operate, perform, act, work *Our printer also functions as a photocopier and scanner.*

fund *noun* account, reserve, supply, store, stock *I put some of the money I earn doing yard work into my college fund.*

fundamental *adjective* essentials, basic, underlying, primary, key, major *Freedom of religion is a fundamental right set forth in the U.S. Constitution.*

fundamentals *noun* basics, essential, underlying principles, rudiments *I explained the fundamentals of American football to my friend from Scotland.*

funny *adjective* 1. amusing, humorous, hilarious, comical, witty *Do you want to hear a funny joke?* boring, dull 2. strange, unusual, odd, peculiar, weird *It's funny that Maureen didn't come to the party.*

fur *noun* hair, coat, fleece, pelt *My rabbit's fur is very soft.*

furious *adjective* 1. angry, mad, enraged, infuriated *My sister was furious with me for borrowing her favorite sweater without asking.* pleased, happy 2. violent, fierce, raging, turbulent, intense *The sailors found themselves caught in a furious gale. There is a furious debate going on in Congress over raising taxes.* calm

furnish *verb* 1. equip, outfit *My brother furnished his college apartment with secondhand furniture.* 2. give, provide, supply *Dad agreed to furnish whatever we need to fix up the shed for a clubhouse.*

further 1. *adverb* additionally, more, to a greater degree *After having a flat tire, we were further delayed by a snowstorm.* 2. *adjective* additional, more, extra, other, new, fresh *Stay tuned for further weather information.* 3. *verb* help, aid, advance, promote, encourage, foster *My brother is taking a class to help him further his interest in photography.* hinder

fury *noun* 1. rage, anger, wrath *The teacher didn't hide her fury at Gary for having cheated.* 2. violence, severity, intensity, force, power *This storm lacked the fury of the hurricane that came ashore three years ago.*

fuse *verb* join, blend, unite, combine, melt *Copper and zinc are fused to make brass.*

fuss 1. *noun* commotion, excitement, bustle, bother, stir, to-do *Lauren made such a fuss when Allie stepped on her toe.* 2. *verb* worry, bother, fret *Mom keeps fussing over the arrangements for my sister's graduation party.*

future 1. *adjective* coming, upcoming, approaching, forthcoming *It is important to protect the environment and conserve our resources for future generations.* 2. *noun* time to come, tomorrow *Alexa says she hasn't decided yet what she wants to be in the future.*

fuzzy *adjective* fluffy, hairy, downy, woolly *My little sister won't go to bed without her fuzzy stuffed lamb.*

G

gadget *noun* device, apparatus, instrument, tool, implement, utensil, appliance, contraption *Dad has a nifty pocket gadget that includes pliers, screwdrivers, knife blades, and a bottle opener.*

gain 1. *verb* get, obtain, acquire, secure, earn, receive *My teacher helped me gain self-confidence by encouraging me to speak up more.* lose 2. *noun* improvement, advantage, increase, advance *Daniels passed to Morgan for a gain of sixteen yards.* loss

gale *noun* high wind, windstorm, tempest, squall *A northeasterly gale trapped explorer Ernest Shackleton's ship the* Endurance *in the ice of Antarctica.*

gallant *adjective* brave, courageous, valiant, bold, heroic *The firefighters made a gallant attempt to save the old barn.* cowardly

gallop *verb* 1. run, trot, canter, sprint *The lead horse galloped to the finish line.* 2. race, speed, fly, zoom *My week at camp just galloped by.*

gamble 1. *verb* bet, wager, risk, chance, venture, speculate, try one's luck *I gambled a dollar that I could beat my brother at one-on-one basketball and lost.* 2. *noun* chance, risk, bet, wager *The coach took a gamble when he allowed me to play in the last quarter of the game.*

game *noun* 1. amusement, pastime, entertainment, recreation *We need to come up with some games to play at the party.* 2. competition, contest, match, event *Did you watch the game on TV last night?*

gang *noun* group, crew, band, ring, company, pack, troop, bunch, crowd *Butch Cassidy and the Sundance Kid were members of a gang of outlaws called "The Hole in the Wall Gang."*

gap *noun* opening, break, hole, space, crack, crevice, cavity *Our dog slipped through the gap in the fence into the neighbor's yard.*

garbage *noun* waste, trash, rubbish, refuse, debris, litter, scraps *Take the garbage out to the curb for tomorrow's pickup.*

garden 1. *noun* plot, patch, yard *We grow flowers in our garden.* 2. *verb* grow, raise, cultivate, plant *We begin gardening in the early spring.*

garment *noun* article of clothing *Our local clothing store refuses to sell garments made in sweatshops overseas.*

gas *noun* 1. gasoline, petroleum, fuel *The car is almost out of gas.* 2. vapor, fume *Air is composed primarily of the gases nitrogen and oxygen.*

gasp 1. *verb* gulp, pant, choke, catch one's breath *I gasped for air when I surfaced after retrieving Mom's sunglasses from the bottom of the pool.* 2. *noun* gulp, pant, wheeze, choke *She let out a gasp of surprise when she saw us.*

gate *noun* entrance, entry, opening, access, doorway, door *A high fence and locked gate were the first obstacles in the video game.*

gather *verb* 1. collect, assemble, congregate, meet, cluster, come together *We gathered around the coach to hear her instructions.* scatter 2. harvest, pick, reap *The children gathered pumpkins from the pumpkin patch to carve for Halloween.* 3. understand, assume, conclude, hear *I gather from your look of disappointment that the team lost.*

gathering *noun* meeting, assembly, congregation, get-together, crowd *We're having a family gathering at the lake over the weekend.*

gauge 1. *verb* measure, estimate, evaluate, judge, determine, test, appraise, assess, size up *It's hard to gauge the effect that TV has on children.* 2. *noun* measure, estimation, test, indication *Happiness is the best gauge of success.*

gaunt *adjective* thin, lean, skinny, scrawny, lanky, bony *Granddad looked a little gaunt for a while after he was sick.*

gay *adjective* happy, merry, lively, cheerful, jolly *Everyone was in gay spirits at the party.*

gaze 1. *noun* stare, look *The cat's gaze was fixed on the mouse.* 2. *verb* stare, gape, eye, gawk, watch *We lay on our backs in the grass gazing at the stars.*

gear *noun* equipment, apparatus, outfit, supplies, things, stuff, paraphernalia *We carried all our gear in backpacks on the two-day hike.*

gem *noun* 1. jewel, precious stone, gemstone *Grandma's ring is set with a blue gem that she says is a sapphire.* 2. treasure, good thing, joy, prize, masterpiece *My baby brother is a real gem.*

general *adjective* 1. common, widespread, universal, broad, accepted *There was general agreement that the plan wouldn't work.* 2. usual, routine, customary, typical, everyday, normal *As a general rule, I am up before 7:00.* 3. universal, sweeping, whole, all-inclusive, total *Smoking is prohibited in enclosed areas open to the general public.*

generally *adverb* 1. usually, normally, customarily, as a rule *Mom generally drops me off at school on her way to work.* 2. commonly, widely, universally *It was generally believed in the past that the earth was flat.*

generate *verb* produce, cause, bring about, create, originate *The sun generates heat and light. Space travel has always generated a lot of excitement.*

generous *adjective* considerate, kind, unselfish, bighearted, giving *A local builder made a generous offer of his time to help build a house for the homeless family.* small, stingy

genius *noun* 1. master, ace, wizard, whiz *My brother will need a genius to help him make the old car he bought run.* 2. intelligence, brilliance, brains, aptitude, talent, ability *Albert Einstein's genius revealed itself at an early age.*

gentle *adjective* 1. mild, soft, moderate, calm, light, low *A gentle breeze made the leaves rustle. He soothed the crying child in a gentle voice.* rough 2. kind, tender, amiable, sympathetic, humane, docile, tame *Our teacher has a patient and gentle disposition. There's no reason to fear the big dog next door—he's very gentle.* harsh, mean

genuine *adjective* real, true, authentic, pure, legitimate *Sometimes it takes an expert to recognize a genuine antique.* fake, phony

germ *noun* microorganism, microbe, bacteria, virus, bug *Germs are the source of many illnesses.*

gesture 1. *noun* motion, movement, sign, signal *The gentleman bowed as a gesture of respect.* 2. *verb* signal, sign, indicate, motion *Dad gestured toward his watch to indicate it was getting late.*

get *verb* 1. obtain, acquire, gain, secure, find *We got tickets for the concert.* 2. become, turn, grow *It's getting cloudy.* 3. bring, fetch, retrieve *Can I get you anything to drink?* 4. persuade, influence, cause, make, induce *We're trying to get Sue and Jeff to come with us.* 5. arrive, reach *We got to the movie after it had started.* 6. understand, grasp, follow, comprehend *I don't get what you mean.* 7. develop, catch, come down with, acquire *I got the flu and missed several days of school.* 8. move, travel, walk, climb *I get to school on the bus.*

ghastly *adjective* horrible, terrible, dreadful, frightful, shocking *Diana looked ghastly when she finally went home sick.* beautiful

ghost *noun* spirit, specter, phantom, spook *Do you believe in ghosts?*

giant 1. *adjective* huge, immense, vast, enormous, tremendous, colossal, monumental, mammoth, gigantic *The whale shark is a giant shark that can grow up to 50 feet long and weigh up to 15 tons.* small, tiny, minute 2. *noun* an imaginary creature, who is very strong and tall 3. someone who is unusually tall or large *The giant in the fairy tale ended up saving the day.*

gift *noun* 1. present, donation, contribution, offering *The philanthropist gave generous gifts to charity.* 2. ability, talent, skill, knack, aptitude *Barbara has a gift for drawing and painting.*

gifted *adjective* talented, skilled, able, exceptional *My sister is taking advanced classes in a program for gifted students.*

gigantic *adjective* huge, immense, vast, enormous, tremendous, colossal, monumental, mammoth *Tyrannosaurus rex was a gigantic dinosaur that weighed between 4 and 7 tons.* small, tiny, minute

giggle 1. *verb* laugh, chuckle, titter, snicker *I can make my brother giggle by tickling him.* 2. *noun* chuckle, laughter, laugh, snicker, titter *Once I get the giggles, it's hard for me to stop.*

girl *noun* female child, young woman, young lady, miss, lass *Both boys and girls play on our softball team.*

give *verb* 1. present, hand over, donate, contribute, bestow *Chandler gave me a book about birds for my birthday.* 2. allow, grant, permit, allot *The walk signal barely gives me enough time to cross the road.* 3. provide, supply, furnish, offer *My sister rarely gives me advice unless I ask for it.* 4. communicate, transmit, convey, send, impart *Aunt Margie gives us news of their travels by postcard.* 5. perform, organize, put on, hold, have *We plan to give a party next Saturday.* 6. yield, bend, collapse, break *The fragile antique chair gave under Uncle Frank's weight.*

glad *adjective* 1. happy, pleased, delighted, joyful, joyous *We're so glad to see you.* sad, unhappy 2. willing, ready, prepared, eager *Dad is always glad to help with the dishes.*

glamorous *adjective* fascinating, charming, alluring, captivating, enchanting, attractive, interesting, appealing *All the glamorous movie stars attended the awards ceremony.* unattractive, unappealing

glance 1. *verb* look, glimpse, peek *Maggie glanced at her watch to see what time it was.* 2. *noun* brief look, glimpse, peek *I took a quick glance in the mirror to be sure I looked all right.*

glare 1. *verb* scowl, glower, frown, stare *Don't glare at me—I didn't do it!* 2. shine, glow, blaze, burn, dazzle, flare, flash *The oncoming car's headlights glared, nearly blinding me.* 3. *noun* scowl, glower, stare, frown *The man gave me an angry glare when I accidentally bumped into him.* 4. blaze, flare, glow, dazzle *The glare from the sun hurt my eyes.*

glaring *adjective* 1. brilliant, blazing, dazzling, blinding *We stepped out of the dark building into the glaring sunlight.* 2. obvious, conspicuous, evident, blatant *I found some glaring errors in my math when I rechecked it.*

glass *noun* tumbler, goblet *I'd like a glass of water, please.*

gleam 1. *verb* shine, glow, glimmer, sparkle, glisten, twinkle *The car gleamed after we washed and waxed it.* 2. *noun* beam, glow, flash, glimmer, twinkle, flare *The travelers saw a gleam of light from a distant farmhouse.*

glee *noun* joy, delight, mirth, happiness, gladness, cheer, elation, bliss, merriment *My sister jumped up and down with glee when she saw the porpoises playing.* sadness

glide *verb* coast, cruise, slide, sail, skim, sweep, fly, move easily *We watched the eagle soar and glide above the lake.*

glimmer 1. *verb* twinkle, flicker, sparkle, gleam, glow, glisten *Stars glimmered in the clear night sky.* 2. *noun* flicker, twinkle, sparkle, gleam, glow *We love watching the glimmer of fireflies on a summer night.* 3. hint, indication, suggestion, trace *The weather forecast offers a glimmer of hope to farmers that rain will soon end the drought.*

glimpse 1. *noun* peek, brief look, glance *I caught a glimpse of the star as he sped away in his limousine.* 2. *verb* see, catch sight of, notice, glance at *I glimpsed my friend in the crowd.*

glisten *verb* sparkle, gleam, twinkle, glimmer, shine *The fresh snow glistened in the moonlight.*

glitter 1. *verb* sparkle, twinkle, shine, glisten, glimmer *The dew on the spiderweb glittered in the sunlight.* 2. *noun* sparkle, twinkle, shine, glisten *We were surprised at the glitter of the stars away from the city's lights.* 3. dazzle, flashiness, glamour, splendor *Our friend Georgia longs for an acting career and the glitter of Hollywood.*

gloat *verb* exult, crow over, revel, delight, triumph *Donna beat me at tennis but was nice enough not to gloat.*

globe *noun* 1. sphere, ball *I have a spinning multicolored light in the shape of a globe in my room.* 2. earth, world, planet *In 1966–67, Sir Francis Chichester was the first person to sail around the globe alone in a small sailboat.*

gloom *noun* 1. darkness, dimness, dreariness, bleakness *We explored the gloom of the cave with our flashlights.* 2. sadness, unhappiness, despair, melancholy, glumness, depression *Yet another loss added to the team members' gloom.* happiness, joy

gloomy *adjective* 1. dismal, dreary, dark, bleak, somber *The big, empty attic was dark and gloomy.* 2. sad, unhappy, melancholy, glum, dejected, depressed *These dark winter days are making me feel gloomy.* cheerful, happy

glorious *adjective* magnificent, splendid, superb, fine, terrific, sensational, wonderful, beautiful, gorgeous, grand *We picked a glorious summer day to go boating.*

glory *noun* 1. magnificence, splendor, grandeur, majesty *We stopped along the road to take in the glory of the mountains at sunset.* 2. fame, prestige, renown, praise, triumph *Carl Lewis won glory as an Olympic athlete.*

glossary *noun* dictionary, word list, thesaurus, lexicon *Look in the glossary at the back of the book for the word's meaning.*

glow 1. *verb* shine, gleam, glimmer, radiate *Lights glowed in all the rooms of the house.* 2. *noun* gleam, glimmer, radiance, light, luminosity *We ate dinner by the glow of candlelight.*

glue 1. *noun* adhesive, paste, cement, gum *We used wood glue to assemble the model sailboat.* 2. *verb* paste, cement, stick, bind, fasten *The children glued hearts to doilies to make valentines.*

glum *adjective* sad, gloomy, dismal, sullen, moody *I was feeling glum after having done badly on my test.* happy, cheerful

gnaw *verb* chew, bite, crunch, munch *Our dog is in the backyard gnawing on a bone.*

go 1. *verb* move, travel, proceed *Go two blocks past the school and turn left.* 2. leave, depart, set off, exit, go away *It's time to go—it's late.* come, arrive 3. become, grow, get *This cheese has gone bad.* 4. extend, stretch, reach, lead *The highway goes north another twenty miles.* 5. progress, develop *How did school go today?* 6. function, operate, work *Dad couldn't get the car going this morning.* 7. belong, have a place *Where do the cups go?* 8. disappear, vanish, stop *My stomachache is gone.* 9. match, harmonize, be compatible *The chair and sofa don't go. Does this sweater go with my skirt?* 10. *noun* energy, vigor *Grandma has a lot of go for her age.* 11. try, attempt (*Slang*—shot, crack) *Both Dad and my brother had a go at fixing the motor scooter, but failed.*

goal *noun* objective, aim, ambition, purpose, destination, end, finish *By exercising and eating less, Dad reached his goal of losing twenty-five pounds.*

gobble *verb* eat fast, devour, gulp down, wolf, gorge (*Slang*—scarf) *Our dog gobbled his dish of food.*

good 1. *adjective* excellent, fine, superior, nice, splendid, great, first-rate *We had a good time at camp.* bad 2. well behaved, proper *The vet said our dog was very good while she examined him.* 3. suitable, appropriate, fitting, right, decent *This is a good book for children.* 4. skilled, able, proficient, talented, accomplished, capable *We took our car to a good mechanic to be repaired.* 5. kind, friendly, gracious, nice, warmhearted, sympathetic *It was good of Danny to visit me when I was sick.* 6. genuine, real, valid, legitimate, authentic, bona fide *I had a good reason for being absent: I was sick.* 7. healthful, wholesome, nutritious, beneficial *Eat your vegetables—they're good for you.* unhealthful 8. *noun* benefit, profit, advantage *The players have to work together for the good of the team.*

good-bye *interjection* farewell, so long, see you later, cheers, bye, adieu *"Good-bye, Mike. I had a great time."* hello, hi

goodwill *noun* friendliness, helpfulness, kindness, willingness, caring, agreeability *The relief agency promotes peace and goodwill among the people it helps.*

gorge 1. *verb* stuff, fill, binge, devour, gulp, gobble *We gorged ourselves on hot dogs and cotton candy at the carnival.* 2. *noun* valley, ravine, gully *The Grand Canyon is a gorge formed, in part, by the Colorado River.*

gorgeous *adjective* splendid, beautiful, ravishing, stunning, glorious, brilliant, dazzling *We had a gorgeous view from our hotel balcony.* hideous, ugly

gossip 1. *noun* rumor, hearsay, idle talk, scandal *You can hear all the local gossip at the coffee shop mornings.* 2. *verb* chat, talk, jabber, chatter *Mom says class reunions are a great place to gossip with old friends.*

govern *verb* rule, control, manage, lead, head, direct, supervise, command, oversee, preside over, regulate, guide *The election will determine who governs the country.*

gown *noun* dress, frock *My sister found a gown to wear to the prom.*

grab 1. *verb* snatch, seize, grasp, grip, clutch *I grabbed my brother's hand before we crossed the street.* 2. *noun* sudden grasp, snatch *Deana made a grab for her hat when the wind blew it off her head.*

grace 1. *noun* charm, elegance, gracefulness, poise, polish *The ballet dancers performed with grace.* 2. kindness, decency, courtesy, consideration, manners *She should at least have the grace to apologize for the insult.* 3. *verb* decorate, adorn, enhance, beautify, honor, dignify *Great masterpieces graced the walls of the mansion.*

graceful *adjective* elegant, poised, smooth, refined, attractive, beautiful *Everyone I* *know thinks that she is one of the most graceful figure skaters of all time.*

gracious *adjective* pleasant, cordial, friendly, generous, courteous, kind, pleasant *The star was gracious in his thanks for the award, giving credit to his family and coworkers.* rude, unkind

grade 1. *noun* score, mark, ranking, rating, evaluation *I got a good grade on the test.* 2. classification, grouping, class, category, position, status, place *A better grade of carpeting will wear longer.* 3. slope, incline, hill, pitch *I'm learning to ski on a hill with very little grade.* 4. *verb* score, mark, rank, rate, evaluate *The teacher promised to grade our papers by tomorrow.* 5. classify, group, categorize, sort, arrange *Eggs in the store are graded by size.* 6. level, flatten, smooth *Our gravel driveway is bumpy and needs grading.*

gradual *adjective* slow, little by little, steady, even, measured *The teacher says he's seeing a gradual improvement in my reading skills.* sudden

graduate *verb* 1. finish, pass, complete, advance *I plan to go to college after graduating from high school.* 2. mark off, measure off, calibrate *A thermometer is graduated in degrees.*

grain *noun* 1. particle, speck, bit *Strong winds cause grains of sand to accumulate and form dunes.* 2. cereal, wheat, corn, barley, oats, rice, rye *Grain is ground to make flour.*

grand *adjective* magnificent, impressive, majestic, stately, opulent *The king and queen live in a grand palace.* insignificant, small

grant 1. *verb* give, present, bestow, award, allot, give out, confer *The mayor granted my dad an award for his volunteer service to the community.* 2. agree, admit, acknowledge, consent to *I grant that you made the right decision.* 3. *noun* gift, donation, present, award, contribution, allotment *Professor Nakamura received a grant to study alternative fuel sources.*

graph *noun* chart, diagram, plot *Our homework assignment is to make a bar graph showing the population of our state over a ten-year period.*

graphic 1. *noun* picture, illustration, image, photograph, chart, map, drawing *Many movies today are made using graphics created by computers.* 2. *adjective* lifelike, vivid, realistic, detailed, clear *The book is a graphic account of Robert Falcon Scott's disastrous South Pole expedition.*

grasp 1. *verb* seize, hold, clutch, clasp, grip *I grasped Jeannie's arm to keep her from falling.* 2. understand, comprehend, follow, get *I find math particularly difficult to grasp.* 3. *noun* understanding, comprehension, knowledge, awareness *Our foreign exchange student already has a good grasp of English.*

grateful *adjective* thankful, appreciative, glad, pleased *Mom was grateful for my help with the dishes.* ungrateful

gratify *verb* satisfy, please, delight *It gratifies me to see you so happy.*

gratitude *noun* thankfulness, gratefulness, appreciation *The neighbors expressed their gratitude to us for finding their lost dog.* ungratefulness

grave 1. *adjective* serious, critical, vital, important, significant, crucial *The report expressed grave concerns about the quality of the air.* unimportant 2. solemn, somber, sober, thoughtful *From the grave expression on Sam's face, I knew he had bad news.* cheerful 3. *noun* burial place, plot *Thomas Jefferson is buried in a grave on his Virginia estate.*

gravel *noun* stones, pebbles *We got a load of gravel for our driveway.*

graze *verb* 1. eat, feed, forage *The cows grazed in the pasture.* 2. touch lightly, scrape, rub, contact, brush, skim *From the way my little brother cried, you'd think he'd done more than just graze his knee.*

grease 1. *noun* fat, lard *Bacon grease is used a lot in traditional Southern cooking.* 2. oil, lubricant *It's hard to remove grease from clothes.* 3. *verb* oil, lubricate *I cleaned and greased my bicycle hubs.*

great *adjective* 1. outstanding, prominent, famous, distinguished, remarkable, important *Picasso is considered a great artist.* unimportant, insignificant 2. large, big, immense, huge, enormous, vast *Great prairies once covered most of the land between the Mississippi River and the Rocky Mountains.* small 3. considerable, substantial, excessive, inordinate *Witnesses were able to describe the accident in great detail.*

greed *noun* craving, hunger, appetite, desire, longing *The dictator was driven by a greed for power.*

green *adjective* 1. unripe, immature, underdeveloped *Those apples are too green to eat.* ripe, mature 2. untrained, inexperienced, new *Most of the players on this year's team are green.* experienced 3. renewable, ecologically sound, environmentally friendly *The wind and sun are green energy sources.*

greet *verb* welcome, meet, hail, salute, acknowledge *Grandma greeted us with hugs.*

grief *noun* sorrow, heartache, misery, sadness, unhappiness *It's okay to cry when you feel grief over the death of a loved one.*

grieve *verb* mourn, sorrow, lament, be sad, be distressed, weep, cry *The whole family is grieving over the death of our old dog, Sparky.*

grill *verb* 1. broil, cook, barbecue *We grilled chicken for dinner.* 2. question, cross-examine, interrogate *I had my sister grill me to see if I was ready for the test.*

grim *adjective* stern, strict, harsh, serious, severe *I knew I was in trouble when I saw the grim expression on my father's face.* relaxed, lenient

grime *noun* dirt, soil, soot, mud, slime, filth *The coal miner was covered in grime after a day's work.*

grimy *adjective* dirty, filthy, grubby, soiled *My clothes were all grimy after having slid into third base.*

grin 1. *noun* smile *The picture showed Dad with a big fish and a big grin on his face.* 2. *verb* smile, beam *Annie grinned and waved to us.*

grind *verb* 1. crush, pulverize, mill, mash, crumble *The mill grinds wheat into flour.* 2. file, sharpen, smooth, polish, sand *Astronomy students learned to grind and polish a lens for a telescope.*

grip 1. *verb* hold, grasp, clutch, clasp, clench, seize *I gripped my bat and waited for the pitch.* release 2. *noun* hold, grasp, clasp, clutch *Mom tightened her grip on my sister's hand as we crossed the street.*

grit 1. *noun* dirt, dust, sand, gravel, grains *The wind blew grit into my eyes.* 2. *verb* grind, grate, clench *I gritted my teeth and dove into the cold water.*

groan 1. *verb* moan, whimper, sigh *The whole class groaned when the teacher announced a pop quiz.* 2. *noun* moan, cry, sigh, whimper *The alarm went off, and with a groan I got out of bed.*

groom 1. *verb* tidy, clean, tend, brush, comb *A cat grooms itself with its tongue.* 2. *noun* newlywed, bridegroom *The groom stood at the front of the church and waited for the bride.*

groove *noun* channel, slot, furrow, track, rut, hollow *Pencils are made by cutting grooves in two wood slats, inserting a rod of graphite in one groove, then gluing the slats together.*

grope *verb* feel around, fumble, poke around *I groped across the unfamiliar room in the dark.*

gross *adjective* 1. blatant, flagrant, glaring, serious, significant *The defendant was accused of gross negligence.* 2. disgusting, unpleasant, revolting, nauseating, vile *Rotten tomatoes smell gross.* pleasant

grotesque *adjective* bizarre, unnatural, odd, monstrous, ugly *The goblin of fairy tales is said to be a grotesque, maliciously evil creature.*

grouchy *adjective* bad-tempered, grumpy, complaining, ill-tempered, crabby, irritable *Don't bother Oscar—he's especially grouchy today.* even-tempered

ground 1. *noun* earth, soil, dirt, sod, land, terrain *The ground is covered in a blanket of snow.* 2. field, arena, park, ballpark, stadium *The band practiced on the parade ground.* 3. *verb* base, support, justify, establish, fix, set, root *The education program is grounded on the principle that children should have a healthy and safe environment in which to learn.*

grounds *noun* 1. basis, foundation, reason, cause, motive, premise *The judge found no grounds for dismissing the case.* 2. land, gardens, lawns, real estate, park *The palace is surrounded by beautiful grounds.* 3. dregs, sediment *Coffee grounds can be used to fertilize your garden.*

group 1. *noun* crowd, gathering, assembly, band, bunch, gang, cluster, collection *A group of friends stopped over after school for a snack.* 2. category, classification, class, set *A balanced diet includes all the food groups.* 3. *verb* arrange, classify, organize, categorize *The books in the library are grouped by subject.* 4. gather, assemble, collect, bunch, cluster *The class grouped together to buy the teacher a birthday present.*

grove *noun* wood, stand, thicket, orchard *We have a small orange grove in the backyard.*

grow *verb* 1. increase, multiply, get bigger, enlarge, expand, swell *If our town keeps growing at the same rate, we will need a new high school in three years.* 2. develop, flourish, prosper, thrive, succeed *Many plants used for medicine grow in tropical forests.* 3. raise, cultivate, produce, breed, farm *We grow our own vegetables in our garden.* 4. become, get, turn *It's growing colder as winter approaches.*

growl 1. *verb* snarl, howl, bark, roar *The dog growled when it saw the cat.* 2. *noun* snarl, howl, bark, roar *Did you hear the growl of the bears at the zoo?*

growth *noun* 1. increase, expansion, rise, development, progress, advance *Interest in organic foods has shown a lot of growth.* 2. something growing, emergence *My brother didn't shave over the weekend and has two days' growth of beard.*

grudge *noun* ill will, dislike, resentment *I hope you won't hold a grudge against me for forgetting about our meeting.*

gruff *adjective* 1. deep, husky, coarse, harsh *"Come in," he said in a gruff voice.* 2. rude, unfriendly, brusque, curt, blunt *Our next-door neighbor has a gruff manner, but he's really very nice.* polite

grumble *verb* complain, protest, mutter, gripe, whine, moan *The kids at school grumble about the food in the cafeteria.*

grumpy *adjective* bad-tempered, irritable, grouchy, cross, crabby, sullen *My brother gets grumpy when I pester him too much.*

guarantee 1. *noun* assurance, promise, pledge, warranty, certification *The thrift shop couldn't give us a guarantee that the VCR works.* 2. *verb* promise, pledge, warrant, certify, back, stand behind *No one can guarantee the team will win.*

guard 1. *verb* watch, defend, shield, protect, secure *Secret Service agents guard the president.* 2. *noun* control, restraint, protection, security, defense *A bicycle helmet is a guard against head injuries.* 3. protector, sentry, lookout, watch, defense *Dogs act as guards for sheep.*

guess 1. *verb* think, believe, suppose, assume, imagine *I guess we can be home by noon.* 2. predict, estimate, reckon, figure out *Connie guessed the answer to the puzzle.* 3. *noun* belief, assumption, opinion, estimate, supposition, conjecture *My guess is that the hard drive has failed in your computer.*

guest *noun* 1. visitor, company, caller *Our weekend guests just left.* 2. lodger, roomer, boarder, customer, patron *The bed-and-breakfast has rooms for twenty guests.*

guide 1. *noun* leader, escort, conductor, usher, attendant *A guide took us on a tour of the cathedral.* 2. model, example, standard, ideal *A dictionary can be used as a spelling guide.* 3. *verb* lead, direct, show, steer, escort, conduct, usher *The flight attendant guided us to our seats.*

guilt *noun* blame, fault, responsibility, culpability *The thief admitted his guilt.*

guilty *adjective* 1. at fault, to blame, responsible, blameworthy, culpable *The jury found the defendant guilty of theft.* 2. ashamed, embarrassed, remorseful, sorry, contrite, mortified *I feel really guilty about being rude to my sister.*

gulf *noun* 1. bay, inlet, harbor, cove *The coast of the Gulf of Mexico is a favorite winter vacation area.* 2. separation, hole, rift, gap, split, division *The issue of slavery created a gulf between the Northern and Southern states that led to the Civil War.*

gullible *adjective* easily fooled, naive, deceivable, trusting, innocent *Hundreds of gullible people are victims of Internet fraud.*

gully *noun* ditch, ravine, valley, gorge, gulf, gulch *The gullies were full of water after the heavy rain.*

gulp 1. *verb* swallow, devour, bolt, wolf, guzzle *I had to gulp down my breakfast so I wouldn't be late for school.* 2. *noun* swallow, mouthful *I finished my milk in four large gulps.*

gun *noun* weapon, firearm, pistol, rifle, revolver, shotgun *My brother is learning how to use a gun at hunter safety class.*

gush *verb* rush out, pour, flow, spout, surge, flood *Water gushed from the fire hydrant.*

gust *noun* blast, rush, gale, blow *A gust of wind blew my hat into the street.*

gutter *noun* channel, groove, trench, ditch *The gutters were clogged with leaves.*

gym *noun* health club, sports club, fitness center, athletic facility *Mom goes to the gym during her lunch hour to work out.*

gymnastics *noun* exercises, calisthenics, acrobatics *Susie's coach at gymnastics says she may someday be good enough for the Olympics.*

H

habit *noun* custom, practice, routine, tradition *My parents are in the habit of taking a long walk every evening. Karen has a bad habit of biting her nails.*

habitual *adjective* regular, usual, customary, accustomed, routine, normal *The teacher greeted the class with her habitual smile. Habitual smokers are likely to have health problems.*

hack *verb* cut, chop, slash, hew *The expedition hacked a path through the dense jungle.*

hail *verb* call, shout to, signal, flag, greet, welcome *It was raining when we left the theater, so we hailed a taxi.*

hall *noun* 1. passageway, hallway, corridor *The principal's office is down the hall to the left.* 2. auditorium, meeting room, assembly room, conference room, chamber *The board holds its meeting once a month in the town hall.*

halo *noun* ring, circle, aura, corona *A halo is produced around the moon when light from the moon strikes ice crystals suspended in the atmosphere.*

halt 1. *noun* stop, standstill, pause, break, cessation *Traffic came to a halt on the freeway due to construction.* 2. *verb* stop, come to a standstill, cease, end, finish, discontinue *The project halted due to lack of money.*

hammer *verb* hit, drive, pound, beat, knock, bang *Gold can be hammered into thin sheets that have many decorative uses.*

hamper *verb* hinder, obstruct, block, impede, restrain, limit *Dad was hampered by rain in his attempt to fix the leaky roof.* help

hand 1. *verb* give, turn over, deliver, transfer, pass *The driver of the delivery truck handed me a package.* 2. *noun* worker, laborer, assistant, employee *Kyle has experience as a ranch hand, tending cattle and mending fences.* 3. assistance, help, aid, support *I need a hand with hooking up my computer.* 4. role, share, part, influence *The accused man claims he had no hand in the robbery.*

handbag *noun* purse, bag, pocketbook *The car keys are in my handbag.*

handicap 1. *noun* disadvantage, hindrance, obstacle, block, disability *My inability to speak Turkish was a handicap during my stay in Turkey.* asset 2. *verb* burden, impede, hinder, hamper *The quarterback's shoulder injury has really handicapped the team.* help

handle 1. *verb* touch, hold, feel, grasp *Handle the kitten gently.* 2. manage, direct, regulate, run, govern, carry on *My mother handles the money in the family.* 3. *noun* grip, handgrip, shaft, knob *Pick up the knife by the handle.*

handsome *adjective* good-looking, attractive, striking, beautiful *My dad is a handsome man. The neighborhood has many handsome old Victorian buildings.*

handwriting *noun* writing, penmanship, script *I can't read your handwriting—is this an "i" or an "e"?*

handy *adjective* 1. useful, helpful, practical, functional *A handheld computer is very handy for keeping track of addresses and appointments.* useless 2. available, accessible, convenient, nearby, ready *It's a good idea to keep several kinds of batteries handy.* inaccessible, inconvenient 3. skillful, adept, clever, proficient *Mom's really handy with a sewing machine and made us Halloween costumes.* unskilled, inept, clumsy

hang *verb* 1. suspend, swing, dangle, attach, fasten, put up, hang up *My baby brother has brightly colored mobiles hanging over his crib. I hung my clothes in the closet.* 2. execute, string up, lynch *Outlaws in America's Wild West were sometimes hanged.*

haphazard *adjective* random, unplanned, disorganized, chance, casual *Papers and magazines were stacked all over the office in a haphazard way.* planned, organized

happen *verb* take place, occur, come about, chance *What will happen if I just push the button to turn off my computer?*

happy *adjective* 1. glad, pleased, delighted, thrilled, contented *I'm so happy to see you.* unhappy 2. joyful, joyous, pleasing, cheerful *The story had a happy ending.* sad

harass *verb* annoy, bother, pester, trouble, torment *Crows will dive-bomb, chase, and harass hawks.*

harbor 1. *noun* port, anchorage, marina, dock, pier *Boats anchored in the harbor during the storm.* 2. *verb* shelter, protect, shield, defend, guard *The Underground Railroad was a network of houses that harbored slaves escaping from the South to the North.*

hard 1. *adjective* firm, solid, rigid, inflexible *On a backpacking trip, my friend slept in his sleeping bag without a mattress on hard ground.* soft 2. difficult, strenuous, laborious, tough, demanding, challenging *I thought the math test was really hard. Construction work involves hard physical labor.* easy 3. forceful, intense, violent, powerful *A big oak came down in last night's hard rain.* 4. *adverb* forcefully, energetically, vigorously, heavily, powerfully, with effort *We pushed hard on the door, but it wouldn't open.* 5. diligently, industriously, earnestly, persistently *The team has worked hard to get to the finals.*

hardly *adverb* barely, just, not quite, scarcely *I can hardly wait!*

hardship *noun* adversity, difficulty, trouble, misfortune, need, misery *The early settlers experienced many hardships.*

hardy *adjective* strong, healthy, fit, robust, sturdy, rugged, tough *Only hardy swimmers plunge into an icy lake on New Year's Day.* weak

harm 1. *noun* damage, hurt, injury, impairment *An occasional treat won't do the dog any harm.* 2. *verb* hurt, damage, injure, spoil, impair, wrong *Energy can be produced from wind without harming the environment.* help, improve

harmful *adjective* damaging, injurious, detrimental, dangerous, unsafe *Does TV violence have harmful effects on children?* harmless, helpful

harmless *adjective* safe, nontoxic, innocuous, innocent *Most snakes found in the United States are harmless.* harmful

harmony *noun* agreement, accord, fellowship, unity, rapport, peace *Our school is working hard to promote racial harmony among its students.*

harsh *adjective* 1. rough, coarse, grating, gruff, jarring, raucous *Ravens have a loud, harsh call.* pleasant 2. cruel, severe, bitter, sharp, cutting, piercing *A cold, harsh wind blew across the plains.* mild

harvest 1. *noun* crop, product, yield *The Pilgrims had a successful harvest in 1621 and celebrated the first Thanksgiving.* 2. *verb* reap, gather, pick, collect, glean *You can harvest your own apples right off the tree at our pick-your-own orchard.*

haste *noun* speed, rapidity, quickness, hurry, rush *In my haste to finish the dishes, I broke a glass.* slowness

hasten *verb* hurry, rush, dash, race, fly, run, speed *I hastened to open the door for my mom.*

hasty *adjective* quick, hurried, fast, swift, speedy, rapid *Our cat made a hasty retreat when he saw the dog.* slow

hat *noun* cap, headgear *The magician removed his hat from his head and pulled a rabbit from it.*

hatch *verb* 1. devise, concoct, make up, invent, originate, plan, plot, scheme *The prisoners hatched an escape plan.* 2. produce, emerge, be born *The tadpoles that hatched from the frogs' eggs were so tiny, we couldn't see them.*

hatchet *noun* ax, tomahawk *We use a hatchet to cut firewood when we're camping.*

hate *verb* dislike, loathe, detest, abhor, abominate *I hate the smell of cigarette smoke in my clothes.* love

hatred *noun* dislike, disgust, hate, animosity, loathing, abhorrence *Salina's hatred of rutabagas was evident from her expression. Some people have an irrational hatred of anyone who is different from them.* love

haughty *adjective* arrogant, conceited, self-important, proud, lofty, vain *The haughty queen in* Snow White *was content as long as her magic mirror told her she was the fairest in the land.* modest, humble

haul 1. *verb* pull, drag, draw, tug, tow *We hauled our baggage from the carousel out to the taxi stand.* 2. carry, transport, ship, convey, move *My brother rented a truck to haul his belongings to his new apartment.* 3. *noun* take, catch, yield *Fishing vessels can process, pack, and freeze their haul onboard.*

haunt *verb* 1. obsess, torment, disturb, trouble, worry *Stage fright has haunted many actors.* 2. inhabit, dwell, visit, frequent, possess *Legends tell of ghosts haunting castles.*

have *verb* 1. hold, possess, own, keep *My sister has a motor scooter.* 2. must, be forced, should, ought, need *I have to get home before dark.* 3. experience, encounter, meet, undergo, endure *I had a great time at camp. Dad's having trouble with his car.* 4. get, receive, obtain, acquire, accept, take *Please have a seat. I had a big breakfast.* 5. contain, comprise, include *Our house has three bedrooms.* 6. permit, tolerate, suffer, put up with, stand for *Our teacher won't have any disruptive behavior in class.*

haven *noun* shelter, safety, harbor, refuge, sanctuary *The tropical rain forest is a haven to more species of animals than any other part of the world.*

hay *noun* feed, fodder, forage *The dairy farmer grows hay for his cows.*

hazard *noun* risk, danger, peril, menace, threat *Road construction workers face life-threatening hazards.*

hazy *adjective* 1. misty, foggy, cloudy, overcast, smoggy *The weather report says it'll be mostly cloudy and hazy with showers likely.* clear 2. vague, obscure, indistinct, unclear, faint, blurred, fuzzy, uncertain, confused, muddled *I have only a hazy recollection of having met her.* clear

head 1. *noun* mind, brain, intellect, mentality, ability, talent, aptitude *Mom says Aunt Doris has a good head for business.* 2. director, manager, supervisor, administrator, leader, boss, chief *Professor Ramos is head of the Spanish Language Department at the university.* 3. front, beginning, start *People camped out overnight in order to be at the head of the line to buy concert tickets.* 4. *adjective* chief, leading, principal, main, top *Assistant Coach Barker was promoted to head coach.* 5. *verb* lead, direct, manage, supervise, administer, run, conduct *Lewis and Clark headed the expedition that explored the American West.* follow 6. go, proceed, move, aim, steer *We headed north out of town.*

heading *noun* title, caption, headline, name, banner *We put the headings in the school newspaper in bold type.*

headquarters *noun* main office, base, command center, center of operations *The headquarters of the United Nations is located in New York City.*

headstrong *adjective* stubborn, willful, obstinate, bullheaded *My sister has trouble controlling her headstrong horse.* docile

headway *noun* progress, advance, improvement, movement *The peace mission still faces problems but appears to have made some headway.* setback

heal *verb* cure, remedy, recover, mend, repair, correct *The doctor says my broken arm should heal in about four weeks.* damage, impair

health *noun* well-being, fitness, wellness, physical condition *It's important to eat right and exercise to maintain your health.* sickness

healthy *adjective* 1. fit, well, in good condition, sound *Granddad is healthy again after being sick for a couple of days.* sick, ill 2. healthful, wholesome, nourishing, nutritious, beneficial *Mom and Dad fix us healthy meals.*

heap 1. *noun* pile, mound, stack, mountain *We took heaps of newspapers and magazines to the recycling center.* 2. *verb* pile, stack, mound, load, gather, fill *Dad told me to put away the clothes heaped on my bed.*

hear *verb* 1. catch, make out, get, perceive *I didn't hear what you said—could you repeat it?* 2. listen to, pay attention to, heed *Hear ye, Hear ye! Court is now is session.*

heart *noun* 1. soul, spirit, temperament, feelings *James is patient and has a kind heart.* 2. warmth, sympathy, kindness, love, affection *In Pat's opinion, anyone who doesn't love animals has no heart.* 3. courage, nerve, enthusiasm, spirit *After Dad prepared a big meal, I didn't have the heart to tell him I wasn't hungry.* 4. middle, center, core, nucleus, hub *The closer you get to the heart of the city, the worse the traffic.* 5. substance, essence, main part, meat *We need to get straight to the heart of the problem.*

hearty *adjective* 1. enthusiastic, sincere, warm, cordial, fervent *The performance received hearty applause.* indifferent 2. substantial, nourishing, filling, ample *Grandma always serves us a hearty meal.*

heat 1. *noun* warmth, hotness, warmness *The heat from the fireplace was welcome after a day of skiing.* cool, cold 2. *verb* warm, make hot, warm up *We heated some milk and made hot chocolate.* cool, cool down

heave *verb* 1. lift, raise, hoist, pull, haul, lug, tug, tow, drag *We heaved our canoes up onto shore.* 2. throw, cast, pitch, fling, hurl, toss, dump *Terry heaved the garbage into the trash cans.*

heaven *noun* paradise, bliss, ecstasy, joy, contentment *It's heaven being able to snuggle under a warm quilt on a cold night.*

heavenly *adjective* blissful, delightful, enjoyable, marvelous, wonderful, fantastic *A roasting turkey on Thanksgiving smells heavenly.*

heavy *adjective* 1. weighty, bulky, hefty, massive, big, large, huge *We dragged the heavy trunk down from the attic.* light 2. laborious, hard, difficult, tough, demanding, tedious *Heavy yard work should be done early in the day, when it's still cool.* light 3. considerable, abundant, plentiful, dense *Traffic is heavy during rush hour.* light

hectic *adjective* frantic, busy, frenzied, bustling, chaotic *Mom came home after a hectic day at work and fell asleep on the sofa.* calm, relaxed

hedge 1. *noun* shrubbery, bushes, border, hedgerow *Dad bought an electric trimmer for the hedge beside our house.* 2. *verb* fence, enclose, surround, ring *Bushes and trees hedged the estate.*

heed *verb* follow, observe, mind, obey, notice, pay attention to *Grandpa is heeding his doctor's advice to eat a healthier diet and get more exercise.* ignore

height *noun* 1. elevation, altitude, tallness, stature *Denver's height is one mile above sea level. I have already grown one inch in height this year.* 2. top, summit, peak, crown, tip, apex, highest point *Michael Jordan left basketball at the height of his career to play baseball.* bottom

hello *interjection* greetings, good day, good morning, good afternoon, good evening, hi *Hello, how are you today?*

help 1. *verb* aid, assist, lend a hand, support *The bag boy helped Mom carry the groceries to the car.* 2. relieve, benefit, soothe, ease, alleviate *All you can do when you have a cold is take something to help the symptoms.* hinder 3. *noun* aid, assistance, hand, support, guidance *If you need any help, just ask.*

helpful *adjective* useful, beneficial, valuable, practical *The teacher gave me several helpful suggestions on ways to improve my writing.* useless

helpless *adjective* powerless, defenseless, weak, vulnerable, feeble *The lost little boy looked frightened and helpless.*

herd 1. *noun* drove, pack, group, crowd, horde, throng, mass *The buffalo herd in Yellowstone National Park has grown to more than four thousand.* 2. *verb* drive, direct, guide, round up, gather, collect *Border collies were bred to herd sheep out of the hills.*

here *adverb* 1. to this place, to this spot *Bring the book here.* there 2. now, at present, at this time *Let's stop here and continue tomorrow.* later 3. present, in attendance *Is everyone here?* absent

heritage *noun* inheritance, legacy, tradition, birthright *Our heritage includes freedom of religion, of speech, and of the press.*

hero *noun* champion, heroine, idol, icon, ideal, example, model *A hero is someone I admire for his or her courage and selflessness.*

heroic *adjective* brave, gallant, valiant, courageous, bold, chivalrous, fearless *Mother Teresa lived a heroic life helping the poorest people in the world.*

hesitate *verb* pause, delay, wait, hang back, waver, falter *I hesitated before asking for the star's autograph.*

hibernate *verb* sleep, slumber, overwinter (*Slang*—hole up) *Bears go into their dens in fall and hibernate until spring.*

hide *verb* conceal, cover up, screen, cloak, veil, mask *Be sure to hide the present we got*

Dad for Father's Day in the hall closet, where he definitely won't find it.

hideous *adjective* ugly, frightful, horrible, horrid, dreadful, terrible, repulsive, ghastly *The actor was made up to look like a hideous monster.* beautiful

high 1. *adjective* tall, lofty, towering, soaring *Mount McKinley, in Alaska, is 20,320 feet high and is the highest mountain in the United States.* low 2. excessive, extreme, elevated, above average *When the temperature is so high, it's uncomfortable without air-conditioning.* low 3. chief, main, important, powerful, leading, prominent, eminent *High government officials meet today to discuss the plan.* unimportant 4. intense, violent, strong, fierce, forceful *High winds damaged a tree in the yard.* light 5. shrill, sharp, piercing *The red-tailed hawk emits a scream at a high pitch while soaring.* 6. *noun* peak, summit, record, maximum *Gas prices reached an all-time high.* low

highway *noun* road, freeway, expressway, interstate, turnpike, thruway *The highway that bypasses the city has less traffic.*

hike 1. *verb* walk, trek, tramp, stroll, ramble, trudge *During summer vacations Emily hiked the Rocky Mountain National Park trails.* 2. *noun* walk, stroll, trek, amble *I like to take an afternoon hike through the woods.*

hilarious *adjective* funny, humorous, comical, amusing, uproarious *My brother thinks British comedy on cable TV is hilarious.*

hill *noun* mound, knoll, rise, slope *In winter my friends and I go sledding on the hill in the park.*

hind *adjective* back, rear *A kangaroo's hind legs are very powerful.* front

hinder *verb* obstruct, impede, stop, check, curb, hold back *Road construction hindered travelers.* help

hinge on *verb* depend on, rest on, revolve around, center on *Whether or not we go to the beach hinges on the weather.*

hint 1. *verb* suggest, imply, intimate, insinuate *Dad hinted that if I helped out with the yard work, we might be able to go out for pizza tonight.* 2. *noun* clue, sign, indication, inkling, suggestion *Just give me a hint—what am I getting for my birthday?*

hire *verb* 1. employ, engage, take on, contract *The school hired a substitute teacher when our teacher had a baby.* fire 2. rent, lease, let, charter *Dad hired a car when we arrived at the airport.*

history *noun* 1. record, chronicle, account, story *Native Americans want to collect and preserve their oral histories and legends for their children.* 2. the past, antiquity, yesterday

We learn from history how to keep from making the same mistakes. the present

hit 1. *verb* strike, knock, punch, poke, slug, sock, bat, swat, whack, smack *The batter hit the ball into the stands for a home run.* 2. affect, impress, strike, touch, move, influence *It suddenly hit me that my sister left for college and I wouldn't see her until Thanksgiving.* 3. *noun* blow, knock, punch, swat, slap, whack, crack *The tree took a direct hit from the lightning.* 4. success, triumph, sensation, smash, winner *The puppet show was a hit with the children.* failure, flop

hitch 1. *verb* fasten, attach, join, unite, couple, hook, tie, bind, clip, snap, latch *Let's hitch the boat to the pickup and go fishing.* 2. *noun* obstacle, block, snag, catch, difficulty, drawback *I installed the game on my computer without a hitch.*

hoard 1. *verb* save, store, collect, accumulate, amass, gather *Red squirrels hoard large quantities of food for winter in burrows, nearby trees, and their nests.* use up 2. *noun* stock, supply, accumulation, mass, cache, collection, stockpile *Early expeditions to Central and South America returned to Europe with hoards of gold.*

hoarse *adjective* rough, harsh, husky, gruff *A bullfrog has a hoarse croak.*

hoax *noun* trick, joke, prank, deception, fraud, swindle, con *A picture that was said to be of the Loch Ness Monster turned out to be a hoax.*

hobby *noun* pastime, leisure interest, recreation, amusement, diversion *Abby collects rocks as a hobby.*

hoe *verb* dig, till, loosen, plow *I like helping Mom hoe the weeds from our garden.*

hoist *verb* raise, lift, elevate, boost *We hoisted the canoe onto the roof of the car.* lower

hold 1. *verb* grasp, grip, clutch, cling to, clasp *Hold my hand while we cross the street.* 2. contain, accommodate, store, comprise, include *How much data does this computer disk hold?* 3. support, bear, take, carry *The ice on the skating pond isn't thick enough to hold our weight.* 4. remain, continue, last, stay, go on, persist, endure *The ceasefire is expected to hold through the winter.* 5. conduct, arrange, have, run, organize *We're holding a graduation party for my sister.* 6. keep, occupy, maintain, engage *The movie didn't hold our interest, so we left early.* 7. consider, think, regard as, view, deem *My parents hold me responsible for my actions.* 8. *noun* grip, grasp, clutch, clasp *Get a firm hold on the ladder.*

hole *noun* 1. hollow, pit, cavity, crater, excavation, depression *The farmer is digging holes for fence posts all around the field.* 2. gap, opening, crack, space, tear *I have a hole in the toe of my sock.*

holiday *noun* 1. vacation, leave, break, time off *We get a holiday this week so teachers can hold conferences with our parents.* 2. celebration, festival, holy day *July 4 is the holiday on which the United States celebrates its independence.*

hollow 1. *adjective* empty, vacant, bare, void *Some owls nest in hollow trees.* 2. *noun* hole, cavity, pit, depression, crater, recess, indentation *Water filled the hollow to form a small pond.* 3. *verb* dig, excavate, scoop, gouge *You can hollow out a gourd to make a bowl.*

holy *adjective* sacred, spiritual, religious, divine *Jerusalem is considered a holy place by Judaism, Christianity, and Islam.*

home *noun* 1. house, dwelling, residence *Our home is at 432 South Adams Street.* 2. institution, residential facility, assisted living, senior housing *Great-Grandpa was playing cards with his friends in the nursing home when we visited.*

homeland *noun* native land, mother country, fatherland, birthplace *My ancestors left their homeland to seek a better life for their families.*

homely *adjective* unattractive, plain, ugly, unlovely *We adopted a homely, but lovable, little dog.*

homework *noun* assignment, schoolwork, lesson, task *We have to read chapter three as our homework for tonight.*

honest *adjective* fair, trustworthy, good, decent, honorable, upright, sincere, truthful *An honest storekeeper will stand behind what he or she sells.*

honesty *noun* fairness, goodness, integrity, honor, truthfulness, trustworthiness *Dad always answers my questions with complete honesty.*

honk *verb* toot, blast, blare, beep, blow *The driver behind us honked his horn the second the light turned green.*

honor 1. *noun* honesty, integrity, decency, morality, virtue *People of honor keep their promises.* 2. distinction, acclaim, praise, commendation, award *Someone who graduates "summa cum laude" from college graduates with highest honors.* 3. *verb* praise, commend, acclaim, pay tribute to *Memorial Day is a holiday to honor U.S. men and women who have died in military service for their country.* 4. *verb* keep, carry out, fulfill *My parents honored their promise to get me a puppy when I was old enough to care for it.*

hook 1. *verb* fasten, attach, secure, clasp, clip, snap, latch *Mom asked Dad to hook her necklace for her.* unhook, unfasten 2. *noun* fastener, catch, clasp, peg *Hang your jacket on the hook in the closet.*

hop 1. *verb* spring, jump, bound, leap, bounce, vault *The rabbit hopped into the woods.* 2. *noun* jump, leap, bound, bounce *The ball took two quick hops before it landed.* 3. trip, journey, flight *It's just a short hop from New York City to Washington, D.C.*

hope 1. *verb* wish, want, expect, desire, look forward to, anticipate *I hope to see you again soon.* 2. *noun* wish, desire, expectation, dream, aspiration, goal *It's our hope that you will succeed. Nell's hope is to become an architect.*

hopeful *adjective* 1. confident, optimistic, expectant *Darrell is hopeful that he will recover from his injury in time to play in next week's game.* 2. promising, encouraging, reassuring, favorable *The return of the robins is a hopeful sign that spring is coming.* discouraging

hopeless *adjective* unpromising, impossible, futile, useless, pointless *Mom says keeping my room clean is a hopeless task.* promising

horde *noun* crowd, swarm, multitude, throng, mob, force, pack *The beaches attract a horde of swimmers on a hot day.*

horizontal *adjective* level, flat, straight, plane *To do sit-ups, lie down on a horizontal surface and bend your knees.* vertical

horrible *adjective* 1. frightful, shocking, terrible, dreadful, ghastly *The creature in the movie was a horrible sight.* 2. bad, nasty, unpleasant, disagreeable *The medicine had a horrible taste.* pleasant

horrid *adjective* disgusting, terrible, dreadful, nasty, vile *The garbage truck has a horrid smell.* pleasant

horror *noun* fear, dread, terror, shock, alarm, panic *Soldiers wrote of their feelings of horror during the war.*

horse *noun* steed, colt, mare, stallion *Cousin Steve let me ride his horse around the corral.*

hose *noun* tube, pipe *I hooked the hose to the outside faucet so Dad could water the garden.*

hospital *noun* medical center, clinic, health-care center *My sister came home from the hospital after having her appendix removed.*

host *noun* hostess, receptionist, entertainer, proprietor *We thanked our hosts before we left the party.*

hostile *adjective* unfriendly, bitter, antagonistic, belligerent, aggressive, militant *The dictator faced a hostile crowd.* friendly

hot *adjective* 1. boiling, steaming, scorching, torrid, sizzling, roasting, sweltering, sultry *The deserts of the Southwest are hot and dry. A hot shower feels good on a cold morning.* cold 2. spicy, peppery, fiery, sharp, biting *I like hot Mexican food.* bland 3. angry, passionate, intense, fiery, fervent, torrid *Andrew sometimes has trouble controlling his hot temper.*

hotel *noun* inn, bed-and-breakfast, motel, lodging, hostel *We spent two nights in hotels on our way to visit my aunt and uncle.*

hound 1. *noun* dog, greyhound, bloodhound, foxhound, wolfhound, basset hound, hunting dog *Buddy is part hound and is a very smart animal.* 2. *verb* harass, pester, bully, badger, press *Fans hounded the star for autographs.*

house 1. *noun* home, residence, dwelling, condominium, abode *Our house has three bedrooms.* 2. building, place, establishment *The old movie house has been replaced with a huge theater showing six movies at a time.* 3. *verb* accommodate, shelter, have room for, lodge, sleep *The cabin at the lake houses six people.*

hover *verb* 1. float, drift, sail, fly, hang, flutter *A hummingbird hovered over the flowers.* 2. linger, hang around, loiter *The cat hovered near the kitchen waiting to be fed.*

however *conjunction* nevertheless, yet, still, although, but *I like chocolate chip cookies; however, brownies are my favorite.*

howl 1. *verb* cry, yell, bawl, bellow, wail, scream, screech, shriek *The wind picked up and began to howl.* 2. *noun* cry, wail, shriek, yowl, bellow *My little sister let out a howl when the nurse gave her a shot.*

hub *noun* center, nucleus, core, heart, focus *Chicago's and Atlanta's airports are traffic hubs for major airlines.*

huddle 1. *noun* cluster, bunch, clump, gathering, group, pack *We sat in a huddle around the campfire to keep warm.* 2. *verb* cluster, bunch, crowd, gather, flock, assemble, congregate *The baby birds huddled together in their nest.*

hue *noun* color, tint, shade *The sky often takes on hues of red, orange, and yellow at sunset.*

hug 1. *verb* hold, clasp, embrace, enfold, squeeze, cuddle *My little brother fell asleep hugging his teddy bear.* 2. *noun* embrace, squeeze, clasp, cuddle *I gave Grandma a big hug when she arrived.*

huge *adjective* very large, enormous, gigantic, immense, tremendous, great, vast, monumental *Whales are huge animals. Some sports stars make huge sums of money.*

hum 1. *verb* drone, buzz, whir, murmur *Bees hummed among the flowers.* 2. *noun* buzz, drone, whir *On a quiet night we can always hear the hum of distant traffic.*

human *noun* person, human being, individual, mortal *Men, women, and children are humans.*

humane *adjective* kind, good, gracious, warmhearted, sympathetic, compassionate, considerate *Laws require the humane treatment of prisoners of war.*

humble *adjective* 1. modest, meek, shy, unpretentious *The star remained humble despite her success.* vain 2. plain, simple, modest, common, lowly, poor *Abraham Lincoln came a long way from his humble beginnings to become president.*

humid *adjective* moist, damp, wet, muggy, steamy *We've had a hot, humid summer.*

humiliate *verb* embarrass, disgrace, shame, mortify, dishonor, disgrace *School bullies try to humiliate others by picking on them.* honor, dignify

humor 1. *noun* wit, comedy, funniness *Slapstick humor makes me laugh out loud.* 2. mood, temper, disposition, frame of mind *Our neighbor is eighty-three and is still healthy, active, and in good humor.* 3. *verb* cater to, give in to, pamper, spoil, coddle, oblige, please, satisfy *Mom and Dad humor me by giving me anything I want when I'm sick.*

hump *noun* bump, bulge, lump, swelling *A dromedary camel has a single hump on its back.*

hunch *noun* feeling, suspicion, impression *I have a hunch that my friends are planning a surprise party for my birthday.*

hunger 1. *noun* appetite, craving, hungriness, starvation *Hunger is making my stomach growl.* 2. *verb* crave, desire, want, yearn, long *Refugees, hungering for a better life, came to the United States.*

hungry *adjective* 1. famished, starving, starved, ravenous *The hikers were tired and hungry at the end of the day.* 2. eager, desirous, yearning, craving, greedy *The soldiers were hungry for news from home.*

hunk *noun* piece, chunk, lump, mass *An apple and a hunk of cheese is my favorite snack.*

hunt 1. *verb* search, look, seek, rummage *I hunted under my bed for the missing sock.* 2. pursue, chase, track, stalk *Lions hunt their prey mostly at night to avoid the heat of day.* 3. *noun* search, quest, expedition, pursuit *Many people went to California to join in the hunt for gold.*

hurdle 1. *noun* obstacle, barrier, difficulty, problem, hitch, catch, snag *Learning English can be a major hurdle for newcomers to the United States.* 2. *verb* leap, jump, vault, bound over *Jamie's horse hurdled the fence.*

~~~~~~

hurl *verb* throw, fling, pitch, toss, cast, heave, launch, propel *He hurled the spear, which glanced off the knight's shield.*

hurricane *noun* typhoon, tropical storm, cyclone, gale, whirlwind *The hurricane caused a great deal of damage along the Gulf Coast.*

hurry 1. *verb* rush, speed, hasten, hustle, dash, run *We hurried to catch the bus.* 2. *noun* rush, haste, bustle, urgency *What's the hurry? We have plenty of time.*

hurt *verb* 1. injure, harm, wound, damage, impair, spoil *Dad hurt his back moving the refrigerator. Oil spills hurt the environment.* help, benefit 2. ache, be sore, be painful, sting *I hurt my knee when I went running.* 3. upset, distress, offend, insult *I didn't mean to hurt your feelings.*

husband *noun* spouse, mate, married man *My uncle George is Aunt Janet's husband.*

husky *adjective* 1. strong, big, sturdy, burly, muscular *Two husky men delivered our new piano.* 2. hoarse, harsh, rough, raspy, gruff *Dad's husky voice is a result of yelling at the ball game.* smooth

hustle *verb* hasten, speed, rush, hurry, dash, run *We need to hustle if we're going to be on time.*

hut *noun* cabin, shed, shack, shanty *Some of the huts used as shelter by expeditions to the South Pole still survive.*

hysterical *adjective* frantic, frenzied, overexcited, upset, beside oneself *Anna is so frightened of mice that she becomes hysterical when she sees one.*

I

ice *noun* frozen water, sleet, frost *The ice on the pond needs to be six inches thick before we skate on it.*

ice cream *noun* frozen dessert, sherbet, ice-cream cone *For dessert we had ice cream with strawberries on top.*

icing *noun* frosting, topping, glaze *My favorite cake is chocolate with chocolate icing on top.*

idea *noun* thought, plan, concept, notion, opinion, view, feeling *I wonder where Dr. Seuss got his ideas for his stories. The idea of skydiving terrifies me.*

ideal 1. *adjective* best, perfect, ultimate, model *A hot summer day is an ideal day to be at the lake.* imperfect 2. *noun* standard, principle, model, value *My parents help me set high ideals to live by.*

identical *adjective* same, alike, matching, like, duplicate, exact *The twins next door always wear identical outfits.* different

identify *verb* recognize, know, distinguish, place, make out, tell, name *I'm able to identify many of the birds at our birdfeeder.*

idiot *noun* fool, dummy *I felt like an idiot when I called your friend Danny by the wrong name.*

idle 1. *adjective* inactive, unoccupied, vacant, at rest, unused *The old factory sits idle. Dad wishes he had more idle hours so he could go fishing.* busy, occupied 2. lazy, loafing, shiftless *Our teacher won't tolerate idle students in his class.* ambitious 3. useless, futile, pointless, worthless, fruitless *Don't make idle promises you don't intend to keep.* worthwhile 4. *verb* loaf, laze, while, fritter, lounge *Jennie idled away the afternoon reading magazines.*

idol *noun* 1. hero, ideal, favorite, star *The astronauts are my idols.* 2. image, icon, statue, symbol, god *The ancient people made sacrifices to their idols.*

igloo *noun* ice hut, Inuit hut, shelter *Igloos are made of snow and ice.*

ignite *verb* burn, set on fire, light, kindle *Dad ignited the charcoal in the backyard barbecue.*

ignorant *adjective* 1. uninformed, unaware, unfamiliar *Explorers set out for the New World, ignorant of what lay ahead.* informed, knowledgeable 2. uneducated, illiterate, unschooled, unenlightened *I felt completely ignorant in Mexico when I couldn't speak Spanish.* educated

ignore *verb* 1. disregard, overlook *I tried to ignore their rude behavior.* 2. snub, slight, avoid, spurn *The salesclerk ignored me when I tried to get his attention.*

ill 1. *adjective* sick, unwell, ailing, unhealthy, indisposed *I was ill and stayed home from school for two days.* healthy 2. unkind, unfriendly, bad, hostile *There were ill feelings between the Hatfield and McCoy families.* good 3. adverse, unfavorable, harmful *Elizabeth had the ill luck to slip on the ice and break her ankle.* good 4. *noun* evil, trouble, harm, misfortune, bad luck *She meant you no ill.* good

illegal *adjective* unlawful, criminal, against the law, forbidden, illicit, illegitimate *Shoplifting is illegal.* legal, lawful

illness *noun* sickness, disease, ailment, disorder, malady, affliction *Gail's illness caused her to miss school.*

illuminate *verb* light, brighten, light up, spotlight *The ice-skating pond is illuminated at night.*

illusion *noun* deception, delusion, misconception, misapprehension, fallacy, error *Many people have the illusion that money can buy happiness. I was under the illusion that I wouldn't have to study for the test.*

illustrate *verb* 1. clarify, explain, show, demonstrate *The speaker illustrated his point with a story.* 2. add pictures to, add graphics to, provide artwork for, decorate *I illustrated a storybook for my class project.*

image *noun* likeness, representation, picture, reflection, resemblance *The images of four presidents are carved into Mount Rushmore.*

imaginary *adjective* make-believe, fictional, made-up, unreal, fantasy *Unicorns are imaginary creatures.*

imagination *noun* 1. creativity, originality, vision, insight, inspiration *The teacher said my poem showed imagination.* 2. illusion, dream, fancy, fantasy *Conrad says it wasn't his imagination—he really saw a ghost.*

imagine *verb* 1. picture, envision, visualize, conceive, dream of, fantasize about *I'm trying to imagine how my grandparents got along without computers.* 2. suppose, assume, guess, presume, gather *I imagine we'll see you at the party.*

imitate *verb* copy, act like, mimic, mirror, reflect, echo, emulate, repeat *My friend's parrot imitates the words it hears.*

imitation 1. *noun* copy, duplicate, reproduction, simulation *The restaurant is an imitation of a Paris café.* 2. *adjective* simulated, mock, synthetic, artificial *Doreen's jacket is imitation leather.*

immature *adjective* childish, babyish, juvenile, infantile *I apologized to my dad for my uncooperative, immature behavior.*

immediate *adjective* 1. instant, prompt, quick, swift, speedy, instantaneous *I got an immediate reply to my e-mail.* 2. near, close, adjacent, adjoining, next *My best friend is also my immediate neighbor.*

immediately *adverb* now, instantly, promptly, right away, at once, without delay *We need to leave immediately or we'll be late for our flight.* later

immense *adjective* huge, large, enormous, gigantic, vast *The Sahara is a huge desert, stretching from the Atlantic Ocean to the Red Sea.* tiny, small

immerse *verb* 1. submerge, plunge, sink, dip, dunk *After skiing, we immersed ourselves in the hot tub.* 2. absorb, engross, occupy, engage, enthrall, fascinate *Carolyn was so immersed in her book that she didn't hear me come in.*

immigrate *verb* enter, come into, settle, relocate *Many Hmong families immigrated to the United States from Laos after the Vietnam War.* leave, emigrate

imminent *adjective* nearing, approaching, coming, impending, forthcoming, close, near *Species listed as endangered are those that are in imminent danger of extinction.*

immoral *adjective* wrong, wicked, evil, bad, sinful *Most people understand that racism and oppression are immoral.*

immune *adjective* resistant, safe, protected, free, spared, exempt *There are some diseases that you are immune to after you have had them once.* susceptible

impact *noun* 1. collision, crash, blow, force, shock, contact *The moon's craters resulted from the impact of asteroids, meteors, and meteorites on its surface.* 2. effect, influence, consequence, result *Personal computers have had a big impact on our lives.*

impair *verb* damage, harm, weaken, hurt, make worse *Loud noises can impair your hearing.* improve, help

impartial *adjective* fair, neutral, unprejudiced, unbiased, uninfluenced *A judge must be impartial.*

impatient *adjective* 1. restless, anxious, eager, excited *I'm impatient for summer to come.* 2. annoyed, irritated, exasperated, agitated, aggravated, intolerant *Drivers stuck in traffic began getting impatient and beeping their horns.*

imperative *adjective* urgent, necessary, compulsory, pressing, crucial, critical, mandatory *It's imperative that you never swim alone.*

imperfect *adjective* defective, faulty, deficient, blemished, marred, incomplete, inadequate *The company will exchange imperfect goods or goods damaged in shipping.*

imperial *adjective* majestic, royal, regal, supreme, stately, magnificent *The emperor lived in the imperial palace.*

impersonal *adjective* unfriendly, cold, unwelcoming, businesslike *The food at the restaurant was good, but the service was impersonal.* friendly

implement 1. *noun* tool, utensil, instrument, apparatus, device, contraption *Hoes, spades, and trowels are garden implements.* 2. *verb* carry out, get done, bring about, complete *Mom implemented a new plan for assigning chores.*

imply *verb* suggest, hint, intimate, infer, insinuate *I didn't mean to imply that you were wrong.*

impolite *adjective* rude, discourteous, disrespectful, ill-mannered, insolent *It's impolite to interrupt someone when he or she is talking.* polite

import *verb* bring in, admit, introduce, receive, take in *The store sells goods imported from countries throughout the world.* export

important *adjective* 1. meaningful, valuable, significant, critical, serious *Knowing how to use a computer is an important skill.* unimportant, insignificant 2. prominent, influential, leading, notable, powerful *The mayor of our city is an important person.* unimportant

impose *verb* 1. put, place, set, charge, levy, burden with, force *The legislature voted to impose a sales tax on goods sold in the state.* 2. be a burden, intrude, take advantage, inconvenience *I don't want to impose, but could you lend me a pen? Please stay for dinner— you won't be imposing on us at all.*

imposing *adjective* impressive, dramatic, spectacular, grand, magnificent, stately, majestic *The Eiffel Tower is an imposing structure.* unimpressive

impossible *adjective* inconceivable, unimaginable, unthinkable, unachievable, absurd *Mom took one look at my room and said it would be an impossible task to clean it.* possible

impostor *noun* fraud, fake, phony, quack, pretender, impersonator *The movie is about an imposter who posed as a doctor, lawyer, and airline copilot before he was finally caught.*

impractical *adjective* unfeasible, unworkable, unrealistic *High-heeled shoes are impractical for hiking.* practical

impress *verb* affect, strike, move, sway, influence, inspire *The exhibits at the National Air and Space Museum really impressed me.*

impression *noun* 1. impact, effect, influence *I want to make a good first impression on my new teacher.* 2. feeling, sense, inkling, suspicion, opinion *I have the impression I've met you before.* 3. indentation, mark, stamp, outline, imprint *You can make a leaf impression by pressing a leaf between two pieces of white paper.*

impressive *adjective* affecting, moving, exciting, rousing, powerful *The symphony orchestra gave an impressive performance.*

improper *adjective* wrong, incorrect, unsuitable, inappropriate, unfit, bad *Dress codes tell you what is considered improper clothing for the classroom.*

improve *verb* better, progress, develop, advance, perfect, mend *The city is trying to improve living conditions for needy families.*

improvement *noun* betterment, advancement, progress, development, enhancement *DVDs are an improvement in quality over videotapes.*

improvise *verb* invent, make up, devise, originate, create, rig *Dad and I improvised a playhouse for my little sister out of a refrigerator carton.*

impulse *noun* sudden thought, notion, whim, urge, desire, wish, inclination, fancy *On an impulse, the whole family went out for pizza and a movie.*

impulsive *adjective* hasty, unplanned, rash, reckless, foolish, spontaneous *My sister made an impulsive purchase of a violin, but has yet to learn to play it.*

in *preposition* into, within, inside *My father is in the house. Your jacket is hanging in the closet.*

inability *noun* incapability, incapacity, incompetence, ineptitude, failure *Mai overcame her inability to speak English after she had been in the United States for only a year.* ability

inaccurate *adjective* incorrect, wrong, mistaken, inexact, erroneous, faulty *Early estimates of the size of the crowd were inaccurate.* accurate

inactive *adjective* idle, sluggish, motionless, still, calm *Many animals find shelter in holes and burrows, and remain inactive throughout the winter.* active

inappropriate *adjective* unfitting, unsuitable, unacceptable, improper, wrong *Talking and laughing during a lesson is inappropriate behavior in a classroom.*

inaugurate *verb* 1. install, induct *Every four years we inaugurate a president of the United States.* 2. begin, start, commence, initiate, introduce *The prime minister inaugurated a conference on economic development.* close, end

incapable *adjective* unable, incompetent, unfit, unqualified, powerless *Dad had to fire an incapable employee today. Our team proved itself incapable of beating the state champions.*

incense *verb* anger, enrage, infuriate, exasperate, provoke, irritate *The cruel treatment of animals incenses me.*

incentive *noun* encouragement, inducement, stimulus, motivation, inspiration *An end-of-season sale was the incentive I needed to buy a new baseball glove.*

incident *noun* happening, event, occurrence, experience *Our assignment today in English class was to write about a strange or amusing incident in our lives.*

incline 1. *verb* lean, tilt, slope, tip, slant *We followed a dirt road that inclined slightly downhill.* 2. *noun* slope, grade, hill *The mountain trail had many steep inclines.*

include *verb* contain, comprise, cover, enclose, incorporate, encompass, take in, add, admit, involve *The group includes students ages eight through twelve. Be sure to include them in the invitation.* exclude

income *noun* earnings, wages, salary, pay, receipts, proceeds, profits *Our landlord's income comes from rent.*

incompetent *adjective* incapable, unfit, unqualified, unsuitable, inept, inadequate, unable *Mom said she was an incompetent cook for at least a year after she and Dad were married.* competent, able

incomplete *adjective* unfinished, deficient, lacking, wanting, partial, imperfect *The lawn work is incomplete because it started to rain.* complete

inconsiderate *adjective* thoughtless, unmindful, unkind, tactless, insensitive *How inconsiderate of him to not ask you to sit down.* considerate, thoughtful

inconvenience 1. *noun* bother, trouble, annoyance, difficulty, nuisance *It's a real inconvenience to have to retrieve the newspaper from the bushes.* 2. *verb* bother, disturb, trouble, annoy *Would it inconvenience you to pick up the kids at school?*

incorrect *adjective* wrong, inaccurate, erroneous, mistaken, false *Jane had only one incorrect answer on the test.*

increase 1. *verb* enlarge, expand, extend, add to, boost, raise *We increased the size of the garden so we can grow more vegetables.* 2. *noun* expansion, growth, enlargement, addition, rise, advance *There has been an increase in the price of gas.*

incredible *adjective* 1. unbelievable, doubtful, preposterous, absurd, ridiculous, implausible *The stories I've heard about people being carried away by aliens seem incredible.* 2. amazing, astonishing, awesome, extraordinary, fantastic, fabulous *The Olympic athletes give incredible performances.*

indeed *adverb* in fact, in truth, really, absolutely, positively, certainly, definitely, surely, of course *She is indeed my favorite author.*

indefinite *adjective* unclear, vague, hazy, uncertain, obscure, confused, general, broad *Donna was indefinite about where we should meet.*

independence *noun* freedom, liberty, self-reliance, self-sufficiency *My parents say that if I continue to use good judgment, I'll be allowed some independence.*

independent *adjective* 1. self-governing, autonomous, sovereign, free *In 1810 Mexico became an independent country.* 2. self-reliant, self-sufficient *My sister found a good job and is completely independent.*

index *noun* guide, catalog, key, table, chart, file *The index tells you where in the book to find the information.*

indicate *verb* show, point out, designate, specify *Road signs indicated the direction of the state park.*

indifferent *adjective* unconcerned, apathetic, uninterested, detached, uncaring *How can they be indifferent to the suffering of the hurricane victims?* concerned

indirect *adjective* roundabout, meandering, out-of-the-way, circuitous, devious *We took the indirect route rather than the main highway in order to enjoy the scenery.* direct

individual 1. *adjective* separate, single, sole, lone, distinct *We wrapped and packed the individual glasses carefully so they wouldn't break.* 2. distinctive, special, personal, peculiar, unique *The twins may look alike, but they have individual personalities.* 3. *noun* human, human being, person, man, woman, being *Many individuals as well as organizations are helping in the relief effort.*

indulge *verb* humor, please, gratify, satisfy, cater to, pamper, coddle, spoil *Now and then I indulge my craving for chocolate.*

industrious *adjective* hardworking, diligent, conscientious, energetic, tireless, busy *Kim is an industrious student and gets good grades.*

industry *noun* business, trade, commerce *Deborah works in the advertising industry.*

inedible *adjective* uneatable *The meat is so tough, it's inedible.* edible

inefficient *adjective* ineffective, useless, unproductive, wasteful *A gas-guzzling car is inefficient.* efficient

inequality *noun* unevenness, imbalance, discrepancy, disparity *Inequality exists between rich and poor in the health-care system.*

inert *adjective* motionless, inactive, unmoving, immobile, still, lifeless *The* *nonpoisonous hognose snake will protect itself by lying inert, belly-up, pretending to be dead until a predator loses interest.*

inevitable *adjective* certain, inescapable, sure, unavoidable, fated, destined *Cold winters are inevitable in the northern Great Plains.*

inexpensive *adjective* low-priced, cheap, reasonable, economical, bargain-priced *My sister found an inexpensive sweater that had never been worn at the resale shop.* expensive

inexperienced *adjective* lacking experience, inexpert, green, new, unskilled, untried *An inexperienced worker can be trained to do the job.* experienced

infant *noun* baby, newborn, small child, tot, toddler *The infant slept in his car seat.*

infected *adjective* contaminated, sick, ill, diseased *Seventy percent of the school became infected with the flu virus.*

infectious *adjective* contagious, communicable, transmittable, catching *Children with infectious diseases should stay home until they're well.*

infer *verb* conclude, deduce, gather, assume, presume, expect, imagine *I inferred from the look on Dad's face when we got home that we were in big trouble.*

inferior *adjective* 1. lower, lesser, worse, subordinate, secondary, minor *The picture quality of this TV is inferior to that of the other one we looked at.* superior 2. poor, substandard, shoddy, bad *The store sold inferior products and soon went out of business.* superior

infinite *adjective* limitless, boundless, endless, eternal, ceaseless, perpetual *Our teacher has infinite patience. Space appears to be infinite.* finite

inflate *verb* expand, swell, blow up *We used a pump to inflate our air mattress.* deflate

influence 1. *noun* effect, impact, control, power *Jan's influence on her younger sister has been good.* 2. *verb* affect, have an impact on, sway, determine, guide, control *Advertising influences what products we choose to buy.*

inform *verb* tell, communicate, advise, enlighten, instruct, notify, report *I e-mailed all my friends to inform them of the party.*

infrequent *adjective* rare, occasional, scattered, irregular, sparse, sporadic *I look forward to my cousin's infrequent visits.* frequent

infuriate *verb* anger, enrage, madden, rile, incense, exasperate *The bully's taunts infuriate me.*

ingenious *adjective* clever, brilliant, imaginative, inventive, original, creative *A robot that will clean my room is an ingenious idea.* unoriginal, dull

ingredient *noun* part, component, constituent, element, factor *Mom always reads the list of ingredients on food packages.*

inhabit *verb* live in, reside in, dwell in, occupy, lodge in, stay in, room in *Foxes inhabit every continent except Antarctica.*

inhale *verb* breathe in, sniff, smell, gasp *I inhaled the fresh morning air.* exhale

inherit *verb* receive, come into, be left *Grandpa inherited the farm from his father.*

initial *adjective* first, earliest, beginning, primary, introductory *The initial letter of the alphabet is "A."* final

initiate *verb* 1. start, begin, originate, comment, lead, launch, pioneer, head, institute *Kevin is so shy, he won't talk unless I initiate the conversation.* 2. admit, install, take in, let in, enroll *The president of the organization initiated the new members.*

injure *verb* harm, hurt, wound, disable, damage, impair *No one was seriously injured in the accident.*

injury *noun* hurt, wound, damage, harm *The doctor said Tom's injury won't take long to heal.*

injustice *noun* unfairness, inequity, wrong, offense, crime, evil *Homelessness is a social injustice.* justice

inn *noun* hotel, motel, bed-and-breakfast, lodge, roadhouse, tavern *It's possible to spend the night in an old inn when you travel in England.*

inner *adjective* interior, inside, middle, central *It's safer to keep your wallet in an inner pocket of your jacket.* outer

innocent *adjective* not guilty, guiltless, blameless, faultless *Under our law, a person is considered innocent until proven guilty.*

inquire *verb* ask, question, query, ask questions, examine *Have you inquired about the price of a hotel room?*

inquisitive *adjective* curious, prying, snooping, meddlesome, nosy *The inquisitive reporter kept trying to get information about the star's personal life.*

insane *adjective* 1. mentally ill *Doctors declared the defendant insane.* 2. foolish, idiotic, absurd, ridiculous, mad, nuts *What an insane plan—it'll never work. You're insane if you think I'll go out in this weather.*

insecure *adjective* unstable, unsteady, flimsy, fragile, weak, rickety *Those bookshelves are too insecure for a set of encyclopedias.* secure

inseparable *adjective* close, devoted, intimate *My friend Joanie and I are inseparable companions.*

insert *verb* put in, enter, introduce, inject *At the ATM, insert your card and follow the instructions. I inserted another sentence in the first paragraph.*

inside 1. *noun* interior, inner part *The inside of the book contains lots of illustrations.* 2. *adverb* in, into, within, indoors *Let's go inside before it rains.* 3. *adjective* interior, innermost, internal *I'll take the inside seat, and you take the aisle seat.*

insignia *noun* emblem, badge, symbol, sign *Members of the armed forces wear insignias showing their rank.*

insignificant *adjective* unimportant, meaningless, small, little, petty, trivial *There's no point in arguing over insignificant details.* important, significant

insincere *adjective* dishonest, deceitful, false, superficial, artificial, phony *He offered an insincere apology, saying he was sorry if he offended anyone.* sincere

insist *verb* urge, press, demand, require *Harold's mother insisted that I stay for dinner.*

inspect *verb* examine, check, observe, study, investigate *Fire department officials inspected the school for safety.*

inspection *noun* examination, check, observation, investigation, assessment, appraisal, survey *The soldiers lined up each morning for their officer's inspection.*

inspiration *noun* 1. motivation, encouragement, stimulus, prompting, influence *The coach's halftime speech was the inspiration the team needed to win the game.* 2. insight, idea, thought, revelation, brainstorm *Many artists get their inspirations from nature.*

inspire *verb* motivate, encourage, influence, prompt, cause *Many of Mark Twain's own experiences on the Mississippi River inspired* The Adventures of Huckleberry Finn.

install *verb* 1. place, put in, fix, set up, position, add *The electrician installed a new microwave in our kitchen. I installed an antivirus program on my computer.* remove 2. establish, inaugurate, instate, induct *The business organization installed my mother as its president.*

instance *noun* example, case, occasion, circumstance *I know of only one instance in which a student in my class was caught cheating.*

instant 1. *noun* moment, second, minute, flash *The rabbit paused for an instant, then hopped off into the woods.* 2. *adjective* immediate, prompt, quick, rapid, sudden *We expect an instant response from a computer.*

instantly *adverb* immediately, promptly, right away, at once *Dad said he recognized his old school buddy instantly.*

instead *adverb* as a substitute, in its place *I'll have chocolate ice cream instead.*

instead of *preposition* in place of, rather than, in lieu of *Instead of doing my homework, I watched TV.*

instinct *noun* feeling, tendency, intuition, sense, impulse, urge *I always regret it when I don't trust my instincts.*

institute 1. *verb* establish, set up, begin, create, organize, form, launch *Our school has had to institute new security measures.* 2. *noun* institution, organization, foundation, establishment, society, school, academy, college *The art institute has an exhibition of its students' paintings.*

institution *noun* organization, foundation, institute, establishment, association, school, college *Banks are financial institutions. Universities are educational institutions.*

instruct *verb* 1. teach, educate, train, coach, tutor, show, guide *The martial arts teacher instructed us in self-defense techniques.* 2. direct, command, order, tell, inform, advise *The doctor instructed me to take aspirin and stay in bed.*

instruction *noun* 1. education, training, guidance, coaching, teaching *Our school has a program of instruction for children with special needs.* 2. command, order, directive, direction, rule *Follow the instructions in the manual.*

instrument *noun* device, tool, implement, utensil, apparatus, gadget, appliance, contraption *The school science lab has all kinds of instruments for conducting experiments.*

insufficient *adjective* inadequate, not enough, deficient, unsatisfactory *The police had insufficient evidence to arrest the woman.* sufficient, enough, adequate

insulate *verb* seal, protect, cover, line, encase, surround *We insulated the walls and ceiling of our house to save energy.*

insult 1. *verb* offend, affront, humiliate, hurt *He insulted me by calling me an idiot.* 2. *noun* offense, affront, slight *Some TV programs are an insult to our intelligence.*

insure *verb* 1. make sure, affirm, vouch, determine *Run the spell-checker to insure your spelling is correct.* 2. protect, safeguard, defend, guarantee, assure, cover *Be sure to check* *the smoke detectors installed in your house regularly to insure your safety.*

integrated *adjective* desegregated, interracial, multiethnic, multicultural, multilingual, mixed, combined, assimilated *Our integrated school offers English as a Second Language classes for Hispanic students.*

integrity *noun* honesty, truthfulness, sincerity, honor, principle, morality, uprightness *She has a reputation for fairness and integrity.*

intellectual 1. *adjective* learned, scholarly, intelligent, academic *The university campus has an intellectual atmosphere.* 2. *noun* thinker, scholar, brain, genius *Leonardo da Vinci was one of the greatest intellectuals of all time.*

intelligence *noun* 1. brains, aptitude, intellect, brightness, cleverness *I think we have the intelligence to solve this problem ourselves.* stupidity, ignorance 2. information, news, reports, data *The spy supplied the army the intelligence it needed to defeat the enemy.*

intelligent *adjective* smart, bright, alert, perceptive, clever, brilliant *Dolphins are intelligent animals.* unintelligent

intend *verb* mean, plan, propose, aim, have in mind, contemplate *I'm sure she never intended to hurt your feelings. What do you intend to do after college?*

intense *adjective* extreme, severe, great, strong, powerful, fierce, harsh *Penguins have thick feathers to protect them from the intense cold.* moderate

intensity *noun* strength, power, force, severity *The intensity of the sunlight is greatest at noon.*

intent 1. *noun* aim, plan, goal, ambition, objective, intention *It is Margaret's intent to travel for a year before settling down.* 2. *adjective* focused, concentrated, fixed, engrossed, occupied, determined *He is intent on finishing the book before bedtime. She bent over her work with an intent expression on her face.*

intentional *adjective* done on purpose, deliberate, meant, planned, premeditated *He gave me an intentional kick under the table to get my attention.*

intercept *verb* interrupt, block, check, stop, cut off, obstruct, seize, catch, deflect *The linebacker intercepted the ball at the fifteen-yard line.*

interest 1. *noun* attention, curiosity, concern, concentration *The mystery story has captured my interest.* unconcern, apathy 2. pastime, activity, hobby, pursuit *Pam's interests include photography and travel.* 3. share, portion, part, stake, investment, percentage *Uncle Charles purchased an interest in a new company.* 4. advantage, good, benefit *It is in our best interests to vote in elections.* 5. *verb* attract, appeal to, fascinate, engross, intrigue *Nothing interests me more than the subject of astronomy.*

interesting *adjective* absorbing, fascinating, engrossing, enthralling, spellbinding, intriguing, appealing, entertaining *Uncle Dave has traveled around the world and met a lot of interesting people. We saw an interesting TV documentary about the return of the whooping crane from near extinction.* uninteresting, boring, dull

interfere *verb* intervene, interrupt, intrude, meddle *The rainy weather interfered with our camping trip.*

interior 1. *noun* inside, middle, heart, core, center, nucleus *The interior of the building was dark.* 2. *adjective* inner, internal, inside *The interior walls of the house are white.*

intermediate *adjective* middle, in-between, midway, halfway, intervening *The school offers classes in beginning, intermediate, and advanced Spanish.*

intermission *noun* pause, break, rest, interruption, respite, interlude *There is a fifteen-minute intermission between acts.*

internal *adjective* inner, inside, interior, innermost *Static electricity can damage the internal components of your computer.*

interpret *verb* explain, clarify, translate, analyze, decipher *You need to be able to interpret the symbols in order to read a map correctly.*

interrupt *verb* break in, intrude, interfere, disturb, stop, hinder *A fire drill interrupted class.*

interval *noun* break, pause, recess, interruption, intermission, interlude, respite *If the interval between seeing lightning and hearing thunder is five seconds or less, go to a safe shelter.*

interview 1. *noun* conference, conversation, dialogue, talk, meeting *My teacher and parents are having an interview about my schoolwork.* 2. *verb* examine, question, interrogate, talk to, test *My sister is being interviewed for a job today.*

intimate *adjective* 1. close, familiar *My mother and Phyllis have been intimate friends since grade school.* 2. private, personal, innermost *The supermarket tabloids claim to have the intimate details of stars' lives.*

intolerable *adjective* unbearable, unendurable *The air-conditioning protected us from the intolerable heat and humidity.* tolerable, bearable

intolerant *adjective* biased, prejudiced, bigoted, unsympathetic, narrow-minded *There are some people who are intolerant of people who are not just like them.* tolerant, understanding, accepting

intoxicated *adjective* drunk, inebriated, under the influence *He was arrested for driving while intoxicated.*

intricate *adjective* complicated, complex, elaborate, involved, tricky *Emily is knitting a sweater with an intricate pattern. With a large telescope you can view the surface of the moon in intricate detail.*

intrigue *verb* fascinate, interest, captivate, charm, enthrall *Children are intrigued to learn how children of other countries live.*

introduce *verb* 1. present, acquaint with, familiarize, announce *The teacher introduced the new student to the rest of the class.* 2. bring in, initiate, originate, launch, inaugurate, establish, institute *The Internet has introduced a whole new vocabulary.*

intrude *verb* interfere, impose, encroach, infringe, meddle, overstep (*Slang*—barge in, butt in) *A ringing cell phone intruded on our conversation during dinner.*

invade *verb* attack, assault, conquer, overrun *In A.D. 43 the Emperor Claudius sent an army to invade Britain.*

invalid *adjective* void, revoked, expired, ineffective *Don't forget to renew your driver's license before it becomes invalid.* valid

invaluable *adjective* priceless, precious, valuable, irreplaceable *The British crown jewels are invaluable.*

invent *verb* originate, create, devise, develop, contrive *Thomas Edison invented the phonograph.*

invention *noun* creation, development, discovery *James Watt is credited with the invention of the steam engine, but he, in fact, improved upon an existing engine to make it practical.*

inventory *noun* 1. stock, collection, supply, merchandise, goods *The store is having a sale to reduce its inventory.* 2. list, catalog, account, register, record *The library made an inventory of all its books.*

invest *verb* devote to, spend on, donate to, give to *The children invested a lot of time in decorating the classroom for the school's open house.*

investigate *verb* explore, examine, probe into, study, review, research *Detectives are investigating the theft.*

invisible *adjective* undetectable, imperceptible, unseen, hidden *Bacteria and viruses are invisible to the naked eye.*

invite *verb* ask, request, bid, summon, call *May I invite Janet to dinner?*

involuntary *adjective* instinctive, automatic, mechanical, spontaneous, unconscious, unintentional *Danielle let out an involuntary gasp of pain when she twisted her ankle.*

involve *verb* 1. include, entail, encompass, require, necessitate *Mom's job involves a lot of travel.* 2. occupy, absorb, engross, preoccupy *I became involved in the TV program and didn't finish my homework.*

irregular *adjective* 1. uneven, unequal, rough, bumpy, jagged, crooked *We followed the road along the irregular coastline.* regular 2. variable, erratic, uneven, unsteady *The patient's breathing was irregular.* regular

irritate *verb* 1. annoy, bother, disturb, anger, agitate, madden, vex, provoke *The barking dog next door is beginning to irritate us.* 2. make sore, hurt, chafe, rub, grate *Scratching will only irritate your poison ivy.* soothe

island *noun* isle, islet, atoll, key *We sailed out to an island in the bay.*

isolate *verb* separate, segregate, set apart, quarantine, seclude *People being treated for leprosy do not have to be isolated from society.*

issue 1. *noun* topic, subject, problem, matter, point, question *The environment is an issue that concerns everyone.* 2. publication, edition, copy *Have you seen this month's issue of the magazine?* 3. *verb* deliver, distribute, give out, hand out, dispense, supply *The postal service issues stamps commemorating people and events.*

itch 1. *verb* prickle, tickle, tingle, be irritated, burn *My mosquito bites itch.* 2. crave, desire, long, want *Dad's just itching to buy a new car.* 3. *noun* irritation, prickling, tickling, tingling, itchiness, burning sensation *Here's some salve for your itch.*

item *noun* 1. thing, article, entry *We need to add a few items to the grocery list.* 2. article, story, report, news, feature, account *I saw an item in the newspaper you may be interested in.*

itemize *verb* list, summarize, total, sum up *Mom itemized our Saturday chores and posted them on the refrigerator.*

J

jab 1. *verb* poke, push, thrust, nudge, prod, punch *I jabbed my pillow a few times to fluff it up.* 2. *noun* punch, prod, nudge, poke, blow *Gene gave me a jab in the ribs to get my attention.*

jail 1. *noun* prison, jailhouse, penitentiary, lockup *The jail holds 100 inmates.* 2. *verb* imprison, incarcerate, lock up *The man was jailed overnight for creating a disturbance.*

jam 1. *verb* cram, crowd, stuff, load, press, squeeze, push, crush *I tried to jam everything into only one suitcase.* 2. *noun* predicament, difficulty, mess, trouble, problem *Tammy got herself into a jam when she couldn't pay off her credit card.* 3. holdup, blockage, congestion, bottleneck, gridlock *An accident caused a traffic jam on the freeway.* 4. jelly, marmalade, preserve, spread *I like lots of jam on my toast.*

jar 1. *noun* bottle, container, vessel, receptacle, jug, vase *Pick up a jar of spaghetti sauce on your way home.* 2. *verb* shake, jolt, bounce, rattle *The truck jarred violently over the bumpy road.* 3. irritate, annoy, upset, grate on *The squealing brakes jarred my nerves.*

jealous *adjective* 1. envious, covetous, desirous *I'm sometimes jealous of my brother because he's old enough to drive.* 2. resentful, bitter, upset, angry, possessive *Our old dog acts jealous because the new puppy is getting so much attention.*

jeer *verb* make fun of, taunt, scoff, mock, ridicule, laugh at *The crowd jeered the candidate.*

jeopardy *noun* danger, risk, difficulty, trouble, peril *Many lives were in jeopardy during the hurricane.*

jerk 1. *verb* pull suddenly, yank, jolt, tug, wrench *I jerked my hand away from the flame.* 2. *noun* jolt, lurch, bump, jar *The tractor started with a jerk.* 3. fool, idiot *I'm sorry—I behaved like a jerk.*

jet *noun* 1. stream, spurt, spray, gush *The fountain's jet of water shoots 150 feet into the air.* 2. airplane, plane, aircraft, airliner *The jet landed safely on the aircraft carrier.*

jewel *noun* gem, gemstone, precious stone, stone, ornament *The queen's crown is set with priceless jewels.*

jiffy *noun* moment, second, instant, flash *I'll be there in a jiffy.*

jingle 1. *verb* ring, chime, tinkle, jangle *Jeff jingled the coins in his pocket.* 2. *noun* ring, tinkle, jangle, chime *I enjoy the jingle of the wind chimes in our garden.*

job *noun* 1. work, employment, occupation, trade, profession, career *My brother found a summer job stocking shelves at the supermarket.* 2. task, chore, assignment, duty, responsibility *It's my job to take out the garbage.*

jog 1. *verb* run, trot *My sister jogs for exercise every morning.* 2. *noun* run *I went for a jog with my dad before breakfast.*

join *verb* connect, fasten, unite, attach *Dad joined the boat trailer to the car.* disconnect, detach 2. merge, unite, combine, band together *The two organizations joined forces to raise funds.* separate, split 3. enroll in, enlist in, sign up for, become a member of *My sister joined a college sorority.*

joint 1. *adjective* shared, common, combined, mutual *Mom and Dad have a joint interest in gardening.* 2. *noun* junction, seam, intersection, coupling *The joint between the two hoses is leaking.*

joke 1. *noun* jest, quip, witticism, gag *My dad told a funny joke.* 2. *verb* kid, tease, jest, fool *Sometimes I can't tell if he's joking or serious.*

jolly *adjective* merry, cheerful, joyful, pleasant, jovial, gleeful *Uncle Jack is a jolly man who laughs a lot.* sad, solemn, glum, serious

jolt 1. *verb* jerk, jar, bounce, shake, bump *A small earthquake jolted the area.* 2. *noun* bounce, bump, shake, jar, jerk *The truck stopped with a jolt.* 3. shock, blow, surprise *It came as a jolt when I realized that my best friend was moving and I may not see him again.*

jostle *verb* push, shove, bump, thrust *People jostled one another trying to get on the bus.*

jot *verb* write, mark down, note, record *I jotted a message to Mom to remember to get some ice cream.*

journal *noun* 1. daily record, log, diary, chronicle *The explorer kept a journal of his travels.* 2. magazine, periodical, publication, newspaper *Our doctor subscribes to several medical journals.*

journalist *noun* reporter, writer, correspondent, columnist, newscaster *Journalists asked the president questions at the press conference.*

journey 1. *noun* trip, voyage, tour, expedition, excursion *The journey in a covered wagon along the Oregon Trail took six months.* 2. *verb* travel, tour, go, trek, make one's way, voyage, roam *The travelers journeyed by foot and horseback.*

jovial *adjective* jolly, cheerful, merry, good-humored *The partygoers were in a jovial mood.* sad, solemn, serious, grim

joy *noun* happiness, delight, pleasure, enjoyment, glee, ecstasy *I couldn't contain my joy at seeing my friend again.* sadness

joyful *adjective* glad, happy, cheerful, blissful, merry, jovial, gleeful *Holidays with the family are particularly joyful times.*

jubilant *adjective* triumphant, overjoyed, elated, delighted, rejoicing, exultant *The hometown fans were jubilant when their team won the Super Bowl.*

judge 1. *noun* justice, magistrate *Everyone rose when the judge entered the courtroom.* 2. critic, reviewer, expert, appraiser, evaluator *The judges at the county fair gave a blue ribbon to my mom's cherry pie.* 3. *verb* decide, assess, consider, form an opinion about, find *Everyone judged the party to be a success.*

judgment *noun* 1. decision, finding, ruling, verdict, conclusion, opinion *The defendant awaited the judgment of the court.* 2. common sense, good sense, wisdom, intelligence *I trust my brother's judgment, so I talk to him when I have a problem.*

juggle *verb* alter, rearrange, change, manage, organize *Mom and Dad juggle their schedules so one of them can be home when we arrive from school.*

jumble 1. *verb* mix, confuse, scramble, muddle *I jumbled the days and missed band practice.* 2. *noun* mess, clutter, disorder, confusion, muddle, disarray *I have to help Dad clean the jumble in the garage over the weekend.*

jumbo *adjective* big, giant, huge, enormous, gigantic, monstrous *I couldn't finish my jumbo burger.* small, little, tiny

jump 1. *verb* spring, leap, bound, vault, hurdle, hop *The deer jumped the fence.* 2. *noun* bound, leap, spring, vault, hop *I made a jump for the ball and missed.*

junction *noun* connection, intersection, joining, meeting, union, convergence *At the junction of I-90 and I-94, follow I-90 east.*

jungle *noun* tropical forest, rain forest, bush, wilderness, wilds *Jungles are home to some of the most unique and rare animals of the world.*

junior *adjective* 1. minor, lesser, lower, subordinate *Kevin is a junior partner in a law firm.* 2. youth, juvenile *Cindy is competing in the junior golf tournament.*

junk *noun* 1. odds and ends, unwanted items, secondhand items, castoffs *We're holding a yard sale to get rid of our junk.* 2. rubbish, trash, litter, garbage, debris, refuse *Our Scout troop is cleaning up the junk in the ditches along the highway.*

just 1. *adjective* fair, impartial, unbiased, objective, honest, ethical, moral *The judge's* *decision was just*. unfair 2. *adverb* exactly, precisely, completely, entirely, perfectly *You look just like your father.* 3. only, scarcely, barely, hardly *We just made it to the airport on time.* 4. recently, not long ago, lately, a short time ago *We just met.*

justice *noun* fairness, rightness, equity, justness, honor *Martin Luther King, Jr., wanted justice for all people.*

jut *verb* stick out, project, protrude, overhang, extend *The pier juts out from the shore into the lake.*

juvenile 1. *adjective* young, youthful, immature, adolescent *Juvenile lions leave their mothers at about eighteen months.* mature, adult 2. *noun* youngster, minor, youth, child, boy, girl *Juveniles are not allowed to vote.* adult

K

keen *adjective* 1. sharp, acute, sensitive, perceptive, discerning *Cats have keen hearing and excellent night vision.* 2. eager, enthusiastic, willing, avid, excited *Will is a keen supporter of the team.*

keep 1. *verb* have, hold on to, retain, save, possess *Can I keep this picture of you?* 2. continue, persist in, remain, stay, carry on *Keep going in the direction you're going for another mile.* 3. store, hold, file, stock *Where do you keep the flour?* 4. honor, fulfill, adhere to, respect *You can trust him to keep his word.* 5. stop, prevent, hinder, hold back, impede, delay, detain *Keep the dog from leaving the yard. You're late; what kept you?* 6. *noun* living, livelihood, support, upkeep *Pets earn their keep with love.*

kennel *noun* doghouse, shelter *Take the dog out of the kennel for a run.*

kettle *noun* pot, pan, cauldron *Mom made a big kettle of chili.*

key 1. *noun* opener, latchkey, passkey *Who has the key to the front door?* 2. answer, explanation, solution, means, guide *Scientists continue to search for the key to the origin of the universe.* 3. tone, pitch, note *That music is played in the key of C.* 4. *adjective* leading, main, vital, crucial, basic, central, fundamental *The economy was a key issue in the campaign.* 5. *verb* type, keyboard, enter *After you've keyed in the information, save the file.*

kick 1. *verb* boot, punt, strike *He kicked the ball between the goalposts.* 2. *noun* boot, punt, blow, strike *Her kick went out of bounds.*

kid 1. *noun* child, youngster, youth, boy, girl *There are three kids in our family.* 2. *verb* tease, mock, joke, rib, fool *My brother and I kid each other all the time.*

kidnap *verb* abduct, take, snatch, carry off *The boy who was kidnapped yesterday was found safe this morning.*

kill 1. *verb* slay, slaughter, murder, execute, exterminate, annihilate *Our cat doesn't kill the mice it catches; it brings them to us alive as gifts.* 2. end, destroy, ruin, eliminate, rule out *Today's loss kills any hope of our winning the championship.* 3. *noun* prey, game *The male lion is the first to eat the lioness's kill.*

kin *noun* family, relative, relations, folks *All our kin were at our family reunion.*

kind 1. *adjective* generous, considerate, warmhearted, sympathetic, thoughtful, caring *It was kind of you to stop by when I was sick.* 2. *noun* sort, type, variety, class, brand, make *What kind of car do you have?*

kindle *verb* 1. light, ignite, set on fire, burn *The cabin was cold, so Dad kindled a fire in the woodstove.* 2. arouse, stir, start, trigger, inspire *My cousin kindled my interest in racing radio control cars.*

kindly 1. *adverb* thoughtfully, generously, helpfully, graciously *It was raining, so Felicia's mother kindly offered me a ride home.* 2. *adjective* kind, nice, good-hearted, kindhearted, thoughtful, generous *Our kindly neighbor brings us flowers from her garden.*

kindness *noun* compassion, sympathy, goodwill, humanity, decency, generosity *During the Great Depression many people had to rely on the kindness of others to survive.*

king *noun* monarch, ruler, sovereign *Did King Arthur and Camelot really exist?*

kink *noun* 1. twist, curl, bend *The garden hose has a kink in it.* 2. pain, twinge, crick, spasm *I sometimes get a kink in my neck if I don't sleep on my own pillow.*

kiss *noun* touch with the lips, buss, peck (*Slang*—smooch, smack) *Grandma always gives me a big kiss when she sees me.*

kit *noun* equipment, set, outfit, gear, tools *I keep a repair kit with me on my bike.*

knack *noun* skill, talent, aptitude, flair, gift *Steven has a knack for computer programming.*

kneel *verb* get down on one's knees, bend, bow, stoop *I knelt down to look under the bed for my slippers.*

knife *noun* cutting tool, blade, sword, dagger, scalpel *I need a sharper knife to cut this steak.*

knit *verb* 1. weave, loop, interweave *My sister knit me a wool scarf for winter.* 2. heal, mend, unite, bind *The doctor says the broken bone will knit in six weeks. The disaster knit the community together.*

knob *noun* handle, dial, button, switch *Turn the knob to the right.*

knock 1. *verb* hit, strike, jab, pound, hammer, rap, tap, bang *Someone's knocking at the back door. Ouch! I knocked my elbow on the corner of the table.* 2. *noun* blow, hit, bump, bang, thump, rap, tap *Do you hear a knock at the door?*

knot 1. *noun* loop, twist, square knot, granny knot, hitch *If you go sailing, you need to know how to tie a variety of knots.* 2. cluster, group, bunch, band, gathering *A knot of students stood outside the classroom door waiting for the bell.* 3. lump, node, bump, mass *A knot in a board shows where a branch grew. He massaged the knot in his muscle.* 4. *verb* tie, bind, loop, twist, join, secure, tether *Knot this rope to the pier.*

know *verb* 1. understand, comprehend, realize, grasp, be aware of, be familiar with *Do you know what this word means? I know from experience that we can count on Jimmy.* 2. recognize, identify, perceive, distinguish, tell *I would know him if I saw him.*

knowledge *noun* 1. information, facts, data, wisdom, learning *We need the knowledge of an expert to get the job done correctly.* 2. understanding, awareness, comprehension, realization *The mechanic says he has no knowledge of any problems with the car.*

L

label 1. *noun* tag, marker, sticker, ticket *I used my computer to make a label for a CD.* 2. *verb* tag, name, identify, classify, categorize *You need to label your luggage, in case it gets lost.*

labor 1. *noun* work, effort, toil, drudgery, exertion *We paid the carpenter for his labor.* 2. workers, employees, staff, workforce, hands *Labor requires safe working conditions.* 3. *verb* work, toil, exert oneself, strive, struggle, endeavor *The crew labored to finish on time.*

lack 1. *verb* be short of, be deficient in, need, want, require *I lacked the time to finish the exam.* 2. *noun* shortage, absence, deficiency, need, scarcity *A lack of sleep made me doze off in class.*

lad *noun* boy, youth, young man, kid *Great-Grandpa likes to tell us stories of how life was when he was a lad.*

laden *adjective* loaded, burdened, weighted down *Camels crossed the desert laden with supplies.*

ladle 1. *noun* dipper, scoop, spoon *We use a ladle to serve soup.* 2. *verb* scoop out, spoon out, dish out *I ladled lots of gravy onto my potatoes.*

lady *noun* woman, female, matron *My brother gave the elderly lady his seat on the bus.*

lag *verb* linger, loiter, dawdle, poke along, trail, delay *We had to wait for my little brother who kept lagging behind.*

lair *noun* den, hole, burrow, nest, refuge, hideaway *The mythical dragon lived in a lair in the side of the mountain.*

lame *adjective* 1. disabled, handicapped, crippled *Glenda's horse has a lame hind leg.* 2. unconvincing, flimsy, feeble, weak, unsatisfactory, inadequate *That's the lamest excuse I ever heard!*

lance 1. *noun* spear, javelin *Knights fought using swords or lances.* 2. *verb* cut, pierce, puncture, prick *We took our cat to the vet to have her lance an infected sore.*

land 1. *noun* ground, soil, sod, earth, property *After the sea voyage she was glad to be back on dry land.* 2. country, nation, homeland, territory, region *Tibet is a mountainous land.* 3. *verb* descend, arrive, touch down, alight *The eagle landed at the top of the pine tree.* 4. secure, get, acquire, obtain, win *Jason landed a good job with a computer company.*

landmark *noun* feature, monument, attraction, sight *Lincoln's home in Springfield, Illinois, is a historic landmark.*

lane *noun* path, road, passageway, alley, track *The lane winds down the hill to the valley.*

language *noun* 1. tongue, dialect, speech *My friend René speaks three languages.* 2. communication, speech, expression, conversation *My hearing-impaired friend taught me sign language.*

lap 1. *noun* circuit, round, loop *Karl ran six laps of the stadium.* 2. *verb* lick, drink *The kitten lapped up the milk.* 3. wrap around, fold over *We lapped the blankets around us to keep warm.*

lapse 1. *noun* error, slip, mistake, blunder *I had a lapse of memory and couldn't remember her name.* 2. interval, gap, pause, break *We began football practice again after a lapse of two months.* 3. *verb* decline, slump, sink, drop, slide *I tried for a while to keep my room clean, but I've lapsed into my messy ways.*

large *adjective* big, considerable, huge, sizable, vast, immense, enormous, massive *Computer hard disks can store a large amount of data.*

lark *noun* fling, spree, celebration, romp, game *Camp last summer was a lark.*

lash *verb* 1. strike, blow, beat, whip, hit, thrash *Six-foot waves lashed the boat.* 2. tie, bind, strap, fasten, attach *Dad lashed our camping gear to the luggage rack.*

lass *noun* girl, young woman, youngster *Great-Grandma was just a lass when she came to the United States from Ireland.*

last 1. *adjective* final, closing, ending, concluding, finishing *You have to wait until the last chapter to find out what happens.* first 2. latest, most recent, newest, previous, preceding *Will you repeat the last thing you said, please.* next 3. *verb* keep, stay fresh, be good, endure, hold up, remain, go on *How long do you think supplies will last? These leftovers won't last for more than a day. How long is the nice weather supposed to last?*

latch 1. *verb* hook, fasten, secure, lock, close, shut *Did you remember to latch the gate?* 2. *noun* hook, clasp, catch, lock, fastener, bolt, bar *We need a new latch on the shed door.*

late 1. *adjective* behind, tardy, overdue, unpunctual, delayed, slow *She's late, and we can't wait any longer.* early 2. *adverb* behind time, belatedly, at the last minute *He always shows up late.* early

lately *adverb* recently, of late, currently *Have you seen any good movies lately?*

latest *adjective* newest, most recent, modern, up-to-date, up-to-the-minute, fashionable *The dress shop carries the latest designer fashions.*

lather *noun* foam, suds, froth *This shampoo doesn't produce much lather.*

latter *adjective* later, last, final, end *It usually cools off in the latter part of the day.* earlier

laugh 1. *verb* chuckle, giggle, snicker, snigger, chortle, roar, howl, crack up *We'd start laughing every time we looked at each other.* 2. *noun* chuckle, giggle, snicker, snigger, guffaw, howl *The comedian's routine got a lot of laughs.*

laughable *adjective* ridiculous, absurd, preposterous, ludicrous *The technology we take for granted today would have seemed laughable 300 years ago.*

launch *verb* propel, fire, shoot, put into orbit *The Soviet Union launched* Sputnik, *the first satellite, in 1957.* 2. begin, start, introduce, commence *Someday I hope to launch my own business.*

launder *verb* wash, clean, dry-clean *My favorite jeans need laundering.*

lavatory *noun* bathroom, washroom, men's room, ladies' room, restroom *Mom always sends us to the lavatory to wash our hands before we eat.*

lavish 1. *adjective* abundant, plentiful, generous, sumptuous, extravagant *The country club serves lavish meals.* 2. *verb* heap, shower, pour, squander, waste *The billionaire lavished gifts on all his friends.*

law *noun* rule, ordinance, regulation, act, bill, statute, decree, directive *There is a law against shoplifting. When you speed, you are breaking the law.*

lawful *adjective* legal, permissible, allowable, authorized, legitimate, just *Soldiers must obey an officer's lawful order.*

lax *adjective* careless, negligent, sloppy, indifferent, slipshod, lazy *I've been lax about keeping my room clean.*

lay *verb* put, place, set, deposit, rest, leave *They lay the blanket on the grass before their picnic.*

layer *noun* coating, coat, covering, film, blanket *There's a layer of dust on the furniture.*

lazy *adjective* idle, inactive, indolent, sluggish, listless, lethargic *He's a lazy fellow who sits in front of the TV all day.*

lead 1. *verb* guide, conduct, escort, steer, usher *The usher led us to our seats.* 2. govern, command, rule, manage, head, direct *George Washington led an army of volunteers during the Revolutionary War.* 3. be the way, go, stretch, extend *This hallway leads to the exit.* 4. *noun* front, first place, advance position *Our team took the lead in the first quarter.*

leader *noun* head, chief, boss, supervisor, manager *My dad has volunteered to be our Scout leader.*

league *noun* alliance, association, society, federation, coalition, union *Area businesses have formed a league to promote a better relationship with the community.*

leak 1. *verb* drip, seep, dribble, trickle, ooze, escape *Water is leaking from the kitchen faucet.* 2. *noun* hole, crack, break, opening, puncture, gash *There's a leak in the canoe.*

lean 1. *verb* slope, slant, incline, tip, tilt *The walls of the old shed lean.* 2. *adjective* thin, slight, slim, slender, skinny, lanky *The runner is tall and lean.*

leap 1. *verb* jump, spring, vault, hop, bound, skip, pounce *The deer leaped over the fence.* 2. *noun* jump, bound, hop, vault, skip *Wally placed third with a leap of twenty-three feet.*

learn *verb* 1. study, absorb, gain knowledge, grasp, master, memorize *My little brother has learned to tie his shoes.* 2. find out, discover, hear, gather *Dad learned from his boss that he's going to be promoted.*

lease 1. *verb* rent, let, charter, hire *We leased a car at the airport.* 2. *noun* contract, agreement *We just signed a one-year lease on a new apartment.*

leash 1. *noun* chain, rope, strap, rein, tether *I put the dog on its leash and took it for a walk.* 2. *verb* tie up, chain, restrain, tether *The law requires that we leash our dog.*

least *adjective* fewest, smallest, slightest, minimum *She gets the least allowance of all her siblings.* most, maximum

leave *verb* 1. go, depart, exit, take off, set off, go away *We have to leave now to be home before dark.* 2. set down, put down, mislay, forget *I must have left my keys in my other pants pocket.* 3. will, hand down, give, transfer, bequeath, endow *The millionaire left her fortune to her children.*

lecture 1. *noun* speech, talk, address, sermon *Our class is going to hear a series of lectures on career choices.* 2. *verb* talk to, speak to, address, make a speech to, preach to *Today the school nutritionist lectured us about healthful eating.*

ledge *noun* shelf, ridge, edge, rim *We attached a bird feeder to our window ledge in order to see the birds close-up.*

legal *adjective* lawful, legitimate, authorized, permitted, allowed, admissible *It's legal to fish in our state only if you have a license.* illegal

legend *noun* story, myth, fable, folklore, tale *We can learn a lot about Native American people from their legends.*

legendary *adjective* celebrated, fabled, mythical, heroic *Did the legendary King Arthur and his Round Table really exist?*

legible *adjective* readable, clear, plain *Your handwriting must be legible for your teacher to read it.* illegible

legion *noun* multitude, crowd, throng, host, mass, group *A legion of screaming fans greeted the rock group at the airport.*

legislation *noun* law, bill, statute, rule, regulation, ordinance *The senator is calling for new legislation to protect the environment.*

legitimate *adjective* valid, sound, just, lawful, rightful, legal, admissible *Illness is a legitimate reason for missing school.* invalid, illegitimate

leisure *noun* spare time, time off, free time, downtime, relaxation, rest *Parents who both work have very little leisure.*

lend *verb* loan, give, let use, provide, supply *Can you lend me a dollar until I get my allowance?*

length *noun* 1. extent, measure, span, reach, distance *A yard is thirty-six inches in length.* 2. time, duration, extent, period, term, span *Scientists think that dinosaurs inhabited the earth for a length of about 160 million years.*

lengthen *verb* extend, make longer, stretch, draw out, increase, expand, prolong *My pants had to be lengthened because I grew an inch over the summer. The president lengthened the time allowed for reporters' questions.* shorten

lenient *adjective* mild, gentle, merciful, lax, relaxed, easy *The accused man hoped for a lenient judge.* harsh, strict

less *adjective* a smaller amount of, not so much as, a reduced amount of *We have less time than I thought.* more

lessen *verb* diminish, decrease, lower, reduce, decline *The massage lessened my back pain. The storm is expected to lessen in a couple of hours.*

lesson *noun* teaching, instruction, education, schooling, study, course *I take piano lessons Thursdays after school.*

let *verb* allow, permit, grant, agree to, consent to *My parents let my friend stay overnight.*

letter *noun* 1. written message, note, written communication, reply *I wrote a letter to Grandma thanking her for my birthday present.* 2. character, symbol *There are twenty-six letters in the English alphabet.*

level 1. *adjective* flat, horizontal, smooth, uniform, even *The floor in the old farmhouse isn't level.* 2. parallel to, even, aligned, flush *Hang the paintings so the tops are level with one another.* 3. *verb* flatten, smooth, plane, grade, even out *The construction crew leveled and blacktopped the road.* 4. demolish, destroy, raze, knock down, wreck *The tornado leveled several buildings, but no one was hurt.* 5. *noun* height, elevation, altitude, point, stage *Hang the mirror at eye level.* 6. rank, position, status, grade, degree, standard *Students at our school have math skills above their grade level.*

liable *adjective* 1. likely, apt, inclined, prone *Don't go near that dog—it's liable to bite.* 2. responsible, accountable, answerable *You are liable for any damage you do.*

liar *noun* fibber, storyteller, perjurer *You can believe Tori—she doesn't lie.*

liberal *adjective* 1. generous, abundant, plentiful, ample, extensive, copious *I put a liberal amount of peanut butter on my sandwich.* 2. tolerant, broad-minded, progressive, freethinking *My parents have liberal attitudes about men's and women's roles in the home.*

liberty *noun* 1. freedom, independence, sovereignty, autonomy, emancipation *The Colonists fought to win liberty from England.* 2. freedom, right, privilege *Freedom of speech, religion, the press, and peaceful assembly are liberties guaranteed us by the First Amendment to the Constitution.*

license 1. *noun* permit, certificate, authorization *My brother just got his driver's license.* 2. *verb* authorize, allow, permit, certify *This restaurant is not licensed to serve alcohol.*

lick *verb* lap, taste *The cat licked my ice-cream bowl clean.*

lid *noun* cover, top, cap, stopper *I always need help opening the childproof lid on the aspirin bottle.*

lie 1. *verb* recline, lie down, stretch out, sprawl, lounge *The dog is outside lying in the shade.* 2. be situated, be located, be, sit, rest *Lake Huron lies between Lake Michigan and Lake Erie.* 3. fib, tell a falsehood, deceive, falsify *Mom says she doesn't lie about her age—she just refuses to tell anyone who asks.* 4. *noun* falsehood, fib, fabrication, untruth, invention *I admit I've told a couple of white lies in my life.*

life *noun* 1. existence, being, living, animation *Our garden comes to life in the spring.* 2. lifetime, life span, existence, days *Grandma says that she never in her life imagined she'd be using a computer.* 3. energy, vitality, vigor, spirit, liveliness *My sister's colt is full of life.* 4. human being, human, person, individual, mortal, soul *Many lives have been lost in wars.*

lift 1. *verb* raise, pick up, hoist, elevate *It took two of us to lift the sofa.* 2. lighten, raise, buoy, brighten *The "A" I got on my paper really lifted my spirits.* 3. rise, disperse, disappear, dissipate *The fog lifted and the sun began to shine.* 4. *noun* boost, hoist, push *Give little Danny a lift so he can reach the candy jar.* 5. ride, transportation *Bob's dad gave me a lift home.*

light 1. *noun* glow, illumination, radiance, brightness, brilliance *The sun provides light and heat.* 2. viewpoint, way, aspect, angle, perspective *People who live in poverty see the world in an entirely different light from those of us more well-off.* 3. *adjective* bright, brilliant, illuminated, sunny *Lots of windows make our house very light during the day.* dark 4. pale, subdued, pastel, whitish, fair *My sister's room is decorated in light colors.* dark 5. lightweight, weightless, insubstantial, slight, underweight, small *She wore light summer clothing. I can carry my bag—it's very light.* heavy 6. gentle, delicate, soft, faint, mild *There's a light breeze off the lake.* strong, harsh 7. simple, effortless, easy, undemanding *Dad gave me a few light tasks to do on Saturday.* demanding 8. *verb* ignite, kindle, set on fire *Dad lit the gas grill, while Mom prepared the burgers.* 9. illuminate, brighten, lighten *The northern lights lit the sky with a wonderful green glow.*

lighten *verb* 1. brighten, illuminate, light up *The sky began to lighten about 5:00 A.M.* darken 2. make lighter, reduce, lessen, ease *The cowboy lightened his horse's load.*

like 1. *verb* enjoy, appreciate, fancy, be fond of, care for, prefer *I like cats, but my sister likes dogs. I like watching football on TV.* dislike 2. *preposition* similar to, resembling, identical to, the same as *Dad bought a digital camera online like the one he saw advertised in the paper.* 3. *adjective* the same, similar, identical, matching *The houses in the new subdivision are all of like design.*

likely 1. *adjective* probable, possible, expected *It's likely we'll leave tomorrow for vacation.* unlikely 2. apt, inclined, liable *If we don't talk to him, he's likely to think we're mad at him.* unlikely 3. reasonable, acceptable, suitable, appropriate *She gave a likely enough explanation for her tardiness.* unlikely 4. *adverb* probably, no doubt, presumably, doubtless *Mom will likely refuse to lend us the money, but we can ask.*

likeness *noun* similarity, resemblance *The likeness between you and your mother is remarkable.* difference

limit 1. *noun* end, boundary, border, perimeter, extent *During recess you must stay within the limits of the playground area.* 2. restriction, limitation, ceiling *There is a limit on how much money we can spend each month.* 3. *verb* restrict, confine, regulate, curb *Limit yourself to only healthy snacks.*

limp 1. *adjective* drooping, sagging, floppy, loose, soft, weak *My clothes were limp from the heat and humidity.* 2. *verb* hobble, stagger, wobble, shuffle *She limped home after spraining her ankle.* 3. *noun* hobble, stagger, wobble, shuffle *My limp is caused by the blisters from my new shoes.*

line *noun* 1. rope, cord, wire, string *Hand me the line, and I'll tie the boat to the pier.* 2. mark, stripe, streak, stripe. *A no-passing zone is indicated by a solid yellow line in the center of the road.* 3. edge, boundary, limit, confines *The fence marks the property line.* 4. row, column, string, file, procession *Girls form a line on this side of the room.* 5. type, kind, brand, sort, range *The store carries a new line of natural products.* 6. note, letter, card, message *Drop me a line from Hawaii.*

linger *verb* remain, stay, persist, hang around, delay, dawdle, loiter *The rain lingered through the morning. Tom and Mary lingered long after the other guests had left.*

link 1. *verb* unite, connect, join, combine, couple, put together *The Mackinac Bridge links lower Michigan with the Upper Peninsula of Michigan.* 2. *noun* connection, association, relationship, attachment, bond *The link between lung cancer and smoking has been proven.*

lip 1. *noun* edge, rim, brim, border *As you stand on the lip of the crater of Maui's dormant volcano, Haleakala, you can watch the sun rise.* 2. one of the two fleshy folds that surrounds the mouth *When she bit her lip, it bled.*

liquid 1. *noun* fluid, solution, juice *Drink plenty of liquids.* 2. *adjective* fluid, flowing, watery, wet, molten, liquefied *Liquid ice is water.*

list 1. *noun* record, register, inventory, catalog *Did you put cat food on the shopping list?* 2. *verb* record, enumerate, itemize, write down, catalog *A thesaurus lists words in alphabetical order.*

listen *verb* pay attention, hear, heed, eavesdrop *Listen carefully to the instructions before you begin.*

literate *adjective* able to read and write, educated *Most jobs require that you be literate.*

literature *noun* writings, works, publications, books, texts, prose, poetry *Kim plans to study American literature in college.*

litter 1. *noun* debris, rubbish, trash, junk, clutter *Volunteers cleaned up the litter left in the park by the crowd after the celebration.* 1. *verb* mess up, cover, clutter *Cans and bottles littered the beach.*

little 1. *adjective* small, tiny, miniature, wee, teeny *Grandma and Grandpa have a little poodle.* big 2. short, brief, small amount *We have only a little time in which to finish the test.* long 3. unimportant, trivial, insignificant, minor *Dad had me fix a little problem with the computer.* significant 4. *adverb* scarcely, barely, slightly, somewhat *Owls are little seen during daylight hours but often heard at night.*

live 1. *verb* be alive, exist, survive, stay alive *We need food and water to live.* die 2. reside in, dwell in, have one's home in, occupy, inhabit *We lived in a house in the country for ten years.* 3. *adjective* alive, living, existing, breathing, conscious, animate *Corals are colonies of tiny live animals.* dead

lively *adjective* active, energetic, spirited, animated, vivacious, spry *Mom took us to see a lively performance of Irish dances.* dull

livestock *noun* farm animals *Prize livestock is shown at the county fair.*

living 1. *adjective* alive, breathing, existing, conscious, animate *The giant sequoia tree is thought to be the largest living plant in the world.* dead 2. *noun* livelihood, income, means of support, keep, employment, occupation, career *Aunt Frieda makes her living as a travel agent.* 3. life, existence, lifestyle *Dad likes the slower pace of small-town living.*

load 1. *noun* burden, pack, cargo, freight, shipment, consignment *A dump truck delivered a load of gravel for our driveway.* 2. *verb* fill, pack, stuff, pile *My brother loaded the trailer with his belongings and set off for college.* unload, empty

loaf *verb* idle, lounge, lie around, loiter, hang around *I just loafed around the house over the weekend.*

loan *noun* credit, advance *I asked Dad for a small loan against my next allowance.*

loathe *verb* hate, dislike, detest, despise, abhor *I loathe turnips.*

lobby *noun* entrance, hall, hallway, passageway, foyer *Meet me in an hour in the hotel lobby.*

local *adjective* neighborhood, nearby, area, community *The local volunteer fire department has an annual picnic to raise money for equipment.*

locate *verb* find, discover, detect, identify *The librarian helped me locate the book I needed.* 2. place, put, position, set, situate, establish *Early pioneers located their homes along streams and rivers.*

location *noun* position, place, site, spot, setting, area, locality *We found a good location for our campsite.*

lock 1. *verb* bolt, bar, padlock, secure *Lock the door on your way out.* unlock, open 2. fasten, connect, join, unite, link, mesh, fit *The pieces of the jigsaw puzzle lock together.* 3. *noun* bolt, bar, padlock, hook, latch, clasp *Students are responsible for providing their own locks for their school lockers.*

lodge 1. *noun* cabin, cottage, house, chalet *Dad and his buddies have a fishing lodge on the lake.* 2. *verb* live, reside, dwell, room, stay *Annie plans to lodge with her aunt until she can find her own apartment.* 3. stick, catch, become fixed, wedge *Someone's kite is lodged in the power lines.*

lofty *adjective* high, soaring, towering, tall *The village is on a plateau surrounded by lofty, snow-covered peaks.*

log *noun* record, account, journal, account, register, catalog *Lewis and Clark kept a log of their journey across the continent to the Pacific Ocean.*

logical *adjective* reasonable, rational, sensible, sound, sane *We need to find a logical solution to the problem.*

loiter *verb* linger, hang around, idle, dawdle *The students loitered at their lockers talking.*

lone *adjective* single, sole, solitary, one *A lone duck hung around our pond after the others flew south for the winter.*

lonely *adjective* 1. isolated, remote, desolate, deserted, uninhabited *On our hike we came upon a lonely cabin in the woods.* 2. alone, solitary, unaccompanied, friendless, lonesome *The artist lived a lonely life in a remote part of the country.*

long 1. *adjective* lengthy, extensive, extended, prolonged, protracted *It's been a long time since we've seen you.* short 2. *verb* want, desire, yearn, wish *My grandfather said that as a kid he longed to be a famous baseball player.*

look 1. *verb* see, observe, stare, gaze, peek, glance, glimpse *Barry kept looking at his watch. Look—there's Susan!* 2. search, seek, hunt *Have you looked in the bottom drawer? I'm looking for Mr. Jankowski.* 3. seem, appear *That house looks deserted.* 4. *noun* glance, glimpse, peek, gaze, view, observation *Take a look at this picture of Mom.* 5. appearance, expression, aspect, air, manner *Have you noticed Kate's stylish new look?*

loom *verb* appear, emerge, come out, materialize *An island loomed out of the mist.*

loop 1. *noun* coil, ring, circle, twist *I slipped a loop around the horse's neck and led it back to the barn.* 2. *verb* circle, coil, wind, twist *She looped a strand of beads around her neck.*

loose *adjective* 1. free, unconfined, untied, unchained, at liberty, at large *The farmer's cows are loose in the road again.* confined 2. unfastened, unattached, wobbly, unsteady, insecure *The legs on this stool are loose.* secure 3. baggy, big, slack, roomy, sloppy *Loose clothes are the most comfortable.* tight

lose *verb* 1. misplace, mislay, forget, drop *I lost my house key.* find 2. be defeated, forfeit, be beaten, yield, surrender *We played badly and lost the game.* win

loss *noun* 1. setback, misfortune, cost, harm, injury *Imagine the loss to the world of thousands of medicinal plants if the rain forests should be destroyed.* 2. reduction, decline, decrease, deficit *The company reported significant losses for the year. Dad's weight loss so far is ten pounds.*

lost *adjective* 1. mislaid, misplaced, missing, vanished, gone, absent *Our cat was lost for two days.* 2. engrossed, absorbed, preoccupied *Sorry, I didn't hear what you said—I was lost in thought.*

lot *noun*. 1. numerous, great deal, great many, great quantity, large amount *I don't have a lot of free time.* 2. plot, tract, parcel, piece of land, piece of property *We bought a lot to build a house on.*

lotion *noun* ointment, salve, cream, balm, oil *Put on some sunscreen lotion before you go outside.*

lots *noun* many, plenty, an abundance, loads *She has lots of friends.*

lottery *noun* raffle, drawing, sweepstakes *What are the odds of your ever winning the lottery?*

loud *adjective* 1. noisy, thunderous, deafening, booming, earsplitting, roaring *The rock concert was so loud, we had to wear earplugs.* quiet, soft 2. bright, flashy, showy, gaudy, garish *Sandy came to the party in a loud, tie-dyed T-shirt.* drab

lounge *verb* rest, relax, laze, sit around, take it easy *My sister and I lounged in front of TV watching videos.*

love 1. *noun* affection, fondness, tenderness, devotion *Karl plans to turn his love for animals into a career by becoming a veterinarian.* 2. *verb* adore, cherish, worship, idolize, be devoted to *I love my little brother.* 3. enjoy, like, fancy, appreciate, relish *Mom loves going out to dinner.*

lovely *adjective* 1. pleasant, delightful, agreeable, wonderful, nice *It's a lovely spring day.* dreary 2. charming, appealing, beautiful, pretty, attractive *My sister wore a lovely dress to the prom.* unattractive

low *adjective* 1. small, short, squat, near the ground *The children had their own low table and chairs.* 2. soft, quiet, subdued, muted, hushed *The librarian asked us to speak in low voices.* 3. inadequate, insufficient, meager, minimal *The gas is getting low in the car.* 4. sad, unhappy, down, glum, depressed *I felt low when I heard our teacher was leaving, but the new one is just as nice.*

lower *verb* decrease, reduce, cut, drop, lessen *The store just lowered the price on the camera I want.* 2. let fall, pull down, sink, drop *Dad lowered the shade so the sun wouldn't wake me.*

loyal *adjective* faithful, true, devoted, dependable, dedicated, trustworthy *The star thanked his loyal fans.*

loyalty *noun* faithfulness, devotion, allegiance, reliability, dependability, trustworthiness *Guide dogs for vision-impaired people are known for their loyalty.*

luck *noun* 1. chance, fortune, fate, destiny *A gambler leaves a lot to luck.* 2. good fortune, good luck, success, prosperity *We wish you luck.*

lug *verb* haul, carry, drag *Lugging around all those books in a backpack can hurt your back.*

luggage *noun* baggage, bags, suitcases *You're each allowed one piece of carry-on luggage.*

lull 1. *verb* soothe, calm, pacify, quiet, ease *The soft music lulled my brother to sleep.* 2. *noun* pause, break, letup, calm, respite *The wind picked up again after a brief lull.*

lumber *noun* wood, boards, planks, timber *A truck delivered the lumber for our deck.*

lump *noun* 1. swelling, bump, bulge *A mosquito bite can cause a large, red, itchy lump on some people.* 2. chunk, hunk, piece, clump, mass, gob *Today in art class I made a bowl from a lump of clay.*

lunge 1. *verb* spring, jump, leap, charge, dive, pounce *The first baseman lunged for the ball.* 2. *noun* spring, leap, jump, dive, pounce *The cat made a lunge for the mouse.*

lure 1. *verb* attract, induce, tempt, draw, pull, lead *The Colorado mountains lure millions of skiers every year.* 2. *noun* attraction, inducement, draw, magnet, bait *The lure of gold brought settlers to California in the 1850s.*

luster *noun* brilliance, brightness, shine, sheen, gloss, glow, gleam *The higher the luster of a pearl, the higher its value.*

luxurious *adjective* elegant, magnificent, grand, splendid, extravagant, lavish *When in Istanbul, you can tour the luxurious palaces where the sultans lived.*

luxury *noun* 1. pleasure, treat, bliss, delight, enjoyment *Mom says a soak in a hot bubble bath is pure luxury.* 2. affluence, prosperity, comfort, grandeur, splendor, opulence *The billionaire lives in luxury.* poverty

M

machine *noun* appliance, device, tool, engine *The washing machine broke down again.*

mad *adjective* 1. angry, furious, enraged, annoyed, irritated, cross, upset, exasperated *Dad got mad when I used his computer to play games.* pleased 2. crazy, insane, foolish, silly, stupid, idiotic *You must be mad to think I'd consider going skydiving.* sane, wise 3. enthusiastic, excited, wild, crazy *My sister is mad about country music.*

magazine *noun* journal, periodical, publication *We subscribe to more magazines than we have time to read.*

magic 1. *noun* wizardry, witchcraft, sorcery, voodoo, enchantment *Do you believe in magic?* 2. illusion, trickery, deception, conjuring *The TV show featured entertainers* *performing magic.* 3. *adjective* enchanting, delightful, charming, wonderful *The songs and the actors' performances in the musical were magic.* dull, boring

magician *noun* 1. illusionist, entertainer, conjurer *Pulling a rabbit out of a hat is a common trick for a magician.* 2. sorcerer, wizard, witch *Merlin was a magician and King Arthur's teacher and adviser.*

magnetic *adjective* attractive, alluring, compelling, charismatic, fascinating, irresistible *The actor was as dashing and magnetic offscreen as on.*

magnificent *adjective* splendid, grand, majestic, wonderful, marvelous, beautiful, impressive *The humpback whale is a magnificent marine mammal.*

magnify *verb* enlarge, expand, intensify, boost, increase, enhance *A telescope magnifies a distant image to make it appear closer.* minimize

maid *noun* servant, helper, domestic, housekeeper *Great-Grandma has a maid come in once a week to help her with the housecleaning.*

mail 1. *noun* letter, correspondence, packages, cards, e-mail, messages *Did I get any mail today?* 2. *verb* send, dispatch, post, ship *If you go past the post office, please mail this package.*

main *adjective* chief, most important, principal, leading, primary, first, foremost *The main entrance to the building is on Second Street. The main thing you need to remember is to save your work often.* secondary

mainly *adverb* mostly, chiefly, largely, generally, essentially *Cynthia is mainly interested in science.*

maintain *verb* 1. keep, uphold, sustain, preserve, continue, protect, retain *Dad says it's important to maintain friendly relations with our neighbors.* 2. keep in good condition, care for, look after, fix, repair, service *An important part of maintaining a car is changing the oil regularly.* 3. claim, argue, insist, assert, state, declare *The defendant maintains he is innocent.*

majestic *adjective* grand, stately, dignified, impressive, imposing, magnificent *We could see the snow-covered peaks of a majestic mountain range in the distance.*

major *adjective* main, chief, leading, principal, senior *Mr. Mendoza is a major government official.*

make 1. *verb* create, build, fashion, form, shape, compose, assemble, manufacture, fabricate *My sister makes her own clothes.* 2. force, compel, cause, require *My parents make me turn off the computer at nine o'clock.* 3. get, receive, acquire, earn, get paid *I'm* *hoping to make enough money this summer to buy a new bike.* 4. equal, come to, add up to, total, amount to *Including tax, that makes $25.20.* 5. *noun* brand, model, sort, kind, type, style, variety *What make is your new car?*

mammoth *adjective* huge, gigantic, immense, enormous, vast, massive *A mammoth highway construction project to bypass the city is under way.* microscopic, miniature

man *noun* male, fellow, gentleman, guy *I can't remember the man's name.* woman

manage *verb* 1. direct, control, supervise, run, administer, govern *We need to hire someone to manage the business.* 2. get by, fare, succeed, survive, get along *Mom thinks we're old enough to manage on our own for an hour after school.*

management *noun* 1. administration, control, supervision, leadership *Mom is responsible for the management of the law firm.* 2. directors, administrators, bosses, board, owners *The union is negotiating a new contract with management.*

manager *noun* administrator, director, supervisor, boss *The salesclerk had to talk to his manager about giving us a refund.*

maneuver 1. *verb* move, manipulate, guide, direct, drive, navigate, negotiate *Dad maneuvered the car into a tight parking space.* 2. *noun* move, movement, play, trick, stunt *The boy executed some amazing maneuvers on his skateboard.*

manner *noun* way, fashion, style, form, means, method *Salesclerks should always treat customers in a courteous, friendly manner.*

manual 1. *noun* instruction booklet, guide, guidebook, handbook *Read the entire manual before you begin assembling the unit.* 2. *adjective* physical, hand *Harvesting vegetables for the market requires a lot of manual labor.* automated

manufacture *verb* make, build, assemble, construct, fabricate, produce, create *Robots are able to manufacture many products.*

many *adjective* numerous, countless, lots of, various, several *Many kids have their own cell phones.* few

map 1. *noun* chart, plot, plan, diagram, atlas *Ellie drew me a map showing the way to her house.* 2. *verb* chart, plot, diagram, record, draw *From 1804–1806, Lewis and Clark mapped their journey from the Mississippi River to the Pacific Ocean.*

marathon *noun* race, relay, athletic event, contest *A marathon is usually a twenty-six-mile run.*

march 1. *noun* parade, procession, rally, demonstration, walk *In 1963 leaders of the* *civil rights movement organized a historic march on Washington, D.C.* 2. *verb* walk, hike, parade, trek, tramp *Our high school band marched at the head of the parade.*

margin *noun* 1. border, edge, rim, leeway, room *I sometimes draw doodles in the margin of my notebook.* 2. room, leeway, space, allowance, slack *You need to allow a margin of thirty minutes in order to get to the office on time during rush hour.*

mark 1. *noun* spot, blemish, stain, streak, scratch, scar, impression *The furniture feet left marks in the carpet.* 2. indication, sign, evidence *"Please" and "thank you" are marks of a courteous person.* 3. target, goal, aim, objective *The charity was trying to raise $50,000, but it missed its mark by $10,000.* 4. grade, score, rating, evaluation, assessment *My parents were pleased with the marks on my report card.* 5. *verb* blemish, stain, scratch, scar, soil, mar *Use a cutting board so you don't mark the countertop.* 6. identify, indicate, show, point out, denote *Prices should be clearly marked on the merchandise.* 7. grade, correct, rate, score, evaluate, assess *The teacher marks us down for misspellings.*

market 1. *noun* store, supermarket, shop, grocery, marketplace *Dad stopped at the market for some milk.* 2. demand, call, trade, business, commerce *The market for organic products is growing.* 3. *verb* sell, trade, promote, advertise *Many people market antiques and collectibles on the Internet.*

marriage *noun* matrimony, wedlock, union *Grandma and Grandpa are celebrating forty years of marriage.*

marshal 1. *noun* law officer, sheriff, officer, deputy *In 1871 Wild Bill Hickok became marshal of Abilene, Kansas.* 2. *verb* arrange, organize, assemble, collect, bring together *The Scouts marshaled a crew of volunteers to clean up the park.*

marvel 1. *noun* wonder, sight, sensation, spectacle, phenomenon *The personal computer is a marvel of technology.* 2. *verb* wonder, be awed, be amazed, admire, gaze *Sky watchers marvel at the northern lights.*

marvelous *adjective* wonderful, extraordinary, awesome, astounding, superb, magnificent, glorious *Andrew had a marvelous vacation in Hawaii.*

mash *verb* crush, squash, smash, purée, pound, pulverize *Dad mashed the avocados for the guacamole while I chopped the tomatoes.*

mask 1. *noun* disguise, cover, camouflage, cloak, veil *I didn't recognize Geoff in his Superman costume and mask.* 2. *verb* disguise, cover, camouflage, hide, conceal *The dark glasses masked his eyes. Karen masked her disappointment with a joke.*

mass 1. *noun* accumulation, batch, quantity, pile, stack, heap, hunk, lump, chunk

Yeast makes a mass of dough rise into a loaf of bread. 2. amount, size, bulk, volume, weight, measure *Only about 10 percent of an iceberg's mass is above water.* 3. *verb* accumulate, gather, collect, join, assemble *Troops massed along the border.* 4. *adjective* widespread, general, universal, wholesale *The Great Depression of the 1930s brought mass unemployment.*

massacre 1. *noun* slaughter, killing, mass murder *The massacre of the most abundant bird on earth, the passenger pigeon, resulted in its extinction.* 2. *verb* slaughter, kill, murder *It is estimated that over six million Jewish people were massacred by the Nazis.*

massage 1. *noun* rub, rubbing, rubdown, bodywork *Mom says a shoulder massage helps her relax after she works at a computer.* 2. *verb* rub, knead, stroke *The therapist massaged the patient's back.*

massive *adjective* huge, enormous, immense, gigantic, mammoth, colossal, heavy, bulky substantial *I watch movies and sports on Jeremy's massive home-theater screen.* little, small

master 1. *noun* leader, chief, ruler, boss, commander, director, controller, owner *Our dog is trained to obey its master.* 2. expert, genius, professional, wonder, wizard, virtuoso *The guest violinist with the orchestra was a master.* 3. *adjective* expert, professional, experienced, skilled, accomplished, proficient, skillful *Michelangelo was a master sculptor, painter, and architect.* 4. main, chief, principal, most important, major *The builder added a new, larger master bedroom with its own master bath onto our house.*

mat *noun* rug, carpet, doormat, bath mat *Wipe your feet on the mat outside the door before you come in.*

match 1. *noun* game, competition, contest, event, tournament *Jessica won the tennis match but told me I played well.* 2. companion, mate, partner, twin, double *The match to my sock got left in the dryer.* 3. equal, equivalent, competitor, rival, competition *Our team was no match for the champions.* 4. *verb* go with, complement, harmonize with *Does this shirt match these pants?* 5. equal, rival, compete with, compare with *Few can match her skill as an actor.*

mate 1. *verb* pair, couple, join *Most cranes mate for life.* 2. *noun* twin, companion, match *Has anyone seen the mate to this glove?*

material 1. *noun* substance, matter, stuff, goods *Dad and I went shopping for building materials for a tree house. I found the material I need for my essay in the encyclopedia.* 2. fabric, cloth, textile *The baby's room has curtains made of bright yellow material.* 3. *adjective* physical, solid, substantial, real, tangible *The material world is filled with familiar objects that we can see, feel, touch, taste, and smell.*

mathematics *noun* math, figures, numbers, calculation, algebra, geometry *Mathematics is Darla's best subject.*

matter 1. *noun* material, substance, stuff, elements *Matter is a solid, liquid, or gas that occupies space.* 2. business, issue, concern, affair, subject, question *I brought up the matter of increasing my allowance.* 3. trouble, problem, worry, difficulty *What's the matter with Doug? He doesn't look happy.* 4. *verb* make a difference, be of concern, count *Your opinion matters a lot to me.*

mature 1. *adjective* adult, full-grown, grown-up *The couple next door have three mature children.* immature 2. ripe, ready, mellow, sweet *Mature tomatoes are deep red.* immature 3. responsible, sensible, wise, experienced, prudent *She's a mature fourteen-year-old, and I trust her to babysit Jimmy.* immature 4. *verb* ripen, develop, mellow, age *An extra-sharp cheddar cheese matures in three years.*

maximum 1. *adjective* largest, highest, greatest, uppermost *You have a maximum time of one hour to complete the test.* minimum 2. *noun* most, highest, greatest, limit, ceiling, top *Two pieces of luggage is the maximum you are allowed to check for free.* minimum

may *verb* be able, can, be allowed *May I have a cookie?*

maybe *adverb* possibly, perhaps, conceivably, it could be *Maybe we'll get some rain tonight.*

maze *noun* network, web, tangle, snarl, muddle, confusion *The town was a maze of alleyways and streets.*

meadow *noun* grassland, pasture, field *Goats browsed in the meadow.*

meager *adjective* scanty, sparse, poor, skimpy, inadequate, insufficient *Because of meager food supplies, harsh weather, and poor pay, many of George Washington's soldiers deserted.* plentiful, abundant

meal *noun* food, breakfast, lunch, dinner, supper, banquet, feast, buffet, picnic *We went out for a meal at our favorite restaurant.*

mean 1. *verb* signify, denote, indicate, imply, suggest *You need to know what road signs mean in order to get a driver's license.* 2. intend, plan, aim, propose, want, have in mind *What do you mean to do when you've finished college?* 3. *adjective* unkind, cruel, malicious, nasty *It's mean to talk about him behind his back.* kind 4. middle, average, medium, normal *The mean temperature for August is 79 degrees.* 5. *noun* average, middle, midpoint, norm *Mom says we must find a mean between getting rid of the TV and watching it four hours a day.*

meaning *noun* sense, idea, message, intent, significance, gist *Allison told her English* *teacher that she was having trouble understanding the meaning of the poem.*

measure 1. *verb* calculate, gauge, compute, assess, estimate, rate, determine *We measured the room to see if my new computer desk would fit.* 2. *noun* amount, quantity, portion, size, extent *The show had equal measures of song, dance, and comedy.* 3. gauge, test, yardstick, standard *Money is not necessarily a measure of someone's success.* 4. step, action, means, procedure, course *We had to take measures to keep the deer out of our garden.*

mechanic *noun* machinist, repairperson, technician *The mechanic replaced the exhaust system on our car.*

mechanism *noun* device, machine, apparatus, system *The mechanism that releases the floppy disk from the drive is broken.*

medal *noun* award, decoration, honor, medallion *Mary Lou Retton won an Olympic Gold Medal in gymnastics with a perfect score of 10.*

meddle *verb* interfere, intrude, intervene, butt in, pry *It's rude to meddle in the affairs of others.*

media *noun* television, broadcasting, radio, newspapers, magazines, journalists, reporters *The actor said that the media's stories about him are untrue.*

mediate *verb* negotiate, settle, resolve, clear up *Mom mediated an argument between my brother and me.*

medicine *noun* medication, drug, prescription, remedy, treatment *I need to take the medicine for my sore throat twice a day.*

meditate *verb* think, reflect, consider, contemplate, ponder *Dad says he meditated a long time before deciding not to take a job in another city. I've been meditating on the perfect birthday gift for Mom.*

medium 1. *adjective* average, intermediate, standard, middle, halfway *My mom thinks I'll probably be of medium height when I'm fully grown.* 2. *noun* method, means, mode, instrument, agent, tool *The Internet has become an important medium of communication.* 3. habitat, environment, setting, substance, conditions *A bucket with hay in the bottom and a heat lamp is the medium we used for incubating the chick eggs.*

meek *adjective* mild, gentle, subdued, humble, modest, timid *Don't be meek about asking for help if you need it.* aggressive, assertive

meet 1. *verb* join, connect, unite, come together, touch, converge, cross, intersect

The earth and sky appear to meet at the horizon. 2. gather, assemble, get together, convene, congregate *The city council meets once a month.* 3. become acquainted, be introduced, get to know *My best friend and I met in kindergarten.* 4. encounter, run into, see, come across *You'll never guess who I met at the mall today.* 5. fulfill, satisfy, take care of, deal with *My brother's part-time job helps him meet the cost of college tuition.* 6. *noun* competition, contest, tournament, event *Sadie is on the relay team for today's track meet.*

meeting *noun* gathering, conference, assembly, get-together, convention *The student council holds its meetings Wednesdays before school.*

mellow *adjective* 1. sweet, soft, smooth, melodious *The cello is a stringed instrument with a rich, mellow tone.* harsh 2. easygoing, relaxed, gentle, good-natured, laid-back *Steven is a mellow person who doesn't worry about much.* tense

melody *noun* tune, song, music *"Danny Boy" is a traditional Irish folk melody.*

melt *verb* 1. thaw, liquefy, dissolve, soften *The ice on the pond is melting and is no longer safe for skating.* solidify 2. disappear, fade, vanish, evaporate *The raccoons melted into the darkness after they had raided our garden.*

member *noun* associate, participant, colleague, part, portion, constituent *Bobbie was chosen as a member of the cheerleading squad.*

memorable *adjective* notable, unforgettable, remarkable, noteworthy, outstanding *On July 20, 1969, we witnessed the memorable event of Neil Armstrong and Buzz Aldrin walking on the moon.*

memorial 1. *noun* monument, statue, plaque, remembrance, reminder, memento *The Tomb of the Unknowns serves as a memorial to those who have died in war.* 2. *adjective* commemorative, remembrance *A memorial service was held for her dad.*

memorize *verb* learn by heart, remember, learn, commit to memory *I have to memorize a poem to recite in class next week.*

memory *noun* recollection, recall, remembrance, retention *I have no memory of the apartment we lived in when I was a baby. Nora has a good memory—she'll remember the man's name.*

menace 1. *noun* threat, danger, hazard, risk, peril, terror *Sea pirates were once a menace to trade.* 2. *verb* threaten, terrorize, endanger, intimidate, frighten, scare *Forest fires menaced area communities.*

mend *verb* 1. repair, patch up, fix, restore *The roof of our garage needs mending.* break, impair 2. heal, recover, get well, improve *The doctor says my broken wrist will mend in six weeks.*

mental *adjective* intellectual, thinking, rational, reasoning *Puzzle-solving and word games are great mental exercise.*

mention 1. *verb* remark, comment, observe, say, tell, note, state *Dad mentioned that his birthday is next week.* 2. *noun* comment, reference, indication, allusion, statement *Fran made no mention of having met you.*

menu *noun* list, listing, index, table *From the File menu, choose Print. My little sister orders her meal from the children's menu.*

merchandise *noun* goods, products, commodities, wares, stock, articles *The thrift store sells secondhand merchandise.*

mercy *noun* kindness, compassion, sympathy, generosity, charity, leniency *The judge showed mercy to the first-time offender.*

merely *adverb* simply, only, purely, just *You merely made a mistake—don't let it bother you.*

merge *verb* combine, unite, join, come together, bring together *After the two highways merge, take the next exit.*

merit 1. *verb* deserve, warrant, rate, earn, justify, be worthy of *Mom's boss said her performance merits a raise.* 2. *noun* value, worth, quality, excellence, distinction, virtue *The art teacher thinks my watercolor has real merit and should be in the student art show.*

merry *adjective* joyful, jolly, cheerful, happy, festive *We had a merry time at the family reunion picnic.* sad, unhappy

message *noun* communication, letter, note, memo, dispatch *When I got home, there was a message that Suzanne had called.*

messenger *noun* courier, runner, emissary, envoy *A messenger brought Cinderella's stepsisters invitations to the ball.*

messy *adjective* untidy, cluttered, disorganized, disordered, sloppy, dirty *I cleaned my messy desk.*

method *noun* means, way, system, procedure, process, manner, mode, fashion *Computers have replaced old methods of typesetting.*

metropolitan *adjective* city, urban, civic, municipal *The Chicago metropolitan area includes Chicago and its surrounding suburbs.*

microscopic *adjective* tiny, minute, minuscule, infinitesimal *Dust mites are microscopic insects that live in the dust of people's homes.*

middle 1. *noun* center, core, heart, hub, nucleus, midpoint *The new software should be ready by the middle of the year. We got stuck in the middle of traffic. I love the cherry in the middle of the chocolate.* 2. *adjective* center, central, mid, intermediate, inner, inside *The napkins are in the middle drawer. The traffic in the middle lane was moving slowly.*

mighty *adjective* strong, powerful, forceful, potent, robust, sturdy, rugged, vigorous *The Aztecs built a mighty empire in Mexico.* weak

migrate *verb* emigrate, move, relocate, travel, journey *The nomadic shepherds migrate annually with their sheep and goats in search of pastureland.*

mild *adjective* 1. gentle, kind, softhearted, good-natured, docile, calm *We're looking for a dog with a mild disposition that is good with children.* 2. warm, pleasant, balmy, temperate, moderate *We've had mild weather all week.*

militant *adjective* aggressive, hostile, antagonistic, combative *Militant members of the organization are willing to go to jail for their beliefs.*

military *noun* armed forces, service, army, navy, air force, marines *Aunt Margaret is an officer in the military.*

mimic *verb* imitate, copy, impersonate, ape, parrot, mock *My brother is able to mimic the voices of TV cartoon characters.*

mind 1. *noun* brain, intelligence, mental ability, intellect *Albert Einstein had one of the best minds of the twentieth century.* 2. *verb* obey, heed, comply with, pay attention to, regard, listen to *Mind the sitter while Mom and I are out.* 3. care, object, disapprove, take offense, be bothered *Do you mind if I use your computer?* 4. care for, take care of, watch, look after, tend, attend to *Will you mind your brother for a few minutes while I go to the store?*

mine 1. *verb* excavate, dig, extract, quarry, dig up *Most U.S. coal is mined from the Appalachian Mountains.* 2. *noun* excavation, quarry, pit, hole, vein *Some of the world's largest diamond mines are in northern Canada.*

mingle *verb* 1. mix, blend, combine, merge, unite *The smells of fresh coffee and frying bacon mingled in the kitchen.* 2. associate, circulate, socialize, mix *On New Year's Eve we mingled with the crowds in Times Square.*

miniature *adjective* small, tiny, minute, little, diminutive *The library has a collection of miniature books, only two inches high.*

minimum *adjective* least, lowest, smallest, slightest, bottom *The minimum price I found on the Internet for a hotel in the city was $138.* maximum

minor 1. *adjective* small, slight, unimportant, insignificant, negligible, trivial *The quarterback suffered a minor injury during practice that won't keep him out of Sunday's game.* major 2. *noun* juvenile, youngster, youth, adolescent, child *Minors are not allowed to vote in U.S. elections.*

minus *preposition* less, excluding, without, lacking, excepting, missing, absent *Dad arrived home from the airport minus his luggage, which the airline had misplaced.*

minute 1. *noun* instant, moment, second, flash, jiffy *I'll be ready to leave in a minute.* 2. *adjective* tiny, small, minuscule, microscopic, negligible, insignificant *The dentist replaced a filling that had a minute crack in it.*

miracle *noun* wonder, marvel, phenomenon, sensation *Cell phones with picture, video, and text messaging are a miracle of modern communication.*

miraculous *adjective* wonderful, marvelous, remarkable, extraordinary, phenomenal, incredible, awesome *The receiver made a miraculous catch.*

miscellaneous *adjective* mixed, assorted, varied, various, jumbled, scrambled *I got together a miscellaneous collection of my old toys and clothes for our garage sale.*

mischief *noun* misbehavior, trouble, naughtiness, disobedience, wrongdoing, harm *If you don't watch my brother every minute, he's bound to get into mischief.*

mischievous *adjective* naughty, bad, misbehaving, troublesome, disobedient, playful, impish *Our two mischievous cats bring live mice home to play with.*

miserable *adjective* 1. sad, unhappy, depressed, dejected, down *I felt miserable when I got a bad grade on my test.* happy 2. bad, poor, lousy, inadequate, unsatisfactory, pitiful *My sister complained that she was paid miserable wages for her summer job.*

misfortune *noun* 1. bad luck, ill luck, mischance *It was our misfortune that it rained the entire week of our vacation.* fortune, good luck 2. disaster, catastrophe, calamity, tragedy, accident *The Kennedy family has endured a series of misfortunes.*

misgiving *noun* doubt, anxiety, concern, uneasiness, qualm, skepticism, suspicion *My parents had some misgivings about my flying alone to visit my cousin.*

mislay *verb* lose, misplace, miss, forget *I'm always mislaying my pen.* find

mislead *verb* deceive, misinform, misdirect, misguide, fool, trick *The sunny morning misled me into thinking I didn't need a raincoat, but by afternoon it was storming.*

misplace *verb* lose, mislay, miss, forget *The technician helped me install my printer after I misplaced the manual.* find

miss *verb* 1. forget, neglect, sacrifice, lose, forfeit, overlook, pass up *I don't want to miss the chance to see that movie.* 2. wish for, want, long for, yearn for *I missed my family a lot the first time I went to camp.* 3. avoid, escape, dodge, evade *Mom leaves work by 4:00 in order to miss rush-hour traffic.*

missing *adjective* lost, absent, vanished, gone, misplaced *Dad found my missing glove on the floor of the car.*

mission *noun* assignment, task, job, duty, chore, errand, work, business *The Mariner 10 spacecraft's mission was to explore Mercury and Venus.*

mist *noun* haze, fog, smog, cloud, vapor, film, blur *A morning mist hung over the valley.*

mistake 1. *noun* error, blunder, fault, slip, oversight *The teacher corrected my spelling mistake.* 2. *verb* misunderstand, confuse, misinterpret, get wrong *It's easy to mistake the meaning of a word or phrase unless you know the context in which it was used.* 3. confuse with, mix up with, take for *I mistook Jack for his younger brother.*

mistaken *adjective* wrong, incorrect, false, inaccurate, erroneous *I had the mistaken idea that the kids at my new school wouldn't be friendly.*

mistreat *verb* abuse, ill-treat, harm, hurt, injure *It's illegal to mistreat animals in our state.*

misunderstand *verb* confuse, misinterpret, misconstrue, misjudge, get the wrong idea *I misunderstood what chapter the teacher said we were to read.*

misunderstanding *noun* 1. mistake, confusion, mix-up, misinterpretation *My brother and I had a misunderstanding about where we were to meet after school.* 2. disagreement, quarrel, dispute, difference of opinion *After their misunderstanding, they both apologized.*

mix 1. *verb* combine, blend, stir together, mingle, join, unite *Mix the sugar and butter, then add the eggs.* 2. *noun* mixture, combination, blend, assortment *Our dog is a collie and Lab mix. The oldies concert attracted a strange mix of people.*

moan 1. *noun* groan, wail, howl, sigh, whimper *There were a lot of moans from the audience at the bad joke.* 2. *verb* groan, wail, howl, sigh, whimper *The wind moaned through the trees.* 3. complain, grumble, whine *There's no point in moaning about the weather.*

mob 1. *noun* crowd, throng, horde, mass, multitude, pack, bunch *The rock group was greeted by a mob of screaming fans.* 2. *verb* crowd around, surround, swarm around, besiege *The president was mobbed by reporters and photographers.*

mobile *adjective* movable, portable, transportable, traveling *Mobile libraries serve small communities that do not have a library building. In the United Kingdom cell phones are called "mobile phones."*

mock 1. *verb* ridicule, scoff at, jeer at, taunt, deride, laugh at, make fun of *Other artists mocked Matisse's early paintings.* 2. *adjective* imitation, fake, artificial, false *His jacket is made of mock leather.*

mode *noun* manner, way, method, means, style, fashion, form *Automobiles are the most popular mode of travel within the United States.*

model 1. *noun* replica, reproduction, duplicate, prototype, copy *Dad helped me build a model of the Wright brothers' original airplane.* 2. type, sort, kind, version, design *We traded in our car for a newer model.* 3. example, standard, ideal, paragon *The farm is a model of good land management.* 4. *verb* copy, design, shape, make, fashion, develop *I try to model myself after my mother.* 5. *adjective* ideal, perfect, classic *Stephen is a model student.*

moderate 1. *adjective* average, normal, modest, reasonable, fair, restrained, conservative *The traffic was traveling at a moderate speed. Jan has moderate political views.* excessive 2. *verb* control, curb, restrain, tone down, subdue, lessen, diminish *The wind moderated late in the afternoon.* intensify

modern *adjective* 1. contemporary, current, up-to-date, recent, new, present *Modern Western medicine and traditional Eastern medicine continue to learn from each other.* old-fashioned 2. leading-edge, innovative, progressive, state-of-the-art *Modern technology continues to change our lives.* outmoded

modest *adjective* 1. humble, shy, quiet, reserved *Albert Einstein was a modest man despite being the most famous scientist of the twentieth century.* arrogant 2. ordinary, plain, simple, unpretentious *The millionaire still lives in his parents' modest two-bedroom home.* showy, pretentious 3. moderate, limited, low, small, fair *The retired couple next door have only a modest pension to live on.*

modify *verb* alter, adjust, change, revise, adapt, vary, fix *The architect modified the design of the house to include another bathroom.*

moist *adjective* damp, wet, humid, dank *If the clothes in the dryer still feel moist, run it for fifteen minutes more.*

moisten *verb* dampen, wet, spray, water *Moisten the soil before planting your seeds.*

moisture *noun* water, liquid, dampness, wetness, humidity *The more moisture there is in the air, the warmer you feel.*

mold 1. *noun* shape, form, model, pattern, cast *You can make candles by pouring melted wax into molds.* 2. mildew, fungus, decay, rot *There's mold on the cheese.* 3. *verb* shape, form, fashion, cast, model *Mold the dough into loaves and bake for forty-five minutes.*

moment *noun* 1. instant, minute, twinkling, jiffy, flash *I'll be with you in a moment.* 2. point in time, instant, time *She's in a meeting at the moment.*

momentous *adjective* important, significant, crucial, great, stirring, historic *Getting married and having children are momentous decisions in a person's life.* unimportant

momentum *noun* motion, speed, velocity, force, energy, push, thrust *The toboggan gained momentum as it went down the hill.*

monarch *noun* ruler, sovereign, emperor, king, queen *Queen Victoria was the longest-reigning monarch in British history.*

money *noun* currency, cash, coins, dollars, legal tender *Do you have enough money for lunch?*

monitor 1. *noun* screen, display, video display, television, TV *My laptop computer has a fifteen-inch flat-panel monitor.* 2. supervisor, overseer, observer, inspector, proctor *Students need to get a pass from the study hall monitor before leaving the room.* 3. *verb* supervise, observe, watch, oversee, examine, inspect *Security cameras monitor the entrances to the building.*

monotonous *adjective* boring, repetitious, tedious, dull, dreary *Listening to my sister practicing piano becomes monotonous.*

monster *noun* beast, creature, ogre, giant *The Komodo dragon is the world's largest lizard, a meat-eating monster up to twelve feet long that lives on the islands of Indonesia.*

monstrous *adjective* 1. huge, enormous, gigantic, massive *A monstrous tree blew down and nearly hit our house.* 2. horrible, dreadful, ugly, hideous, grotesque, shocking *The mythical fire-eating dragon was a monstrous creature.*

monument *noun* memorial, shrine, tribute, marker *The 550-foot-tall obelisk that stands on the National Mall is a monument to President George Washington.*

monumental *adjective* huge, important, enormous, weighty, immense *We face the monumental task of preserving the environment for future generations.*

mood *noun* feeling, temperament, humor, disposition, nature, frame of mind *Almost any kind of music puts me in a happy mood.*

moody *adjective* gloomy, sullen, glum, sulky, grumpy *My brother has been a little moody since his girlfriend went away to college.* cheerful

moor *verb* anchor, fasten, secure, dock, tie *We moored the boat near the island and swam ashore.*

mop *verb* wipe, wash, clean, scrub, scour, swab *I mopped up the spilled orange juice.*

mope *verb* sulk, brood, fret, pout *Do you plan to stay inside and mope all day?*

moral 1. *adjective* right, just, ethical, honorable, good, decent, virtuous *The moral thing to do is tell the truth.* immoral 2. *noun* lesson, message, meaning, significance, teaching *Most fairy tales have a moral that teaches right and wrong.*

morale *noun* spirit, attitude, confidence, self-esteem, assurance *The team's morale has improved a lot since our win.*

more 1. *adjective* additional, extra, added, new *I need more space in my room for all my computer equipment.* 2. *adverb* in addition, additionally, further, to a greater extent *I've been studying more this year.* 3. *noun* extra, addition, another, increase *We're out of milk; can you get more on the way home?*

morsel *noun* bit, scrap, piece, crumb, shred *Ginny and I devoured every morsel of food on our plates.*

mortal 1. *adjective* deadly, fatal, lethal, terminal *The bite of a coral snake can be mortal.* 2. *noun* human being, person, individual, man, woman *The glamorous star is just an ordinary mortal like the rest of us.*

most 1. *adjective* greatest, best, maximum *That's the most fun I've had in a long time.* 2. *adverb* very, highly, extremely, truly *The last two minutes of the game were the most exciting.* 3. *noun* the majority, nearly all, almost all, the bulk *Colleen did most of the work.*

mostly *adverb* mainly, chiefly, almost all, nearly *My homework is mostly finished.*

mother *noun* female parent, mom, mommy, mama *Dana's mother and my mother are friends.*

motion 1. *noun* movement, activity, action, flow, stir *The motion of the rocking boat made me feel sick.* 2. suggestion, proposal, recommendation, proposition *Felicia made a motion to adjourn the meeting.* 3. *verb* signal, gesture, wave, beckon *My friend motioned for me to follow.*

motive *noun* reason, cause, ground, basis, motivation *Grandma's motive for traveling to Poland was to learn about her Polish ancestors.*

motor 1. *noun* engine, machine *A hybrid car has both a gasoline engine and batteries that power an electric motor.* 2. *adjective* motorized, moving, mobile *Our family has three motor vehicles: a car, a motorcycle, and a small truck.*

motto *noun* saying, maxim, proverb, adage *The United States' motto "E pluribus unum" is Latin for "One out of many."*

mound *noun* heap, hill, pile, stack *Our teacher has a mound of papers to correct before tomorrow.*

mount *verb* 1. rise, increase, gain, grow, swell, intensify *Pressure has been mounting on the community to build a new elementary school.* decrease 2. ascend, go up, climb, scale *Dad mounted the ladder while I held it.* descend 3. place, fix, set, position, display, exhibit *About 1,300 diamonds are mounted on Queen Victoria's small diamond crown, which is displayed at the Tower of London.*

mountain *noun* 1. peak, mount, elevation, height, hill *The highest mountain in North America is Alaska's Mount McKinley.*

mourn *verb* grieve, sorrow, weep, cry *It's okay to mourn when a pet dies.*

move 1. *verb* shift, shove, stir, budge, change, rearrange, transport, transfer *Let's move out of the sun. We moved the furniture so we could paint the walls.* 2. relocate, transfer, leave, go away *My grandparents retired and moved to a condominium in Florida.* 3. influence, sway, prompt, persuade, induce, inspire, convince *What moved you to run for student council president?* 4. affect, touch, impress, disturb, upset *We were deeply moved by the warm welcome we received. The sad story moved me to tears.* 5. *noun* motion, movement, shift, step *Don't make a move; a butterfly landed on your head.* 6. turn, chance, opportunity, play *It's your move.*

movement *noun* 1. motion, move, shift, action, activity *Kyle's sudden movement frightened the deer.* 2. campaign, crusade, drive, effort, program *The civil rights movement led to laws guaranteeing basic civil rights for all Americans.*

movie *noun* film, motion picture, show, moving picture *Danny's parents' new car has a backseat DVD player for watching movies on long trips.*

mow *verb* cut, clip, crop, trim, shear *The grass needs mowing.*

much 1. *adjective* a lot of, lots of, abundant, plentiful, ample *Hurry—we don't have much time.* 2. *noun* a great deal, a lot *I didn't do much over the weekend.* 3. *adverb* often, frequently, a lot, regularly *She doesn't stop to visit her old friends that much.*

mud *noun* muck, mire, slime, dirt *Mom made us clean up the mud we tracked into the house.*

muffle *verb* soften, mute, dampen, hush, deaden, silence, suppress, stifle *The sound barrier along the freeway muffled the traffic noise.*

muggy *adjective* humid, damp, sticky, stuffy, close *It's nice to have air-conditioning on a hot, muggy day.*

multiply *verb* increase, grow, rise, swell, accumulate, reproduce *My computer problems multiplied when I tried to install new software.*

mumble *verb* mutter, murmur, speak indistinctly, whisper *Evan mumbled to himself as he tried to remember where he'd put his book bag.* shout

munch *verb* chew, crunch, chomp, eat, snack *The airline gave us pretzels to munch on during the flight.*

murder 1. *noun* homicide, killing, slaying, assassination, massacre, slaughter *The penalty for murder can be life in prison.* 2. *verb* kill, slay, assassinate, massacre, slaughter *Most people alive at the time remember where they were when they learned that President John F. Kennedy had been murdered.*

murmur *verb* 1. whisper, mumble, mutter *I murmured an apology to Rick after accidentally bumping into him.* shout 2. babble, burble, whisper *The stream murmured as it flowed over the rocks.*

muscle *noun* 1. strength, power, brawn *He lacks the muscle to run for class president.* 2. a tissue in the body that can contract and produce movement *I've been working out to build up my muscles.* weakness

music *noun* tune, melody, harmony, song, orchestration *Mom listens to music on her CD player while jogging.*

must *verb* should, ought to, have to, need to, be obliged to, be forced to *We must turn in our assignments tomorrow.*

mutiny 1. *noun* rebellion, uprising, revolt, riot, revolution, insurrection *A hostile crew staged a mutiny after the captain refused their demands.* 2. *verb* rebel, revolt, riot, protest *Half of Columbus's crew mutinied while they were stranded on the island of Jamaica waiting for help.*

mutter *verb* 1. mumble, murmur, whisper *I couldn't hear what Sam muttered under his* *breath*. shout 2. grumble, complain, moan, gripe *Consumers are muttering about the high price of gas.*

mutual *adjective* common, joint, shared, reciprocal *My dog and I have mutual affection for each other.*

mysterious *adjective* 1. unexplained, puzzling, strange, baffling *The universe is still a mysterious place.* known 2. secretive, evasive, vague, cagey *I guessed about the surprise party because my friends were so mysterious about their plans.* open

mystery *noun* puzzle, problem, riddle, question, unknown, secret *The existence of the Loch Ness monster remains a mystery.*

myth *noun* legend, story, fable, folktale *The ancient Greeks' myths gave explanations for natural phenomena.*

mythical *adjective* fabled, legendary, imaginary, imagined, fantastic *The unicorn is a mythical white horse with one horn.*

mythology *noun* myth, legend, folklore, lore, tradition *In ancient Greek mythology Athena was the goddess of wisdom.*

N

nag *verb* pester, bother, badger, annoy, harass, trouble *My little sister kept nagging me to play with her.*

nail 1. *verb* fasten, hold, secure, fix, attach, hammer *The carpenter nailed the deck boards to the joists.* 2. *noun* pin, spike, tack *Mom pounded the nail into the wall and hung the painting.*

naked *adjective* 1. uncovered, exposed, nude, bare, undressed *The little children at the beach swam naked.* clothed 2. plain, unaided, simple, bare *Kelly was completely trustworthy, always telling the naked truth. Bacteria and viruses cannot be seen with the naked eye.*

name 1. *noun* title, label, tag, appellation *We're trying to decide on a name for our kitten.* 2. reputation, renown, fame, distinction *He made a name for himself in the computer industry.* 3. *verb* call, label, term, entitle *I am named after my grandmother.* 4. identify, specify, give, cite *Can you name all the planets?* 5. nominate, appoint, select, choose, pick, designate, elect, vote *Our teacher was named teacher of the year by the school district.*

nap 1. *noun* doze, sleep, rest, snooze, catnap *My little brother takes a nap every afternoon.* 2. *verb* doze, sleep, rest, snooze *Our cat likes to nap in the sun.*

narcotic *noun* drug, medicine, painkiller, sedative *Your doctor may prescribe a narcotic if you are in severe pain.*

narrate *verb* tell, relate, recount, report, recite, describe *In* A Connecticut Yankee in King Arthur's Court, *Mark Twain narrates the story of a nineteenth-century factory employee who is sent back in time 1,300 years to Camelot.*

narrow 1. *adjective* cramped, restricted, confined, close, tight *We wound down a narrow, one-lane dirt road.* wide 2. close, small, limited, meager *The mayor won the election by a narrow majority.* wide, large 3. *verb* close in, taper, constrict, tighten *The trail narrows as you climb higher.*

nasty *adjective* 1. mean, cruel, vicious, malicious, disagreeable *In his last movie the actor played a nasty character with no redeeming qualities.* 2. disgusting, offensive, foul, repulsive, sickening *That ashtray smells nasty.* 3. serious, severe, dangerous, bad *The figure skater took a nasty fall.*

nation *noun* country, land, state, kingdom, realm, republic, commonwealth *The nation of Canada is a federation of ten provinces and three territories.*

native *adjective* indigenous, original, aboriginal, natural *The native people of New Zealand are the Maori.*

natural *adjective* 1. innate, inborn, inherent, inherited, instinctive *Cats have a natural tendency to sleep during the day and hunt at night.* 2. real, authentic, characteristic, true, normal *It's important that we protect the natural habitat of endangered species.* 3. unprocessed, untreated, pure, organic *Mom thinks natural foods are healthier.*

naturally *adverb* 1. of course, plainly, certainly, surely, indeed *Naturally, I accepted her offer of ice cream.* 2. normally, authentically, genuinely, sincerely, unpretentiously *My brother has trouble behaving naturally around his new girlfriend.*

nature *noun* the environment, the outdoors, the wilderness, natural surroundings, the earth, the world, the universe *Many artists get their inspiration from nature.*

naughty *adjective* disobedient, bad, mischievous, misbehaving *Once when I was naughty, Mom told me she had Santa Claus on her speed-dial.* obedient

~~~~~~

nausea *noun* indigestion, upset stomach, sickness, motion sickness, queasiness *Some people suffer from nausea when flying on an airplane.*

nautical *adjective* naval, marine, sailing, boating, maritime *A nautical term for a rope that controls a sail is "sheet."*

navigate *verb* steer, guide, pilot, sail, cruise *Ferdinand Magellan's expedition was the first to navigate a ship through the strait connecting the Atlantic and Pacific oceans at the southern tip of South America.*

navy *noun* fleet, armada, naval force, flotilla *The British navy dominated the seas during the eighteenth and nineteenth centuries.*

near *adjective* 1. close, nearby, neighboring, adjacent, adjoining *The nearest supermarket is only two blocks from our house. The bus stop is quite near.* far 2. approaching, coming, close, imminent, at hand *The time is near for us to shop for school clothes.* far

nearly *adverb* almost, approximately, just about, close to *It's nearly noon.*

neat *adjective* 1. clean, orderly, organized, tidy, trim, well kept, shipshape *I keep the drawers in my dresser neat.* messy 2. good, great, terrific, excellent, clever *Dad bought me a neat new bicycle helmet. Alex has a neat idea for a new computer game.*

necessary *adjective* essential, required, crucial, needed, urgent, important *Mom says it's necessary for me to eat a healthful breakfast every morning.* unnecessary

necessity *noun* essential, requirement, must, basic, fundamental *Food and water are necessities.*

need 1. *verb* want, require, call for, demand *My bike needs a new tire.* 2. *noun* essential, necessity, requirement, want, basic, fundamental *The community is trying to meet the educational needs of the children.* 3. necessity, call, obligation *The dentist told me there was no need to be frightened.*

needless *adjective* unnecessary, pointless, useless, unwanted *If you don't have virus-protection software on your computer, you're taking a needless risk.*

needy *adjective* disadvantaged, poor, in need, destitute, poverty-stricken *Our local food bank collects food for needy families.*

negative *adjective* bad, disapproving, critical, adverse *I liked the first movie, but I had a negative opinion of the sequel.*

neglect 1. *verb* omit, forget, overlook, ignore, disregard *My brother Carl neglected to close the gate, and the dog got out.* 2. *noun* inattention, disregard, negligence, carelessness *The house, which had been abandoned a long time ago, suffered from neglect.* care

negligent *adjective* careless, neglectful, inattentive, indifferent, irresponsible, remiss *A negligent driver caused the accident.* careful

negotiate *verb* arrange, talk over, discuss, settle, agree on *Union and company leaders have negotiated an end to the strike.*

neighborhood *noun* area, community, district, locality, vicinity, block, street *We just moved to a new neighborhood.*

nerve *noun* courage, daring, bravery, mettle, bravado *It takes a lot of nerve to stand up to a bully.*

nervous *adjective* anxious, agitated, tense, edgy, strained, shaken, flustered *The actor said she becomes nervous before every performance.*

nestle *verb* snuggle, cuddle, hug, hold closely *I nestled the kitten in my arms.*

net *noun* mesh, web, webbing, lacelike cloth *The trapeze artists had a safety net stretched beneath them.*

neutral *adjective* 1. impartial, detached, unprejudiced, independent, cool, indifferent *It's hard to remain neutral in a dispute between your two best friends.* 2. drab, pale, colorless, indistinct, bland *I told Mom and Dad I want my room painted a bright color, not a neutral color.* colorful, bright

nevertheless *adverb* however, regardless, anyway, nonetheless *It was late, but I watched the movie nevertheless.*

new *adjective* 1. brand-new, unused, recent, modern *We need to keep our pets off the new furniture.* old 2. novel, original, fresh, different, creative *Does anyone have any new ideas for this year's float in the parade?* old 3. unknown, unfamiliar, strange, different *My sister is nervous about starting a new job next week.* old

newly *adverb* recently, lately, just *A newly discovered planet has three suns.*

news *noun* information, story, report, word, bulletin, announcement *We got a letter from Aunt Jessie full of the latest news about her family.*

next 1. *adjective* following, coming, succeeding, successive, subsequent *Don't forget your dentist appointment next Monday.* 2. adjacent, adjoining, bordering, closest, nearest *The next house on our block is for rent.* 3. *adverb* later, after, afterward, then, subsequently *We had pizza, and next we went to a movie.*

~~~~~~

nibble 1. *verb* chew, munch, bite *Randy nibbled nervously on his pencil during the test.* 2. *noun* bite, taste, morsel, crumb, piece *The fish took one nibble of the bait and swam away.*

nice *adjective* 1. pleasing, agreeable, enjoyable, fine, good *We had a nice time at the beach.* 2. friendly, pleasant, likable, agreeable *Your new friends are very nice.* 3. polite, kind, gracious, courteous, thoughtful, good *It's so nice of you to offer to help.*

nick 1. *noun* chip, cut, notch, scratch, mark *There's a nick in this glass; throw it out.* 2. *verb* chip, scratch, dent, mark *I dropped my bike on the pavement and nicked the paint.*

night *noun* nighttime, dark, darkness, nightfall, sunset *Owls have large eyes that gather a lot of light, enabling them to see very well at night.*

nimble *adjective* lively, light, quick, active, agile, spry *Fred Astaire and Gene Kelly were nimble dancers.*

noble 1. *adjective* honorable, moral, decent, self-sacrificing, virtuous *Sir Lancelot of Arthurian legends was known for his bravery and noble deeds.* 2. aristocratic, titled, highborn, upper-class *The king chose as a wife a woman of noble birth.* common 3. grand, majestic, lofty, magnificent, stately *The Capitol building in Washington, D.C., is a noble structure.* 4. *noun* aristocrat, nobleman, noblewoman, lord, lady, duke, duchess *Nobles who supported the king were given land.* commoner

nod *verb* bow, bob, tip, bend, signal, gesture *The principal nodded a greeting as he passed.*

noise *noun* sounds, racket, din, clamor, clatter, uproar, tumult, hubbub, commotion *The noise from the thunderstorm woke us at 2:00 A.M.* quiet

noisy *adjective* loud, blaring, blasting, earsplitting, deafening *My friend Clyde lives near a noisy airport.* quiet

nominate *verb* name, appoint, select, choose, designate *Victoria Woodhull was nominated by the Equal Rights Party in 1872 as the first woman candidate for the U.S. presidency.*

nonsense *noun* foolishness, ridiculousness, folly, absurdity, rubbish, gibberish *I don't believe the nonsense about the house on the hill being haunted.*

normal *adjective* usual, regular, average, standard, ordinary, typical, characteristic, true to form *It's about fifteen degrees above the normal temperature for this time of year.* abnormal, unusual

notable *adjective* important, remarkable, noteworthy, memorable, special, famous *Galileo made the notable discovery of the four major moons of Jupiter in 1610.*

notch 1. *noun* indentation, dent, nick, cut, slit *The edge of a quarter has notches in it.*
2. level, degree, step *Valerie's work is several notches above the work of the rest of the class.*
3. *verb* cut, nick, dent, slit *Start making your kite by notching the ends of two sticks tied together in the form of a cross.*

note 1. *noun* message, letter, memo, card *Don't forget to send Grandpa a thank-you note for the check.* 2. record, comment, notation, remark, observation, reminder *I made a note of the assignment.* 3. hint, indication, suggestion, clue, sign, evidence *Dad had a note of concern in his voice when I told him I didn't feel well.* 4. *verb* notice, observe, see, be aware of, perceive *Please note that the password is case-sensitive.*

nothing *noun* not anything, naught, nil, zero *My sisters look nothing alike. The score is fourteen to nothing.*

notice 1. *verb* note, observe, regard, see, heed *Have you noticed Katie's new haircut?*
2. *noun* announcement, sign, poster, bulletin, advertisement *The notice on the door says the store opens at 9:00.* 3. warning, announcement, notification, information *We gave notice to our landlord that we would be moving out in thirty days.* 4. attention, observation, heed, regard, consideration *A slight movement in the brush caught my notice.*

notify *verb* inform, advise, report, tell, instruct, remind, warn *If the school district decides to close schools because of the weather, it will notify local TV and radio stations.*

notion *noun* idea, belief, view, thought, opinion, impression, understanding *Different scientists have different notions about how dinosaurs became extinct.*

notorious *adjective* infamous, disreputable, ill-famed, well-known *The James brothers were notorious outlaws of the Wild West.*

nourish *verb* feed, nurture, sustain, strengthen, maintain *Sunlight nourishes living things.*

nourishment *noun* food, nutrition, sustenance *Children who have the proper nourishment are more likely to do well in school.*

novel 1. *adjective* new, original, fresh, unique, unusual, different *Scientists are continuing to find novel uses for recycled materials.* 2. *noun* book, fiction, story, tale *I can hardly wait to read the next novel in the series.*

novelty *noun* originality, newness, freshness, unusualness *The novelty of a new video game wears off after playing it for a while.*

now *adverb* 1. at once, immediately, right away *Dad says to clean up your room now.* later 2. presently, today, at this time *We don't have any in stock right now.*

noxious *adjective* harmful, poisonous, damaging, toxic *The factory released noxious chemicals into the stream and killed the fish.*

nucleus *noun* middle, core, heart, kernel, hub, focus *Forts often became the nucleus of growing towns in America.*

nudge 1. *verb* push, prod, shove, poke, jab *Jackie nudged me with her elbow when it was time for me to say my lines.* 2. *noun* push, prod, shove, poke, jab *The mother dolphin gave her baby a nudge with her nose.*

nuisance *noun* annoyance, irritation, bother, pest *Mosquitoes are not only a nuisance, but some species spread disease.*

numb 1. *adjective* unfeeling, deadened, dead, frozen, asleep *My toes were numb from the cold.* 2. *verb* deaden, freeze, dull, anesthetize *The dentist numbed my jaw with an injection.*

number *noun* 1. numeral, digit, figure, symbol *Pick a number between one and ten.* 2. quantity, sum, amount, count *What's the maximum number of people the auditorium will seat?*

numeral *noun* number, digit, figure, symbol *I am learning to read and write Roman numerals.*

numerous *adjective* many, abundant, several, various, myriad *We took numerous photographs while on vacation.*

nurse *verb* care for, take care of, tend, look after, nurture *Mom nursed me back to health after the flu.*

nutrition *noun* food, nourishment, sustenance *Good nutrition is essential to good health.*

nutritious *adjective* nourishing, wholesome, healthy, healthful, beneficial *Mom and Dad only let me eat nutritious snacks.*

nuzzle *verb* snuggle, cuddle, nestle, rub against, press against *I like nuzzling my cat's soft fur.*

O

oath *noun* promise, pledge, vow, commitment *Witnesses in court take an oath that they will tell the truth.*

obedient *adjective* dutiful, compliant, submissive, yielding, loyal *Our dog has been trained to be obedient and will wait for a command.* disobedient

obese *adjective* fat, overweight, heavy, plump, large *See a veterinarian before you put an obese cat on a diet.* thin, lean

obey *verb* yield, submit, follow, comply, mind, heed, listen to *A soldier is required to obey all lawful orders given by an officer.* disobey

object 1. *noun* thing, article, item *The museum has thousands of objects on display from ancient Rome and Greece.* 2. purpose, end, goal, target, intent, aim *The object of the game is to capture all the other players' pieces.* 3. focus, target, subject *A sunken treasure ship was the object of the divers' search.* 4. *verb* protest, challenge, oppose, complain, disapprove *Dad objected to our playing video games indoors on such a nice day.* approve

objection *noun* protest, challenge, complaint, criticism, disapproval, dissent *Objection to the British Tea Act of 1773 led to the Colonists' rebellion known as the Boston Tea Party.* approval

objective 1. *adjective* fair, impartial, unprejudiced, unbiased, neutral *If you want an objective opinion, ask someone other than a friend.* 2. *noun* goal, aim, intention, desire, hope *My objective this summer is to learn to water-ski.*

obligation *noun* duty, responsibility, requirement, commitment, task, job *Parents have an obligation to supervise their children's online activities.*

oblige *verb* require, compel, force, make, obligate *George Washington's army was obliged to retreat across the Delaware River from New York in 1776.*

obliging *adjective* helpful, considerate, thoughtful, accommodating *The clerk was very obliging in suggesting another store where I might find what I was looking for.*

obscure 1. *adjective* vague, indefinite, unclear *The meaning of this poetry is really obscure.* clear 2. faint, dim, blurred, shadowy, hazy, indistinct *An obscure shape loomed out of the fog.* clear 3. unknown, unheard of, minor, insignificant, unimportant *I read an excellent book by an obscure author who has never had a best seller.* 4. *verb* hide, cover, conceal, block *Snow obscured the roadway.*

observation *noun* 1. examination, study, inspection, scrutiny, contemplation, review *Through his observation of the planets, Galileo was convinced the sun, not the earth, was the center of the solar system.* 2. comment, remark, thought, opinion, statement *Mark Twain's amusing observations about people and places make enjoyable reading.*

observe *verb* 1. see, notice, watch, perceive, inspect, examine *Did you observe anything unusual?* 2. obey, follow, comply with, heed, abide by *Drivers are expected to observe the rules of the road.*

obsolete *adjective* old-fashioned, out-of-date, outmoded, discontinued, antiquated *Computer technology that was brand-new ten years ago is obsolete today.* recent

obstacle *noun* barrier, obstruction, block, hindrance, deterrent, impediment *Our different cultural backgrounds are no obstacle to Serafino's and my friendship.*

obstinate *adjective* stubborn, willful, headstrong, unyielding, inflexible *We're taking our obstinate puppy to obedience school.*

obstruct *verb* block, hinder, impede, delay *Construction on the highway is obstructing traffic.* help, aid

obstruction *noun* barrier, obstacle, hindrance, deterrent, impediment, bar *Beaver dams can be an obstruction to salmon migrating upstream.*

obtain *verb* get, acquire, secure, gain, earn, receive *I obtained the information I needed for my report from the encyclopedia.*

obvious *adjective* plain, apparent, clear, evident, distinct, explicit, understandable *Rock climbing has some obvious risks.* hidden

occasion *noun* 1. event, happening, occurrence, time, circumstance *Great-Grandma's ninetieth birthday was a happy occasion.* 2. opportunity, chance, possibility *The family gathering gave us an occasion to catch up on one another's activities.*

occasional *adjective* infrequent, irregular, intermittent, rare *During the winter we have snow but only an occasional blizzard.*

occupant *noun* inhabitant, resident, tenant, renter, lodger *The new occupant of the house next door came over to introduce herself.*

occupation *noun* 1. job, work, career, trade, business, profession, employment, function *Grandpa's occupation is farming.* 2. possession, rule, invasion, takeover, conquest *Poland was under German occupation between 1939 and 1945.*

occupy *verb* 1. live in, inhabit, dwell in, reside in *A young couple occupies the upstairs* *apartment.* 2. fill, engage, employ, take up, use up *Schoolwork, sports, and music lessons occupy most of my time.* 3. conquer, capture, control, take possession of, take over *The Romans occupied Britain between the first and fifth centuries.*

occur *verb* 1. happen, take place, come about, transpire *Northern lights occur when a strong magnetic patch on the sun erupts in a flare, shooting charged particles into space.* 2. come to mind, cross one's mind, strike *It suddenly occurred to her that today was her father's birthday.*

occurrence *noun* event, happening, incident, experience, occasion *Freezing temperatures are a rare occurrence in southern Florida.*

odd *adjective* 1. strange, unusual, peculiar, unique, weird, bizarre *It's odd he hasn't called.* usual, ordinary 2. extra, left over, remaining, spare, unmatched *Mom ended up with one odd sock after doing the laundry.* 3. various, miscellaneous, occasional, irregular *Dad had several odd jobs for me to do around the house.*

odor *noun* smell, scent, aroma, fragrance, stink, stench *Cigarette smoke leaves an unpleasant odor in your hair and clothes.*

offend *verb* displease, anger, upset, annoy, irritate, insult, disgust *The destruction of the rain forests offends environmentalists.*

offense *noun* 1. crime, violation, wrongdoing, misdeed, sin *Cruelty to animals is a criminal offense.* 2. insult, slight, snub, injury, harm, affront *I'm sorry—I meant no offense.*

offensive 1. *adjective* disgusting, distasteful, unpleasant, nasty, foul, repulsive *That garbage truck has an offensive smell.* pleasant 2. *adjective* rude, discourteous, impolite, insulting *Jokes about peoples' ethnic backgrounds are offensive.* courteous, polite 3. *noun* attack, assault, charge, drive, invasion *The army launched a major offensive against the insurgents.*

offer 1. *verb* propose, suggest, submit, volunteer *Dad offered to buy pizza in return for our help.* 2. provide, supply, furnish *Mom's new job offers excellent pay and benefits.* 3. *noun* proposal, suggestion, proposition, bid, deal *We accepted the buyer's offer of $3,000 for our old car.*

office *noun* 1. room, workplace, headquarters, studio, department *The waiting room of the doctor's office was full.* 2. position, post, function, role, capacity, duty, job *An election for the office of president takes place every four years.*

official 1. *adjective* authorized, approved, allowed, legal, formal *You will need to get official permission from your teacher whenever you want to leave the classroom.* 2. *noun* officer, administrator, executive, director *The governor is a state official.*

often *adverb* repeatedly, many times, frequently *Do you come here often?* seldom, infrequently

old *adjective* 1. senior, aged, elderly, mature, ancient, antique *Grandma and Grandpa claim they're getting old and would like to retire.* 2. former, previous, last, other *Our old house had a smaller yard than the one we live in now.* 3. worn-out, stale, out-of-date, abandoned, obsolete *It's time to throw out this old food.*

omen *noun* sign, indication, warning, prophecy *To find a horseshoe is an omen of good luck.*

omit *verb* leave out, exclude, neglect, skip, miss, overlook *Mom has to omit nuts from recipes because my brother is allergic to them.*

once *adverb* 1. formerly, previously, in the past, then *The prairie once stretched across a million square miles of North America.* 2. when, after, as soon as *You may watch TV once you have finished your homework.*

only 1. *adverb* just, merely, simply, no more than *I ate only two brownies.* 2. *adjective* single, lone, one, sole *I am the only girl in the family.*

onward *adverb* further, farther, forward, ahead *The store gets busy from about 5:00 onward.*

ooze *verb* leak, seep, flow, drip *The toothpaste is oozing from the tube.*

open 1. *adjective* not shut, unlocked, unclosed, ajar *It rained in the open window.* closed 2. uncovered, unsealed, unfastened *The open carton spilled all over the floor.* closed, covered 3. unoccupied, vacant, available *If the job is still open, my sister might be interested in applying.* closed, unavailable 4. undeveloped, unenclosed, uncluttered, spacious, clear *We took a walk in the open countryside.* built-up, developed 5. public, general, accessible, not exclusive, shared *The meeting is open to everyone.* exclusive 6. direct, honest, frank, candid, sincere *Dorothy is very open about her opinions.* guarded 7. *verb* begin business, start, commence *The grocery store opens at 7:00 A.M.* close 8. unlock, unfasten, unseal, unwrap, uncover *I opened the present from Grandma first.* close

operate *verb* 1. manage, conduct, handle, run, carry on, direct *Mr. Barton operates a construction business.* 2. work, run, function, act, perform *The machines operate twenty-four hours a day.*

operation *noun* functioning, performance, process, procedure, action, use *The job requires a knowledge of basic computer operation.*

opinion *noun* belief, judgment, attitude, estimation, view, idea, thought, conviction *In my opinion, that's the best chocolate cake I've ever tasted.*

opponent *noun* enemy, foe, adversary, competitor, rival, contender *The mayor defeated her opponent and will serve another term.*

opportunity *noun* chance, occasion, time, opening, turn *The walk signal is too brief to give much opportunity to cross the street.*

oppose *verb* disagree with, dispute, object to, fight, resist, contest *I wouldn't oppose a longer summer vacation.*

opposition *noun* disagreement, objection, resistance, hostility *There is overwhelming opposition by parents to closing the neighborhood school.*

optimistic *adjective* hopeful, positive, confident, cheerful, happy, bright *I am optimistic about our team's chances of winning.* pessimistic

optional *adjective* voluntary, elective *An optional longer-life battery is available for the laptop computer.* required

oral *adjective* spoken, verbal, voiced, sounded *I gave an oral book report to the class today.*

orbit 1. *noun* revolution, circuit, circle, path, route, trajectory *There are hundreds of communications satellites in orbit around the earth.* 2. *verb* circle, revolve around, encircle *The earth orbits the sun in a little over 365 days.*

orchestra *noun* band, ensemble *Julia plays the saxophone in the school orchestra.*

ordeal *noun* difficult experience, test, trial, tribulation *Ernest Shackleton's Antarctic expedition became trapped in ice and suffered a twenty-month ordeal.*

order 1. *noun* condition, state, shape, arrangement *I put my room in good order before Mom got home.* 2. arrangement, organization, classification, sequence *The books in the store are in alphabetical order by author.* 3. command, instruction, direction, directive *The sergeant gave the order to halt.* 4. peace, calm, discipline, law, control *The substitute teacher maintained order and kept the students on task.* 5. *verb* command, instruct, direct, require, bid *Dad ordered my sister and me to stop arguing.* 6. request, ask for, buy, send for, purchase *I ordered a new backpack over the Internet.*

orderly *adjective* 1. neat, tidy, organized, arranged *Our classroom desks are in orderly rows.* disorderly 2. well behaved, disciplined, nonviolent, peaceful, calm *The environmental group staged an orderly demonstration.*

ordinarily *adverb* usually, normally, regularly, typically, as a general rule *We ordinarily go out to eat on Friday evenings.*

ordinary *adjective* 1. usual, common, normal, average, regular, standard *The day started like any ordinary day.* 2. plain, simple, unimpressive, commonplace, mediocre, dull *For all the money they spent on the house, I thought it was very ordinary.*

organization *noun* 1. association, group, society, club, body, company *The organization hopes to raise money for housing for homeless people.* 2. arrangement, coordination, planning, development, management *The organization of my sister's wedding took a lot of time.* 3. structure, design, form, arrangement *Scientists want to better understand the organization of the universe.*

origin *noun* beginning, start, birth, source, basis, derivation *The origin of the word "astronaut" comes from two Greek words meaning "star" and "sailor."*

original *adjective* 1. first, initial, primary, early, previous *The original owner of our house kept it in excellent repair.* 2. creative, new, unique, unusual, innovative, imaginative, fresh *Barbara's art teacher says her paintings and drawings are truly original.*

originate *verb* begin, start, commence, initiate, create, invent, develop *Does anyone know where the rumor originated?*

ornament 1. *noun* decoration, adornment, trimming, embellishment *Some of our Christmas tree ornaments belonged to my great-grandparents.* 2. *verb* decorate, adorn, trim, embellish *The wedding dress is ornamented with pearls.*

other *adjective* different, distinct, additional, extra, further, fresh, new *Can you give me a few other examples?*

ought *verb* should, must, need, have, be obliged *You ought to call to let your parents know where you are.*

out 1. *adverb* outside, outdoors *Please let the cat out.* 2. elsewhere, away *The boss is out of the office today.* 3. *adjective* unfashionable, old-fashioned, outdated, unstylish, out-of-date *Shocking pink hair is out this year.* 4. extinguished, dead *The fire in the fireplace is out.*

outbreak *noun* epidemic, plague, eruption, outburst, torrent *A lot of the teachers and students are absent from school because of an outbreak of the flu.*

outburst *noun* eruption, outbreak, torrent, outpouring *Except for an occasional outburst of laughter, the class was quiet while we worked at our computers.*

outcome *noun* result, conclusion, end, consequence, effect, upshot *What was the outcome of last night's game?*

outdated *adjective* old, old-fashioned, outmoded *I donated my outdated computer to an organization that will upgrade it and give it to a disadvantaged child.*

outdo *verb* surpass, exceed, outshine, defeat, beat *Serena outdid her opponent at tennis.*

outer *adjective* outside, external, exterior, surface *A crab's shell is, in fact, an outer skeleton.*

outfit 1. *noun* clothing, dress, suit, garb *I got a new outfit for the wedding.* 2. *verb* equip, furnish, prepare, rig, fit *The troop outfitted itself for the camping trip.*

outing *noun* trip, journey, jaunt, excursion, tour *We went on a weekend outing to the lake.*

outlaw 1. *noun* criminal, crook, robber, villain, bandit *Butch Cassidy was a legendary outlaw of the Wild West.* 2. *verb* ban, forbid, prohibit, suppress *In 1920 a constitutional amendment came into effect that outlawed the sale of alcoholic beverages.*

outlet *noun* opening, passage, exit, channel, vent *This alley has no outlet at the far end. One-on-one basketball with my dad is a good outlet for my energy.*

outline 1. *noun* plan, sketch, diagram, chart, draft, summary *The teacher suggested we first do an outline to organize the information for our reports.* 2. profile, contour, silhouette, shape *We could see the outline of a ship along the horizon.* 3. *verb* plan, sketch out, make a draft, summarize *The teacher outlined her lesson plan for the fall term.*

outlook *noun* 1. view, attitude, position, point of view *Studies show that people with an optimistic outlook on life live longer and healthier lives.* 2. forecast, prediction, prospect, likelihood, chance *The outlook for rain to end the drought is not good.*

outnumber *verb* exceed, be more than *The girls outnumbered the boys at the dance.*

output *noun* yield, production, proceeds, crop, harvest *Companies that produce ethanol for use as a gasoline additive are increasing their output.*

outrage *noun* anger, shock, rage, fury, indignation *Public outrage forced the dishonest official to resign.*

outrageous *adjective* disgraceful, shameful, scandalous, shocking, despicable *Some outrageous stories appear in the supermarket newspapers near the checkout.*

outside 1. *noun* exterior, outer surface, face, external surface *We painted the outside of the house.* inside 2. *adjective* outer, external, exterior *Black walnuts have a hard shell surrounded by a thick outside husk.* inside

outspoken *adjective* frank, open, straightforward, direct, candid, unrestrained *My parents are outspoken critics of television violence.* shy, reserved

outstanding *adjective* excellent, superior, exceptional, remarkable, impressive *The actor gave an outstanding performance as the villain.* poor

over 1. *preposition* across, above, past, beyond *The hikers disappeared over the hill.* 2. more than, greater than, larger than, in excess of, faster than *He is over six feet tall. Don't go over the speed limit.* 3. *adjective* ended, finished, done, through *Baseball season is over for the winter.*

overcast *adjective* cloudy, dark, gloomy, bleak, hazy *The sky was overcast earlier but has cleared.* clear, sunny, bright

overcome *verb* conquer, defeat, upset, overpower, surmount *Franklin D. Roosevelt overcame a crippling illness to become president.*

overdo *verb* carry too far, go to extremes *You overdid your exercises if you're still sore after a couple of days.*

overdue *adjective* late, tardy, behind, unpaid *My overdue library books cost me two dollars in fines.* on time

overflow *verb* flood, run over, spill over, cascade over, pour over *The river overflowed its banks.*

overhaul *verb* repair, service, fix, mend, recondition *I helped Dad restore the antique car and overhaul its engine.*

overhead 1. *adverb* above, high, aloft *A flock of geese flew overhead.* 2. *noun* expenses, costs *Running a business from your home keeps overhead low.*

overjoyed *adjective* delighted, ecstatic, elated, jubilant, thrilled *I was overjoyed when I realized that I hadn't lost my wallet.*

overlook *verb* miss, forget, neglect, skip, pass over, ignore, disregard *The teacher caught a spelling error I had overlooked.* notice, note

overrule *verb* reject, disallow, veto, override, overturn *The appeals court judge overruled the lower court's decision.*

oversight *noun* error, mistake, omission, slip, failure to notice *Through an oversight, I didn't get my books back to the library on time.*

overtake *verb* catch up with, pass, surpass, outdistance *We all watched the horse that* *was in second place overtake the leader and end up winning the race.*

overthrow 1. *verb* defeat, overpower, overturn, unseat, conquer, destroy *In 1917 the Russian people overthrew the czar.* 2. *noun* defeat, downfall, collapse *Several times, conspirators plotted the overthrow of King James I of England.*

overturn *verb* capsize, tip over, topple over, keel over *The canoe overturned when Gordie tried to get in.*

overweight *adjective* heavy, fat, plump, stout, obese, chubby, large, chunky *The vet recommended we put our overweight dog on a diet.*

overwhelm *verb* 1. crush, defeat, conquer, vanquish *The government army overwhelmed the rebels in only two hours of fighting.* 2. move, overcome, stun, awe *The generous gifts overwhelmed the needy family.*

owe *verb* be in debt, be liable for *How much do you owe on your credit card?*

own *verb* have, possess, hold, maintain *My grandparents owned the house we live in before my parents bought it from them.*

P

pace 1. *noun* rate, speed *Cheetahs can run as fast as seventy miles per hour but cannot sustain this pace for long.* 2. stride, step, gait *My little brother followed a few paces behind.* 3. *verb* stride, gait, step, walk, tread *The dogs paced restlessly at the door, waiting for their walk.*

pacify *verb* quiet, calm, soothe *I felt sorry for the woman in the crowd who was unable to pacify her crying baby.* provoke, anger

pack 1. *verb* fill, load, stuff, cram, jam, stow *We just managed to pack all our camping gear in the trunk of the car.* unpack, empty 2. *noun* package, parcel, box, carton, container *The batteries cost less if you buy them by the twelve-pack.* 3. backpack, rucksack, knapsack, bag, bundle *The hikers carried everything they needed in packs on their backs.* 4. gang, band, mob, group, crowd, bunch, herd *Wolves hunt in packs.*

package *noun* carton, box, container, parcel, bundle, pack *Please take this package to the post office to be mailed.*

pact *noun* agreement, contract, understanding, bargain, deal *The member nations of NATO have a pact to defend one another against attack.*

pad *noun* 1. cushion, pillow, mat *I put a pad on the floor to do my yoga exercises.* 2. notebook, tablet, notepad, scratch pad *I jotted the phone number on a pad near the phone.*

page *noun* sheet, paper, leaf *I'm on page 114 of the book.*

pageant *noun* show, spectacle, display, entertainment, exhibition, presentation *Our class was in charge of the pageant to celebrate Mexican Independence Day.*

pail *noun* bucket *The pioneer women carried pails of water in which to wash their clothes from the stream.*

pain 1. *noun* ache, soreness, hurt, pang, discomfort, irritation *I still have pain in my ankle from having twisted it.* 2. suffering, sorrow, sadness, grief, anguish, agony *The loss of someone we love causes us great pain.* 3. *verb* distress, sadden, upset, grieve *It pains me to see so much suffering in the world.*

paint 1. *noun* coloring, dye, stain, tint, pigment *We put a fresh coat of paint on the house.* 2. *verb* coat, color, cover, decorate, trim *What color would you like to paint your room?*

painting *noun* picture, artwork, watercolor, oil, canvas, landscape, portrait *The Mona Lisa, perhaps the most famous painting in the world, hangs in the Louvre, a museum in Paris.*

pair 1. *noun* two, couple, duo, twosome, set *I can find only one of my pair of gloves. Bob and Maggie make an attractive pair.* 2. *verb* team up, combine, join, match up *Grant paired with Eric in the doubles championship.*

pal *noun* friend, companion, comrade, colleague, buddy, chum *Dad and Charlie have been pals since college.*

palace *noun* castle, mansion, villa, château *The millionaire's house is as big as a palace.*

pale *adjective* dim, colorless, faint, indistinct, pallid, whitish *Pale moonlight is filtering through the clouds.*

pamper *verb* indulge, spoil, coddle, cater to, favor *Mom says we pamper my baby brother too much.*

pamphlet *noun* booklet, brochure, leaflet, folder *We're studying travel pamphlets to decide where to go on vacation.*

panel *noun* group, forum, board, committee, council *A panel of judges will decide the competition.*

pang *noun* twinge, spasm, pain, cramp, stitch, ache, discomfort *I got a pang in my side after running.*

panic 1. *noun* fear, fright, alarm, terror, dread *The snake caused me a moment of panic until I realized it wasn't a rattlesnake.* 2. *verb* frighten, scare, terrify, alarm *I panicked when my computer locked up and I hadn't saved my report.*

pant *verb* puff, huff, gasp, wheeze, breathe *We were all panting hard after the race.*

pants *noun* slacks, trousers, jeans, blue jeans, capris *Are you going to wear pants or a skirt to the party?*

paper *noun* 1. report, essay, composition, piece, article *Our assignment is to write a paper on the Civil War.* 2. document, contract, instrument, deed *Anna received her citizenship papers last week.* 3. newspaper, gazette, journal, publication, periodical, tabloid *I always read the comics in the Sunday paper.* 4. writing paper, blank paper, stationery, sheet, page *I need a piece of paper on which to write a letter.*

parade 1. *noun* procession, march *My brother is in charge of the class float for the homecoming parade.* 2. *verb* march, file, walk, strut *The troops paraded before the general.*

paradise *noun* heaven, bliss, glory, ecstasy *Mom claims a bubble bath is sheer paradise.*

parallel 1. *adjective* side-by-side, aligned, equidistant *The lines on ruled paper are parallel to each other.* 2. similar, like, corresponding, comparable *Parallel efforts are under way by environmental groups to restore wetlands.* 3. *noun* similarity, resemblance, likeness, comparison, correspondence *The art critic sees parallels between the artists' works.* 4. *verb* resemble, correspond to, compare to, be similar to *The second witness's account of the accident parallels that of the first witness.*

paralyze *verb* cripple, disable, incapacitate, immobilize, numb *A spider paralyzes or kills its prey with venom by puncturing it with its fangs.*

parcel *noun* package, bundle, pack, container, box *The mail carrier delivered a parcel for you today.*

parched *adjective* dry, dehydrated, scorched, arid *The cornfields are parched after the long drought.*

pardon 1. *verb* forgive, excuse, absolve, overlook *Pardon my interruption, but there's a phone call for you.* 2. *noun* forgiveness, exoneration, reprieve, mercy *He received a pardon after serving twelve years for a crime he did not commit.*

pare *verb* peel, trim, skin, strip, scrape *I helped my mom pare apples for a pie.*

park 1. *noun* public land, grounds, sanctuary, common, green, recreation area, playground *The children played in the park after school.* 2. *verb* stop, place, leave, put *I'll let you out here and look for a place to park the car.*

part 1. *noun* portion, section, division, segment, component, fraction, piece *My favorite part of the movie was the chase scene.* 2. role, duty, job, responsibility, function *Everyone on the team has a part to play.* 3. *verb* divide, separate, split, open *Jon parted the curtains to see who was at the door.*

partial *adjective* 1. part, limited, incomplete, fragmentary, fractional *Our class's fund-raising campaign was only a partial success; we were $25 short of our goal.* 2. biased, prejudiced, unjust, unfair, discriminatory *The contest's losers claimed the judges were partial.*

participate *verb* take part, enter, join, have a hand, contribute, partake *Children and their parents are invited to participate in story hour at the library.*

particle *noun* fragment, speck, spot, bit, crumb, flake, grain *Dust particles make up the part of a comet's tail most easily seen from earth.*

particular 1. *adjective* special, unusual, especial, exceptional, specific, thorough *Pay particular attention to the instructions.* 2. fussy, finicky, fastidious, exacting, meticulous, discriminating, critical *Dad is on a diet and is very particular about what he eats.* 3. *noun* detail, item, point, fact, specific *The news report didn't give any particulars.*

partition 1. *noun* division, divider, wall, barrier *The dining area and the kitchen are separated with a waist-high partition.* 2. *verb* divide, separate, wall off, split off, segregate *The entire floor of the building is partitioned into tiny cubicles for the office workers.*

partly *adverb* somewhat, in part, partially, to some degree *The forecast is for a partly sunny day.*

partner *noun* companion, colleague, comrade, associate, coworker, mate *Mom and Ms. Ashford are partners in a new business venture.*

partnership *noun* alliance, association, collaboration, company, business, joint venture *The university and the school board have formed a partnership to provide tutors for students.*

party *noun* 1. celebration, festivity, social event, get-together *We had a party to celebrate my grandmother's seventieth birthday.* 2. group, crew, gang, company *We'd like reservations for a party of four.*

pass 1. *verb* go, travel, move, proceed, progress *Very little traffic passes along our street.* 2. go by, go past, overtake, get ahead *The left lane is for passing other vehicles.* 3. succeed in, do well in, meet the requirements of *My sister passed all her final exams.* 4. hand over, deliver, transfer, give *Please pass me the salt.* 5. approve, adopt, ratify, authorize *The Civil Rights Act, passed in 1964, prohibits job discrimination based on race, color, religion, sex, or national origin.* 6. *noun* throw, toss, pitch *The quarterback completed three passes in the first quarter.*

passage *noun* 1. corridor, hallway, hall, lane, tunnel, channel, passageway *The Mammoth Cave system has about 350 miles of underground passages.* 2. advance, flow, movement, progress *With the passage of time, I've grown to like Thomas.* 3. section, paragraph, chapter, excerpt, selection *The teacher asked me to read aloud a passage from the book.* 4. voyage, cruise, crossing, trip, trek *After a stormy ocean passage, the travelers arrived in the United States.*

passenger *noun* rider, commuter, traveler *All airline passengers must go through a metal detector.*

passion *noun* emotion, enthusiasm, strong feeling, fervor *He has a passion for soccer.*

past 1. *adjective* former, previous, preceding, ended, over, gone by *Where have you been for the past few days? Winter is past, and spring has arrived.* 2. *noun* former times, times gone by *Archaeological discoveries help us understand the past.* 3. *preposition* beyond, by *I walk past her house on my way to school.*

paste 1. *noun* glue, adhesive, cement, mucilage *The paste has dried up in the bottom of the jar.* 2. *verb* stick, glue, attach, fasten, fix *In art class we made a collage by pasting magazine cutouts on poster board.*

pastime *noun* recreation, amusement, enjoyment, relaxation, diversion *Waterskiing is my favorite summer pastime.*

pasture *noun* grassland, field, meadow, range *Cows grazed in roadside pastures.*

pat *verb* tap, stroke, touch, caress *Corey gave our dog a friendly pat on the head.*

patch 1. *verb* mend, repair, fix, service *Mom wanted to patch my torn blue jeans.* 2. *noun* area, spot, streak, bit *We stopped to rest under a tree in a patch of shade.*

pathetic *adjective* pitiful, touching, moving, sad *They looked pathetic, thoroughly drenched, dripping water on the floor, their hair plastered to their heads.*

patience *noun* serenity, calmness, composure, restraint, tolerance, indulgence *Building a model ship in a bottle requires a lot of patience.*

patient *adjective* serene, calm, composed, restrained, tolerant, understanding *We might as well be patient—there's nothing we can do about a flight delay.*

patriotic *adjective* loyal, nationalistic *After the Boston Tea Party, patriotic Colonists came up with a substitute for English tea made from sweet goldenrod.*

patrol *verb* watch, guard, protect, defend, keep vigil *Security guards patrol the building after closing.*

pattern 1. *noun* arrangement, design, illustration, picture, form, outline, shape *I chose wallpaper with a sailboat pattern for my room.* 2. model, example, standard, guide, prototype *Mom used a paper pattern to make a rabbit costume for my sister.* 3. *verb* model, style, fashion, form, mold *The state capitol building is patterned after the U.S. Capitol in Washington, D.C.*

pause 1. *verb* wait, stop, rest, cease, halt *The speaker paused to take a question from the audience.* 2. *noun* break, rest, stop, halt, delay, intermission *After a pause for gas and lunch, we continued on our way.*

pave *verb* cover, surface, floor *We paved our walkway with bricks.*

pay 1. *verb* compensate, give, reward, reimburse, remunerate *Our neighbor pays me to mow the lawn and shovel the sidewalk.* 2. *noun* compensation, wages, salary, earnings, fees, money, remuneration *Dad receives extra pay for overtime.*

peace *noun* 1. harmony, accord, truce, goodwill, friendship *The agreement brought peace to the two nations.* 2. calm, quiet, tranquillity, serenity *We enjoy the peace of living in the country.*

peaceful *adjective* 1. calm, quiet, still, tranquil, placid, untroubled, serene *The cabin is set in peaceful surroundings.* 2. nonviolent, peaceable, harmonious, cordial, friendly *The Hopi people are a peaceful people who have had good relations with their neighbors.*

peak *noun* 1. top, crest, summit, hilltop, pinnacle, crown, tip, apex *The peaks of the mountains are covered with snow at this time of year.* 2. climax, zenith, top, height, high point *He's at the peak of his career as a quarterback.*

peculiar *adjective* 1. strange, odd, unusual, curious *The extinct dodo bird was a peculiar, flightless bird native only to the island Mauritius in the Indian Ocean.* 2. special, distinctive, characteristic, typical, representative *The people use a weaving technique for their rugs that is peculiar to the region.*

pedal *verb* bike, cycle, ride, propel *I pedaled hard up the hill.*

peddle *verb* sell, hawk, vend, market *In the nineteenth century, medicine shows came to town to peddle bottles of a liquid guaranteed to cure everything.*

pedestrian *noun* walker, hiker, person on foot *Pedestrians should cross the street only in marked crosswalks.*

peek 1. *verb* glance, glimpse, peep, look *I stood on tiptoe and peeked over the fence.* 2. *noun* glance, glimpse, quick look *I took a peek in the oven to see what was cooking.*

peel *verb* strip, pare, skin *I helped with dinner by peeling the potatoes.*

peer 1. *noun* equal, match, like, equivalent *As a writer, she has few peers.* 2. *verb* look, gaze, stare, examine, scrutinize *I peered under the bed in search of the cat.*

pelt 1. *verb* attack, strike, pound, beat, hit, knock, bombard, pepper *We pelted each other with snowballs. The rain pelted the metal roof.* 2. *noun* hide, skin, fur, coat *Trade in animal pelts flourished in North America from the seventeenth to early nineteenth centuries.*

pen 1. *noun* enclosure, coop, cage, pound, corral *Let the dog out of his pen to run.* 2. writing instrument, ballpoint, felt-tip, quill, fountain pen *Our teacher uses a red pen to correct our mistakes.* 3. *verb* enclose, confine, shut in, surround, coop up *Did you remember to pen the dogs for the night?* 4. write, draft, jot, inscribe *Choose a poem penned by your favorite poet to read aloud in class.*

penalize *verb* punish, discipline, reprimand, correct, fine *Speeders on city streets are penalized.* reward

penalty *noun* punishment, fine, discipline, consequence *I was grounded as a penalty for neglecting my chores.*

penetrate *verb* 1. pierce, enter, puncture, bore, perforate *A sliver penetrated the palm of my hand.* 2. understand, perceive, figure out, solve, decipher *I couldn't even begin to penetrate the scientist's explanation.*

pennant *noun* flag, banner, streamer, ensign, standard, colors *The pirate ship flew a pennant with a skull and crossbones.*

pension *noun* retirement income, allowance, benefit, support *After my grandparents retire, they'll receive company pensions and Social Security.*

people *noun* 1. persons, human beings, humans, individuals, folks *About 300 people attended the concert.* 2. public, community, society, citizens, populace *The people objected to taxation without representation.*

perceive *verb* 1. observe, detect, see, notice, recognize, distinguish *Some people*

~~~~~~

are color-blind and do not perceive colors the way the rest of us do. 2. understand, grasp, comprehend, sense, realize *I perceived immediately that she wasn't interested.*

percentage *noun* proportion, part, ratio, share, fraction *A large percentage of the students were absent with the flu.*

perch *verb* sit, rest, settle, land *A wren was perched nearby, scolding the cat.*

perfect 1. *adjective* flawless, faultless *The actors gave a perfect performance.* flawed 2. correct, accurate, exact, true, precise *The forgery was a perfect copy of the original painting.* inexact 3. ideal, excellent, wonderful, exemplary *Genevieve is a perfect student.* 4. *verb* improve, refine, better, polish *Jan is taking lessons to perfect her guitar playing technique.* spoil

perform *verb* 1. execute, accomplish, carry out, achieve, complete *A. A. Michelson performed a series of experiments to determine the speed of light.* 2. act, present, enact, stage, put on *Shakespeare's plays are easier to understand when you see them performed.*

perhaps *adverb* possibly, maybe, conceivably *Perhaps we'll have better weather tomorrow.*

peril *noun* danger, hazard, risk, threat, jeopardy, endangerment *The coast guard braves the same perils of the sea as the people it rescues.*

period *noun* interval, span, time, spell, stretch *A teenager may grow three to four inches over a period of a year.*

periodical *noun* magazine, journal, gazette, newsletter, bulletin *We subscribe to a number of online periodicals that cover such things as news, science, and entertainment.*

perish *verb* die, succumb, expire, pass away, depart *Thousands of people perished when Mount Vesuvius erupted in A.D. 79 and destroyed the cities of Pompeii and Herculaneum.*

permanent *adjective* lasting, durable, enduring, long-lasting, constant, unchanging, stable *Following his defeat at Waterloo, Napoleon went into permanent exile on the island of St. Helena.*

permit 1. *verb* allow, let, authorize, approve, consent to, grant *My parents permit me to stay up late on Saturday nights.* forbid 2. allow, make possible *When time permits, Dad and I go golfing together.* 3. *noun* license, authorization, approval, permission *We had to get a building permit in order to build an addition onto our home.*

perpendicular *adjective* upright, vertical *The divers dove from a 135-foot perpendicular cliff into the ocean below.*

perplexed *adjective* puzzled, bewildered, baffled, mystified, confused, confounded, stumped *Dad was totally perplexed by the highway exit signs.*

persecute *verb* oppress, harass, torment, badger, intimidate *Women were persecuted as witches during the Salem witch trials of 1692.*

persist *verb* last, stay, continue, endure, prevail, go on, persevere *If the drought persists, there will likely be forest fires.*

persistent *adjective* 1. insistent, stubborn, obstinate, determined *The workers were persistent in their demands for safer working conditions.* 2. continuing, enduring, constant, lasting, incessant *Computer viruses are a persistent problem and can seriously damage your system.*

person *noun* human, human being, individual, man, woman, child, somebody, someone *Each person must decide for himself or herself what to do.*

personal *adjective* private, individual, own, specific, particular, special *The health club has lockers in which we can store our personal belongings.* public

personality *noun* character, nature, disposition, identity, individuality *Dr. Martin Luther King, Jr., used his powerful personality to fight injustice.*

perspective *noun* outlook, viewpoint, view, attitude, standpoint, angle, slant *Parents view life from a different perspective than do their children.*

perspire *verb* sweat, be dripping, be drenched *When you're exercising strenuously and perspiring, you need to drink water.*

persuade *verb* convince, encourage, influence, coax, plead with, urge *No one can persuade my sister to change her mind once she has made it up.* dissuade

pertain *verb* relate, refer, apply, concern, belong, be appropriate, be connected *I have a question pertaining to our homework assignment.*

pessimistic *adjective* cheerless, joyless, gloomy, unhappy, negative, cynical *Some farmers are pessimistic about the future of small family farms.* optimistic

pest *noun* annoyance, bother, nuisance, irritation, tease *Our puppy can be a real pest when it wants to play.*

pester *verb* annoy, trouble, torment, bother, harass, badger, tease, nag, vex *The mosquitoes were pestering me, so I had to go indoors.*

pet 1. *noun* animal, domestic animal, tame animal *Our pets include a dog, a cat, and* *two hamsters.* 2. favorite, darling, dear *Grandma calls me her pet.* 3. *adjective* favorite, cherished, dearest, precious, special *The city's pet project is the renovation of the old downtown.* 4. *verb* stroke, pat, caress, fondle *When I pet the cat, it rubs against my legs.*

petite *adjective* little, small, slight, tiny *My sister may be petite, but she's very strong.* large

petition 1. *noun* request, demand, appeal, plea, requisition *Over 800 residents have signed a petition to ban smoking in restaurants.* 2. *verb* request, demand, ask, appeal to, plead with *Teachers have petitioned the school board for more money for textbooks.*

petrify *verb* 1. terrify, frighten, scare, horrify, shock *When I was small, it petrified me to walk past the cemetery at night.* 2. harden, solidify, fossilize, set, become stone *An ancient forest of petrified giant redwood trees can be seen in California.*

petty *adjective* 1. unimportant, small, trivial, minor, insignificant *Forget about your petty problems and enjoy yourself.* important 2. mean, spiteful, resentful, narrow-minded, small-minded *Only a jealous, petty person would spread such rumors.*

phantom *noun* ghost, spirit, specter, spook, apparition *There are many stories of phantoms haunting mansions on hills.*

phase *noun* stage, time, period, part, chapter, state *The environmental group is in the initial phase of a prairie restoration project.*

phenomenal *adjective* extraordinary, exceptional, remarkable, marvelous *The class play was a phenomenal success: Every seat in the auditorium was filled.*

phony 1. *adjective* fake, artificial, simulated, false, fraudulent, bogus *Authorities have arrested a man for selling phony designer merchandise.* 2. *noun* fake, impostor, fraud, quack *Several men, who turned out to be phonies, claimed to be the heir to the French throne who disappeared during the French Revolution.*

photograph 1. *noun* picture, photo, snapshot, print *We have a printer that can print photographs straight from our digital camera.* 2. *verb* take a picture, film, shoot, snap *Dad likes to photograph nature scenes.*

phrase 1. *noun* clause, expression, saying, idiom, slogan *Phrases such as "have it made" and "buckle down" are hard for people who are just learning English to understand.* 2. *verb* express, say, word, put into words, formulate *I would phrase it differently, or she may misunderstand.*

physical 1. *adjective* bodily *I like to get some physical exercise every day.* 2. real, tangible, solid, substantial, material *A physical object is something you can see or touch.* 3. *noun* medical examination, physical examination *I had to have a physical before going to camp.*

physician *noun* doctor, surgeon, medical doctor, general practitioner *Dr. Lopez is our family physician.*

pick 1. *verb* choose, select, elect, decide on *I'm small, so I'm usually the last one picked for the sports team.* 2. harvest, gather, collect, pluck, reap *We picked cherries, and Mom made a pie.* 3. *noun* choice, selection, preference, option *We had our pick of five different desserts.*

picnic *noun* outdoor meal, cookout, barbecue *After our swim, we had a picnic at the beach.*

picture 1. *noun* image, photograph, painting, drawing, illustration, depiction *The book has pictures of fire engines used over the past 150 years.* 2. movie, film, motion picture, show *The movie won seven awards, including one for best picture.* 3. *verb* imagine, visualize, see, envision *Picture what it was like to cross the country in a covered wagon.* 4. represent, illustrate, portray, depict, describe, characterize *The ancient Greek god Hermes, the messenger of Zeus, is often pictured as a youth wearing winged sandals and a winged helmet.*

piece *noun* part, bit, portion, segment, section, share *I ate two pieces of cake.*

pier *noun* dock, wharf, breakwater, quay, landing *Passengers lined up on the pier to take the ferry.*

pierce *verb* penetrate, puncture, perforate, stab, bore *A nail pierced my bicycle tire.*

pile 1. *noun* heap, stack, mound, collection, accumulation, batch *I left a pile of dirty clothes on the floor.* 2. *verb* stack, heap, mound, collect, accumulate *Blowing snow piled against the fences.*

pillar *noun* column, support, post *The library has decorative pillars on either side of the entrance.*

pillow *noun* cushion, headrest, bolster *We threw some pillows on the floor and lay down to watch TV.*

pilot 1. *noun* aviator, flyer, captain *The pilot announced that we had reached our cruising altitude of 30,000 feet.* 2. navigator, guide, operator *The river pilot must navigate carefully through the locks on the Mississippi River.* 3. *verb* navigate, guide, operate, steer *Women have piloted airplanes since before they could vote.*

pin 1. *verb* fasten, attach, join, secure, affix, fix, stick, tack *The coach pinned a notice on the board saying that practice was canceled.* 2. hold, restrain, immobilize *The bully tried to pin him up against the wall.* 3. *noun* brooch, ornament, stickpin, safety pin *Mom fastened the hem up with pins. She wore a pin in the shape of a butterfly.*

pinch 1. *verb* squeeze, press, tweak, nip *These new shoes pinch my toes.* 2. *noun* squeeze, tweak, nip *The nurse said I'd only feel a little pinch when she gave me the shot.* 3. bit, trace, small amount, dash, little *Add a pinch of salt.* 4. emergency, time of need, predicament *The recipe calls for fresh tomatoes, but canned tomatoes will do in a pinch.*

pioneer *noun* 1. settler, colonist, frontiersman, frontierswoman, explorer *Pioneers began settling the Midwest in the 1790s.* 2. forerunner, leader, innovator, originator, creator, groundbreaker *Henry Ford was a pioneer in the automobile industry.*

pious *adjective* religious, devout, reverent, spiritual, holy *Truly pious people in all religions condemn violence.* atheistic

pipe *noun* tube, channel, duct, pipeline *Water pipes burst when the water in them freezes and expands.*

piracy *noun* stealing, theft *Duplicating a copyrighted piece of software is piracy.*

pistol *noun* gun, firearm, handgun, revolver *Police officers are trained to use pistols.*

pit 1. *noun* hole, cavity, crater, hollow, mine, quarry *The gravel pit has marred the landscape.* 2. *verb* set to compete, match, oppose *The sisters were pitted against each other in the final round.*

pitch 1. *verb* throw, fling, hurl, toss, sling, cast, heave *The children pitched stones into the lake.* 2. put up, erect, set up *We pitched our tent at the edge of the woods.* 3. fall, topple, tumble *Gary tripped and pitched forward down the hill.* 4. sway, lurch, roll, rock *The ship pitched in the storm.* 5. *noun* slope, angle, slant, incline *The mountain road has a steep pitch.* 6. toss, throw, cast, fling, heave *The first pitch was a fly ball to the shortstop.* 7. talk, argument, offer, proposal *The clerk delivered a good sales pitch.* 8. level, degree, height, intensity *The fans' excitement was at a high pitch with only ten seconds left in the game and the home team on the one-yard line.*

pitiful *adjective* pathetic, wretched, sad, miserable *The dripping wet cat looked pitiful.*

pity 1. *noun* sympathy, sorrow, compassion, mercy *We all feel pity for the victims of the tornado.* 2. misfortune, shame, disappointment *It's a pity we have to be in school on such a beautiful spring day.* 3. *verb* sympathize with, feel compassion for, show concern for, feel sorry for *Dad pitied the stray kitten and brought it home with him.*

pivot *verb* turn, swivel, swing, rotate, revolve *The basketball player pivoted left and shot the ball to make three points.*

place 1. *noun* location, area, spot, position, site *We found a nice, quiet place in the shade to sit.* 2. district, region, locality, city, town, neighborhood *Florida is a place where* *northerners go in winter to get away from the cold.* 3. house, home, residence, apartment, dwelling *Come over to my place after school.* 4. rank, position, standing, status, grade, class, station *He received first place in the state speech contest. Mrs. Daly has a high place in the law firm.* 5. *verb* put, set, position, leave, lay, locate, situate *Place the books back on the shelf.* 6. identify, recognize, remember, know *I've seen you before, but I can't place you.*

placid *adjective* calm, peaceful, quiet, still, tranquil, smooth, untroubled *The only ripples on the placid lake were from a fish jumping.*

plague 1. *noun* disease, sickness, epidemic, pestilence *In 1793 a yellow fever plague hit Philadelphia, killing 10 percent of the population.* 2. affliction, disaster, adversity, scourge, evil *Hunger is a plague that still exists throughout the world.* 3. *verb* annoy, bother, torment, harass, pester, trouble, afflict *Flies plagued the picnickers. President Theodore Roosevelt was plagued by poor health as a youngster.* soothe, comfort

plain 1. *adjective* clear, understandable, simple, distinct, obvious, evident *Your meaning is plain.* obscure, complex 2. ordinary, unadorned, basic, simple, average, normal, everyday *She wore a plain white T-shirt and blue jeans.* 3. honest, straightforward, candid, direct, frank, forthright *The officer asked for a plain statement of the facts.* 4. *noun* meadow, grassland, prairie, pasture, field *We could see across the plain all the way to the horizon.*

plan 1. *noun* idea, scheme, design, procedure, aim, goal, intention, proposal *I've already laid out my plans for the summer. Things were not going according to plan.* 2. *verb* arrange, design, devise, aim, propose, intend *There are many things to keep in mind when you're planning a rafting trip.*

plane *noun* 1. airplane, aircraft, jet, airliner *On average, planes take off or land every fifty-six seconds at the busy airport.* 2. level, stage, rank, position, grade *Albert Einstein was on a different intellectual plane from the rest of us.*

plant 1. *noun* shrub, bush, tree, flower, herb, vegetable, seedling, houseplant *It's my job to water the plants in the sunroom.* 2. *verb* grow, root, seed, sow, raise *We plant lots of vegetables in our garden.*

play 1. *verb* amuse oneself, entertain oneself, enjoy oneself, have fun, frolic *Dad suggested we play outside until dinner.* 2. act, perform, portray, be, act the part of *Carlin is playing the lead in the school play.* 3. participate, take part, join, compete *Tim got to play in yesterday's game.* 4. *noun* production, drama, comedy, show, performance *The community theater is rehearsing its new play.* 5. fun, amusement, entertainment, recreation *I prefer play to doing my chores.*

playful *adjective* frisky, spirited, lively, mischievous *We have two playful kittens.*

plea *noun* request, appeal, petition *The charity made a plea for donations for the hurricane victims.*

plead *verb* beg, appeal, petition, implore, entreat, request, ask *The prime minister pleaded for peace.*

pleasant *adjective* pleasing, enjoyable, agreeable, delightful *A swim on a hot day is a pleasant experience.*

please *verb* 1. make happy, delight, satisfy, gratify *The flowers I got for Mom for Mother's Day pleased her.* 2. want, wish, choose, prefer, desire *I can do as I please after I finish my chores.*

pleasure *noun* enjoyment, happiness, delight, joy, satisfaction, gratification *Our teacher says he gets great pleasure out of teaching.*

pledge 1. *noun* promise, vow, oath, assurance, guarantee, commitment *My parents made a pledge of fifty dollars to the library building fund.* 2. *verb* promise, vow, swear, guarantee, give one's word *I pledged that I would report to my parents anything on the Internet that makes me feel uncomfortable.*

plenty *noun* an abundance, a lot, lots, a great deal, enough, sufficient *We have plenty of snacks for the party.*

plod *verb* trudge, slog, tramp, drag, lumber, walk *We plodded up the hill pulling our sleds.*

plot 1. *noun* plan, scheme, conspiracy, intrigue *In 1605 there was a plot to murder King James and blow up Parliament.* 2. story, story line, narrative, scenario, theme *This novel's plot is so exciting, I stayed up past my bedtime reading.* 3. lot, land, parcel, patch *People without garden space can rent a plot in the village park.* 4. *verb* plan, scheme, conspire, contrive *Macbeth and his wife plotted to kill King Duncan.*

plow *verb* 1. cultivate, work, till, furrow *The farmer plowed his fields after the corn was harvested.* 2. plunge, crash, smash, run *The car slid on the ice and plowed into a snowbank.*

plug 1. *noun* stopper, cork, top, seal *I put a plug in the bathtub and turned on the water.* 2. *verb* block, stop, seal, cork, close, fill *We plugged the air leaks around the door with weather stripping.*

plump *adjective* fat, round, stout, stocky, chunky, chubby, fleshy *We harvested plump, juicy tomatoes from our garden all summer.*

plunder 1. *verb* rob, steal, loot, pillage, ransack *Pirates plundered ships of their cargo.*

2. *noun* booty, loot, spoils, stolen goods *They divided the plunder from their raid on the village among themselves.*

plunge 1. *verb* dive, plummet, jump, fall, drop, swoop down *The bald eagle plunged and snatched a big fish out of the water with its talons.* 2. drop, fall, dip, sink, tumble, descend *The temperature plunged to minus 20 degrees last night.* 3. *noun* dive, jump, leap, dip *I like to take a plunge in the lake on a hot night before I go to bed.*

plush *adjective* luxurious, elegant, grand, sumptuous, expensive *The magazine showed pictures of plush apartments owned by the wealthy.*

pocket 1. *noun* compartment, pouch, receptacle *My backpack has lots of zippered pockets.* 2. *verb* take, steal, swipe, appropriate *Marie got caught pocketing a CD as she left the store.* 3. *adjective* miniature, small, portable, compact, concise, abridged *Emilio carries a pocket Spanish-English dictionary to look up words he doesn't understand.*

poetry *noun* verse, rhymes, poems, lyrics, odes, limericks *Edward Lear's nonsense poetry makes me laugh.*

point 1. *noun* tip, end, top, summit, peak *The point of my pencil needs sharpening.* 2. promontory, headland, peninsula, cape *The ship sailed around the point into the harbor.* 3. position, location, spot, site *Boston has many points of historic interest.* 4. instant, moment, time, stage, period *My parents say I don't have to decide on a career at this point in my life.* 5. detail, item, aspect, element, step *We reviewed the important points in preparation for the test.* 6. purpose, objective, aim, meaning, idea, significance *I think you're missing the point of the story.* 7. *verb* direct, aim, turn, face, train *In your first lesson you will learn to point your ski tips inward toward each other to slow down.*

point out *verb* indicate, show, identify, designate, call attention to *The teacher pointed out the spelling errors in my report.*

poise 1. *noun* composure, confidence, self-assurance, calmness, dignity *She immediately regained her poise after stumbling on the stairs.* 2. *verb* balance, hang, float, hover *The hawk was poised nearly motionless in midair, ready to attack its prey.*

poisonous *adjective* toxic, harmful, noxious, deadly, lethal, venomous *We got rid of all our houseplants that are poisonous to pets.*

poke *verb* 1. jab, prod, stab, thrust, stick *Janice poked me in the ribs with her elbow.* 2. search, look, rummage *We poked through the drawer for fresh batteries for the flashlight.* 3. push, thrust, shove *The groundhog poked its head out of its hole.*

pole *noun* stick, bar, post, rod, beam *Our power was out for a few hours while a crew* *replaced the telephone poles that ran on both sides of our street.*

police 1. *noun* law enforcement, police officers, police force, the law, policemen, policewomen *The police stopped the car for speeding.* 2. *verb* control, watch, monitor, patrol, guard, oversee *Deputies policed the grounds during the rock festival.*

policy *noun* plan, program, procedure, guideline, principle, rule *The day-care center has a strict policy that sick children must be cared for at home.*

polish 1. *verb* rub, buff, shine, burnish, wax *I helped Mom polish the silverware before Thanksgiving dinner.* 2. improve, perfect, refine, practice, work on *I spent the summer polishing my diving skills.* 3. *noun* shine, luster, gloss, brilliance *The car had a great polish on it after Dad waxed and buffed it.* 4. elegance, grace, refinement, sophistication, style *The dancer's performance lacked polish.*

polite *adjective* courteous, gracious, respectful, well mannered, tactful, refined *It is not polite to interrupt someone who is talking.* rude

poll 1. *noun* survey, sampling, census, market survey *The school conducted a poll to see if the students liked the cafeteria food.* 2. *verb* survey, canvas, sample, question *A reporter polled the voters as they left the voting place to see whom they voted for.*

pollute *verb* contaminate, taint, foul, defile, poison *Environmental organizations have united to clean up the industrial chemicals that have polluted the river.*

ponder *verb* consider, contemplate, reflect on, think over, study *Let's ponder the possibility that life exists elsewhere in the universe.*

pool 1. *noun* pond, lake, swimming pool, puddle, reservoir *Let's go for a swim in the pool.* 2. *verb* combine, share, merge *Let's pool our money and get a pizza.*

poor *adjective* 1. needy, impoverished, destitute, penniless, poverty-stricken *The food bank distributes food to poor families.* rich, wealthy 2. defective, bad, inferior, substandard, inadequate, unsatisfactory *I wouldn't shop there if I were you; their merchandise is of poor quality.* superior 3. pitiful, unfortunate, wretched, miserable *We found a poor, wet, shivering kitten in our garden.* fortunate

popular *adjective* 1. common, prevalent, conventional, standard, widespread *It is a popular myth that a cat has nine lives.* unusual 2. well liked, admired, favorite, accepted, in favor *The music teacher is popular with the students. Music sites are among the popular Internet sites.* unpopular, disliked

popularity *noun* admiration, approval, acceptance, fame, recognition, renown *The popularity of gas-electric hybrid cars has been increasing.*

population *noun* inhabitants, populace, residents, people *The entire population of our town was affected by the disaster.*

port *noun* harbor, dock, wharf, pier, anchorage *San Diego is a major West Coast port for the U.S. Navy.*

portable *adjective* movable, transportable, handy, compact, lightweight, light *Airline regulations restrict the use of portable electronic devices such as cell phones on airplanes.*

portion *noun* part, share, piece, section, fraction, percentage *The millionaire left a large portion of his estate to charity.*

portion out *verb* divide, distribute, split, parcel out, dole out *Dad portioned out the candies among the trick-or-treaters.*

portray *verb* 1. represent, picture, depict, illustrate, characterize, describe *Laura Ingalls Wilder's books portray life growing up on the Western frontier.* 2. play, act the part of, impersonate *The actor portrayed Hamlet on the stage.*

pose 1. *verb* model, sit, stand, position oneself *The king posed for his portrait.* 2. present, cause, create *Road construction caused problems for commuters.* 3. *noun* position, attitude, stance, posture *We all struck silly poses for the photo.*

pose as *verb* impersonate, pretend to be, masquerade as, play the part of *The movie is the true story of a man who posed as an airline pilot, a doctor, and a lawyer before the FBI caught him.*

position *noun* 1. place, location, spot, area, setting *We took positions around the campfire.* 2. job, function, role, post, office, situation *Sandra Day O'Connor became an associate justice of the U.S. Supreme Court in 1981, the first woman appointed to that position.* 3. situation, state, circumstance, condition *Dad says we're not in a financial position to buy a new car.* 4. opinion, view, attitude, outlook, belief, feeling, thinking *What is your position on the issue?*

positive *adjective* 1. certain, sure, definite, convinced, confident *I'm positive we've met before.* 2. optimistic, constructive, helpful, encouraging, productive *The art teacher had some positive suggestions on how to improve the picture I was painting.*

possess *verb* own, have, hold, control, maintain *The ancient library at Alexandria, destroyed around A.D. 400, possessed the largest collection of manuscripts in the world.*

possession *noun* 1. ownership, control, custody *The United States took possession of the Louisiana Territory in 1803.* 2. belonging, asset, personal effect, property *Mom says her most treasured possession is the valentine I made her in kindergarten.*

possibility *noun* chance, likelihood, probability *There's a possibility it will rain this weekend.*

possible *adjective* likely, conceivable, imaginable, feasible, probable *Anne has proposed a possible solution to our problem.*

post 1. *noun* pole, column, pillar, stake, support *The cowboys tied their horses to the hitching post in front of the saloon.* 2. position, office, duty, job, assignment *My cousin accepted a post with a bank in London.* 3. *verb* put up, attach, fix, fasten *Mom posts our weekend job assignments on the refrigerator.* 4. notify, inform, advise, fill in, brief *Keep us posted on the family's activities.* 5. station, position, place, put *Guards were posted at the gate.*

postpone *verb* put off, delay, defer, suspend, hold over, table, shelve *The game was postponed because of rain.*

posture *noun* carriage, bearing, stance, position *Yoga exercises can improve your posture.*

potential 1. *adjective* possible, likely, conceivable, promising, hidden *Exercise and a healthful diet can reduce the potential risk of disease.* 2. *noun* ability, capability, aptitude, promise *The music company recognized the singer's potential and gave him a contract.*

pounce *verb* jump, leap, spring, swoop, bound, dive *The cat pounced on the mouse.*

pound *verb* strike, hit, hammer, beat, rap, bang, batter, drum *I had to pound on my sister's door in order for her to hear me over the loud music.*

pour *verb* drain, flow out, stream, spill, gush, run *Water poured into the streets from the open fire hydrant.*

pout *verb* sulk, mope, frown, scowl *My little brother pouts when he doesn't get his way.*

poverty *noun* neediness, need, want, hardship, deprivation *The mayor says her goal is to rid the city of poverty.*

powder *noun* fine particles, dust, fine grains, talcum, talc *During the long drought the soil was as dry as powder.*

power 1. *noun* strength, might, force, energy, potency, ability, capability, capacity *Overuse of antibiotics can reduce their power to cure infections.* 2. authority, right, control, command, mastery, dominion *Congress has the power to enact laws.* 3. *verb* run, control, operate *Our car is a hybrid, powered by gas and electricity.*

powerful *adjective* effective, strong, forceful, influential, authoritative, potent *The speaker made a power case for the development of wind and solar energy.*

practical *adjective* useful, sensible, sound, workable, realistic *Shorts and a T-shirt are not practical clothes for freezing weather.*

practically *adverb* nearly, almost, essentially, fundamentally, basically *We're practically home.*

practice 1. *verb* train, drill, exercise, prepare, condition, rehearse *I practiced two hours every day during the week before my piano recital.* 2. carry out, perform, follow, observe, apply *My parents see to it that we practice good eating habits.* 3. *noun* drill, training, preparation, rehearsal *The team has practice every day after school.* 4. habit, custom, procedure, routine, tradition *It's a good practice to read the instructions before installing new software.*

praise 1. *noun* compliments, congratulations, acclaim, approval *My parents give me plenty of praise and encouragement when they know I'm doing my best.* 2. *verb* compliment, commend, applaud, acclaim, congratulate *The teacher praised us for decorating the room so nicely for school family night.*

prank *noun* trick, joke, stunt *My best friend and I play harmless pranks on each other all the time.*

pray *verb* wish, long, hope, appeal, beg, ask, plead *I'll bet the team is praying for a win today.*

precaution *noun* safety measure, preventive measure, safeguard, care *I took the precaution of carrying an umbrella because it looks like rain.*

precede *verb* lead, head, come before, go before, lead to, usher in *We learned today about the events that preceded the Revolutionary War.* follow

precious *adjective* 1. valuable, expensive, costly, priceless, prized *Diamonds, rubies, emeralds, and sapphires are precious stones.* 2. dear, loved, cherished, special *My old teddy bear is still precious to me.*

precise *adjective* exact, accurate, specific, definite, detailed, meticulous, clear-cut *It's best to have precise room measurements when buying furniture.*

precision *noun* accuracy, exactness, correctness, care, meticulousness *Satellite imagery has brought greater precision to weather forecasting.*

predicament *noun* mess, jam, difficulty, trouble, problem, complication, plight, dilemma *We were in a real predicament when our canoe with all our gear in it tipped over.*

predict *verb* forecast, foretell, prophesy, foresee, divine, tell *No one can predict with* *any certainty when the volcano on the island will become active again.*

preface *noun* introduction, forward, preamble, beginning *The author explains in the preface what led him to write the book.*

prefer *verb* choose, like better, desire, wish *Which do you prefer, the blue or the white?*

prejudice 1. *noun* bias, intolerance, bigotry, discrimination, unfairness, narrow-mindedness *His dislike of anyone who doesn't look or sound like him is just prejudice.* 2. *verb* influence, sway, bias, predispose *Don't let Connie's poor opinion of him prejudice you.*

preliminary *adjective* introductory, beginning, prior, opening, preceding, initial *After some preliminary announcements, the principal introduced the assembly speaker.*

premature *adjective* early, too soon, hasty, untimely *It was premature to start celebrating the team's victory before the game ended.*

prepare *verb* get ready, arrange, plan, organize *We spent the day preparing for Mom's birthday party.*

presence *noun* attendance, being, existence, occurrence, appearance *The presence of fish in the river is a sign that the quality of the water has improved.*

present 1. *adjective* current, contemporary, existing, present-day *Before we moved to our present home, we lived in an apartment.* 2. here, at hand, near, nearby, in attendance *Everyone in our class was present.* 3. *verb* give, offer, donate, grant, bestow, award *We presented Mom with a big bouquet of flowers for Mother's Day.* 4. introduce, acquaint with, make known *Pocahontas was presented to King James I in London in 1616.* 5. furnish, produce, submit, offer *The committee presented its report to the council.* 6. *noun* gift, donation, offering, award, contribution *Everyone pitched in for his birthday present.*

presently *adverb* soon, shortly, directly, before long *Don't be so impatient—she'll be here presently.*

preserve 1. *verb* protect, maintain, defend, guard, shelter, sustain, save, conserve *In order to preserve the natural habitat, pedestrians and bicyclists must stay on designated trails.* destroy 2. *noun* sanctuary, refuge, reserve, park, protected habitat *Hunting is not permitted in the wildlife preserve.*

preserves *noun* jam, jelly, marmalade *I like cherry preserves on my toast.*

press *verb* 1. push, force, squeeze, depress *Press the large button to turn on the computer.* 2. iron, smooth, flatten *My shirt needs pressing before I can wear it.* 3. urge, insist, prod, coax *We pressed our friends to stay for dinner.*

pressure *noun* 1. force, weight, heaviness, load *The pressure of the snow collapsed the roof.* 2. stress, anxiety, tension, strain *It's difficult to think clearly under pressure.*

prestige *noun* importance, distinction, prominence, significance, greatness, superiority, influence, authority *Her prestige as an actor has enabled her to get great roles.*

presume *verb* suppose, assume, guess, think, imagine *I presume I'll see you at school tomorrow.*

pretend *verb* 1. make believe, act, play, imagine, fantasize *The children were running around the yard with their arms outstretched pretending to be airplanes.* 2. fake, feign, affect, imitate, simulate *I pretended I liked my sister's haircut so I wouldn't hurt her feelings.*

pretty 1. *adjective* attractive, good-looking, lovely, beautiful, handsome, cute *What a pretty baby!* ugly, homely 2. *adverb* rather, fairly, quite, somewhat *It's getting pretty late—time for bed.*

prevent *verb* stop, keep from, block, hinder, inhibit, thwart *The flu prevented me from going to school today.* allow, permit

previous *adjective* earlier, prior, preceding, former *In the previous episode the crew had just landed on the planet Vega.* following, succeeding

prey *noun* game, kill, quarry, target, victim *When a lion gets near its prey, it charges and knocks the prey down.*

prey on *verb* live on, eat, hunt, kill *Owls prey on rodents, reptiles, and small game at night.*

price 1. *noun* cost, value, amount, rate, charge, worth, expense *Digital camera prices range from under $200 to over $1,000.* 2. *verb* set value on, rate *We need to price hotel rooms for our trip to Paris.*

priceless *adjective* valuable, invaluable, precious, expensive, costly, dear *The priceless British crown jewels are on display at the Tower of London.*

prickly *adjective* 1. sharp, spiny, thorny, bristly *Roses have prickly stems.* 2. stinging, tingly, smarting, itchy *My skin feels prickly when I wear wool.*

pride *noun* 1. self-respect, self-esteem, dignity, honor *Restoring the historic downtown area gave the community a sense of pride.* 2. satisfaction, pleasure, enjoyment, delight, happiness, joy *Parents take pride in their children's accomplishments.* 3. vanity, egotism, arrogance, conceit, self-importance, superiority *Her pride made her think she could get away with anything she wanted.*

primary *adjective* 1. first, beginning, initial, earliest, introductory *The project is in the primary stages of development and should be completed in three years.* 2. chief, most important, main, principal, foremost, basic, fundamental *The school's primary function is to ensure that the children get a good education.*

primitive *adjective* simple, basic, elementary, early, original, ancient, prehistoric *Chimpanzees have the ability to use primitive tools.*

principal 1. *adjective* chief, main, most important, leading, foremost, primary *The principal mode of transportation in the United States is the automobile.* secondary 2. *noun* leader, administrator, head, director, manager, boss *The principal called a meeting of the teachers and staff.*

principle *noun* standard, rule, law, belief, doctrine, truth *The Declaration of Independence sets forth the principles under which the United States was founded.*

print 1. *verb* stamp, imprint, mark, engrave, etch *The wallpaper is printed with flowers.* 2. publish, issue, put out *The publisher plans to print over a million copies of the book.* 3. *noun* type, lettering, letters, writing *Newspaper headlines are in large print.* 4. imprint, mark, impression *The paw prints in the garden confirmed our belief that raccoons ate our sweet corn.* 5. picture, etching, engraving, photograph, drawing, illustration *In art class we cut a design into half a potato, dipped it in paint, and stamped it on paper to make a potato print.*

prior *adjective* earlier, before, previous, former *The job requires that you have prior experience.* later

prison *noun* jail, penal institution, penitentiary, reformatory *She was sentenced to three years in prison after being found guilty.*

privacy *noun* solitude, seclusion, peace, isolation, retreat *I enjoy having the privacy of my own room.*

private *adjective* 1. personal, individual, own, exclusive *Her parents respect that her diary is for her private thoughts.* 2. confidential, secret, classified, hidden *The officials held private talks in an unknown location.* public

privilege *noun* advantage, benefit, right, liberty, freedom, opportunity *Aunt Frieda gets free air travel as a privilege of working for the airline.*

prize 1. *noun* reward, award, medal, trophy, honor *Colleen won first prize in the spelling bee.* 2. *verb* appreciate, value, treasure, cherish, hold dear, revere, respect *Oak trees have been prized for their shade, beauty, and lumber since the earliest settlement of North*

America. 3. *adjective* winning, champion, choice, best, top *My grandfather grows prize roses.*

probable *adjective* likely, possible, feasible, apparent *Heavy traffic seems the most probable cause of his being late.* unlikely

probe 1. *verb* search, examine, explore, investigate *I probed my memory for her phone number.* 2. *noun* search, examination, investigation, exploration *The charges of wrongdoing warrant a thorough probe by the committee.*

problem *noun* 1. question, mystery, puzzle *Were you able to figure out that last math problem?* 2. difficulty, trouble, complication, predicament, mess, issue *Mom is having problems with her car, so can you take me to school? The drought is causing problems for farmers.*

procedure *noun* process, means, method, way, course, practice, plan *Insert your CD and follow the procedure described below.*

proceed *verb* advance, progress, continue, go forward, go ahead *School buses must come to a full stop at the railroad tracks before proceeding.*

proceeds *noun* receipts, income, profits, earnings *The proceeds from the bake sale will enable the library to purchase a new set of encyclopedias.*

process 1. *noun* procedure, method, system, way, means, technique *Alchemists claimed to have developed a process for changing any metal into gold or silver.* 2. *verb* deal with, handle, manage *The U.S. State Department processes applications for passports.* 3. treat, alter, prepare, refine *Some cheeses are processed so that they are spreadable.*

proclaim *verb* declare, announce, decree, state, pronounce *Napoleon I had himself proclaimed emperor of France.*

procure *verb* obtain, get, acquire, secure, purchase, buy *I was able to procure the last of the baseball cards I needed to complete my collection.*

prod *verb* 1. poke, jab, nudge, dig *She prodded the horse gently with her knee.* 2. goad, stir, urge, prompt *Mom prodded my brother to get his homework done before Sunday night.*

produce 1. *verb* make, manufacture, build, assemble, construct *Automobile manufacturers are using robots to help produce cars.* 2. supply, furnish, yield, provide *Cows produce milk.* 3. show, present, offer *The prosecutor has not produced enough evidence to convict the man.* 4. *noun* fruit, vegetables, crops, food *We grow organic produce in our garden.*

product *noun* merchandise, item, article, commodity, result, outcome *We purchase lots of products online.*

productive *adjective* fruitful, profitable, gainful, worthwhile, rewarding *We had a very productive weekend—we got all the yard work done.*

profanity *noun* swearing, cursing *Neither my teacher nor my parents allow profanity.*

profess *verb* claim, maintain, proclaim, assert, declare, state *The defendant professed his innocence.*

profession *noun* occupation, job, vocation, career, work, business *The nursing profession requires skill and caring.*

professional *adjective* expert, skilled, adept, skillful, excellent, fine *Dad did a professional job of refinishing our table so that it looks brand-new.*

profile *noun* side view, silhouette, outline *His head was turned, so all we saw was his profile.*

profit 1. *noun* earnings, returns, receipts, proceeds, income *Our profits from the garage sale came to $123.* loss 2. gain, benefit, advantage *There's no profit in worrying about something you can do nothing about.* loss 3. *verb* benefit, gain, be of use, help, improve, earn *Dad says he hopes we profited from our mistake and won't make it again.*

program *noun* 1. plan, system, procedure, agenda, schedule *The community has launched a program for helping homeless people.* 2. show, broadcast, presentation, performance *I missed my favorite TV program last night.*

progress 1. *noun* development, advancement, growth, improvement, headway *My teacher discussed my progress with my parents.* 2. *verb* advance, proceed, go ahead, move forward *Peace talks are progressing slowly.*

prohibit *verb* forbid, ban, bar, deny, restrict, deter, prevent, disallow *The sale of cigarettes to anyone under eighteen is prohibited.* allow

project 1. *noun* plan, job, undertaking, enterprise, venture, scheme, activity *For art class we have to come up with a project that uses recycled materials.* 2. *verb* protrude, stick out, extend, bulge *The peninsula projects into the lake 500 feet.*

prolong *verb* extend, stretch out, lengthen, draw out, drag out *A snowstorm prolonged our drive home.* shorten

prominent *adjective* 1. well known, important, distinguished, outstanding, great, eminent, famous, popular, celebrated *Prominent entertainers lent their support to the* *relief effort.* unknown 2. noticeable, visible, obvious, conspicuous *She has a picture of her children hanging in a prominent place in her office.*

promise 1. *verb* pledge, swear, vow, assure, guarantee *I can't go to the movie—I promised I would stay home and babysit.* 2. *noun* pledge, oath, vow, word, guarantee, assurance *I gave my friend my promise that I would keep his secret.* 3. indication, sign, hint *There's a promise of spring in the air.* 4. talent, ability, potential, possibility *His first novel shows real promise.*

promising *adjective* hopeful, encouraging, favorable *The game got off to a promising start when our team returned the kickoff for a touchdown.* hopeless

promote *verb* 1. advance, elevate, move up, raise *The store promoted him from assistant manager to manager.* demote 2. aid, help, advance, further, encourage, support, foster *A good diet promotes good health.*

prompt 1. *adjective* punctual, quick, timely, immediate, on time *The phone company expects prompt payment of their bills.* slow, late 2. *verb* remind, hint, suggest, coach *Gina prompted me when I forgot my lines.* 3. cause, encourage, motivate, inspire, stimulate *An opportunity for Mom to teach prompted us to move to another city.*

prone *adjective* 1. face down, flat, horizontal, prostrate, reclining *I lay prone while my dad gave me a massage.* vertical, standing 2. inclined, liable, apt, subject, disposed, given *Flights in this weather are prone to delay.*

pronounce *verb* 1. say, utter, sound, articulate, enunciate, express *The Hmong students in our class taught us to spell and pronounce their names.* 2. announce, declare, decree, proclaim *The doctor pronounced Dad to be in excellent physical health.*

pronounced *adjective* distinct, marked, clear, obvious, evident, definite *She spoke with a pronounced French accent.*

proof *noun* evidence, certification, verification, validation *The airlines require a picture ID as proof of your identity.*

prop *verb* brace, support, lean, rest, balance *I propped my bike against the garage wall.*

propel *verb* drive, push, move, thrust, force *Hawaiian outrigger canoes are propelled by paddle or sail.*

proper *adjective* correct, fitting, appropriate, suitable, right *If you're going hiking, you need to wear the proper shoes.* improper

property *noun* 1. belongings, possessions, effects, things, assets, holdings *These* *books are the library's property.* 2. land, real estate, acreage, plot, lot, estate *My uncle owns some wooded property on a lake.* 3. quality, attribute, feature, characteristic, power *Many plants that grow in the rain forest are known to have healing properties.*

prophecy *noun* prediction, foretelling, foresight, forecast, divination *Merlin had the power of prophecy and predicted that Arthur would one day be king.*

prophesy *verb* predict, foretell, foresee, forecast, divine, see the future *The seer prophesied the king's rise to power.*

proportion *noun* 1. ratio, measure, amount, percentage, share, portion *Mix equal proportions of yellow and blue to get green.* 2. balance, relation, harmony, symmetry, agreement, correspondence *In your drawing, his feet are too large in proportion to the rest of his body.*

proposal *noun* 1. plan, scheme, idea, suggestion, recommendation, motion *The school board is considering a proposal to remove vending machines from schools.* 2. offer, request, proposition, invitation *She accepted his proposal of marriage.*

propose *verb* 1. suggest, recommend, offer, present, advocate, submit *Dad proposed we go out for a movie and pizza.* 2. plan, intend, aim, mean, have in mind *She proposes to leave at 4:00.*

prospect 1. *noun* expectation, hope, likelihood, chance, possibility *The prospect of competing in the Olympics was thrilling.* 2. *verb* search, explore, hunt, look, explore *Thousands traveled to Alaska to prospect for gold after successful prospectors arrived in Seattle in 1897.*

prosper *verb* thrive, flourish, succeed, do well, make good *Many companies doing business on the Internet have prospered.*

prosperity *noun* success, good fortune, wealth, riches, affluence *Their prosperity enabled them to donate large sums of money to charities.*

protect *verb* defend, guard, shield, safeguard, shelter *We put on sunscreen to protect our skin from sunburn.*

protest 1. *verb* object, complain, dispute, dissent, oppose, challenge *My little brother protested when he was told it was time for bed.* 2. *noun* objection, complaint, opposition, challenge, demonstration *College students all over the country joined the protests against the Vietnam War.*

protrude *verb* project, stick out, bulge *When Jinnie pouts, her lower lip protrudes.*

proud *adjective* 1. pleased, elated, gratified, delighted, satisfied *I was proud to be chosen for the team.* 2. arrogant, haughty, vain, conceited, stuck-up *Just because she was famous didn't mean she was too proud to associate with her old friends.* modest, humble

prove *verb* show, verify, check, confirm, certify, establish *Galileo proved that gravity pulls all objects downward at the same speed.*

proverb *noun* saying, adage, maxim *A proverb meaning that you shouldn't count on something that hasn't happened yet is "Don't count your chickens before they've hatched."*

provide *verb* supply, give, furnish, grant, make available, deliver, contribute *The organization provides hot meals for senior citizens.*

provoke *verb* 1. anger, irritate, annoy, antagonize, disturb, aggravate *Hornets are easily provoked and will sting, so avoid their nests.* 2. motivate, stir, prompt, excite, rouse, spur, induce *The clowns' antics provoked the children's laughter.*

prowl *verb* creep, sneak, lurk, slink, steal, skulk *Raccoons prowled around our campsite looking for food.*

prudent *adjective* careful, cautious, sensible, judicious, wise *It's prudent to back up your computer regularly.* careless

pry *verb* 1. meddle, snoop, interfere, intrude *Don't pry if he doesn't want to talk about it.* 2. loosen, force, wrench, jimmy *The window was painted shut, so we pried it open with a screwdriver.*

public 1. *adjective* community, civic, social *It was her strong sense of public duty that motivated her to run for mayor.* 2. *noun* people, citizens, populace, society, population, inhabitants *The public should know about any health issues that affect it.*

publish *verb* issue, print, circulate, release, distribute *Six books in the series have already been published.*

pull 1. *verb* haul, tow, drag, draw *The tractor pulled the plow behind it.* 2. remove, extract, pluck, take out, draw out *The dentist pulled one of my brother's wisdom teeth.* 3. tear, rip, separate, destroy, demolish *The puppies immediately pulled their toys to pieces.* 4. attract, draw, bring, lure *The band always pulls in large audiences.* 5. *noun* tug, jerk, yank *In the tug of war, we gave a strong pull on the rope and didn't budge the other team.*

pulse *noun* beat, throb, rhythm, pounding *We tapped our feet to the pulse of the music.*

punch 1. *verb* hit, strike, knock, box, jab, slug *Kevin punched me playfully in the arm.* 2. *noun* blow, hit, jab, slug *Both boxers landed a few good punches.*

punctual *adjective* on time, prompt, timely *My mother insists we be punctual for dinner.* late

puncture 1. *verb* pierce, perforate, penetrate, stab, bore *A sharp rock could puncture your kayak.* 2. *noun* hole, perforation, cut, break, leak *Our inflatable boat came with a repair kit for punctures.*

punish *verb* discipline, penalize, chastise, reprimand, admonish, correct *Any student using a cell phone on school grounds will be punished.*

punishment *noun* discipline, penalty, admonishment, correction *Drawing graffiti on the walls is subject to punishment.*

pupil *noun* student, schoolchild, schoolboy, schoolgirl, scholar *Sachi is the best pupil in our class.*

purchase 1. *verb* buy, acquire, obtain, get *We purchased a new computer.* 2. *noun* acquisition, buy *That CD was a really good purchase.*

pure *adjective* 1. genuine, real, authentic, unmixed, uncontaminated *Sterling silver is 95.2 percent pure.* impure 2. complete, absolute, utter, sheer, total, downright *That's pure nonsense!*

purify *verb* cleanse, clean, refine, sterilize, decontaminate, filter *If you get water from a stream, you need to purify it before drinking it.* pollute, contaminate

purpose *noun* plan, aim, intention, objective, goal, design *The purpose of our shopping trip was to find a birthday present for Will.*

pursue *verb* 1. chase, follow, go after, track, trail, shadow, tail *The police pursued the escaped prisoner and persuaded him to give himself up.* 2. strive for, work toward, aspire to, follow, engage in *Anne is pursuing her goal of becoming a doctor.*

pursuit *noun* 1. chase, tracking, trailing, following, hunt, search *Lions spend about two or three hours a day in pursuit of food.* 2. activity, hobby, pastime, interest, occupation *The state park offers boundless opportunities for anyone interested in outdoor recreational pursuits.*

push 1. *verb* press, depress, force, nudge, thrust, shove, drive *Push the green button on the remote to turn on the TV. Jack pushed me into the swimming pool.* pull 2. urge, encourage, prod, coax, spur *Mom's been pushing me all weekend to straighten up my desk.* discourage 3. *noun* shove, nudge, thrust, ram *Give the door a push.* 4. attempt, drive, effort, initiative *The state is supporting a push to discourage teens from smoking.*

put *verb* 1. place, set, lay, deposit, position, arrange *Put your coat in the closet.*
2. express, say, word, phrase, state, formulate *Can you put that more simply so I can understand it?* 3. set, employ, apply, utilize, assign *She put her skill as an artist to good use. The teacher put us all to work solving the math problem.*

puzzle 1. *noun* mystery, riddle, brainteaser, problem *Each clue led us closer to the solution to the puzzle.* 2. *verb* mystify, bewilder, perplex, baffle, confuse *The reason for the Mayans' abandonment of their cities has long puzzled archaeologists.*

Q

quaint *adjective* old-fashioned, picturesque, charming, appealing, pretty *We took a drive through a quaint little seaside village.* modern

quake *verb* shake, tremble, quiver, shiver, shudder, vibrate *The ground quaked with the explosions.*

qualification *noun* 1. requirement, condition, certification, skill, ability, experience, training *One of the qualifications for the job is a college degree.* 2. limitation, exception, restriction, reservation *I agree with everything you said without qualification.*

qualify *verb* 1. entitle, allow, permit, certify, enable, equip, prepare, make suitable *His age qualifies him for a pension. Your training qualifies you to teach.* disqualify 2. restrict, limit, modify, change *He qualified his statement that he would help with a "maybe."*

quality *noun* 1. characteristic, feature, trait, attribute, property *One quality of water is wetness.* 2. value, merit, worth, caliber, grade, excellence *The products the store sells are always of high quality.*

quantity *noun* amount, number, measure, volume, sum *Shipping will be free if you buy quantities of ten or more.*

quarantine *noun* isolation, separation, segregation, confinement, seclusion *Quarantine was the first line of defense against the spread of disease before vaccines were developed.*

quarrel 1. *noun* argument, disagreement, dispute, squabble, row, fight *Craig and I had a quarrel, but we made up and are best friends again.* agreement 2. *verb* argue, disagree, squabble, fight *The children quarreled over the toys.* agree

queen *noun* monarch, ruler, sovereign *Buckingham Palace is the official London residence of the kings and queens of the United Kingdom.*

queer *adjective* odd, strange, peculiar, unusual, curious, out of the ordinary *Pangolins, sometimes called scaly anteaters, are queer-looking animals covered with scales.* ordinary

quench *verb* stop, extinguish, put out, suppress, quell *I quenched my thirst with a big glass of lemonade. The firefighters quenched the fire in minutes.*

query 1. *noun* question, inquiry, uncertainty, doubt *The customer had a query about the price of the item.* 2. *verb* question, inquire, ask, interrogate, quiz *"Are you absolutely certain?" the lawyer queried.*

question *noun* 1. inquiry, query *I have a question about our assignment.* answer 2. doubt, uncertainty, reservation, hesitation, debate *There's no question that you're too sick to go to school today.* certainty 3. issue, matter, subject, problem, topic *The question of whose turn it is to wash dishes came up over dinner.*

quick *adjective* fast, swift, hasty, speedy, rapid, prompt, immediate *She had a quick response to the teacher's question.*

quicken *verb* speed up, hasten, hurry, accelerate, go faster *I quickened my pace so I wouldn't be late.*

quiet 1. *adjective* still, silent, hushed, noiseless *The night was perfectly quiet except for an owl hooting in the distance.* noisy 2. peaceful, restful, tranquil, calm *We spent a quiet evening at home.* noisy 3. *noun* stillness, hush, silence, tranquility, calm *I study best in the quiet of my own room.* noise 4. *verb* silence, hush, calm, settle *If we don't quiet down, the neighbors will complain.*

quit *verb* 1. stop, end, halt, discontinue, cease, refrain from *Grandpa quit smoking twenty-five years ago.* begin 2. leave, withdraw, depart, abandon, vacate, retreat *General Washington and his troops quit New York and New Jersey and crossed the Delaware River into Pennsylvania.* return

quite *adverb* 1. completely, absolutely, entirely, totally, wholly *She hasn't quite recovered from her illness.* 2. rather, somewhat, fairly, moderately *I'm quite achy after that workout.* 3. very, exceedingly, really *He's quite strong to lift so much weight.*

quiver *verb* shake, shiver, tremble, vibrate, quake, quaver, shudder *My little brother's lower lip quivers when he's about to cry.*

quiz 1. *noun* test, exam, examination *We had a math quiz today.* 2. *verb* question, examine, test, ask, interrogate, query *The teacher quizzed us on the chapter we read yesterday.*

quota *noun* allotment, proportion, share, ratio, percentage, ration *Mom says I've had my quota of sweets today.*

quotation *noun* passage, line, quote, citation, reference, excerpt *"The course of true love never did run smooth" is a quotation from Shakespeare.*

quote 1. *verb* cite, repeat, refer to, recite *The newspaper quoted from the president's speech.* 2. *noun* passage, quotation, citation, reference, excerpt *Be sure to enclose quotes from other people's work in quotation marks.*

R

race 1. *noun* competition, contest, relay, marathon *Sandra ran in a charity race to raise money for the children's hospital.* 2. *verb* run, dash, rush, hurry, speed, scurry, bolt, sprint *He raced to catch the bus.*

rack *noun* frame, framework, stand, support, shelf *Dad built a rack to hold our CDs.*

racket *noun* noise, din, commotion, tumult, hubbub, clamor, uproar, ruckus *We made too much racket and woke my baby sister.* quiet, peace

radiant *adjective* 1. bright, brilliant, shining, gleaming, luminous, lustrous *The sky was a radiant blue.* dull, dim 2. happy, beaming, joyful, delighted, blissful, glowing *The little boy who is holding the huge fish has a radiant smile on his face.*

radical 1. *adjective* extreme, revolutionary, fanatical, militant, complete, thorough, sweeping *The group is calling for radical change.* moderate 2. *noun* extremist, revolutionary, fanatic, activist *Galileo was considered a radical for using experiments to find scientific truths.* moderate

rag *noun* cloth, dust cloth, remnant *Use a damp rag to clean the fingerprints off the door.*

rage 1. *noun* anger, fury, wrath, frenzy, furor *He tried to control the rage in his voice.* 2. fad, craze, style, latest trend *Disco music was all the rage in the 1980s.* 3. *verb* lose one's temper, blow up, seethe, fume, rant, rave *The angry customer raged about the store's service.*

ragged *adjective* torn, worn, shabby, tattered, frayed *She wore her ragged blue jeans everywhere.*

rags *noun* tattered clothing, tatters, shreds, torn clothing *The homeless man was dressed in rags.*

raid 1. *noun* attack, invasion, assault, strike *The commander ordered a raid on the enemy's camp.* 2. *verb* attack, invade, assault, plunder, pillage, seize *Pirates raided the villages along the coast.*

rain *verb* 1. pour, shower, sprinkle, drizzle, precipitate *It rained all day, so we stayed inside.* 2. lavish, shower, bestow, pour *The critics rained praise on the author's latest book.*

raise 1. *verb* lift, elevate, boost *If you know the answer, raise your hand.* lower
2. increase, inflate, boost, escalate *The university has raised the price of tuition.* reduce
3. improve, advance, better, increase, upgrade *I raised my grade from a B to an A.* lower
4. bring up, rear, foster, grow, produce, cultivate *Grandma and Grandpa raised five children. They raise corn on their farm.* 5. collect, accumulate, get, gather, amass *The Scout troop raised money to buy toys for needy children.* 6. *noun* increase, advance, boost *Ellen got a promotion and a raise in salary.*

rally 1. *verb* assemble, meet, gather, congregate, collect, unite *The students rallied to support the team.* 2. improve, recover, recuperate, mend, get better *Grandma rallied quickly after her surgery.* 3. *noun* gathering, assembly, meeting, get-together *Supporters attended a rally for their candidate.*

ram *verb* strike, collide with, slam, run into *The getaway car rammed the roadblock and came to a stop.*

ramble 1. *verb* walk, amble, stroll, wander, roam, meander *We rambled around in the woods.* 2. chatter, babble, talk aimlessly *The speaker rambled on and put me to sleep.* 3. *noun* walk, stroll, amble, roam, saunter *Dad and I went for a ramble around town to see if anything interesting was happening.*

ranch *noun* farm, homestead, estate, spread *Uncle Robert runs a cattle ranch in Montana.*

random *adjective* haphazard, chance, unorganized, unsystematic, hit-or-miss *The photographs I took on vacation are in random order now, but I will arrange them in an album.*

range 1. *noun* variety, choice, assortment, selection, array *The T-shirts come in a wide range of colors.* 2. row, line, chain, string, series *We saw a range of snowcapped peaks in the distance.* 3. pasture, grazing land, grassland, plains *Buffalo herds can once more be seen on the range.* 4. *verb* extend, reach, stretch, go, vary *Temperatures range from 30 degrees below 0 to 95 degrees above 0.*

rank 1. *noun* grade, class, position, status, level *Salaries are based on rank. President*

Ronald Reagan achieved the rank of captain in the U.S. Army during World War II. 2. *verb* classify, arrange, group, categorize *The computer programs are ranked according to ease of use.* 3. rate, place, grade, stand *Flying ranks among the safest ways to travel.* 4. *adjective* offensive, foul, nasty, bad, disgusting, vile *Rotten tomatoes have a rank smell.*

rap *verb* knock, tap, strike, hammer, bang *Is that someone rapping at the door?*

rapid *adjective* quick, swift, fast, speedy, brisk, fleet, hasty *I made a rapid retreat when I saw the big dog.*

rapture *noun* joy, delight, bliss, elation, happiness *She gazed with rapture at the magnificent snowcapped mountains.* distress, sorrow

rare *adjective* scarce, uncommon, unusual, sparse, infrequent *Many rare and endangered species of plants and animals live in tropical rain forests.*

rarely *adverb* infrequently, seldom, scarcely, hardly ever *I rarely see my cousins who live in Alaska.*

rascal *noun* mischief-maker, scamp, devil *Come here, you rascal—it's nap time.*

rash *adjective* hasty, careless, reckless, impetuous, impulsive, brash *It was rash of me to shut down the computer when I hadn't saved my file.* careful, cautious

rate 1. *noun* speed, pace, velocity, tempo *You can measure your heart rate when you use the gym's treadmill.* 2. charge, cost, price, fee, amount *We found good hotel rates on the Internet.* 3. *verb* grade, rank, evaluate, appraise, value *How would you rate this video game?*

ratify *verb* approve, endorse, confirm, support, accept, pass *The nations ratified an arms reduction treaty.* veto, refuse

ratio *noun* proportion, percentage, comparison, relation *A low student-to-teacher ratio gives students an advantage.*

ration 1. *noun* allowance, portion, share, quota, allotment, measure, supply, amount *Mom says I've had my cookie ration for today.* 2. *verb* allot, distribute, allocate, give *Food and water were rationed to the public during the disaster.*

rational *adjective* sensible, reasonable, logical, sound, level-headed *When it's raining, the rational thing to do is wear your raincoat.*

rattle 1. *verb* clatter, clank, bang, jangle, knock *Wind rattled the windows.* 2. *verb* confuse, disturb, upset, fluster *Our teacher is even-tempered and not easily rattled.* 3. *noun* clatter, clanking, banging, jangling, knocking *The rattle of trash cans in the alley meant that our garbage was being picked up.*

rattle off *verb* recite, list, run through, say quickly *Harriet can rattle off the names of all the states.*

raw *adjective* 1. uncooked, fresh *Raw fruits and vegetables are part of a healthful diet.* 2. inexperienced, untrained, unskilled, new, green, immature *The sergeant's job was to train the raw recruits.* 3. cold, bitter, piercing, biting, penetrating, freezing, harsh *A raw wind blew in over the lake.*

ray *noun* beam, stream, shaft, gleam *Rays of sunlight filtered through the trees.*

reach 1. *verb* arrive at, come to, approach, achieve, get to *We should reach our destination by 2:30. The negotiators say they have reached an agreement.* 2. extend, stretch, go, span, run *At one time the Great Plains reached across a quarter of the continental United States.* 3. contact, get in touch with, communicate with *Dana said she tried to reach you by cell phone but couldn't get a good signal.* 4. *noun* grasp, range, touch, stretch *Matches should be kept out of the reach of children.*

react *verb* respond, answer, reply, behave, act *Katy and I reacted to Dad's joke with groans.*

reaction *noun* response, reply, answer, behavior *What was Mom's reaction when you told her you broke the vase?*

ready 1. *adjective* prepared, set, organized, arranged, equipped *We're all packed and ready to leave for vacation.* unprepared 2. *verb* prepare, equip, arrange, organize, get set *The team readied itself for the first game of the season.*

real *adjective* actual, true, genuine, authentic, legitimate, valid *Her latest book is based on real events.*

reality *noun* actuality, existence, fact, truth, certainty *The town's dream of having a public library has become reality.*

realize *verb* 1. understand, grasp, comprehend, conceive, appreciate *I realize how fortunate I am to have such a caring family.* 2. accomplish, achieve, fulfill, reach, attain, complete, make happen *After years of training, Diane realized her goal of becoming a master chef.*

realm *noun* domain, kingdom, country, state, principality, province, territory *In the medieval feudal system, the king divided his realm into plots of land that he gave to noblemen in return for their support.*

reap *verb* gather, acquire, gain, obtain, get, earn, glean *She has reaped the benefits of having an excellent education.*

rear 1. *noun* back, end, tail *The only seats remaining were in the rear of the theater.* front 2. *verb* raise, care for, bring up, train, nurture *Abraham Lincoln was reared by his father and stepmother.*

reason 1. *noun* cause, explanation, grounds, justification, basis, motive *What's your reason for not having your homework done?* 2. logic, sense, judgment, intelligence, reasoning, thinking *His decision was based on reason, not emotion.* 3. *verb* work out, solve, think through, analyze, figure out *Aristotle, who lived in the fourth century B.C., reasoned incorrectly that if the earth rotated on its axis, we would fly off into space.* 4. talk over, discuss, argue, consider, debate *If you reason with them, you may get them to change their minds.*

reasonable *adjective* 1. logical, sensible, rational, intelligent, wise, practical *I'm sure Darrell has a reasonable explanation for being absent.* unreasonable 2. fair, acceptable, satisfactory, realistic, justifiable *You can find clothing that has never been worn for a reasonable price at the thrift store.* unreasonable

rebel 1. *verb* revolt, rise up, resist, defy, mutiny, disobey, protest *In 1848 women rebelled and organized the first woman's rights convention.* 2. *noun* revolutionary, mutineer, insurgent, freedom fighter *During the Revolutionary War, Nathan Hale spied on the British for the American rebels.*

rebellion *noun* revolution, revolt, mutiny, uprising, resistance, insurgence *Government troops tried to put down the rebellions.*

recall 1. *verb* remember, recollect, call to mind, think of *I can't recall which street he lived on.* forget 2. call back, take back, withdraw *The manufacturer recalled the vehicle to correct the problem.* 3. *noun* memory, recollection, remembrance *She has total recall of people's names.*

recede *verb* retreat, withdraw, ebb, subside, diminish, lessen *After the tide recedes to its lowest point, it rises for the next six hours and thirteen minutes.* advance

receive *verb* take in, get, obtain, acquire, secure, gain, accept *I receive an extra allowance when I do extra chores around the house.* give

recent *adjective* new, modern, up-to-date, latest, current *Make sure you have recent backups of all the important data on your computer.* old

reception *noun* 1. gathering, party, function, get-together, social *After the wedding there will be a reception at the country club.* 2. welcome, greeting, response, reaction, acceptance *The celebrity received a warm reception.*

recess *noun* break, rest, pause, intermission, respite, time off *We spent recess this afternoon playing volleyball.*

recipe *noun* instructions, directions, formula, procedure *I made the brownies by following my mom's recipe.*

recite *verb* narrate, tell, relate, recount, rehearse, review, repeat *Sue recited a poem to the class.*

reckless *adjective* careless, heedless, rash, thoughtless, inconsiderate, hasty, unmindful *Mom warned us not to be reckless on our skateboards.*

reckon *verb* calculate, compute, estimate, figure *I reckoned we had walked five miles.*

recline *verb* lie down, repose, lounge, rest, stretch out *I found the cat reclining in my favorite chair.*

recognize *verb* 1. know, identify, distinguish, place, be familiar with *I recognized her immediately from her picture.* 2. acknowledge, appreciate, understand, accept, admit, allow *The teacher recognized that Vera needed extra help.*

recollect *verb* remember, recall, think of, call to mind *I don't recollect ever having been here; I must have been very young.*

recommend *verb* suggest, advise, guide, direct, propose *The server recommended the grilled salmon.*

reconcile *verb* settle, mend, fix up, patch up *They reconciled their differences and shook hands.*

record 1. *noun* account, chronicle, document, file, log, diary, journal *Dad keeps a record of his business expenses.* 2. top score, best, top performance, best time *The women's relay team was fast enough to beat the school record.* 3. *verb* mark down, note, log, enter, chronicle *The teacher records our grades in her grade book.*

recover *verb* 1. regain, get back, reclaim, retrieve, rescue *The gold stolen from the stagecoach was never recovered.* lose 2. get better, improve, rally, heal, recuperate *She recovered quickly from the flu and returned to school.*

recovery *noun* improvement, recuperation, healing *He made a quick recovery after his surgery.*

recreation *noun* amusement, entertainment, relaxation, pastime, diversion, fun, play, sport *For recreation, our family goes camping, fishing, and hiking.* work

recruit *verb* enlist, sign up, enroll, draft, take on, employ *The company is recruiting only those employees who have computer skills.*

reduce *verb* lessen, lower, decrease, diminish, cut, moderate *Competition has reduced the price of cell phone service.* increase

reel *verb* sway, rock, wobble, lurch, stumble, stagger, pitch *The boxer reeled backward from the punch.*

refer *verb* 1. send, direct, transfer, pass on, recommend *The salesclerk referred the unhappy customer to the customer service department.* 2. mention, allude to, bring up, comment on *He referred to a book he'd read but didn't give the title.* 3. consult, check, examine, look at, use *I referred to the encyclopedia for the information I needed for my report.*

referee *noun* umpire, judge, arbitrator, mediator *The coach challenged the referee's call.*

refine *verb* purify, process, clean, filter *Whole grains have greater nutritional value than those that have been refined.*

reflect *verb* 1. mirror, send back, return *The glass skyscraper reflected the sunset.* 2. consider, contemplate, think, ponder, deliberate, mull over *I took time to reflect before answering the question.*

reform 1. *verb* change, improve, revise, correct, make better *The new government promises to reform the health-care system.* 2. *noun* change, improvement, development, progress, reorganization *Opposition leaders are calling for democratic reforms.*

refrigerate *verb* cool, chill, ice *Milk must be refrigerated to keep it from becoming sour.* heat

refuge *noun* sanctuary, shelter, haven, protection, asylum, retreat, port, harbor *The organization is restoring the land for a wildlife refuge. We took refuge from the rain in our tent.*

refund *verb* repay, reimburse, pay back *The store will refund your money if you're not satisfied.*

refuse 1. *verb* decline, reject, say no, turn down, rebuff *Fred refused my offer of help. The star refused to comment on the rumors.* 2. *noun* waste, garbage, trash, rubbish, litter, junk *Our Scout troop cleaned up the refuse that had accumulated in the empty lot.*

regard 1. *verb* consider, think of, judge, view, observe *He regarded the snake from a safe distance before concluding it was harmless.* 2. *noun* respect, admiration, esteem, opinion, affection *The students in Ms. Ortega's class have high regard for her.* 3. notice, attention, thought, thoughtfulness, consideration *The people in the next apartment turn up the volume on their radio with no regard for their neighbors.*

region *noun* place, area, location, district, zone, territory, section, space, vicinity *Northern Italy is a very mountainous region.*

register 1. *verb* sign up, enroll, log in, check in, enter one's name *My brother registered to vote right after his eighteenth birthday.* 2. *noun* list, record, catalog, index *Teachers keep a register of students' attendance.*

regret 1. *verb* be sorry, feel sorry, feel contrite about *Dad regretted having been impatient with me and apologized.* 2. *noun* sorrow, remorse, disappointment *Dad says he has no regrets about turning down the offer of a higher-paying job in another town.*

regular *adjective* 1. usual, customary, habitual, everyday, common, typical, normal, routine *Ten o'clock is her regular bedtime.* 2. uniform, even, orderly, balanced, symmetrical *The foghorn sounded at regular intervals of forty-five seconds.* irregular

regulate *verb* control, adjust, set, modify, remedy, correct, manage, direct *Water regulates the temperature of the earth through evaporation.*

rehearse *verb* practice, train, prepare, drill, repeat *The school orchestra rehearsed for their concert.*

reign 1. *noun* rule, power, dominion, regime, monarchy, government *Queen Victoria's reign lasted for sixty-three years.* 2. *verb* rule, govern, lead, control, prevail *Queen Elizabeth II has reigned since her father's death in 1952.*

reinforce *verb* strengthen, fortify, brace, support, bolster *Crews are reinforcing the dikes for better flood control.* weaken

reject *verb* 1. refuse, deny, veto, decline, eliminate, discard, scrap, throw out *The school board rejected a plan for a new school. Reject anything that doesn't look fresh.*

rejoice *verb* celebrate, be happy, delight, revel, exult *Crowds rejoiced at the fall of the Berlin Wall on November 9, 1989.*

relate *verb* 1. tell, report, recount, narrate, convey, communicate *In* Life on the Mississippi, *Mark Twain relates his experiences as a riverboat pilot.* 2. apply, associate, be relevant, refer, pertain, connect *The police have received new information relating to the theft.*

relation *noun* 1. connection, association, link, relationship, affiliation *Scientists say that astrology has no relation to science.* 2. family member, relative, kin, family *Yes, of* *course I know Gordon—in fact, he's one of my relations.*

relax *verb* rest, unwind, take it easy, calm down, loosen up *We have the whole weekend to relax.*

release *verb* 1. free, let go, set free, set loose, liberate, discharge *The eagle was fitted with a tracking device before it was released. We released him from his promise of secrecy.* hold 2. circulate, issue, publish, distribute, make available *Her new book will be released in the spring.*

relent *verb* yield, bend, submit, give in *My parents finally relented and let me paint stars on my bedroom ceiling.*

relevant *adjective* applicable, pertinent, connected, related, suitable, fitting *We need relevant information on which to base a decision.* irrelevant, unconnected

reliable *adjective* trustworthy, dependable, faithful, loyal, steadfast *He's always reliable, so if he said he'd help, he will.* unreliable

relic *noun* antique, artifact, thing from the past *The amateur archaeologist dug for relics at the site believed to be Troy.*

relief *noun* 1. ease, release, freedom, alleviation, cure *The pharmacy shelves are full of products that claim to provide relief for cold symptoms.* 2. assistance, aid, help, support *Several agencies got relief to the hurricane victims.*

relieve *verb* 1. help, ease, soothe, reduce, lessen, alleviate *We phoned to relieve our parents' concern about our whereabouts.* 2. take over for, substitute for, replace *The clerk waited for someone to relieve him so he could take his break.*

religion *noun* belief, faith, creed, denomination *Buddhism and Taoism are two of many traditional Chinese religions.*

religious *adjective* pious, devout, reverent, faithful *A religious Muslim prays five times a day.*

reluctant *adjective* unwilling, disinclined, hesitant, averse *I am reluctant to get out of bed early on weekends.* willing

rely on *verb* depend on, count on, trust, expect *You can rely on me to support you for class president.*

remain *verb* continue, endure, last, keep on, stay, persist *Snow remains on the mountaintops all year around.*

remark 1. *verb* comment, mention, observe, note, say, state *Mom remarked about how nice I look when I dress up.* 2. *noun* comment, observation, mention, statement *During her opening remarks the speaker thanked us all for coming.*

remarkable *adjective* unusual, noteworthy, extraordinary, exceptional, notable *The fund-raising campaign has been a remarkable success.*

remedy *noun* cure, treatment, therapy, tonic, antidote *There is evidence that some herbal remedies are effective.*

remember *verb* recall, recollect, think of, bring to mind *I can't remember where I put my softball.*

remind *verb* prompt, suggest *Remind me to stop for milk on the way home.*

remnant *noun* remainder, remains, scrap, leftover *Grandma used remnants of fabric to make me a patchwork quilt for my bed.*

remorse *noun* sorrow, regret, guilt, shame *He has never shown any remorse for his crime.*

remote *adjective* 1. far, distant, secluded, isolated, hidden *Rosario's family came from a remote mountain village in Mexico.* 2. slight, slim, small, outside, unlikely *There's a remote possibility we'll visit you in July.*

removal *noun* elimination, withdrawal, taking away, disposal, exclusion *The removal of stones and stumps from the field was necessary before the farmer could plow it.*

remove *verb* 1. take away, move, withdraw, transfer, transport *We removed the books from the shelves before moving the bookcases.* 2. eliminate, get rid of, discard, dispose of, erase *I removed my typing errors before I sent the e-mail.* 3. dismiss, fire, eject, expel, oust *She was removed as president of the organization.*

renew *verb* 1. restore, renovate, repair, mend, make like new *Mom renewed the finish on an antique desk.* 2. extend, continue *This prescription needs to be renewed.* 3. revive, refresh, revitalize *Spring renews my spirits.*

renovate *verb* redo, renew, recondition, remake, modernize, restore, repair, fix up *We have renovated our kitchen with new cupboards, flooring, and appliances.*

renowned *adjective* well-known, famous, celebrated, distinguished, popular *Linus Pauling was a renowned, two-time Nobel Prize winner.*

rent 1. *verb* hire, lease, charter *We rented a car at the airport.* 2. *noun* payment, fee, charge, rental *The rent is due the first of the month.*

repair 1. *verb* fix, restore, mend, overhaul, service, patch up *I repaired the bent wheel rim on my bicycle myself.* 2. *noun* overhaul, patching, restoration, fixing *Our roof is in need of repairs.*

repeal *verb* withdraw, abolish, revoke, annul, invalidate, rescind, take back *The law prohibiting the manufacture, sale, or distribution of alcoholic beverages was repealed in 1933.*

repeat *verb* say again, recite, reiterate, retell *Please repeat your question so everyone can hear it.*

repel *verb* 1. drive away, hold off, keep away, chase off, deter *The Great Wall of China was designed to repel invaders.* 2. offend, disgust, repulse, revolt, sicken *TV violence repels me.*

reply 1. *verb* answer, respond, acknowledge, react, counter *It took Francis a week to reply to my e-mail.* 2. *noun* answer, response, acknowledgment *I knocked on the door, but there was no reply.*

report 1. *noun* account, article, story, narrative, description, summary, broadcast *The evening news report showed the damage from the tornado.* 2. *verb* describe, tell, announce, broadcast, communicate, narrate, state *The park rangers reported that there was a bear in the campground.* 3. appear, arrive, come, check in, show up, present oneself *Barbara reports for work at the downtown office every morning at exactly nine o'clock.*

represent *verb* 1. stand for, symbolize, signify, denote, portray, depict *The @ symbol stands for "at" in e-mail addresses.* 2. act for, speak for, stand in for, appear for *Lawyers represent their clients.*

representative 1. *noun* delegate, ambassador, envoy, spokesperson, agent *The number of representatives from each state in the House of Representatives is determined by the state's population.* 2. *adjective* elected, chosen *The United States has a representative form of government.*

repulsive *adjective* disgusting, offensive, foul, revolting *Don't let the dog in until we get the repulsive smell of skunk out of him.*

reputation *noun* standing, status, name, character, position *Abraham Lincoln had a reputation for honesty.*

request 1. *verb* ask for, seek, apply for, call for, petition *The pilot requested permission to land.* 2. *noun* appeal, call, demand, plea, application, petition *The bank granted her request for a loan.*

require *verb* 1. need, lack, want, have need of *A Canadian citizen does not require a visa to visit the United States.* 2. demand, order, command, oblige, instruct, compel *You are required to check in at the office if you are late.*

rescue 1. *verb* save, free, release, liberate, recover, retrieve, salvage *Josh rescued the kitten from the top of the tree.* 2. *noun* recovery, salvation, retrieval, release, assistance, aid *The helicopter team came to the rescue of the stranded mountain climbers.*

research 1. *noun* investigation, study, examination, analysis, inquiries *After hours of research, I finally had enough information to write my paper.* 2. *verb* investigate, study, examine, inquire into, look into, explore, dig into, delve into *Glenda is researching her family's history.*

resemblance *noun* likeness, similarity, sameness *I see no resemblance between Ivan and his sister.*

resentment *noun* displeasure, irritation, annoyance, bitterness, anger *She felt a lot of resentment toward her boss for being passed over for a promotion.*

reservation *noun* 1. booking, arrangement, engagement, appointment *She made a reservation at the restaurant for 6:00 P.M.* 2. doubt, reluctance, hesitation, unwillingness *I have reservations about letting the children stay out so late on a school night.*

reserve 1. *verb* hold back, save, put aside, keep, retain, store, preserve *I reserved the frosting for last.* 2. book, engage, arrange for, make a reservation for *Did you reserve a table for tonight?* 3. *noun* supply, stockpile, store, cache *We keep a reserve of rainwater in barrels to water our garden during dry weather.* 4. aloofness, self restraint, self-control, detachment, coolness *He's really very nice, but his reserve tends to put people off.*

reside *verb* live, dwell, inhabit, occupy *Dad has resided in the same town all his life.*

residence *noun* home, house, apartment, condominium, dwelling, abode *My grandparents' residence is in Arizona.*

resident *noun* inhabitant, occupant, tenant, dweller, citizen *There are fewer than 10,000 residents of our town.*

resign *verb* quit, leave, leave office, give notice, retire, abdicate *Richard Nixon was forced to resign as president of the United States in August of 1974.*

resist *verb* oppose, challenge, stand firm against, withstand, counteract *Britain was unable to resist the Roman invasion.* comply, yield

resistance *noun* opposition *Women met a lot of resistance to their demand to vote.*

resolve *verb* 1. determine, decide, make up one's mind *I've resolved to study harder this year.* 2. settle, solve, answer, work out, clear up *We need to resolve the problem of disposing of our trash.*

resort *noun* 1. vacation spot, retreat *Resorts along the Gulf Coast are popular with Northerners in winter.* 2. choice, possibility, hope, chance, alternative *As a last resort, we'll sleep in the van if no motel rooms are available.*

resort to *verb* use, turn to, utilize, fall back on *If you don't know the spelling of a word, you may have to resort to a dictionary.*

resource *noun* 1. source, aid, help, means, way *The Internet is a resource for finding information about nearly any subject.* 2. asset, fund, wealth, capital, reserve *Trees are an important renewable resource. Mom says we haven't the resources to buy any more expensive high-tech gadgets.*

respect 1. *noun* admiration, regard, esteem, reverence, appreciation, approval, honor *Many societies have more respect for their senior citizens than we do.* 2. *verb* admire, esteem, appreciate, value, revere, honor *The students respect their teacher.* 3. show consideration, observe, recognize *My sister and I respect each other's privacy.*

respond *verb* answer, reply, acknowledge, counter, react *Sandy hasn't responded to the message I left on her answering machine.*

response *noun* answer, reply, acknowledgment, reaction *My brother is waiting for a response to his job application.*

responsibility *noun* duty, task, role, charge, obligation *It's my responsibility to clean up the kitchen after dinner.*

responsible *adjective* 1. dependable, reliable, trustworthy *The club chose a responsible member as treasurer.* irresponsible, undependable 2. accountable, answerable, liable *I'm responsible for my own actions.* exempt

rest 1. *noun* break, pause, breather, lull, time-out, intermission *Let's stop for a rest here on the park bench.* 2. sleep, slumber, relaxation, peace, quiet *Eat a healthful diet, drink plenty of water, exercise daily, and get plenty of rest.* 3. remainder, balance, excess, surplus, leftovers *There's only one piece of cake left—who ate the rest?* 4. *verb* lie down, relax, lounge, repose, take it easy, sleep, nap *We rested for an hour, then went back to work.* 5. lean, lay, set, support, place *We rested the ladder against the garage.*

restless *adjective* uneasy, troubled, agitated, fidgety, nervous, anxious *The dog gets restless when it hears thunder.* calm, composed

restore *verb* repair, renew, recondition, fix, refurbish *Uncle Phil restores antique cars.*

restrain *verb* hold back, control, check, curb, restrict *Restrain the dog while I see who is at the door.*

restrict *verb* confine, limit, restrain, control, bound, hamper, impede *Ordinances restrict industrial development in residential areas.*

restriction *noun* limitation, limit, restraint, control, bound, regulation *There are restrictions on watering our lawns during a drought.*

result 1. *noun* consequence, end, effect, outcome, upshot, product *We were pleased with the results of the class election.* 2. *verb* end, culminate, terminate *Anne's hard study resulted in an excellent test score.*

resume *verb* continue, begin again, carry on, proceed, restart *The concert resumed after a fifteen-minute intermission.*

retain *verb* keep, hold, maintain, preserve, save *A well-insulated house retains heat in the winter.*

retire *verb* stop working, resign, quit *Grandpa plans to play a lot of golf when he retires from his job.*

retreat 1. *verb* withdraw, fall back, flee, escape, leave *General George Washington's army retreated after being defeated in the Battle of Long Island.* advance 2. *noun* withdrawal, departure, escape, flight *The troops made a quick retreat to behind their defenses.* advance 3. haven, sanctuary, refuge, escape *Dad and Uncle George have a retreat in the mountains where they go to relax and fish.*

retrieve *verb* get back, recover, regain, reclaim *You can retrieve lost items at the front desk.*

return 1. *verb* go back, come back, revisit, reappear *My brother is returning home from college for the summer.* 2. give back, repay, reimburse *Connie returned the dollar I lent her.* keep 3. *noun* reappearance, homecoming *I'm looking forward to Connie's homecoming.* 4. profit, gain, income, earnings, yield *She had a good return on her real-estate investments.*

reunion *noun* gathering, get-together, meeting, social event *My parents are getting all dressed up for Dad's high school class reunion.*

reveal *verb* disclose, tell, divulge, give away, let slip, expose *Don't reveal to anyone what our Halloween costumes will be.*

reverse 1. *adjective* opposite, back, rear, other, contrary, counter *The list of ingredients* *is on the reverse side of the package.* 2. *verb* overturn, turn around, undo, change, repeal *The appeals court reversed the lower court's decision.* 3. *noun* opposite, contrary *We did something wrong because the reverse of what we intended to happen happened.*

review 1. *verb* go over, check, look over, reexamine, reassess *I made sure to review my paper for mistakes before I handed it in.* 2. evaluate, study, assess, rate, judge *The critic reviewed the book and didn't have anything good to say about it.* 3. *noun* study, examination, look *The test will be easy now that I've done a thorough review of the subject.* 4. criticism, assessment, evaluation, judgment, rating *Let's go to the movie that has the best reviews.*

revise *verb* change, alter, amend, reconsider *I revised my opinion of Joyce after I got to know her better.*

revive *verb* restore, refresh, renew, revitalize *The air-conditioning revived us after we spent hours working outdoors in the heat.*

revoke *verb* repeal, cancel, withdraw, recall, rescind *His driver's license was revoked for receiving too many traffic tickets.*

revolt 1. *verb* rebel, riot, mutiny, rise up *In November 1917 Vladimir Lenin and his followers revolted against the government of Russia.* 2. offend, horrify, appall, disgust, sicken *Cruelty to animals revolts me.* 3. *noun* rebellion, riot, mutiny, uprising *Spartacus led the slave revolt against Rome.*

revolution *noun* 1. rebellion, revolt, uprising, riot, overthrow *The Stamp Act was one of the major causes of the American Revolution.* 2. circle, circuit, orbit, cycle, turning *It takes 365 days for the earth to make one revolution around the sun.*

revolve *verb* turn, go around, circle, orbit *At least seventeen moons revolve around the planet Jupiter.*

reward 1. *verb* compensate, pay, repay, award *Mr. Hernandez rewarded us for our help by taking us out for pizza.* 2. *noun* payment, bonus, award, prize, tip *The nice man gave me a $10 reward for returning his lost wallet.*

rhythm *noun* beat, pulse, throb, tempo, meter *Joel loves listening to the calypso rhythm of steel drums.*

rich *adjective* 1. wealthy, well-to-do, prosperous, affluent *Some rich people own homes with as many as twelve bedrooms.* 2. fertile, productive, fruitful, lush *The family has farmed the rich land for decades.* 3. creamy, fatty, buttery, heavy *Grandpa is supposed to avoid rich food.*

rid *verb* clear, free, do away with *We had to rid our garden of weeds when we returned from vacation.*

riddle *noun* puzzle, question, mystery, brainteaser, enigma, problem *Scientists are still trying to solve the riddle of the origin of the universe.*

ride 1. *verb* travel, be carried on, drive, control, manage *Men rode horses nearly 2,000 miles between St. Joseph, Missouri, and Sacramento, California, carrying mail for the Pony Express.* 2. *noun* trip, drive, journey, spin, jaunt *The Clarks took us for a ride in their new speedboat.*

ridicule *noun* 1. mockery, scorn, derision, laughter, jeering, taunting, teasing *Inventors frequently have to endure ridicule.* 2. *verb* mock, deride, laugh at, scoff at, jeer, taunt, sneer at *Over a year after the Wright brothers flew, an article appeared in a magazine ridiculing their "alleged" flights.*

ridiculous *adjective* foolish, preposterous, outrageous, bizarre, unbelievable, ludicrous, nonsensical *Pterodactyls were ridiculous-looking flying reptiles.*

rig *verb* fit, equip, outfit, furnish, prepare, make ready *It takes a while to rig our sailboat with sails before we can go sailing.*

right 1. *noun* goodness, justice, fairness, honesty, truth, morality *Nate should know by now the difference between right and wrong.* 2. freedom, power, privilege, license, permission *He has the right to fire you if you don't do your job.* 3. *adjective* correct, true, accurate, exact, perfect, faultless *Kurt had the right answer for question three; mine was wrong.* 4. good, just, lawful, fitting, suitable, proper *You did the right thing to admit the accident was your fault.*

rigid *adjective* stiff, firm, hard, unbending, inflexible *The CDs come with clear, rigid, plastic cases.*

rim *noun* edge, border, margin, fringe *The hike from the North Rim to the bottom of the Grand Canyon is nearly fifteen miles.*

ring 1. *noun* circle, loop, band, hoop *I keep my house key on a key ring.* 2. peal, chime, tinkle, jingle, ringing *When you hear the ring of the timer, take the cake out of the oven.* 3. *verb* sound, peal, toll, chime, tinkle, jingle *Did the phone ring?* 4. circle, enclose, encircle, surround *The campers ringed the campfire, singing and toasting marshmallows.*

riot *noun* uprising, disturbance, demonstration, protest, rebellion, revolt *Police were called to deal with the riot.*

rip 1. *verb* tear, split, shred, cut, slash *She ripped the letter open and found she had been* *accepted at the university.* 2. *noun* tear, split, slit, hole *Do you know you have a rip in the seat of your pants?*

ripe *adjective* developed, ready, mature, full-grown *We picked the ripe cherries for a pie.* unripe, immature, green

rise 1. *verb* go up, climb, ascend, come up, lift *The sun rises earlier and sets later in the summer. Every hand in the class rose when the teacher asked who was ready for recess.* descend 2. increase, grow, gain, mount, get higher, swell, expand *Noise levels rose when the band came onstage.* decrease 3. *noun* increase, gain, upsurge, climb, escalation *The hospital has seen a rise in the number of flu cases.* decrease 4. advancement, ascent, improvement, progress *His rise to president of the company surprised no one.*

risk 1. *noun* chance, gamble, hazard, peril, jeopardy *You reduce your risk of getting sick by eating healthful food.* 2. *verb* endanger, jeopardize, imperil, gamble *She risked her life to save her friend.*

rival 1. *noun* competitor, opponent, adversary, challenger, enemy, foe *My best friend and I are rivals in the next tennis match.* 2. *verb* match, compete with, equal, compare to *Nobody's grilled hamburgers rival my dad's.* 3. *adjective* competing, opposing, challenging, contending *The rival department stores both had big sales.*

road *noun* street, highway, freeway, avenue, boulevard, thoroughfare, lane, route *Follow the road to the right.*

roam *verb* wander, drift, stray, meander, ramble *We roamed around town looking into shop windows.*

roar 1. *verb* bellow, bawl, howl, cry, yell, shout *The crowd roared as the gladiators fought.* 2. *noun* bellow, howl, growl, yell, cry *At night on Africa's Serengeti Plain, you can hear the roar of lions.*

rob *verb* burglarize, hold up, stick up, steal from, loot, raid *Jesse James and his gang robbed banks, trains, and stagecoaches all across the West.*

robust *adjective* strong, healthy, sturdy, rugged, hardy, vigorous *President Theodore Roosevelt overcame asthma to become a robust outdoorsman.*

rock 1. *noun* stone, boulder, pebble *The rocks along the shore were worn smooth by the waves.* 2. *verb* sway, swing, roll, pitch, shake *Grandpa gently rocked my baby brother to sleep. Don't stand up—you'll rock the boat.*

role *noun* part, character, position, function, capacity *Tanya got the lead role in the play.*

roll 1. *verb* turn, revolve, rotate, spin, move *The ball rolled into the street.* 2. coil, turn, fold, twist, wrap *Roll the dough into a ball.* 3. *noun* list, register, lineup, attendance record *The teacher calls the roll at the start of class.* 4. reel, spool, cylinder *With a digital camera, you no longer need a roll of film.* 5. bun, biscuit, pastry, croissant *We had freshly baked rolls with butter.*

romance *noun* adventure, mystery, excitement, love *I thought that* The Adventures of Robin Hood *was a classic story of daring and romance.*

room *noun* 1. chamber, bedroom, accommodations, lodging *We each have a room of our own. The hotel has no rooms available.* 2. space, area, expanse *Move over, Terry—you're taking up too much room.*

root *noun* cause, source, origin, basis *If we can get to the root of the problem, we can solve it.*

rot 1. *verb* decay, spoil, go bad, disintegrate *We need to pick the apples before they rot.* 2. *noun* decay, decomposition, mold, blight *We checked the boat for rot before we bought it.*

rotate *verb* spin, turn, revolve, swivel, pivot *A toy top rotates on an axis.*

rough *adjective* 1. coarse, uneven, irregular, bumpy, jagged *Oak trees have rough, furrowed bark.* 2. incomplete, basic, sketchy, inexact, vague, hasty, quick *Here's a rough idea of what we have in mind.* 3. difficult, tough, hard, unpleasant *We had a rough time against the opposing team.*

round 1. *adjective* circular, spherical, ball-shaped, ring-shaped *The earth is round.* 2. curved, smoothed, convex, rounded *An arch is a structure that is round at the top.* 3. *noun* series, succession, string *College freshmen attend a round of activities to become familiar with the campus.* 4. *verb* go around, travel around, turn, circle *Before the Panama Canal, ships had to round Cape Horn.*

rounds *noun* circuit, tour, schedule, routine, beat *The doctor makes her hospital rounds every day at 7:30 A.M. and 4:00 P.M.*

rout 1. *noun* defeat, drubbing, beating, thrashing *Today's game was a complete rout for our team.* 2. *verb* defeat, conquer, crush, overwhelm, beat *Government forces routed the insurgents.*

route 1. *noun* course, way, path, road, itinerary *The tour guide has the route all planned.* 2. *verb* direct, guide, send, move *Traffic was routed around the road construction.*

routine 1. *noun* habit, custom, practice, schedule, system, order *He goes to the gym every day as part of his routine.* 2. *adjective* usual, common, customary, normal, ordinary, everyday *Backing up your computer data should be a routine procedure.*

row *noun* line, file, string, series, succession, column *Rather than sitting at desks in a row, we sit in a circle in our classroom.*

rowdy *adjective* rough, disorderly, boisterous, rambunctious *Dad said we were getting too rowdy and should go outside to play.*

royal *adjective* 1. aristocratic, imperial, regal, noble *The royal family moved to their country palace for the summer.* 2. wonderful, splendid, grand *Grandma and Grandpa always give us a royal welcome when we visit.*

rub 1. *verb* massage, stroke, knead *I rubbed Mom's shoulders to get the tension out.* 2. *noun* massage, kneading, rubdown *I'd like a back rub, please.*

rubbish *noun* trash, garbage, waste, refuse, scrap, debris, litter, junk *We need to keep the rubbish and the recyclables separate.*

rude *adjective* 1. impolite, discourteous, disrespectful, inconsiderate, insolent, ill-mannered *A rude man barged in front of us and took our taxi.* 2. rough, crude, primitive, simple *Chimpanzees make rude tools in order to get at their favorite foods.*

ruffle *verb* disturb, tousle, rumple, upset, dishevel, mess up *A breeze ruffled his hair.*

rug *noun* mat, floor covering, carpet *I took the rugs outside and shook them while my brother swept the floor.*

rugged *adjective* 1. rough, harsh, rocky, uneven, jagged *We hiked through rugged terrain to get to the mountain stream.* 2. strong, sturdy, tough, hardy, durable *Rodney has a rugged case to protect his laptop computer.*

ruin 1. *verb* destroy, demolish, wreck, spoil, mess up *I ruined my new white T-shirt by spilling spaghetti sauce on it.* 2. *noun* destruction, devastation, collapse *During the Great Depression the economy was in a state of ruin.* 3. rubble, remains, debris, relics *The ruins of the Parthenon, built in the fifth century B.C., stand on a hill overlooking Athens, Greece.*

rule 1. *noun* regulation, instruction, guideline, principle, standard, law *The rules of this card game are very simple.* 2. government, regime, control, reign, administration, command *During Queen Victoria's rule, Britain expanded into an empire.* 3. *verb* govern, reign, control, lead, direct, command, administer *George III ruled during the Revolutionary War.* 4. decree, order, judge, decide, settle *The judge ruled in favor of the defendant.*

rumble 1. *verb* roar, thunder, boom, roll, resound, growl, grumble *The sound of thunder rumbled through the valley.* 2. *noun* boom, roar, roll, growl, grumble *The rumble of my stomach seemed really loud in the quiet room.*

rummage *verb* search, look through, poke through, delve *I rummaged through my backpack for my keys.*

rumor 1. *noun* gossip, talk, story, report, opinion *The principal denied the rumor that she was resigning.* 2. *verb* gossip, say, suggest, spread *It was rumored that a lost city of gold existed in South America.*

run 1. *verb* hurry, race, speed, rush, hasten, scurry, dash, jog *Some mornings we have to run to catch the school bus.* slow down 2. go, operate, function, work, move *A diesel engine can be modified to run on vegetable oil.* 3. stretch, extend, reach, range, lie, spread *The highway runs north and south along the coast.* 4. flow, stream, pour, gush, discharge *A water main broke and water is running in the street.* 5. continue, last, endure, persist *The Broadway play has been running for many years.* stop, end 6. campaign, compete, electioneer *The governor is running for reelection.* 7. conduct, manage, lead, direct, regulate, govern, administer, supervise *Mr. Mulhern runs the bookstore.* 8. *noun* jog, sprint, dash, race, trot, gallop *We took the dog out for a run along the beach.* 9. streak, spell, period, stretch, series, succession *The team is having a run of good fortune this season.*

rupture 1. *noun* break, breach, fracture, crack *A bruise is caused by a rupture of a small blood vessel under the skin.* 2. *verb* break, burst, fracture, crack *Darcy had to have her appendix removed before it ruptured.*

rural *adjective* country, countryside, pastoral, agricultural, rustic, provincial *People who live in rural areas have less access to health care.* urban, city

rush 1. *verb* hurry, hasten, hustle, speed, dash, scurry, run *He rushed to the bank to deposit his check before it closed.* slow down 2. *noun* haste, hurry, bustle *We have plenty of time, so what's the rush? She was in a rush to finish her homework.*

rusty *adjective* 1. corroded, eroded, oxidized *Rusty cars littered the salvage yard.* 2. out of practice, unpracticed *Paula says her guitar picking is pretty rusty.*

ruthless *adjective* cruel, merciless, heartless, cold, unfeeling, brutal *Civil rights activists criticized the ruthless dictator.* kind

S

sack *noun* 1. bag, pack, shopping bag *I bought a sack of potato chips.* 2. destruction, burning, plundering, robbing, ransacking, looting *The story of the siege and sack of Troy is told in Homer's* Iliad.

sacred *adjective* holy, blessed, hallowed, spiritual, divine *The feathers of eagles are sacred to Native Americans.*

sacrifice 1. *noun* loss, surrender, forfeiture, self-sacrifice *Our parents are making many sacrifices in order for us to get good educations.* 2. offering, gift *The tribe made sacrifices of gold and silver to the gods.* 3. *verb* give up, surrender, forego, forfeit *He sacrificed a good job to join the Peace Corps.*

sad *adjective* unhappy, dejected, blue, glum, depressed, melancholy, gloomy *I was sad when my sister had to return to college.* happy, glad

safe 1. *adjective* secure, unharmed, protected, guarded, sheltered *A smoke alarm outside your bedroom is a safe thing to have.* unsafe, endangered 2. *noun* strongbox, vault, safe-deposit box, lockbox *Our important papers are stored in a safe.*

sag *verb* droop, sink, hang, dangle, slump, drop, wilt *The mattress on my cot at camp sags in the middle.*

sail 1. *verb* navigate, steer, pilot, captain *I would like to learn to sail a sailboat.* 2. set sail, cruise, voyage *The* Titanic *sailed on April 10, 1912.* 3. drift, float, glide, fly *The balloons sailed upward until they disappeared.* 4. *noun* cruise, boat trip, voyage *The breeze was perfect for a sail.*

salary *noun* pay, wages, earnings, compensation *Dad's boss just increased Dad's salary.*

sale *noun* 1. trade, exchange, transfer, transaction *She receives a commission on every sale.* purchase 2. bargain, discount, closeout, reduction, deal *We got all our school supplies at the back-to-school sales.*

same *adjective* identical, alike, matching, equivalent, similar, equal *She and I have the same first names.*

sample 1. *noun* example, model, representative, specimen, instance *I chose the carpeting for my room from samples that Mom brought home.* 2. *verb* test, try, try out, experiment with, taste *Dad let me sample his coffee.*

sanctuary *noun* refuge, shelter, haven, reserve, preserve *I have heard that millions of* *birds stop at the sanctuary each day during peak migration.*

sand *verb* smooth, polish, rub, scrape, grind *She sanded the table carefully before she varnished it.*

sane *adjective* sensible, sound, rational, reasonable, responsible *The only sane thing to do in this downpour is pack up our camping gear and go home.*

sanitary *adjective* clean, hygienic, spotless, healthful, sterile, antiseptic *Hospitals must maintain sanitary conditions.*

sanity *noun* reason, mental health, stability, judgment, common sense *I doubted my sister's sanity when she came home with orange hair.*

sarcastic *adjective* scornful, sneering, mocking, cutting, bitter, caustic *Kevin made a sarcastic remark about my new haircut.*

satisfaction *noun* contentment, happiness, pleasure, enjoyment, gratification *I felt a lot of satisfaction at having done well on my math test. My dad gets satisfaction from working in the garden.*

satisfactory *adjective* adequate, acceptable, sufficient, all right, passable *I haven't gotten a satisfactory solution to my computer problems.*

satisfy *verb* 1. please, gratify, appease, content *An afternoon snack satisfied my hunger.* 2. convince, persuade, assure, relieve *The prosecutor must satisfy the jury that the defendant is guilty.*

saturate *verb* soak, wet, drench, douse, flood, inundate *The heavy rain saturated the farmers' fields.*

savage *adjective* fierce, cruel, vicious, ferocious *Grizzly bears are capable of making savage attacks on humans, so keep your distance.*

save *verb* 1. keep, conserve, store, accumulate, gather, reserve *We save our change in a jar until we have enough for the family to eat out.* 2. rescue, help, protect, recover, retrieve *My brother saved a kitten that was too frightened to come down from a tree.*

say 1. *verb* speak, utter, articulate, express, comment, mention, declare, state *Did you say "thank you"? She said she'd call tonight.* 2. *noun* vote, opinion, voice, input, two cents *We all have our say in family decisions.*

saying *noun* proverb, motto, expression, adage *"An apple a day keeps the doctor away" is an old saying.*

scald *verb* burn, scorch, singe, blister *Be careful the boiling water doesn't scald you.*

scan *verb* examine, inspect, look at, check, search, study, review, scrutinize *I scanned the website but found nothing helpful.*

scandal *noun* disgrace, humiliation, shame, dishonor, outrage *The break-in at Democratic National Committee headquarters in the Watergate Hotel was a scandal that forced President Nixon to resign.*

scant *adjective* meager, scarce, sparse, small, slight, skimpy, negligible, inadequate *I paid scant attention to the instructions and am unsure now what to do.*

scar 1. *noun* mark, blemish, wound, injury *Darcy has a scar from the surgery to remove her appendix.* 2. *verb* blemish, mar, mark, deface, wound, damage *The landscape is scarred by strip mines.*

scarce *adjective* scant, rare, uncommon, in short supply, insufficient *Water is scarce in desert regions.* plentiful

scarcely *adverb* barely, just, hardly *I scarcely got in the house before it began to pour.*

scare 1. *verb* frighten, alarm, startle, terrify, shock, panic *The dog scared the rabbit out of the garden.* 2. *noun* fright, start, shock, panic *You gave me a scare when you sneaked up on me that way.*

scatter *verb* disperse, distribute, spread, strew *The wind scattered the leaves across the lawn.* gather, collect

scene *noun* 1. setting, site, place, area, location *Police arrived at the scene of the accident.* 2. view, scenery, picture, sight, vista, landscape *Grandma Moses painted rural scenes of upstate New York.* 3. act, division, part, section *Derek appeared in every scene of the play.*

scenic *adjective* beautiful, picturesque, pretty, charming *We took the scenic back roads rather than main highways.*

scent 1. *noun* fragrance, odor, smell, aroma, whiff, bouquet *This lotion has a lavender scent.* 2. *verb* smell, sniff, detect, sense, become aware of *The animal must have scented our presence and took off.*

schedule 1. *noun* list, program, lineup, calendar, timetable *We have a busy schedule this weekend. My brother's schedule of courses includes chemistry and biology.* 2. *verb* arrange, plan, organize, reserve, book *Mom scheduled a dentist's appointment for me to have my teeth cleaned.*

scheme 1. *noun* plan, procedure, program, idea, strategy, plot *When John Muir* *was young, he devised a scheme by which his bed would tilt him to a standing position each morning.* 2. *verb* plan, plot, conspire, contrive, intrigue *The thieves schemed to steal the jewels from the palace treasury.*

scholar *noun* learned person, intellectual, sage, academic, student *Confucius was a famous Chinese scholar and philosopher.*

school 1. *noun* educational institution, college, university, academy, institute, elementary school, middle school, high school *I started school when I was five years old.* 2. *verb* educate, teach, instruct, tutor, train *He was schooled in ballet.*

scoff *verb* mock, laugh, jeer, ridicule, make fun of *Before you scoff at my suggestion, see if it will work.*

scold *verb* reprimand, admonish, talk to, lecture *Dad scolded me for not calling when I was going to be late.*

scoop 1. *noun* ladle, spoon, dipper *I'd like two scoops of ice cream.* 2. *verb* lift, ladle, pick up *She scooped up water with her hands and splashed it on her face.*

scope *noun* extent, degree, measure, range, sphere, reach *It's hard to even imagine the scope of the Internet's impact on society.*

scorch *verb* burn, singe, blacken, char *I scorched my marshmallow in the campfire.*

score 1. *noun* grade, mark, total, count, result, outcome *I got a better score on this test than on the last.* 2. *verb* achieve, gain, win, get *Ted scored the first goal for our team.*

scour *verb* scrub, rub, polish, clean, wash, buff, shine *When I finished my bath, I scoured the tub.*

scout 1. *noun* guide, lookout, spy, agent *The scout returned with information about the enemy's location.* 2. *verb* search, hunt, look, explore, survey *The Mars orbiter's mission is to scout for future landing sites.*

scowl *verb* frown, glare, glower *The librarian scowled at us for talking.*

scramble 1. *verb* mix, jumble, disorganize, mess up, mingle *The children's toys were all scrambled together in a box.* 2. hurry, scurry, rush, hustle, scoot, dart *Everyone overslept and had to scramble to get ready for school and work.* 3. *noun* competition, struggle, commotion, rush, stampede, free-for-all *There was a scramble among sports fans to get tickets to the Super Bowl.*

scrap 1. *noun* small amount, shred, piece, fragment, particle, speck *Grandma sews scraps of fabric into beautiful quilts.* 2. *verb* throw away, discard, dispose of, get rid of, abandon

My sister scrapped her plans to travel this summer because she hadn't saved enough money.

scrape 1. *verb* clean, scrub, rub, brush, remove *I scraped the food from the dishes and put them in the dishwasher.* 2. scratch, scuff, abrade, cut, hurt, injure *Protective gear helps skateboarders to avoid scraping their knees and more serious injuries.* 3. *noun* scratch, scuff, abrasion, cut, injury *He had a few scrapes and bruises from the fall but nothing serious.*

scratch *verb* scrape, scuff, abrade, tear, nick, cut *We got our cat a post that it can scratch.*

scrawny *adjective* skinny, thin, undernourished, bony, gaunt *Our dog Sparky was just a scrawny puppy when we brought him home from the shelter.* husky, chubby

scream 1. *verb* yell, shout, howl, cry, shriek, screech, bawl *The fans were on their feet screaming as the receiver caught the pass for the winning touchdown.* 2. *noun* shriek, cry, yell, shout, screech, howl *We listened to the children's screams of delight as they played in the waves.*

screech 1. *noun* shriek, scream, squeal, yell, cry, shout, howl *Harry's screech brought us running.* 2. *verb* shriek, squeal *Our brakes screeched as we came to a sudden stop to avoid the deer crossing the road.*

screw 1. *noun* fastener, bolt *You tighten a screw by turning it clockwise.* 2. *verb* fasten, tighten, twist, turn, rotate *The instructions say to screw the cabinets to the wall, then install the doors.*

scribble *verb* scrawl, scratch, doodle, draw, write *I scribbled in the margins of my notebook.*

scrub *verb* 1. wash, clean *Be sure you scrub your hands well before dinner.* 2. rub, cleanse, scour, wash, polish *She scrubbed the floors clean.*

scuffle *noun* struggle, fight, tussle *The players got into a scuffle for possession of the ball.*

sculpture *noun* carving, statue, figure, figurine, shape, form *We made a sand sculpture of a castle on the beach.*

scurry *verb* scamper, dash, dart, run, race, tear *A mouse scurried under the refrigerator.*

seal 1. *noun* emblem, symbol, insignia, mark, stamp *The governor affixed his seal to the document.* 2. *verb* fasten, close, shut, secure *She sealed the package with packing tape.*

search 1. *verb* look for, hunt for, seek, track down, investigate, probe *Mom was searching for her glasses when all the time she was wearing them.* 2. *noun* hunt, pursuit, exploration, investigation, probe *We were about to give up the search for our missing dog when Jenny found him playing fetch with kids in the park.*

season 1. *noun* time, period, time of year *The best part of the fall season in the north is seeing the leaves change color.* 2. *verb* flavor, spice, add seasoning to *Quinn seasons his food with a lot of pepper.*

secluded *adjective* remote, isolated, private, undisturbed, hidden, concealed *We spend summer weekends at a secluded cabin in the woods.* accessible, open

secret 1. *noun* confidence, confidential information, private matter, mystery *You swore you wouldn't tell anyone my secret.* 2. *adjective* confidential, classified, mysterious, hidden, concealed, private *The Allies broke the Germans' secret code during World War II after capturing several German coding devices.* open

section 1. *noun* part, portion, segment, division, slice, piece *She jumped to the last section of the book because she couldn't wait to see what happened.* 2. *verb* split, cut, divide, slice, partition *Marcie sectioned the apple into quarters.*

secure 1. *adjective* safe, protected, sheltered, shielded *We keep valuable papers in a secure place.* unsafe 2. reliable, steady, sure, assured, guaranteed, stable *My parents say they want a secure future for their children.* 3. *verb* close, fasten, shut, lock, seal, fix, attach *Be sure to secure all the doors and windows before we leave.* 4. get, obtain, acquire *The publisher secured the rights to her books.* 5. make safe, guard, protect, safeguard, shield, shelter *Soldiers secured the embassy from attack.*

see *verb* 1. catch sight of, glimpse, spot, perceive, observe, notice, recognize *Have you seen Sally?* 2. understand, realize, comprehend, appreciate *I see what you mean.* 3. find out, ascertain, discover, learn, check, establish *I'll see if I can come over tonight.* 4. make sure, make certain, ensure, guarantee *See that you're home by 10:00.*

seek *verb* hunt for, search, look for, pursue, explore *Congress is seeking changes in the law.*

seem *verb* appear, look, give the impression *He seems to be a polite young man.*

seep *verb* ooze, trickle, leak, drip *Water is seeping from the leaky faucet.*

segment *noun* part, division, section, piece, portion, fraction *The chocolate bar can be broken into segments and shared.*

seize *verb* grab, grasp, clutch, grip, snatch, catch *I seized my brother's arm and pulled him back onto the curb.* release

seldom *adjective* rarely, infrequently, hardly, not often *I seldom get sick.* often

select 1. *verb* pick, choose, decide on *I usually select the chicken when we go out to* *eat.* 2. *adjective* choice, prime, best, top-quality, exclusive *He was one of the select few admitted into the prestigious school.*

selection *noun* assortment, collection, range, variety *The cell phones are available in a selection of colors.*

self-conscious *adjective* timid, bashful, shy, nervous, embarrassed *I felt self-conscious when I got up to speak in front of the whole school.*

selfish *adjective* self-centered, possessive, stingy, greedy, egotistical *It was selfish of the boy not to share his toys with the other children.* generous

sell *verb* market, vend, peddle, offer, auction *A garage sale is a good place to sell your old stuff.* buy

send *verb* dispatch, mail, transmit, transfer, forward, convey, relay *Dad sent me on an errand. Did you send Aunt Sally a thank-you note?*

senior 1. *adjective* elder, elderly, old, older, oldest, aged *Some senior citizens don't have enough to live on.* 2. *noun* older, elder *Dad is my uncle's senior.*

sensational *adjective* exciting, amazing, astounding, superb, magnificent, marvelous, fantastic *The July 4 fireworks display was sensational.*

sense 1. *noun* feeling, sensation, perception, faculty *A dog has a good sense of smell.* 2. appreciation, awareness, feeling, consciousness, understanding *I had a strong sense of accomplishment when I finished my science project.* 3. intelligence, judgment, brains, wisdom *Chris had the good sense to stay out of Joan and Amy's argument.* 4. *verb* feel, perceive, understand, realize, follow, grasp, comprehend *Sue sensed I was worried about something.*

senseless *adjective* foolish, silly, stupid, irrational, idiotic *It's senseless to try to change Dad's mind when he's made it up.* bright, sensible

sensible *adjective* intelligent, wise, rational, logical, practical, realistic *The sensible thing to do if you need help is to ask for it.* senseless

sensitive *adjective* responsive, receptive, understanding, perceptive, considerate *Mom and Dad are sensitive to our needs.* insensitive

sentimental *adjective* emotional, loving, tender, mushy *Grandma gets all sentimental when she looks at our baby pictures.*

separate 1. *verb* divide, part, disconnect, split, detach, break up *The river separates the east side of town from the west. The teacher separated the boys who were fighting.* join, unite 2. *adjective* distinct, different, independent, isolated, individual, single *My sister and I have separate rooms in our new house.*

sequel *noun* continuation, follow-up, conclusion *Do you plan to see the movie's sequel?*

sequence *noun* series, succession, string, progression, chain, run *What is the next number in the sequence 2, 4, 8, 16, 32?*

serene *adjective* peaceful, calm, tranquil, quiet, untroubled *The cabin in the woods is a serene retreat.*

series *noun* sequence, succession, string, chain, course, set *A series of concerts will be presented in the park.*

serious *adjective* 1. thoughtful, grave, reflective, solemn, somber *You're looking serious today—is something troubling you?* 2. important, momentous, profound, significant, crucial, urgent, major *Drinking is a serious problem among college students.* unimportant, minor 3. sincere, honest, earnest, determined *If you're serious about getting better grades, you'll have to study.* 4. critical, acute, dangerous, grave, alarming *An oil spill is a serious threat to the environment.*

sermon *noun* lecture, talk, address *Our class read one of Dr. Martin Luther King Jr.'s sermons on the holiday commemorating his life.*

serve *verb* 1. function, work, act, perform *Phyllis serves as president of our class.* 2. supply, present, furnish, provide *Mom served roast beef for dinner.* 3. assist, wait on, attend, help *We had to wait while the salesclerk served another customer.*

service 1. *noun* help, assistance, aid, benefit, use *How can I be of service to you?* 2. ceremony, celebration, observance, rite *My sister was a bridesmaid in my cousin's wedding service.* 3. armed forces, military, army, navy, air force, marines, coast guard *Granddad was in the service in Vietnam.* 4. *verb* repair, fix, overhaul, tune, maintain *We took our lawn mower into a shop to be serviced.*

set 1. *verb* place, position, lay, put, rest, deposit *Set the dirty dishes next to the sink.* 2. harden, solidify, congeal, gel, thicken *Let the glue set for twenty-four hours.* 3. arrange, prepare, fix, adjust *Set the clock ahead an hour for daylight saving time.* 4. settle on, agree on, establish, fix, specify, name *Bill and Joanne have set the date for their wedding.* 5. *noun* collection, group, arrangement, selection, batch, assortment *We get out our best set of dishes for Thanksgiving dinner.*

setting *noun* location, scenery, surroundings, background *Claude Monet used gardens as the setting for his most famous paintings.*

settle *verb* 1. decide, determine, arrange, agree on, establish, choose *Let's settle on a time to meet.* 2. resolve, reconcile, mend, clear up *Dan and I settled our argument with no hard feelings.* 3. occupy, locate, inhabit, populate, colonize *Many homesteaders settled in South Dakota.* 4. sink, drop, descend, fall *The ship settled to the bottom of the sea with a cargo of gold.* 5. calm, quiet, soothe, relax *This medicine will settle your upset stomach.*

several *adjective* some, a few, various, assorted *I found several books about whales in the library for my report.*

severe *adjective* 1. strict, harsh, stern, serious, grave, rigorous *The crime is subject to a severe penalty.* easy, lenient 2. bitter, harsh, fierce, brutal, intense *Severe thunderstorms are forecast for tonight.*

shabby *adjective* worn, ragged, shoddy, tattered, frayed *Mom says our living room sofa looks shabby, and we should replace it.*

shack *noun* hut, shanty, shed, cabin *She grew up in a shack with no electricity or indoor plumbing.*

shade 1. *noun* shadow, cloud cover, dimness, dark, gloom *We had our picnic in the shade of an oak tree.* light 2. color, tint, hue, tone *Bodies of water are usually shown on maps in shades of blue.* 3. *verb* cover, shield, protect *I shaded my eyes from the glaring sunlight.*

shadow 1. *noun* image, shape, silhouette, outline *Our shadows grew longer as the sun set.* 2. shade, darkness, dimness, gloom *Something moved in the shadows and startled us, but it was only our cat.* light 3. *verb* to follow closely *The police shadowed the suspect for two days before arresting him.*

shady *adjective* shaded, shadowy, dim, sheltered, sunless *We found a shady parking space for our car.* sunny

shaggy *adjective* long-haired, bushy, thick, tousled, disheveled *Our shaggy dog sheds on the furniture.*

shake 1. *verb* jiggle, rattle, agitate, mix *Shake the salad dressing before you pour it on your salad.* 2. tremble, shiver, quiver, quaver, vibrate *The earth shook from the quake.* 3. disturb, distress, upset, unsettle, unnerve *Nothing you say will shake my confidence.* 4. *noun* shaking, jiggle, wobble, wag *He indicated no with a shake of his head.*

shallow *adjective* not deep, low *We waded in the shallow water along the shore.*

shame 1. *noun* embarrassment, humiliation, guilt, discomfort, disgrace *He felt shame at having lied to his best friend.* 2. bad luck, misfortune, pity *What a shame it is that you can't stay for the weekend.* 3. *verb* humiliate, disgrace, dishonor, embarrass *In Colonial* *times people were shamed for their crimes by being put in stocks.*

shape 1. *noun* form, outline, contour, figure, appearance *People are all shapes and sizes.* 2. condition, state, health, order *Our car is in bad shape and needs to be replaced.* 3. *verb* form, fashion, mold, design, develop, adapt *The potter shaped the clay into a vase.*

share 1. *verb* divide, split, apportion, distribute *We share the chores in our family.* 2. *noun* part, portion, piece, segment *We each got a share of the pie.*

sharp 1. *adjective* cutting, razor-edged, sharp-edged, pointed, pointy *That knife is sharp—be careful.* dull 2. bright, smart, intelligent, clever, alert, shrewd, brainy *It takes someone sharp to do these crossword puzzles.* unintelligent 3. severe, bitter, harsh, intense, angry *The country's government has faced sharp criticism for its human rights violations.* mild 4. abrupt, sudden, quick, rapid *We're expecting a sharp drop in the temperature tonight.* gentle 5. *adverb* on time, promptly, exactly, precisely, punctually *Arrive at 8 o'clock sharp.*

sharpen *verb* make sharp, hone, grind, file *This knife needs sharpening.*

shatter *verb* smash, break, fragment *The glass shattered when it hit the floor.*

shed 1. *verb* cast off, throw off, molt, slough off *Snakes shed their skin as they grow.* 2. radiate, emit, cast, spread *My reading lamp sheds a lot of light.* 3. *noun* outbuilding, shack, hut *We keep our garden tools in a shed in the backyard.*

sheen *noun* luster, shine, gloss, glow, gleam, brightness *Our brand-new car had a beautiful sheen.*

sheer *adjective* 1. transparent, translucent, clear, thin, see-through *Sheer curtains let in a lot of sunlight.* 2. pure, complete, plain, absolute, total, utter *The children watched in sheer amazement as the magician performed his magic.* 3. steep, abrupt, sharp, precipitous *There is a sheer drop of thousands of feet from the cliffs of the Grand Canyon to the river below.* gentle

shelter *noun* 1. cover, protection, refuge, safety *We sought shelter from the rain under a shop awning.* 2. home, housing, refuge, sanctuary, haven *The Jacksons run a shelter for homeless people.*

shield 1. *verb* protect, guard, shelter, screen, hide, defend *Our immune systems shield us against disease.* 2. *noun* protection, safeguard, cover, defense *My parents insist I use sunscreen as a shield against sunburn.*

shift 1. *verb* change, move, transfer, switch, alter, vary *When the wind shifts from the south to the north, the weather gets cooler.* 2. *noun* change, switch, alteration, modification *We had to make a shift in plans when our flight was canceled.* 3. work period, duty, assignment, crew, staff *The night shift works from eleven o'clock until seven o'clock.*

shimmer *verb* gleam, glimmer, shine, twinkle, sparkle, glisten *The moonlight shimmered on the surface of the lake.*

shine 1. *verb* glow, gleam, glimmer, twinkle, sparkle, glisten, beam, flash, radiate *The sun was shining through my bedroom window. The eye doctor shined a light in my eyes.* 2. polish, buff, brush, wax *I need to shine my shoes.* 3. excel, do well at, be skilled at *Erica shines at math and science.* 4. *noun* gleam, glow, twinkle, sparkle, radiance, luster, polish *The car had a shine like new after we washed and waxed it.*

ship 1. *noun* vessel, craft, boat, passenger liner, freighter *Dozens of ships were lined up waiting to unload their cargo.* 2. *verb* send, dispatch, transport *We shipped the package overnight express.*

shiver 1. *verb* shake, quiver, quaver, tremble, quake *Take my sweater—you're shivering.* 2. *noun* quiver, shudder, tremor, tremble *A shiver went down my spine when we passed the house that Jeff said is haunted.*

shock 1. *noun* surprise, blow, jolt, upset, fright *The news that my best friend was moving came as quite a shock.* 2. *verb* startle, frighten, horrify, appall, stun, surprise *The devastation caused by the earthquake shocked everyone.*

shoot 1. *verb* fire, discharge, launch, let fly *The circus performer was shot from a cannon.* 2. race, speed, run, dash, dart *We shot down the hill on our bikes.* 3. *noun* sprout, bud, branch, stem, leaf *Shoots are beginning to emerge from the seeds I planted in the garden.*

shop 1. *verb* go shopping, look to buy, look *Mom and I shopped for school clothes.* 2. *noun* store, boutique, outlet *The shops in the mall are having a sale this week.*

shore *noun* coast, beach, waterfront, coastline *We walked along the shore looking for shells.*

short 1. *adjective* small, little, slight, tiny, petite *My older sister is short—only about five feet tall.* tall 2. brief, concise, quick, succinct *The speaker kept her speech short.* long, lengthy 3. *adverb* suddenly, abruptly, quickly, unexpectedly *The car in front of us stopped short.* gradually

shortage *noun* deficit, deficiency, lack, absence, scarcity, want *A seven-year drought has caused a shortage of food and water.*

shortcoming *noun* fault, defect, flaw, weakness, failing, imperfection, inadequacy, deficiency *Dad's only shortcoming is he can't cook.*

shorten *verb* cut, trim, abbreviate, condense, abridge, reduce, decrease *The expressway shortens the commute into the city. My new pants need to be shortened.*

shout 1. *verb* yell, call, cry out, scream, shriek, howl, bellow *The drivers got out of their cars and began shouting at each other.* 2. *noun* yell, cry, shriek, howl, roar, bellow *We heard shouts of laughter coming from the party next door.*

shove 1. *verb* push, thrust, heave, jostle, nudge, move *We shoved the furniture out of the way to make space to dance.* 2. *noun* push, nudge, thrust, heave *Brian gave me a shove into the pool.*

show 1. *verb* direct, point, steer, guide, accompany, escort *The usher showed us to our seats.* 2. display, present, exhibit, reveal *Anna is showing her watercolors at the art gallery.* 3. explain, demonstrate, illustrate, indicate, clarify *The science teacher showed us what lightning is.* 4. *noun* display, exhibit, exhibition, demonstration *Sandy will be riding her horse in the show.* 5. performance, program, production, entertainment *The shows I enjoy most are musicals.*

shred 1. *noun* scrap, piece, tatter, strip, bit, fragment, particle *She tore the paper into shreds.* 2. *verb* tear up, cut up, rip up, grate, slice, chop *Dad shredded cheese for the top of the pizza while I sliced the pepperoni.*

shrewd *adjective* clever, smart, keen, sharp, intelligent, wise, astute *He was a shrewd politician in order to be elected to four terms as governor.*

shriek 1. *noun* yell, cry, scream, screech, squeal *My little sister let out a shriek of excitement when she saw she got a bicycle for her birthday.* 2. *verb* yell, cry, scream, screech, squeal *Chris shrieked when he saw the mouse.*

shrink *verb* 1. become smaller, shrivel, contract, wither *The hot water shrank the wool sweater.* 2. withdraw, pull back, retreat, cringe, recoil, flinch *I shrank from the idea of touching the snake.*

shrivel *verb* wither, shrink, dry up, wrinkle *Drought shriveled the grass.*

shudder 1. *verb* tremble, quiver, shiver, shake, quake *The clap of thunder made the windows shudder.* 2. *noun* tremble, shiver, quiver, tremor *A shudder passed through me when I thought of how close I came to the rattlesnake.*

shuffle *verb* 1. drag one's feet, scuff one's feet, scuffle, hobble *We shuffled along the icy sidewalk.* 2. mix up, scramble, jumble, rearrange, reorder *She shuffled the stack of papers on her desk.*

shut *verb* 1. close, fasten, seal, lock, bolt, secure *Shut the screen door to keep out the flies.*

open 2. enclose, confine, cage, fence, pen, imprison *Shut the dogs in the kennel before you go to bed.*

shy *adjective* 1. bashful, reserved, withdrawn, timid *Juan is shy until he's known someone for a while.* 2. lacking, short, missing, deficient *This deck of cards is shy two cards.*

shy away *verb* back away, avoid, shrink from, recoil from, balk at *The stray kitten shied away from me when I tried to pet it.*

sick *adjective* ill, unwell, under the weather, ailing, indisposed *I missed two days of school because I was sick with a cold.* well

side *noun* 1. surface, face, part *Which side should be up?* 2. edge, boundary, margin, border *Our Scout troop picks up trash along the side of the road as a community project.* 3. opinion, position, view, viewpoint, angle, aspect *Let me hear your side of the argument.* 4. team, squad, group, gang, party, camp, sect *We chose sides for the game.*

sift *verb* filter, screen, strain, sort *The archaeologists sifted the sand looking for bits of pottery.*

sight 1. *noun* vision, eyesight *Owls have keen sight and hearing.* 2. view, range, notice *The moon disappeared from sight beyond the horizon.* 3. scene, spectacle, display, show *An eclipse of the sun is a memorable sight.* 4. *verb* notice, glimpse, observe, see, perceive, spot *The Spanish Armada was first sighted off the English coast on July 29, 1588.*

sign 1. *noun* hint, clue, indication, evidence, trace, symptom *The peace talks have shown no signs of progress.* 2. signal, gesture, motion, movement, code *The librarian made a sign for us to be quiet.* 3. poster, notice, placard, billboard, signpost *The sign says this is Oak Street.* 4. *verb* write, autograph, endorse, initial *Sign the check on the back.*

significance *noun* importance, consequence, value, meaning *Mom says the gifts we make for her have special significance.* unimportance, insignificance

significant *adjective* important, noteworthy, major, big, meaningful *The teacher says I've made significant progress in math.* insignificant

silence 1. *noun* hush, quiet, stillness, peace, calm, tranquility *The night's silence was broken by the hoot of an owl.* 2. *verb* quiet, hush, still, calm, pacify *Mom's threat of sending us to our rooms silenced my sister's and my argument.*

silent *adjective* 1. still, hushed, quiet, soundless, noiseless *The orchestra conductor raised his baton, and the audience became silent.* 2. unspoken, understood, implied *Jake and I nodded in silent agreement.*

silhouette *noun* shape, form, shadow, outline, contour, profile *The silhouette of a large ship could be seen against the sunset.*

silly *adjective* foolish, ridiculous, absurd, stupid, childish, crazy, nutty, dumb *The movie is full of silly slapstick scenes that I find hilarious.*

similar *adjective* alike, like, comparable, corresponding, equivalent, close *My brother and I are similar in appearance.*

simple *adjective* 1. easy, effortless, uncomplicated, straightforward, elementary *The teacher gave us some simple math problems to solve.* difficult 2. plain, ordinary, basic, modest, unornamented, unadorned, classic *I prefer eating simple food at home to eating at a fancy restaurant. Mom wears simple clothes and very little jewelry.* fancy

sin *noun* wrongdoing, evil, misconduct, offense, crime *Lying, stealing, and cruelty are sins in most people's eyes.*

sincere *adjective* honest, genuine, real, earnest, heartfelt, authentic *The candidate expressed her sincere thanks to those who supported her.*

sing *verb* vocalize, chant, carol, croon, serenade *I sing in the school chorus.*

single *adjective* one, lone, solitary, sole, only, individual *I'll have a single scoop of ice cream.*

sink *verb* 1. go down, go under, submerge, drop, descend, fall, settle *It took less than three hours after the* Titanic *hit the iceberg for it to sink. The sun sinks in the west.* rise 2. dig, drill, bore, mine, excavate *Edwin Drake was the first man to sink a commercial oil well in the United States.*

sip 1. *verb* drink, taste *Grandma was on the porch sipping iced tea.* gulp 2. *noun* taste, swallow, drop, mouthful *May I just have a sip of your coffee?*

siren *noun* alarm, whistle, signal, warning *If the National Weather Service issues a tornado warning for our area, the sirens will sound for three minutes.*

sit *verb* 1. be seated, sit down, take a seat, perch *The photo shows Dad sitting on the arm of Grandpa's chair.* 2. be located, be situated, be placed, be positioned *Pictures of the family sit on Dad's desk. The house sits on a hill overlooking the river valley.*

site *noun* place, location, position, spot, whereabouts *Gettysburg was the site of the most important battle of the Civil War.*

situation *noun* circumstances, condition, state of affairs *In your situation I would have done the same thing you did.*

size *noun* dimension, measurement, proportion, extent, volume, range, scope *Cell phones used to be the size of a brick. Do you have a size ten? The town's size has grown in area and population.*

sketch 1. *noun* drawing, picture, representation, diagram, draft, outline *This is just a rough sketch of the house.* 2. *verb* draw, outline, draft, depict *There's only time to sketch the main points of the plan.*

skill *noun* ability, aptitude, talent, competence, expertise *The functioning of the hospital relies on the nurses' skills and dedication.*

skillful *adjective* expert, adept, talented, able, capable, clever *She is a talented songwriter and a skillful performer.* incompetent

skim *verb* 1. glide, coast, sail *The speedboat skimmed across the surface of the water.* 2. scan, glance at, flip through *I skimmed the magazines in the dentist's waiting room.*

skinny *adjective* thin, scrawny, lean, gaunt, bony *The skinny puppy we brought home from the shelter has begun to gain weight.* chubby

skip *verb* 1. bounce, spring, jump, leap, hop *The children skipped merrily down the street ahead of their parents.* 2. cut, miss, avoid *The kids who skipped class got detention for a week.* 3. omit, pass over, bypass, leave out *I skipped one question on the test because I couldn't think of the answer.*

skirt *verb* border, bypass, circle, go around, avoid *The new highway skirts the city.*

slack *adjective* 1. loose, lax, baggy, hanging, limp, relaxed *The wind on the lake died and the sails went slack.* 2. slow, inactive, quiet, sluggish *Business at northern resorts is slack during the winter.*

slam *verb* bang, fling, throw *A sudden gust of wind slammed the door shut. Ken slammed his books down on his desk.*

slant 1. *verb* slope, incline, lean, tip, tilt *The picture on the wall slants to the left.* 2. *noun* slope, incline, pitch, angle *The roof has a sharp slant so that the snow slides off.*

slap 1. *verb* hit, smack, strike, whack, spank *Beavers slap the water with their tails to warn of danger.* 2. *noun* smack, blow, whack, spank, pat *Mac greeted me with a slap on the back.*

slash *verb* 1. cut, hack, slice, chop *The story's hero slashed the ropes that tied her to the chair.* 2. reduce, drop, lower, decrease, cut, mark down *The stores slashed their prices after Christmas.*

slavery *noun* bondage, servitude, serfdom *The Thirteenth Amendment to the U.S. Constitution abolished slavery in the United States.*

slay *verb* kill, destroy, put to death, murder *In fairy tales the knight always slays the dragon.*

sleek *adjective* smooth, glossy, shiny, polished *My friend Jeremy's older brother has a sleek, new sports car.*

sleep 1. *verb* slumber, doze, drowse, nap, rest, snooze *Newborn babies sleep about sixteen hours a day.* 2. *noun* slumber, nap, snooze, doze, rest, siesta *My parents insist that I get at least eight hours of sleep on school nights.*

slender *adjective* thin, slim, lean, narrow, svelte *Weeping willow trees have slender branches and narrow leaves.*

slice 1. *noun* piece, sliver, wedge, chunk, serving, portion *I'd like a slice of cheese, please.* 2. *verb* cut, split, carve, divide, sever, slit *Plywood is composed of layers of wood that are sliced and have been glued together.*

slick *adjective* slippery, smooth, glossy, sleek, polished *Freezing rain was making the roads slick.*

slide *verb* glide, coast, skim, skid, slip *The children slid down the hill on their saucers.*

slight 1. *adjective* small, tiny, minor, unimportant, insignificant, trivial *The forecast is for a slight chance of showers.* 2. slender, thin, dainty, petite, frail, delicate *She's nearly an adult but is so slight, she can fit into children's clothes.* 3. *verb* snub, insult, ignore, disregard, neglect, overlook *I hope you didn't feel slighted when I sat with Jason at lunch.*

slim *adjective* slender, thin, lean, slight *The ballet dancer had a slim figure.*

sling 1. *verb* throw, cast, fling, hurl, pitch, toss, heave *Just sling all that junk into the trash.* 2. *noun* bandage, support *He had his arm in a sling after dislocating his shoulder.*

slip 1. *verb* skid, slide, lose one's balance *She slipped on a patch of ice and fell.* 2. sneak, steal, slide, creep *The thief slipped out of the art museum with the famous painting.* 3. decrease, decline, fall off, drop *The temperature slipped below freezing last night.* 4. *noun* mistake, error, oversight, blunder *He made a slip of the tongue and said "fire distinguisher" for "fire extinguisher."*

slit 1. *noun* opening, gap, slot, slash, cut, split, tear *She peeked out through a slit in the window blinds.* 2. *verb* cut, split, slash, tear, slice *I slit the envelope open with a knife.*

slogan *noun* motto, expression, phrase, saying *The motto of the state of Hawaii is "Ua* *mau ke ea o ka aina I ka pono,"* which means in English *"The life of the land is perpetuated in righteousness."*

slope 1. *verb* slant, incline, tilt, lean, dip *The path slopes gradually upward.* 2. *noun* angle, incline, slant, tilt *The ball rolled away down the slope.*

sloppy *adjective* 1. messy, untidy, disorderly, haphazard, careless, slovenly *I can't read Kay's sloppy handwriting.* neat, careful 2. wet, soggy, slushy *A sloppy mixture of rain, snow, and mud covers the parking lot.* dry

slow 1. *adjective* unhurried, leisurely, relaxed, gradual, lingering, delaying, dawdling *Mom and I jogged along at a slow pace.* fast 2. *verb* reduce speed, decrease speed, decelerate, brake *The driver slowed when he saw the police car.*

sluggish *adjective* slow-moving, inactive, listless, lethargic *Sloths are sluggish animals that move slowly and only when they must.*

slumber 1. *verb* sleep, doze, drowse, nap, rest, snooze *The lions slumbered in the shade of a tree.* 2. *noun* sleep, nap, rest, snooze *I awoke refreshed from my slumber.*

sly *adjective* shrewd, clever, crafty, cunning, smooth, sneaky, tricky *Tom Sawyer was very sly in getting his friends to paint his aunt Polly's fence for him.*

smack 1. *verb* hit, slap, strike, whack *My sister and I had great fun smacking each other with pillows.* 2. *noun* blow, hit, slap, whack, rap *He gave his horse a smack on the rump.*

small *adjective* 1. little, tiny, petite, minute, miniature, puny *The Chihuahua is the world's smallest breed of dog.* 2. insignificant, unimportant, minor, trivial *I need to ask you a small favor.* 3. limited, modest, scant, slight *There's only a small amount of milk left in the carton.*

smart 1. *adjective* bright, intelligent, clever, quick, alert, brainy *Adam is a smart, hard-working student.* 2. stylish, fashionable, chic, elegant, well dressed *We all wore smart new clothes to my cousin Jamie's wedding.* 3. *verb* ache, hurt, sting, throb *The smoke from the campfire made my eyes smart.*

smash *verb* 1. shatter, break, destroy, demolish, ruin, crush, fragment *I think smashing a beautiful guitar during a rock concert is stupid.* 2. collide, clash, bump, strike, knock, bang *The driver walked away unhurt after his race car smashed into the wall.*

smear 1. *verb* spread, coat, cover, daub, apply *Denny smeared butter on his bread.* 2. smudge, streak, stain, mark, dirty, soil *The eraser smeared the paper when I tried to correct my mistake.* 3. *noun* stain, mark, soil, smudge, spot, streak *The windshield wipers leave smears on the windshield.*

smell 1. *verb* sense, sniff, detect, get a whiff of *Do you smell something burning?* 2. stink, reek *Take the garbage out—it really smells.* 3. *noun* scent, odor, fragrance, essence *I love the smell of the Thanksgiving turkey roasting.*

smile 1. *verb* grin, beam, smirk *Everyone in the photograph is smiling.* 2. *noun* grin, smirk, beam *Our teacher always greets us with a friendly smile.*

smog *noun* pollution, smoke, fog, haze *It was a humid, windless day, and smog hung over the city.*

smooth 1. *adjective* even, level, flat *Sand the wood to make it smooth before you paint it.* 2. glossy, silky, soft, sleek, slick, polished *Juanita has smooth, long black hair.* 3. easy, effortless, trouble-free, uneventful *The astronauts had a smooth launch.* 4. *verb* flatten, level, even, straighten *She tried to smooth her windblown hair.*

smother *verb* 1. extinguish, put out, snuff out, suffocate, choke *Rain kept smothering our small campfire. We were smothering in the stuffy room.* 2. stifle, muffle, suppress, repress *She tried hard to smother a yawn.*

smudge 1. *verb* smear, streak, mark, soil, stain, spot *The child's face was smudged with tears and dirt.* 2. *noun* smear, streak, stain, spot, mark *I got a smudge on my pants when I knelt to tie my shoe.*

snag *verb* trap, hook, catch, snatch, snare *Dad snagged a fish, but it was too small and he threw it back.*

snake 1. *verb* wind, bend, meander, twist *The river snakes through the valley.* 2. *noun* a reptile with a long body and no limbs *The snake slithered through the grass.*

snap 1. *verb* break, burst, split, crack *I snapped my candy cane in half and gave one half to Dan.* 2. bite, nip *A snapping turtle has powerful jaws with which it snaps at prey.* 3. *noun* crack, crackle, pop *"I've got it!" she said with a snap of her fingers.* 4. fastener, clasp *I offered to help with the snaps on my little brother's shirt, but he likes to dress himself.*

snare *verb* trap, catch, capture *We snared a rabbit in our live trap and set it loose in the country.*

snatch 1. *verb* grab, seize, grasp, snag, take, catch *The hawk swooped down and snatched a mouse out of the grass.* 2. *noun* small amount, bit, scrap, shred *We overheard only a snatch of their conversation.*

sneak *verb* 1. creep, steal, prowl, slink, lurk *We thought we heard someone sneaking around outside.* 2. slip, smuggle *The children sneaked the kitten into the house.*

snip *verb* cut, clip, trim, prune *I snipped the tag off my new shirt.*

snoop *verb* spy, sneak, pry, meddle, intrude, interfere *Dad caught me snooping around the closet looking for my birthday present.*

snooze 1. *verb* doze, sleep, nap, slumber *The dog is snoozing on the front porch.* 2. *noun* sleep, doze, nap, siesta *I took a short snooze on the sofa.*

snub *verb* avoid, ignore, shun, spurn, slight, offend, insult *The actor snubbed his old friends after he became a star.*

snug *adjective* 1. comfortable, warm, cozy, sheltered *The cat is curled up in a snug corner behind the woodstove.* 2. tight, close-fitting *Last winter's jacket is too snug this year.*

snuggle *verb* cuddle, nestle, huddle, curl up, nuzzle *Carolyn snuggled close to Dad on the sofa to have a story read to her.*

soak *verb* wet, drench, saturate *We were soaked through from the rain.*

soak up *verb* absorb, take up, sop up, mop up *She soaked up her spilled juice with a sponge.*

soap *verb* wash, lather, shampoo, cleanse, clean *I soaped the dog, then rinsed him off with a bucket of water.*

soar *verb* fly, sail, coast, glide, hover *The bald eagle soared high over the treetops.*

sob *verb* cry, weep, bawl, wail, howl, sniffle, blubber *The little girl sobbed when her playmate took her toy.*

sober *adjective* serious, solemn, somber, grave, thoughtful *The Puritans who settled in America were sober, frugal, and hardworking.*

sociable *adjective* friendly, amiable, congenial, cordial, gregarious *My parents are sociable people and often entertain friends.*

social *adjective* 1. community, civic, public *Health care for elderly citizens is an important social issue.* 2. friendly, cordial, sociable *Our next-door neighbor is a social person who enjoys chatting over the fence.* unfriendly

society *noun* 1. the people, the public, the populace, the community, the world *Society needs to become more energy-efficient.* 2. organization, association, group, club, union, alliance *Our local library society organizes events that will help raise money for the library.*

soft *adjective* 1. delicate, smooth, silky, velvety *The baby's hair is really soft.* rough

2. flexible, pliable, elastic, yielding *Balsa is a soft light wood used for carving.* hard
3. spongy, mushy, squashy *The river bottom is soft and muddy.* hard 4. mild, gentle, calm, hushed, pleasant, delicate, faint, quiet *A soft breeze rustled the leaves. We spoke in soft voices in order to not wake the baby.*

soggy *adjective* wet, soaked, saturated, sopping, waterlogged *All our camping gear got soggy in last night's rain.* dry

soil 1. *noun* dirt, earth, ground, clay, humus, loam, topsoil *Adding compost or rotted manure to the garden improves the soil.* 2. *verb* dirty, muddy, stain, smudge, foul *My baseball uniform got soiled when I slid into home plate.* clean

soldier *noun* fighter, combatant, warrior *Women disguised themselves as men and served as soldiers in Civil War battles.*

sole *adjective* only, single, one, individual, unique *The sole purpose of their research is finding a cure for cancer.*

solemn *adjective* serious, grave, somber, gloomy, glum *Memorial Day is intended to be a solemn occasion for remembering those who have died serving our country.* happy, cheerful

solid *adjective* 1. hard, firm, rigid, substantial, sturdy, strong, durable *The travelers were glad to be back on solid ground after having flown for sixteen hours.* flimsy, soft 2. whole, entire, continuous, complete *Paula has been practicing the same tune on the piano for a solid hour.* 3. reliable, dependable, trustworthy, stable *My sister and I have a solid relationship with our parents.*

solitary *adjective* single, individual, lone, isolated, unaccompanied *The lions slept in the shade of a solitary tree. Henry David Thoreau lived a solitary life on Walden Pond.*

solution *noun* 1. explanation, answer, resolution, outcome *Jenny came up with the solution to the math problem.* 2. mixture, blend, compound, liquid *My eye doctor recommended a solution in which to clean my contact lenses.*

solve *verb* answer, work out, figure out, decipher, decode, explain *Scientists are still trying to solve the mystery of what happened to the dinosaurs.*

somber *adjective* dark, gloomy, dismal, dreary, melancholy, bleak, solemn, grim *Everyone was in a somber mood after the space shuttle's accident.* cheerful

sometimes *adverb* occasionally, now and then, at times *Sometimes Dad gives me a ride to school, but usually I ride my bike.* always

song *noun* tune, melody, jingle, hymn, anthem, ballad, number, piece *The chorus* *teacher helped our class choose the songs we would sing at the concert.*

soon *adverb* promptly, quickly, shortly, presently, directly, before long *A new school year will be starting soon.*

soothe *verb* calm, comfort, quiet, ease, relieve, pacify *By making silly faces, I can soothe my little sister when she's upset.*

sore 1. *adjective* painful, aching, tender, hurting, smarting *My arm is sore where the nurse gave me the shot.* 2. angry, mad, offended *My sister is sore at me for borrowing her sweater without asking.* 3. *noun* injury, wound, bruise, blister, infection *I have a sore on my heel from my new shoes rubbing.*

sorrow *noun* sadness, unhappiness, grief, anguish, regret *We expressed our sorrow to our elderly neighbor when her husband died.* happiness

sorry *adjective* 1. apologetic, regretful, sympathetic, sad *I'm sorry that I hurt your feelings.* happy 2. poor, wretched, pitiful, pathetic *What a sorry sight it was to see our team lose so badly.*

sort 1. *noun* kind, type, variety, class, category *I read all sorts of books, but mysteries are my favorite.* 2. *verb* arrange, classify, organize, categorize, group, divide, catalog *We sort our laundry into piles by color and fabric.*

sound 1. *noun* noise *I get up in the morning when I hear sounds coming from the kitchen.* silence, quiet 2. *verb* make noise, ring, signal *When the fire alarm sounds, all students must leave the building.* 3. utter, pronounce, voice, be pronounced *The words "night" and "knight" sound the same.* 4. appear, seem, look *It sounds as if you had fun at the pool.* 5. *adjective* strong, safe, secure, stable, firm, solid *Parts of the Great Wall of China are as sound as they were nearly 2,500 years ago when it was built.* weak 6. reasonable, sensible, logical, rational, correct *I welcomed the teacher's sound advice on how to improve my writing skills.*

sour 1. *adjective* acidic, tart, tangy, biting, sharp, bitter *Lemons are sour.* sweet 2. spoiled, fermented, curdled, bad *Dad ruined his coffee by adding sour milk to it.* 3. *verb* curdle, ferment, spoil, go bad, turn *Connie left the milk on the counter and it soured.*

source *noun* 1. origin, beginning, start, rise, commencement *The source of the Nile River was a mystery for centuries* 2. resource, supply, authority, reference *The Internet is not always a good source of information.*

souvenir *noun* keepsake, memento, token, remembrance *Fran brought back a miniature totem pole as a souvenir of her trip to Alaska.*

sovereign 1. *noun* monarch, king, queen, emperor, ruler *Before 1603 England and Scotland each had their own sovereigns.* 2. *adjective* supreme, royal, imperial, regal, reigning *In Russia, sovereign power once belonged to the czar.* 3. independent, self-governing, free *Indian tribes are recognized by the U.S. government as sovereign nations.*

space 1. *noun* area, expanse, room, extent *My bed, desk, and dresser take up all the space in my room.* 2. gap, opening, break *Leave a space of one inch between boards.* 3. the solar system, the universe, outer space *Someday I'd like to travel in space.* 4. *verb* arrange, set, place, separate *Space the plants a foot apart.*

spacious *adjective* roomy, large, big, expansive *Our yard is spacious enough for us to play volleyball.* small, confining

span 1. *noun* period, interval, spell, time *We charted the high and low temperatures over a span of thirty days for science class.* 2. *verb* cross, stretch over, reach over, cover, bridge *The Golden Gate Bridge spans the opening between the Pacific Ocean and San Francisco Bay.*

spare 1. *verb* part with, give up, afford, give, lend, provide *Can you spare a few minutes to help me with my schoolwork?* keep 2. save, free, release, protect *The loggers spared the tree where the woodpeckers were nesting.* destroy 3. *adjective* extra, additional, replacement, unused, surplus *Did you check to see that the spare tire has air in it?* 4. lean, slender, skinny, thin, lanky *He has the spare build of a long-distance runner.* stout

sparkle 1. *verb* glitter, glimmer, twinkle, flash, shine, shimmer, glisten, gleam *The waves on the lake sparkled in the moonlight.* 2. *noun* twinkle, gleam, glint, glitter, glow, shimmer *She had a sparkle in her eyes.* 3. liveliness, spirit, energy, enthusiasm, vitality *His performance lacked sparkle.*

sparse *adjective* scattered, meager, scarce, scant *Deserts have sparse vegetation.* dense

spasm *noun* contraction, twinge, seizure, convulsion *A muscle spasm prevented her from finishing the marathon.*

spatter *verb* splash, spray, sprinkle, shower *Passing cars spattered water on pedestrians.*

speak *verb* 1. talk, communicate, converse, chatter *My little brother is learning to speak.* 2. say, tell, express, utter, state *He always speaks the truth.*

spear 1. *noun* lance, javelin, harpoon, pike *The knight's shield deflected the spear.* 2. *verb* pierce, stab, puncture, stick, impale *He speared a potato with his fork.*

special *adjective* unusual, exceptional, rare, extraordinary, specific, particular, unique *We only go out to eat on special occasions. My brother has food allergies, so he's on a special diet.* ordinary, usual

specialty *noun* skill, talent, gift, field of expertise, line *Dad's specialty is cooking on the grill.*

species *noun* kind, sort, type, variety, class *We have many species of birds come to our bird feeder.*

specific *adjective* definite, precise, particular, exact *He never gave me a specific reason for not coming to the party.* general

specimen *noun* sample, example, type, representative, instance *Darlene collects flower specimens, presses them, and glues them on paper to make greeting cards.*

speck *noun* tiny bit, particle, fleck, spot *You have a speck of food on your tie.*

spectacle *noun* sight, show, display, exhibition, pageant *The huge humpback whales breaching and slapping their tails is quite a spectacle to see.*

spectacular *adjective* dramatic, sensational, exciting, amazing *Photographs taken from satellites give us a spectacular view of earth.* dull, unexciting

speculate *verb* reflect on, ponder on, think about, guess at, surmise *We can only speculate what life on another planet might look like.*

speech *noun* 1. language, talking, talk, speaking, communication, conversation, dialogue *Computers are able to understand human speech and convert it to written text.* 2. lecture, address, talk, sermon, oration *People who give public speeches often begin with a joke or amusing story.*

speed 1. *noun* pace, rate, velocity *Traffic was moving at a slow speed.* 2. haste, hurry, swiftness, quickness, rapidity *She worked with speed to finish her project on time.* 3. *verb* race, fly, zoom, rush, hurry, hasten *The plane sped down the runway.*

spell *noun* 1. charm, enchantment, power, fascination, attraction *We fell under the spell of the beautiful music.* 2. period, time, stretch, interval *The cold spell only lasted a couple days.*

spend *verb* 1. pay, pay out, lay out, expend *I spent only $3.00 of my allowance this week.* 2. consume, use up, fill up, occupy, use, devote, employ *I spent a lot of time cleaning my room Saturday.*

sphere *noun* 1. ball, globe, orb *Most of our Christmas tree ornaments are colorful glass spheres.* 2. area, field, domain, realm, extent, scope *She's an expert in the sphere of economics.*

spice 1. *noun* seasoning, flavoring, herb *Cinnamon, ginger, allspice, and nutmeg are spices* *used in pumpkin pie.* 2. *verb* flavor, season, enhance *We spiced our taco filling with extra chili powder.*

spill 1. *verb* overflow, run over, brim over, pour, slop *My soda spilled when I bumped it reaching for the popcorn.* 2. *noun* fall, tumble *She took quite a spill skateboarding.*

spin 1. *verb* turn, twirl, twist, rotate, revolve, pivot *The earth spins on its axis.* 2. tell, relate, narrate, recount *Laura Ingalls Wilder spun tales of pioneer life on the prairie.* 3. *noun* turn, rotation, twirl, whirl *One spin of the earth on its axis takes one day.* 4. drive, ride, trip, journey, outing *We're going for a spin in our new car.*

spirit 1. *noun* soul, heart, mind *Many people believe the spirit continues to exist after death.* 2. ghost, apparition, phantom, specter *The vacant house on the hill is said to be haunted by a spirit.* 3. courage, energy, strength, vigor, life, enthusiasm, vivacity *The racehorse has a lot of spirit.* 4. *verb* take, whisk, remove, carry *The movie star was spirited away in a limousine.*

spiritual *adjective* religious *He has strong spiritual beliefs.*

spite 1. *noun* animosity, ill will, malice, hostility, resentment *He said you didn't deserve to win the award out of spite because he didn't win.* 2. *verb* annoy, irritate, provoke, upset *Ignore his remark—he said it just to spite you.*

splash 1. *verb* splatter, spatter, sprinkle, spray *My little sister splashed water all over the floor during her bath.* 2. *noun* slap, smack, plop *He jumped into the pool with a big splash.*

splatter *verb* splash, sprinkle, spatter *A passing car splattered mud on us.*

splendid *adjective* fine, excellent, brilliant, glorious, magnificent, great, grand *The gardens surrounding the palace were splendid.*

splendor *noun* glory, magnificence, grandeur, brilliance, radiance *You can observe the night sky in its full splendor at a planetarium.*

split 1. *verb* break, crack, separate, cut, carve, sever *He split the log into firewood for the fireplace.* 2. divide, share, distribute, allocate, allot *We split the bag of candy among the trick-or-treaters.* 3. *noun* tear, rip, crack, break, separation, division *There's a split in the seam in the seat of my pants. There's a split among family members over where we should go for vacation.*

spoil *verb* 1. ruin, botch, mess up, damage, wreck, destroy *The rainstorm spoiled our hike.* 2. decay, rot, go bad, decompose, mold, sour *We'd better eat these leftovers before they spoil.* 3. indulge, pamper, baby, make a fuss over, coddle *We like to spoil Mom on Mother's Day.*

sponsor 1. *noun* backer, promoter, supporter, underwriter, financer, contributor *The local business organization is a sponsor of scholarships for outstanding students.* 2. *verb* back, finance, support, fund, underwrite *Ten people have already offered to sponsor me in the race for a cure for childhood cancer.*

spontaneous *adjective* natural, automatic, unplanned, instinctive, impulsive *The astronauts were greeted with spontaneous applause when they stepped off the plane.* planned

sport *noun* game, contest, competition, amusement, pastime, recreation, athletic activity *Mom's favorite sport is tennis.*

spot 1. *noun* mark, speck, dot, fleck, smudge, stain *You have a grease spot on your tie.* 2. place, location, area, site, setting *Let's find a spot in the shade to sit down.* 3. *verb* pick out, recognize, notice, spy, catch sight of, identify, distinguish *I spotted my friend Jane in the crowd. The teacher spotted a spelling mistake in my paper.*

sprawl *verb* spread, stretch out, lounge, lie *We sprawled on the floor to watch TV.*

spray 1. *noun* mist, spray, shower, drizzle *We were wet with ocean spray.* 2. *verb* shower, sprinkle, spatter, splash *The dog shook himself and sprayed us with water.*

spread 1. *verb* stretch out, unfold, extend *We spread the map out in front of us. The bird spread its wings and flew off.* 2. cover, coat, smear, apply *The butter is too hard to spread.* 3. circulate, broadcast, publicize, make known, distribute *Spread the news that we're raising money for the flood victims.* 4. *noun* increase, growth, advance, expansion *You can reduce the spread of disease by staying home when you're sick.* 5. range, extent, expanse, span, reach *A pterodactyl's wings had a spread of twenty feet from tip to tip.* 6. ranch, farm, estate, plantation *My uncle owns a big cattle spread in Montana.* 7. bedspread, cover, coverlet, throw, quilt *I got a new spread for my bed.*

spree *noun* outing, fling, bout, indulgence *We went on a shopping spree for new school clothes.*

spring *verb* leap, jump, bounce, bound, hop, hurdle, vault *The dog sprang into the air and caught the ball.*

spring up *verb* appear, emerge, come into existence, pop up, crop up *New homes have been springing up on the edge of town.*

sprinkle 1. *verb* rain, shower, drizzle *It sprinkled this morning, but the sun is shining now.* 2. scatter, spread, shake over, dust *She sprinkled salt and pepper on her potatoes.* 3. *noun* drizzle, rain, shower *After the sprinkle there was a beautiful rainbow.*

sprinkling *noun* dash, dusting, scattering, trickle, pinch, trace *Johnny didn't want to* *be too daring, so he put just a sprinkling of hot pepper and garlic on top of his pizza.*

sprout 1. *verb* grow, come up, shoot up, emerge, develop, bud *The radishes were the first seeds to sprout in the garden.* 2. *noun* shoot, bud, seedling *I like alfalfa sprouts on my salad.*

spur *verb* motivate, inspire, prompt, encourage, stimulate, urge, prod *Spurred by reports of poor health care for British soldiers, Florence Nightingale volunteered as a nurse and reformed the nursing profession.*

squabble *verb* quarrel, disagree, argue, dispute, fight, bicker *My brother and I squabbled over whose turn it was to wash dishes.*

squad *noun* unit, company, band, group, crew, troop, body *A squad of soldiers patrolled the town.*

squall *noun* storm, gale, windstorm, gust, blow, blizzard *The sailors got caught in a squall.*

square *noun* 1. four-sided figure, rectangle *After the brownies have cooled, cut them into squares.* 2. plaza, place, marketplace *We walked around the square until we found a café.*

squash *verb* crush, mash, smash, press, flatten *She squashed the bugs that were eating her plants.*

squat *verb* crouch, stoop, bend *I squatted down to tie my shoe.*

squeak *verb* squeal, whine, screech *My bike's brakes squeak.*

squeal 1. *verb* yell, cry, scream, shriek, squeak, screech *My little brother squealed with delight when he saw his new bike.* 2. *noun* yell, scream, screech, shriek *Corey let out a squeal when he saw the spider.*

squeeze 1. *verb* press, crush, twist, force, extract *We squeeze fresh juice from oranges for breakfast.* 2. stuff, cram, pack, jam, force *You'll never squeeze all those clothes into one suitcase.* 3. *noun* hug, embrace, cuddle, clasp, hold *Dad put his arm around my shoulders and gave me a squeeze.*

squirm *verb* wriggle, twist, wiggle, writhe *The little boy squirmed in his seat.*

squirt 1. *verb* jet, gush, spurt, spray, surge, spout *The water from the fountain squirts 135 feet in the air.* 2. *noun* jet, spray, stream, spurt *She soaked me with a squirt from the hose.*

stab 1. *verb* pierce, jab, spear, stick, poke, puncture, impale *She stabbed the piece of* *meat with her fork.* 2. *noun* attempt, try, effort *I took a stab at painting but wasn't very good at it.*

stable *adjective* 1. steady, firm, sound, solid, secure, immovable *Dad made sure our new swing set was stable by anchoring it firmly in the ground.* 2. unchanging, steadfast, settled, established, secure, lasting *The new prime minister is promising a stable government.* unsettled, changing

stack 1. *noun* pile, heap, mound, load *There's a stack of unopened junk mail on the desk.* 2. *verb* pile, heap, mound, collect, accumulate *We stack our old newspapers and magazines in the garage to be taken to the recycling center.*

staff *noun* 1. group of employees, crew, workforce *The small country school has a staff of only ten people.* 2. stick, pole, rod *The shepherd leaned on his staff while watching his sheep.*

stage 1. *noun* period, interval, point, phase, time *We are still in the planning stage of our project.* 2. platform, podium, stand, rostrum *The crowd cheered when the band took the stage.* 3. *verb* dramatize, present, produce, perform, enact, put on *The high school drama club staged a musical revue.*

stagger *verb* 1. sway, reel, waver, flounder, stumble, lurch *She staggered down the hall carrying a huge stack of books.* 2. amaze, astound, astonish, shock, overwhelm *I was staggered by the size of the city when we moved here from the country.*

stagnant *adjective* foul, dirty, polluted, sluggish, still, standing *Mosquitoes breed in stagnant water.*

stain 1. *verb* spot, soil, mark, smudge, discolor *The spilled grape juice stained the tablecloth.* 2. *noun* spot, smudge, mark, discoloration *I got grass stains on my pants.*

stake *noun* pole, post, stick, rod, peg *We used a rock to pound in the tent stakes.*

stake out *verb* mark, define, bound, limit *The homesteaders staked out 160 acres for their farm.*

stale *adjective* old, dry, hard, moldy, not fresh *The refrigerator smells of stale cheese.* fresh

stalk 1. *noun* stem, twig, branch, shoot *Asparagus stalks are beginning to emerge in our vegetable garden.* 2. *verb* pursue, hunt, chase, follow, track *Several lions worked together stalking their prey.*

stall 1. *verb* stop, quit, halt, shut down *A car stalled on the expressway and caused a traffic jam.* 2. delay, dawdle, hesitate *I stalled while trying to think of an answer.* hurry 3. *noun* booth, stand, kiosk *The orchard has a stall at the farmers' market where it sells its* *apples.* 4. pen, cage, enclosure, coop *I take my horse out of his stall every day for exercise.*

stammer *verb* stutter, falter, stumble *He stammered nervously when he was introduced to his hero.*

stamp 1. *verb* mark, seal, label, brand, engrave, print *The official stamped our passports when we entered the country.* 2. trample, stomp, tread, crush, pound, mash *Mom tried to teach me to dance, but I kept stamping on her feet.* 3. *noun* mark, label, emblem, seal *The document bore the stamp of the king.*

stampede 1. *noun* rush, dash, flight, charge *There was a stampede for the door when the bell rang.* 2. *verb* rush, dash, flee, take flight, panic, scatter *A clap of thunder caused the cattle to stampede.*

stand 1. *verb* rise, get up, get to one's feet *Everyone stood when the judge entered the courtroom.* sit, lie down 2. endure, bear, tolerate, put up with *My parents can't stand this music.* 3. remain, last, continue, stay, persist *The dress code still stands.* 4. be situated, be located *A statue of Peter Pan stands in Kensington Gardens in London.* 5. set, put, place *Stand the lamp in the corner.* 6. *noun* stall, shop, booth, store *She bought a magazine at the newspaper stand on the corner.* 7. rack, frame, shelf, support *I need a stand for my new flat-screen TV.* 8. attitude, opinion, position, view, viewpoint, policy *The candidate challenged his opponent to take a stand on health-care reform.*

standard *noun* 1. model, pattern, example, guide, criterion, ideal *"Treat others as you want to be treated" is a good standard by which to live.* 2. flag, banner, pennant, emblem, symbol, colors *The Royal Standard is the monarch's official flag in the United Kingdom.*

standstill *noun* stop, halt, pause, impasse *Traffic came to a standstill. The peace talks have come to a standstill.*

stanza *noun* verse, section, unit of poetry *Each stanza of this poem has four lines.*

staple *adjective* important, main, principal, essential, basic *Bread is a staple food around the world.*

star 1. *noun* heavenly body, celestial body *The Milky Way galaxy contains hundreds of billions of stars.* 2. celebrity, big-name, lead, headliner, superstar *Many Hollywood stars will appear in a show to raise funds for hurricane victims.* 3. *verb* be the lead, be featured, headline *The actor starred in many movies.*

stare 1. *verb* look, gape, gaze, gawk, glare *The little girl stared at the puppies in the pet shop window.* 2. *noun* look, glare, gaze, glower *Our Halloween costumes received lots of stares from people on the street.*

stark *adjective* complete, utter, absolute, outright *Why, that's stark nonsense!*

start 1. *verb* begin, commence, originate, initiate, open *I didn't start the argument—she did.* 2. set out, leave, depart, get under way, be off *We need to start by 9:00 in order to be there by noon.* 3. create, found, establish, set up, organize, launch *Mr. Grant started the company in 1995.* 4. *noun* beginning, opening, commencement, launch, onset *She exercises at the start of the day.* 5. surprise, shock, fright *You gave me quite a start when you came up behind me.*

startle *verb* frighten, surprise, alarm, shock *The loud noise startled me.*

starving *adjective* famished, hungry, ravenous *When do we eat? I'm starving.*

state 1. *verb* tell, express, say, declare, relate, report, announce, tell *The senator stated her objections to the proposal.* 2. *noun* condition, position, status, situation, circumstance *The building is in a state of disrepair.* 3. country, nation, land, republic *Each member state of the United Nations has one vote in the General Assembly.*

stately *adjective* dignified, imposing, noble, grand, majestic, grandiose, impressive, magnificent, splendid *The Lincoln Memorial in Washington, D.C., is a stately monument.*

statement *noun* account, report, announcement, proclamation, declaration, notice *His lawyers instructed him to make no statements to reporters.*

station 1. *noun* place, position, location, site, post *The security guards are at their stations.* 2. headquarters, office, base *Our class toured the fire station, where we saw all kinds of firefighting and rescue equipment.* 3. depot, terminal *The bus arrived at the station on time.* 4. *verb* place, post, position, locate, base *My uncle is a fighter pilot stationed on an aircraft carrier.*

stationary *adjective* fixed, immovable, immobile, motionless, still *A satellite whose speed matches the speed of the earth's rotation appears from earth to be stationary.* moving, movable

stationery *noun* writing paper, notepaper, paper *I need a piece of stationery so I can write to my pen pal in Germany.*

statue *noun* sculpture, figure, bust, monument *The Statue of Liberty stands in New York Harbor.*

status *noun* standing, position, rank, grade, station *He has achieved high status as a political leader.*

stay 1. *verb* remain, wait, linger, pause, delay *He had to stay late at work.* leave 2. reside,

live, dwell, visit, lodge *I stayed at my friend's while my parents were out of town.*
3. *noun* visit, stopover, vacation, holiday *Did you enjoy your stay at the resort?*

steady 1. *adjective* constant, ceaseless, unending, continuous, incessant *There's a steady stream of traffic on the expressway during rush hour.* 2. fixed, still, motionless, unmoving *Hold the camera steady and snap the picture.* 3. regular, uniform, even *We jogged along at a steady pace.* 4. *verb* hold, support, balance, stabilize *Jim steadied the ladder while Jack climbed onto the roof.*

steal *verb* 1. rob, take, thieve, pilfer, filch, swipe, shoplift *Raccoons raided our garden and stole our sweet corn.* 2. sneak, slip, creep, tiptoe, slink *I heard my sister steal out of the room to see if Santa had come.*

steam *noun* 1. vapor, gas, mist *The steam from the hot shower condensed on the bathroom window.* 2. energy, vigor, power, force *She ran out of steam before she finished her work.*

steep *adjective* vertical, perpendicular, sheer, precipitous, high *Most of the Grand Canyon is inaccessible because of rugged terrain and steep cliffs.*

steer *verb* control, guide, drive, navigate, maneuver, pilot *The farmer steered the tractor down the rows of corn.*

step 1. *noun* footstep, pace, stride *I took a quick step backward when I saw the snake.*
2. act, move, action, measure, procedure, effort, stage *The school has taken steps to ensure that children have a safe environment in which to learn.* 3. *verb* walk, tread, stride, move, proceed *I stepped to the front of the class when the teacher called on me.*

sterilize *verb* clean, disinfect, decontaminate, sanitize *We sterilized the water from the stream by boiling it for ten minutes.* contaminate

stern 1. *adjective* severe, strict, harsh, firm, hard, exacting, austere *The police officer issued a stern warning to the driver.* 2. *noun* back, rear, tail *They waved to us from the stern of the boat as they pulled away from the dock.* bow

stick 1. *verb* pierce, jab, stab, spear, poke, puncture *Be careful not to stick your finger on that thorn.* 2. fasten, attach, glue, fix, affix, paste *Can you stick this picture on the paper with glue?* 3. *noun* twig, branch, stem, pole *We collected sticks for the campfire.*

stick out *verb* extend, protrude, poke out *I've grown so much that my arms stick out of the sleeves of last winter's jacket.*

sticky *adjective* 1. gummy, gluey, tacky, gooey *She licked her sticky fingers.* 2. humid, muggy, clammy, sultry, close *A cool shower feels good before bed on a sticky July day.* dry

stiff *adjective* 1. rigid, inflexible, firm, hard, unbending *You can mail a CD or a DVD in an envelope made out of stiff cardboard.* flexible 2. tense, taut, tight, aching *I have stiff muscles from yesterday's exercise.* 3. tough, intense, strong, challenging, formidable *We had stiff competition in today's soccer match.* easy

stifle *verb* stop, suppress, control, smother *I was sleepy but tried hard to stifle my yawns.*

still 1. *adjective* quiet, silent, calm, tranquil, placid, serene, peaceful, motionless, untroubled *By 10:00 P.M. the house was still. Bugs skimmed along the still surface of the water.* 2. *verb* quiet, calm, soothe, pacify, silence *She stilled the baby with a lullaby.* 3. *adverb* yet, even now, until now, so far *It's after 10:00, and they still haven't arrived.* 4. nevertheless, however, nonetheless *I should be in bed; still, I want to see how the movie ends.*

stimulate *verb* encourage, motivate, prompt, spur, rouse, inspire *The chemistry set my parents got me has stimulated my interest in chemistry.*

sting *verb* burn, hurt, pain, wound, inflame, smart, prick *The cigarette smoke stings my eyes. The nurse's needle stung when she gave me the shot.*

stingy *adjective* ungenerous, cheap, miserly, tight, penny-pinching *Charles Dickens's A Christmas Carol is the story of stingy Mr. Scrooge, who becomes charitable after being visited by ghosts of his past, present, and future.* generous

stink 1. *verb* smell bad, reek, smell *The garbage truck really stinks.* 2. *noun* bad smell, foul odor, stench, smell *We didn't let the dog in the house until we got the stink of skunk off of him.*

stir 1. *verb* mix, blend, beat, whip, whisk *Stir the batter vigorously for one minute.* 2. move, budge, wake up, rouse, awaken, get up *He refuses to stir before 10:00 on Saturdays.* 3. *noun* excitement, commotion, fuss, disturbance *Having a movie crew in town caused quite a stir.*

stock 1. *verb* supply, store, collect, accumulate, amass, stockpile, gather, hoard *We stock enough firewood to burn in our fireplace over the winter.* 2. *noun* supply, store, reserve, accumulation, hoard *It's a good idea to keep a stock of food, water, and first-aid supplies in your home for emergencies.* 3. livestock, animals, cattle *Cowhands are employed by ranchers to look after the stock.* 4. ancestry, descent, family, parentage *We're looking for a puppy that comes from healthy stock.*

stocky *adjective* thickset, chunky, stout, sturdy, solid, strapping *Mom says I'll probably grow up to be stout like my dad.* lean, thin

stomach *noun* belly, abdomen, gut, tummy *I'm hungry, and my stomach is growling.*

stone *noun* 1. rock, pebble, boulder *The farmers picked stones from their fields and used the stones to build fences.* 2. gem, gemstone, jewel, precious stone *The ring is set with three stones: two rubies and a diamond.*

stool *noun* seat, chair, bench, footstool *We sat on stools in the kitchen to eat our snacks.*

stoop 1. *verb* bend forward, crouch, squat, lean down *I stooped to pick up a quarter from the sidewalk.* 2. lower oneself, sink, descend, resort *She'd never stoop to cheating.* 3. *noun* hunch, slouch, bow, droop of the shoulders *The elderly man walked with a stoop.*

stop 1. *verb* end, halt, cease, discontinue, conclude, terminate *We couldn't stop laughing. Work at the factory stops at 5:00.* start, begin 2. block, check, prevent, obstruct, plug up, hinder *An accident on the highway stopped traffic.* 3. *noun* pause, halt, delay, finish, close, conclusion, end *Work on the project has come to a stop.*

store 1. *noun* shop, market, mart, outlet, retailer, supermarket *Stop at the store on your way home and get some bread.* 2. supply, accumulation, stock, stockpile, collection, hoard *Grandma and Grandpa have a store of oldies rock music.* 3. *verb* accumulate, save, stock, keep, amass, gather, hoard *Dad says we need to get rid of the junk stored in the attic.*

storm 1. *noun* tempest, snowstorm, gale, thunderstorm, hurricane, tornado, blizzard, downpour, rainstorm *The storm blew down a tree in our yard.* 2. outburst, outcry, furor, flood, disturbance *There was a storm of angry protest against the new tax.* 3. *verb* blow, rain, hail, snow *It stormed throughout the night.* 4. attack, besiege, raid, charge, assault *The king's army stormed the castle.*

story *noun* 1. account, report, description, record, version *The stories of the witnesses to the accident differed.* 2. tale, narrative, legend, myth, novel, anecdote, epic, saga *My little sister asked Dad to read her a bedtime story.* 3. floor, level, tier *Our house has two stories.*

stout *adjective* large, stocky, heavyset, thickset, heavy, sturdy, brawny *Stout horses were used by the pioneers for farmwork and to pull heavy loads.* thin

straggle *verb* trail, lag, linger, stray, drift, wander *We stopped to wait for the smaller children, who were straggling behind.*

straight 1. *adjective* in line, horizontal, vertical, even, unswerving, unbending, direct *Is this picture straight? Use a ruler to draw a straight line.* crooked 2. honest, frank, truthful, candid, sincere, direct *Now give me a straight answer.* 3. successive, consecutive, in a row, uninterrupted *The team has had three straight wins.* 4. *adverb* directly, immediately, without delay, right *Come straight home after school.*

strain 1. *verb* sprain, wrench, injure, hurt, pull *She strained a leg muscle in yesterday's race.* 2. try hard, struggle, strive, work, labor *He had to strain to hear the speaker.* 3. *noun* stress, worry, anxiety, pressure *Police work can cause a lot of strain.*

strange *adjective* unusual, peculiar, odd, curious, bizarre *Ostriches are strange birds that cannot fly but can run up to forty miles per hour for as long as thirty minutes.* ordinary

stranger *noun* unknown person, newcomer, outsider *Two of the students in my class this year are strangers.*

strangle *verb* choke, suffocate, smother *The collar on this shirt is strangling me.*

strap 1. *noun* band, tie, belt, strip *The strap on my sandal broke.* 2. *verb* tie, bind, belt, fasten, secure *Dad strapped my little sister into her car seat.*

strategy *noun* plan, tactic, scheme, procedure, policy *The coach's strategy was to run the ball as much as possible.*

stray 1. *verb* wander, meander, roam, ramble, drift *If you stray from the path, you could get lost.* 2. *adjective* lost, abandoned, homeless, wandering *The stray cat we adopted has become my favorite pet.*

streak 1. *noun* line, mark, stripe, band *The striped skunk is black with two broad white streaks down its back.* 2. spell, period, stretch, run *The team has had a four-game winning streak.* 3. *verb* mark, stripe, smear *Janice had her hair streaked with blond.* 4. dash, run, speed, fly, race, zoom *Cars streaked past us as we changed a flat tire by the side of the road.*

stream 1. *verb* flow, pour, surge, rush, gush, flood *The onion made tears stream from my eyes.* 2. *noun* creek, brook, river *We fished from the bridge that crosses the stream.* 3. flow, flood, rush, surge, jet, torrent *A stream of water poured from the open fire hydrant.*

street *noun* road, highway, avenue, boulevard, drive, lane *My brother is not allowed to cross the street on his own. What street do you live on?*

strength *noun* power, force, vigor, might, stamina *Ballet requires a lot of strength.* weakness

strengthen *verb* make stronger, reinforce, brace, support, fortify, toughen *Calcium in the diet strengthens bones.* weaken

strenuous *adjective* active, energetic, vigorous, demanding, tough, hard *Shoveling snow is a strenuous activity.* easy

stress 1. *noun* tension, pressure, worry, anxiety, strain *Regular exercise such as jogging or yoga can reduce stress.* 2. emphasis, importance, value, weight, significance *My parents put a lot of stress on getting a good education.* 3. *verb* emphasize, accentuate, underscore, highlight *Our teacher stresses the importance of reading skills.*

stretch 1. *verb* extend, draw out, lengthen, elongate, spread, expand *The cat stretched its legs, then curled up and went to sleep.* 2. *noun* expanse, extent, length, area, sweep *We detoured around a twenty-mile stretch of road that is under construction.*

strew *verb* scatter, throw, spread, distribute *Mom told me to pick up the clothes that were strewed all over my room.*

strict *adjective* 1. firm, harsh, rigorous, severe, exacting, stern *The school enforces strict discipline.* lenient 2. complete, absolute, exact, perfect *He told me the secret in strict confidence.*

strike 1. *verb* hit, knock, rap, whack, pound, smack, punch, sock, slap, swat *The boat struck the rocks near shore. She said, "I forgot!" and struck her forehead with the palm of her hand.* 2. affect, impress, seem to, appear to, occur to, hit *His idea doesn't strike me as being very good.* 3. discover, find, come upon *Edwin Drake struck oil in August of 1859 after drilling to 69 feet.* 4. walk out, protest, stop work *Workers are striking for better health benefits.* 5. *noun* attack, assault, bombing *The general ordered an air strike on the enemy.*

striking *adjective* noticeable, obvious, conspicuous, pronounced *She bears a striking resemblance to her mother.*

string *noun* 1. twine, thread, cord, rope *Our cat likes to play with a ball of string.* 2. series, run, succession *The singer has had a string of successful albums.*

strip 1. *verb* remove, peel off, take away *We stripped the paint from the woodwork, then varnished it.* 2. *noun* band, ribbon, piece, sliver *The paper shredder cuts sheets of paper into strips.*

stripe *noun* band, bar, streak, line *My new curtains have green stripes on a white background.*

strive *verb* try, endeavor, attempt, make an effort, struggle, labor *She's striving to improve her backhand in tennis.*

stroke 1. *verb* pet, pat, caress, rub, massage *When I stroke my cat, he purrs.* 2. *noun* blow, hit, strike, rap, knock, whack *He split the log with one stroke of the ax.* 3. feat, accomplishment, act, action *Your plan is a stroke of genius!*

stroll 1. *verb* walk, saunter, amble, ramble, wander *We strolled along the beach looking for shells.* 2. *noun* leisurely walk, saunter, ramble *Let's go for a stroll down to the ice-cream shop after dinner.*

strong *adjective* 1. powerful, vigorous, forceful, mighty, hardy, muscular, brawny *Are you strong enough to lift that by yourself?* 2. sturdy, solid, durable, tough, heavy-duty *Dad built some strong shelves to hold our books.*

structure *noun* 1. building, construction, edifice *Many modern structures are built of glass and steel.* 2. form, shape, configuration, design, system, organization, arrangement *The structure of the human body is very complex.*

struggle 1. *verb* endeavor, strive, attempt, try, labor, toil, battle, fight *The settlers struggled to grow enough food for their families* 2. *noun* battle, fight, scuffle, effort, endeavor *The regiment was engaged in a struggle to take the fort.*

stubborn *adjective* obstinate, willful, headstrong, adamant, rigid, unyielding, inflexible *The stubborn mule refused to get out of the road.* yielding, flexible

student *noun* pupil, scholar, schoolchild, schoolboy, schoolgirl *There are twenty-one students in my class.*

study 1. *verb* read, learn, review, go over, cram, examine *Our assignment is to study chapter four.* 2. *noun* examination, investigation, analysis, research *Biology is the scientific study of living things.* 3. office, den, studio, library, workroom *Our study is a quiet place to go to read.*

stuff 1. *noun* things, objects, articles, items, belongings, possessions *We need to get rid of some of the stuff we've stored in the attic.* 2. *verb* pack, cram, jam, fill, load *After I stuffed everything into my suitcase, I couldn't close it.*

stuffy *adjective* 1. stifling, airless, close, oppressive, suffocating *Let's open some windows—it's stuffy in here.* 2. blocked, congested, clogged, stopped up *My allergies make my nose stuffy.*

stumble *verb* trip, slip, tumble, falter, stagger, blunder *It was dark and I stumbled over the clothes I'd left on the floor.*

stump *verb* baffle, perplex, mystify, bewilder, puzzle, confound *The final question on the test stumped me.*

stun *verb* amaze, astound, shock, overwhelm, daze *She was stunned when she heard she had won the talent contest.*

stunning *adjective* astounding, astonishing, amazing, spectacular, magnificent, superb *The actor gave a stunning performance in this adaptation of Shakespeare's play.*

stunt 1. *verb* restrict, slow, impede, hold back, hinder, check, stop *Lack of water will stunt the plant's growth.* 2. *noun* feat, trick, act, exploit *The stunts performed by the trapeze artists were amazing.*

stupid *adjective* foolish, silly, dumb, senseless, asinine, unintelligent *I'd like to ask what may sound like a stupid question.*

sturdy *adjective* strong, firm, solid, well-built, stable, sound, substantial, durable *Is this chair sturdy enough to hold my weight?*

stutter 1. *verb* stammer, falter, stumble, hesitate *I sometimes stutter when I'm nervous.* 2. *noun* speech impediment, stammer *A therapist is helping my sister overcome her stutter.*

style *noun* 1. design, manner, fashion, mode *She has a unique style of dressing.* 2. elegance, flair, stylishness, polish, class, sophistication *The dancer impressed me with his style and grace.*

subdue *verb* suppress, control, check, restrain, overcome, hold back, soothe, calm *She subdued her urge to giggle. My apology subdued his anger.*

subject *noun* 1. topic, theme, issue, text, question, point *What is the subject of your paper? He kept changing the subject.* 2. field of study, course, class *English is my best subject.*

submerge *verb* 1. dip, sink, immerse, plunge, dunk *I submerged myself in a tub of hot water.* 2. flood, inundate, engulf, swamp *Floodwaters submerged the city streets.*

submit *verb* 1. yield, surrender, comply, obey, heed, give in *The government refused to submit to the demands of the protestors.* 2. hand in, offer, turn in, give, present, propose *The architect submitted his plan for the building.*

subsequent *adjective* following, later, succeeding, future *The foul and subsequent fight among the players resulted in penalties for both teams.*

subside *verb* decrease, diminish, lessen, decline, let up *When the noise from the party next door subsided, I fell asleep.*

substance *noun* 1. material, matter, stuff, element, ingredient *Nicotine is a hazardous substance contained in cigarettes.* 2. essence, basis, meaning, significance, validity *His ideas don't seem to have much substance.*

substantial *adjective* large, considerable, significant, great, major *Dave's contribution to the success of the project is substantial.*

substitute 1. *verb* replace, change, exchange, switch, swap *We substituted whole wheat flour for white flour in the recipe.* 2. *noun* replacement, alternative, stand-in *Ms. Delaney was the substitute today for our teacher, who was sick.*

subtle *adjective* not obvious, slight, fine, delicate, faint *There's a subtle fragrance in the air, and I can't tell what it is.*

subtract *verb* deduct, take away, remove, withdraw, discount *The salesclerk subtracted 20 percent from the price because the jeans were on sale.* add

succeed *verb* be successful, prosper, do well, thrive, flourish *In order to succeed today, you need computer skills.* fail

success *noun* accomplishment, achievement, victory, triumph, hit, sensation *The auction to raise money for the senior center is a success.* failure

successful *adjective* 1. effective, fruitful, productive, profitable *The after-school tutoring program has proven to be successful.* unsuccessful 2. prosperous, wealthy, famous, well-known, popular *Her best-selling books made her the world's most successful writer of children's literature.* unsuccessful

sudden *adjective* unexpected, unforeseen, abrupt, quick, impulsive *The sudden drop in temperature caught us without our jackets. He had a sudden change of plans.* gradual

sue *verb* prosecute, take to court, charge *He was sued for downloading copyrighted music from the Internet without permission.*

suffer *verb* endure, experience, bear, stand, tolerate, undergo *She suffered disappointment when she learned that she had not been chosen for the Olympic team.*

sufficient *adjective* enough, ample, plenty, adequate, satisfactory *My cousin visited from Florida and didn't have sufficient clothing for our cold northern winter.* insufficient, unsatisfactory

suffocate *verb* smother, stifle, choke *Plastic bags can suffocate people.*

suggest *verb* propose, advise, recommend, put forward *I suggest we go out for pizza.*

suggestion *noun* proposal, recommendation, idea, advice, offer, plan *Have you any suggestions for a birthday present for Dad?*

suit *verb* agree with, satisfy, fit, please, be acceptable *The slower pace of living in a small town suits us.*

suitable *adjective* appropriate, acceptable, fitting, proper, favorable, satisfactory *Jeans and a sweatshirt are not suitable clothes for a business meeting.* unsuitable

sulk *verb* mope, pout, brood, be in a huff *Vicky sulks when she can't have her way.*

sullen *adjective* grim, gloomy, sulky, moody, angry, bad-tempered *The clerk was sullen and uncooperative when we tried to return the merchandise.* cheerful, pleasant, happy

sum *noun* total, whole, entirety, quantity, amount *Our purchases came to the sum of $24.80.*

summarize *verb* outline, review, go over, brief, recap *Our teacher summarized yesterday's chapter before going on to the next.* expand on, detail

summit *noun* top, tip, peak, crest, crown, apex *Edmund Hillary and Sherpa Tenzing Norgay were the first people to reach the summit of Mount Everest.* base

sunny *adjective* bright, cheerful, pleasant, radiant *My sister has a sunny smile.* dull

sunrise *noun* dawn, daybreak, sunup, crack of dawn, daylight *Gordon gets up at sunrise to deliver the newspapers.*

sunset *noun* sundown, dusk, evening, nightfall *The moon sometimes rises before sunset.*

superb *adjective* splendid, fine, excellent, marvelous, wonderful, magnificent *My grandparents are both superb cooks.* inferior

superior *adjective* excellent, fine, first-class, choice, better, greater, higher *Photographs taken with the latest digital cameras are of superior quality.* inferior

superstition *noun* misconception, fallacy, fantasy, false belief *A common superstition is that the number thirteen is unlucky.*

supervise *verb* direct, manage, oversee, administer, head, lead, govern, regulate *Ms. Grindle supervises the school cafeteria during lunch.*

supplement 1. *noun* addition, extra, enhancement, add-on, appendix, addendum *The Sunday newspaper contains dozens of advertising supplements.* 2. *verb* add to, complete, fortify, augment, reinforce, increase *We take vitamins to supplement our diet.* subtract from

supply 1. *verb* furnish, provide, give, contribute, stock, outfit, equip *Our garden supplies us with vegetables all summer.* 2. *noun* amount, quantity, stock, store, source *We keep a supply of batteries on hand for our portable devices.*

support 1. *verb* hold up, bear, prop up, bolster, brace *How a bridge is supported* *determines the length of its span.* 2. care for, provide for, take care of, maintain, sustain *Both of my parents work to support the family.* 3. encourage, help, foster, be in favor of, aid, assist, back, defend, champion *My parents support the school's decision to get rid of vending machines.* 4. *noun* encouragement, backing, assistance, help, aid *My family always gives me love and support.* 5. reinforcement, brace, prop, buttress, post, pillar, column *The tree's branches are the supports for the tree house.*

suppose *verb* imagine, think, believe, assume, presume, expect, reckon *I suppose we should leave. I don't suppose he'll forget, will he?*

suppress *verb* hold back, check, control, restrain, subdue *She suppressed an urge to laugh.* encourage

supreme *adjective* highest, greatest, uppermost, foremost, chief, top *He's the supreme commander of the armed forces.*

sure *adjective* 1. certain, positive, absolute, definite *Are you sure you locked the door?* uncertain 2. reliable, dependable, effective, foolproof *The only sure way to protect your computer is to have a firewall and all the latest software updates.* unreliable

surface 1. *noun* outside, exterior, face, top *Wipe the surfaces of all the counters.* interior 2. *verb* cover, coat, pave, overlay, top *The gravel road is being surfaced with blacktop.*

surge 1. *verb* gush, rush, flow, flood, stream, swell *The river surged over its banks.* 2. *noun* rise, swell, flood, rush, gush *A storm surge happens when winds around the eye of a hurricane push water toward shore.*

surpass *verb* exceed, go beyond, outdo, outshine, better, top *The success of the website has surpassed their wildest dreams.*

surplus *adjective* excess, extra, remaining, leftover *The supermarket donates its surplus and outdated products to the food bank.*

surprise 1. *verb* astonish, amaze, astound, catch unaware, awe *Dad surprised Mom with a new car for her birthday.* 2. *noun* astonishment, amazement, awe, disbelief, shock *Janet looked up in surprise when she saw me.*

surrender 1. *verb* give up, submit, yield, abandon, relinquish *When the opposing team scored in the last 30 seconds, we surrendered all hope of winning.* 2. *noun* submission, yielding, giving up *The enemy's surrender ended the war.*

survey *verb* examine, inspect, observe, view, study, scan *They surveyed the countryside from the top of a hill.*

survive *verb* live, endure, persist, stay alive, last, continue, remain *The plants survived the first light frost of autumn.* die

suspect *verb* 1. think, guess, suppose, assume, imagine, gather *I suspect you're right about that.* 2. doubt, distrust, mistrust, question, challenge, dispute *I suspected the truth of her story—it just didn't sound believable.* trust

suspend *verb* 1. hang, dangle, swing, sling *Dad suspended our swing from a large tree limb.* 2. interrupt, break off, delay, postpone, put off, defer, adjourn *Road construction is suspended in the North during the winter months.* continue

suspense *noun* anticipation, expectation, tension, uncertainty, doubt, anxiety *The mystery story kept me in suspense until the last page.*

suspension *noun* interruption, delay, halt, pause, break, adjournment *Peace talks have resumed after a brief suspension.* continuation

suspicion *noun* 1. distrust, mistrust, doubt, misgiving *I view a lot of what I read in supermarket newspapers with suspicion.* trust 2. guess, feeling, hunch, notion, thought, idea *My suspicion is that it will rain tomorrow.*

sustain *verb* 1. bear, carry, support, prop up, hold up *The roof wasn't built to sustain the weight of all that snow.* 2. keep up, maintain, continue, keep going *Her sense of humor sustained her through some hard times.*

swallow 1. *verb* eat, drink, consume, gulp down, ingest *My sore throat made it difficult to swallow food.* 2. *noun* gulp, sip, drink, mouthful, bite *I got the pill down in one swallow.*

swamp 1. *noun* marsh, bog, lowland, wetland, everglade, slough, bayou *We can hear the bullfrogs croaking in the swamp at night.* 2. *verb* flood, overwhelm, deluge, drown, inundate *Online bookstores were swamped with orders for the popular author's new book.*

swap *verb* trade, exchange, switch, barter, make a deal *I swapped one of my duplicate baseball cards for one of Sam's.*

swarm 1. *noun* crowd, throng, mob, mass, horde *Swarms of shoppers showed up for the big sale.* 2. *verb* crowd, flock, teem, overrun, throng, flood *Fans swarmed onto the field to celebrate.*

swat *verb* hit, strike, slap, whack, smack *I swatted at the mosquitoes that were trying to bite me.*

sway *verb* 1. swing, rock, wave, shake, wobble, move back and forth, bend, lean *The pines swayed in the breeze.* 2. persuade, convince, influence, win over, induce

The candidate's persuasive arguments eventually swayed many voters to vote for her.

swear *verb* promise, pledge, vow, give one's word *I swear I won't do it again.*

sweep 1. *verb* clean up, brush, vacuum *I swept up the dirt I tracked in.* 2. move, glide, coast, skim *The wind swept down the valley.* 3. *noun* movement, gesture, wave, stroke *The farmer indicated his fields with a sweep of his arm.* 4. stretch, extent, range, scope *Understanding the broad sweep of history helps us to understand our place in the world.*

sweet *adjective* 1. sugary, syrupy, sweetened *I am allowed to eat sweet foods only in moderation.* sour, bitter 2. nice, kind, considerate, friendly, pleasant, agreeable *It was sweet of Jen to stop by when I was sick.* inconsiderate, unpleasant

swell *verb* grow bigger, increase, expand, enlarge, inflate, bulge, billow *I put ice on my sprained ankle to keep it from swelling a lot. The population of our small village has swelled to over 2,000.* shrink, decrease, deflate

swelter *verb* sweat, perspire, feel too hot, roast, boil *We sweltered in the hot sun.*

swerve *verb* dodge, veer, shift, swing, turn aside *We swerved in order to avoid hitting a deer crossing the road.*

swift *adjective* fast, quick, rapid, fleet, speedy, hasty *The river became swift and dangerous at the rapids.* slow

swim *verb* bathe, go swimming, take a dip, float, paddle around *The children swam in the shallow water near shore.*

swindle 1. *verb* cheat, con, deceive, trick, dupe, defraud *The corporate executive swindled investors in his company and fled the country.* 2. *noun* fraud, deception, trick, con, racket, hoax *Beware of e-mail swindles that ask you to verify credit card numbers on the Internet.*

swing 1. *verb* hang, dangle, be suspended, sway *The gate swung on rusty hinges.* 2. turn, curve, circle, wind, twist *The road swings to the right in about a mile.* 3. *noun* blow, strike, stroke, hit *He took a swing at the ball and missed.*

swirl *verb* twist, whirl, spin, reel, wheel, curl *The wind swirled the fallen leaves around the yard.*

switch 1. *verb* change, exchange, trade, swap, substitute, shift, replace *Dad and I switched seats in the movie theater so I could see better.* 2. *noun* change, adjustment, shift, substitution, trade, swap, exchange *My sister made a switch from chemistry to biology as her college major.* 3. button, lever, control, key *He couldn't find the on-off switch on his computer.*

swoop *verb* dive, plunge, fly, drop *The eagle swooped down and caught a fish in its talons.*

symbol *noun* sign, representation, mark, token, emblem, figure *The dove is a symbol of peace.*

sympathize *verb* express concern for, feel sorry for, understand, show compassion for *I sympathized with my sister who had to go to the doctor for a shot.*

sympathy *noun* understanding, sensitivity, compassion, kindness, mercy, pity *I didn't get any sympathy when I complained about having to wash the dishes.*

symptom *noun* sign, indication, characteristic, indicator *Mom sent me to bed when I showed symptoms of the flu.*

synthetic *adjective* artificial, fake, imitation, simulated *This jacket is made of synthetic leather.* authentic, real

system *noun* 1. plan, method, procedure, scheme, technique, way, approach *Alchemists claimed they had a system for changing any metal into gold.* 2. set, unit, arrangement, organization, structure *The stomach is part of the digestive system.*

T

table *noun* list, chart, index, catalog, schedule *The periodic table lists all the chemical elements known to scientists.*

tablet *noun* pill, capsule, dose, dosage *Take one tablet twice a day.*

tack *verb* attach, affix, fasten, stick, pin, staple, nail *The coach tacked a notice to the bulletin board canceling today's practice.*

tackle *verb* 1. undertake, begin, get busy on, go to work on, deal with, attack, embark upon *We have decided to tackle the task of painting the outside of the house.* 2. bring down, stop, seize, halt *He was tackled at the fifteen-yard line.*

tact *noun* grace, diplomacy, sensitivity, consideration, thoughtfulness, care *It takes tact to tell someone it's time for him or her to leave.*

tag 1. *noun* label, sticker, ticket, badge *We all were given name tags to wear on the first day of camp.* 2. *verb* label, name, identify, mark, ticket *We tagged all the items in the rummage sale with a price.*

tag along *verb* follow, trail behind, accompany, go with, shadow *When I go to the park, my little sister often tags along.*

tail 1. *noun* back, rear, end, tip *Tails of comets are made up of dust particles and gas.* 2. *verb* follow, pursue, shadow, trail *The police tailed the suspected thief.*

take *verb* 1. get, obtain, gain, receive, secure, procure, seize, capture *Our team took the championship.* 2. bring, carry, convey, transport, haul *I took a book along to read on the plane.* 3. require, need, involve, entail *It takes about fifteen minutes for me to walk home from school.* 4. tolerate, endure, bear, stand, put up with *I can't take any more of his complaining.* 5. choose, select, decide on, pick out *I had a choice between chocolate and strawberry, so I took chocolate.* 6. understand, interpret, comprehend, gather, guess, suppose, assume *She took his remarks as a compliment. I take it you agree.* 7. eat, drink, consume *She takes milk in her coffee.* 8. subtract, deduct, remove, eliminate *The store took 20 percent off the regular price.*

tale *noun* story, account, narrative, yarn, fable, anecdote *Our elderly neighbor likes to tell us tales of his boyhood in Ireland.*

talent *noun* ability, skill, gift, aptitude, capability, genius *Bill shows remarkable talent as a musician.*

talk 1. *verb* speak, converse, discuss, chat *Everyone was talking at once. What were you and Dad talking about?* 2. *noun* conversation, discussion, chat, dialogue *I had a nice talk on the phone with my cousin.* 3. lecture, speech, address, sermon *Jerome's father gave a talk to our class about his job as a pilot.*

tall *adjective* high, towering, soaring, lofty, big, long, lengthy *Most of the tallest mountains in the world are in the Himalayas.* short

tally *verb* calculate, compute, count, figure *Kelly tallied the score of each player to see who had won.*

tame 1. *adjective* gentle, obedient, docile, disciplined, domesticated *The birds that come to our feeder are so tame, they will eat out of our hands.* wild 2. *verb* domesticate, train, break, discipline, subdue, control *People have caught and tamed wild horses for at least 6,000 years.*

tamper *verb* meddle, fool around, monkey around, mess, tinker, interfere *Someone tampered with my printer and it won't print.*

tang *noun* flavor, taste, bite, sharpness *The mustard has quite a tang to it.*

tangle 1. *verb* twist, knot, snarl, intertwine, jumble *The vines became tangled in the fence.*

2. *noun* jumble, mass, knot, snarl, twist, web *The narrow streets and alleys were a tangle.*

tantrum *noun* outburst, fit, scene, rage, fury *My little brother threw a tantrum at the supermarket when Mom wouldn't buy him candy.*

tap 1. *noun* faucet, spigot, valve *We connected a hose to the outdoor tap and watered the garden.* 2. rap, knock, touch, pat *I felt a tap on my shoulder.* 3. *verb* rap, knock, beat, pat *Roger has an annoying habit of tapping his fingers on his desk.*

tape 1. *noun* strip, band, ribbon, binding, adhesive tape, packing tape, masking tape, duct tape *I need some tape to seal this package.* 2. *verb* wrap, bind, tie, fasten, seal, bandage *I taped the torn page in my book.* 3. record, videotape, copy, tape-record *We taped our favorite TV show so we could watch it later.*

taper off *verb* lessen, diminish, decrease, dwindle *The summer tourist season tapers off at the end of August.*

tardy *adjective* late, delayed, overdue *I overslept and was tardy for school.* early, on time

target *noun* goal, mark, objective, aim, end, purpose *They set a target of one week in which to finish the project.*

tarnish 1. *verb* discolor, corrode, dull, dim, fade, stain *The silver candlesticks are beginning to tarnish.* 2. *noun* discoloration, corrosion, stain *We used a special cleaner to remove the tarnish from the silverware.*

tart *adjective* sour, tangy, sharp, bitter *The cherries are tart.* sweet

task *noun* job, assignment, responsibility, chore, duty, function, work *My task is to fold the laundry.*

taste 1. *verb* sample, try, test, sip, experience, sense *Taste this and tell me if you think it needs salt.* 2. *noun* flavor, savor, tang *I love the taste of fresh strawberries.* 3. bite, piece, sip, swallow, drop, spoonful, bit, sample *May I have a taste of your coffee?* 4. judgment, polish, style, class, sophistication *Jordan has good taste in clothes.*

tasteless *adjective* 1. flavorless, bland, flat, unappetizing, unsavory *The food on the restaurant buffet was tasteless.* tasty 2. rude, crude, offensive, vulgar, improper *Our browser is set up to block tasteless websites.*

taut *adverb* tight, tense, firm, rigid *Jim pulled the rope taut and tied it to the dock.*

tax 1. *noun* duty, tariff, levy, toll, assessment *Public schools are paid for by taxes.* 2. *verb* charge a tax on, levy a tax on, deduct a tax from *The government taxes salaries.* 3. strain, exhaust, wear on, drain, stretch, burden, overload *Waiting in line taxes my patience.*

taxi *noun* cab, taxicab *We took a taxi to the airport.*

teach *verb* educate, instruct, train, tutor, coach, direct, guide, enlighten *I've been teaching our dog some new tricks.*

teacher *noun* schoolteacher, educator, instructor, trainer, professor, coach, tutor *Our class is learning Spanish from a language teacher who comes in every day.*

team *noun* group, crew, band, gang, squad, unit, party, company *Teams of scientists continue to study the ocean floor, where creatures live without sunlight.*

team up *verb* combine, band together, join, unite, get together, work together *The neighborhood kids teamed up to remove the trash from a vacant lot.*

tear 1. *noun* teardrop, drop, droplet *Tears of laughter rolled down my cheeks.* 2. split, rip, slit, hole, slash, gash, cut *I lost my lunch money through a tear in my pocket.* 3. *verb* rip, shred, pull apart, split, slice, slit, cut *I tore open the box containing my new guitar.* 4. dash, run, rush, race, charge *I tore home to get out of the rain.*

tease *verb* annoy, pester, bother, badger, harass, torment *Some kids were teasing our neighbor's dog and it bit one of them.*

technique *noun* method, style, procedure, means, skill *In recent years doctors have developed new surgical techniques using lasers.*

tedious *adjective* dull, dreary, boring, monotonous, slow, tiring, wearisome *Raking leaves in the autumn is a tedious task.* interesting, exciting

televise *verb* broadcast, telecast, show, air *The game will be televised only on cable channel 301.*

tell *verb* 1. say, express, speak, communicate, state, convey *The airline told us our flight was delayed.* 2. narrate, relate, describe, recount, report *Mom told us what happened at work today.* 3. disclose, reveal, inform, expose, divulge *I haven't told your secret to anyone.* 4. instruct, direct, order, command, require *The teacher told us to sit down.* 5. distinguish, recognize, know, identify, determine *I've known the twins long enough to tell the difference between them.*

temper *noun* 1. disposition, nature, character, attitude, mood *Our cat has a very sweet temper.* 2. anger, annoyance, irritation, rage, fury *That was a very childish display of temper.*

temporary *adjective* passing, momentary, short-lived, transient *During a temporary power failure my uninterruptible power supply keeps my computer running.* lasting, permanent

tempt *verb* attract, interest, appeal to, invite, lure, tantalize *The freshly baked chocolate-chip cookies tempted me, but I knew I had to wait till after dinner.*

temptation *noun* attraction, lure, draw, pull, enticement *I resisted the temptation to hunt for my hidden birthday present.*

tenant *noun* renter, occupant, resident, lodger *There's a new tenant in the apartment next door.*

tend *verb* 1. be likely, be inclined, be apt, lean *My parents tend to get up early.* 2. care for, look after, mind, watch over *My cousin tends the chickens on his parents' farm.*

tendency *noun* inclination, leaning, habit, disposition *I have a tendency to be disorganized.*

tender *adjective* 1. soft, chewable, delicate, not tough *Tender lettuce from the garden makes the best salad.* tough 2. gentle, kind, affectionate, loving, caring, warm *Her tender feelings toward animals caused her to become a vegetarian.* harsh, rough 3. sensitive, sore, painful, aching, raw, bruised *My elbow is still tender from bumping it.*

tense *adjective* 1. anxious, nervous, worried, stressed, apprehensive *I had a tense moment when I thought I'd lost my homework assignment.* relaxed 2. strained, stretched, tight, rigid, taut *The therapist massaged his tense shoulder muscles.* relaxed

term *noun* 1. period, time, duration *The president of the United States is elected for a four-year term.* 2. word, expression, phrase, name, designation *The Internet has provided us with thousands of new terms.* 3. condition, provision, requirement *One of the terms of the agreement to purchase the Louisiana Territory was that the United States pay France $15 million.*

terminal *noun* station, depot, airport *The gate for our flight home is at the far end of the terminal.*

terrible *adjective* 1. dreadful, horrible, awful, appalling, bad, poor, rotten *He's always been terrible at golf.* 2. severe, serious, intense, frightening, terrifying *A terrible storm destroyed several buildings.*

terrific *adjective* 1. excellent, great, superb, magnificent, marvelous, wonderful, sensational *We went to a terrific concert last night.* 2. extreme, intense, extraordinary, considerable, tremendous *The police car was going at a terrific speed when it passed us.*

terrify *verb* frighten, scare, horrify, appall, shock, petrify *The first time I tried the rock-climbing wall, I was terrified I would fall.*

territory *noun* land, region, area, zone, place, district *The Northwest Territory included* the present states of Ohio, Indiana, Illinois, Michigan, Wisconsin, and part of Minnesota.

terror *noun* fear, fright, dread, horror, alarm, shock *The inhabitants of Pompeii fled in terror on August 24, A.D. 79, when Mount Vesuvius erupted.*

test 1. *noun* exam, examination, quiz *I have to study for my English test.* 2. *verb* examine, investigate, analyze, assess, check *The doctor tested my eyesight.*

testimony *noun* statement, declaration, evidence, proof *The court testimony of the two witnesses agreed.*

text *noun* 1. contents, subject matter, wording, transcript *The text of the president's speech is available on the Internet.* 2. book, schoolbook, reader, primer, textbook, manual *The teacher assigned us the second chapter of our social studies text.*

textile *noun* cloth, material, fabric, yard goods, weaving *The museum has an exhibit of antique Oriental textiles and rugs.*

texture *noun* feel, touch, finish, grain, composition, structure *Velvet has a soft texture.*

thankful *adjective* grateful, appreciative, glad, happy, pleased *We're thankful everything worked out well.*

thaw *verb* melt, defrost, liquefy, warm *Salt on the highways thaws the ice.* freeze

theater *noun* playhouse, cinema, auditorium, hall *The movie opens at a theater near you on Friday.*

theft *noun* stealing, robbery, burglary, shoplifting *She was arrested for theft as she left the store.*

theme *noun* 1. subject, topic, issue, point, idea *The theme of this year's homecoming parade is "A Night at the Movies."* 2. report, paper, essay, article, composition *Our themes have to be turned in tomorrow.*

theory *noun* hypothesis, idea, opinion, speculation, supposition, view *Louis Pasteur developed the theory that germs cause disease.*

therefore *adverb* so, consequently, hence, accordingly, for that reason *It's late and therefore I'm going to bed.*

thick *adjective* 1. broad, wide, deep, big, massive, bulky, fat *The village was surrounded by a thick stone wall.* thin, narrow 2. dense, crowded, packed, abundant, concentrated *The area is covered in thick forest.* thin 3. stiff, heavy, firm, solid, gooey *I don't like thick oatmeal.* runny, watery, thin

~~~~~~

thief *noun* robber, burglar, shoplifter, crook *The thief escaped with only $15 in cash.*

thin 1. *adjective* slender, lean, slim, slight, lanky, skinny, gaunt *Carlos is very tall and thin.* 2. fine, delicate, light, narrow *The furniture was covered with a thin layer of dust. The cup has a thin crack in it.* 3. scanty, sparse, meager, scattered *The concert attracted a thin crowd.* 4. watery, diluted, runny, weak *This gravy is too thin.* 5. *verb* water down, dilute, weaken *She thinned the soup with some chicken broth.* 6. decrease, diminish, lessen, dwindle *The crowd at the party thinned around 11:00.*

thing *noun* 1. object, item, article, device, machine, gadget *What is that thing over there?* 2. action, act, deed, task, job, feat *That's a difficult thing to do.* 3. point, detail, matter, idea, fact *There is one more thing we should discuss.*

things *noun* 1. possessions, belongings, clothes, stuff *Mom told me to put all my things away.* 2. affairs, matters, circumstances, conditions *How are things going?*

think *verb* 1. consider, contemplate, reflect, ponder, deliberate, reason *Let me think awhile before I make up my mind.* 2. believe, expect, imagine, presume, gather, guess, suppose *I thought they would be here by now.*

thirsty *adjective* 1. dry, parched, dehydrated *Give the dog some water—he's thirsty.* 2. eager, hungry, desirous, craving, yearning *The children are thirsty for knowledge of the rest of the world.*

thorough *adjective* complete, full, sweeping, total, detailed, all-out, intensive *Teachers today need a thorough understanding of how to use the Internet. The doctor gave me a thorough physical exam.*

though *adverb* however, in any case, nevertheless, notwithstanding *I plan to come to the party; I might be a little late, though.*

thought *noun* 1. consideration, deliberation, contemplation, reflection *Give my suggestion some thought before you decide.* 2. idea, notion, belief, opinion, thinking *My thought is that we should go to the mall.* 3. concern, regard, care, attention *He dove into the water and rescued the child with no thought for his own safety.*

thoughtful *adjective* 1. caring, considerate, kind, sympathetic, helpful, courteous *It was thoughtful of you to bring me flowers.* thoughtless, inconsiderate 2. contemplative, reflective, pensive, meditative *She was in a thoughtful mood and preferred to be alone.*

threat *noun* 1. warning, caution, admonishment, alert *Mom's threat to send us outside to play in the rain quieted us down.* 2. danger, menace, hazard, risk *Pollution is a threat to our health.*

threaten *verb* 1. menace, intimidate, frighten, bully, terrorize, harass *A bully has been threatening younger children during recess.* 2. endanger, put at risk, jeopardize *Rising flood waters are threatening the homes along the river.*

thrifty *adjective* economical, frugal, careful, prudent, economizing, saving *A thrifty shopper can find lots of bargains at yard sales.* wasteful

thrill 1. *verb* excite, delight, enthrall, elate, stimulate, please *The carnival rides thrilled the children.* bore 2. *noun* joy, delight, pleasure, exciting experience *Getting his baseball hero's autograph was a thrill.* bore

thrive *verb* prosper, grow, develop, succeed, flourish, boom *Water parks thrive during a hot summer.* shrivel, fade, fail

throb 1. *verb* beat, pulsate, pound, thump, vibrate *The climb up the steep hill made her heart throb.* 2. *noun* beat, pounding, thump, rhythm *We could feel the throb of the rock music coming from upstairs.*

throng 1. *noun* crowd, mass, mob, multitude, gathering, congregation *A throng of fans gathered at the airport to greet the team.* 2. *verb* crowd, cluster, gather, collect, assemble *People thronged to the theater to see the new movie.*

throw 1. *verb* pitch, toss, cast, fling, heave, sling *I threw the ball for our dog to fetch.* 2. *noun* pitch, toss, fling *The first baseman caught the throw from the shortstop.*

thrust *verb* push, shove, ram, jam, drive, force *He thrust his hands into his coat pockets.*

thus *adverb* therefore, hence, consequently, accordingly, so *We ran into heavy traffic and thus were delayed.*

ticket *noun* 1. admission, pass, permit, receipt, voucher *We purchased tickets to the concert online.* 2. label, tag, sticker, price tag *The ticket on the shirt says $15.95.*

tickle *verb* 1. touch, stroke, pat, pet *He tickled his little sister's feet and made her squirm and laugh.* 2. amuse, delight, entertain, charm, please *She was tickled by her big brother's silly faces.*

tidy 1. *adjective* neat, orderly, organized, well kept, trim, shipshape *He keeps his dresser drawers very tidy.* sloppy, messy 2. *verb* neaten, straighten up, organize *I tidied the kitchen before Mom and Dad got home.*

tie 1. *verb* fasten, attach, bind, lash, secure, knot *She tied the package with a red ribbon.* 2. be equal, be even, draw *The teams tied and had to go into overtime.* 3. *noun* fastener, fastening, string, cord, rope, ribbon, line, wire *Twist the tie securely to close the trash bag.*

4. bond, connection, relationship, friendship, link *My parents still have close ties to their high school classmates.* 5. draw, dead heat, deadlock, standoff *The game ended in a tie.*

tier *noun* row, layer, level, story, deck *A four-tier parking garage is connected to the hotel.*

tight *adjective* 1. taut, tense, stretched, rigid, stiff *He made certain the ropes holding the boat were tight.* loose 2. snug, close-fitting, narrow, small *Last year's school clothes are too tight this year.* loose, roomy 3. secure, firm, fast, strong, fixed *I kept a tight grip on my little sister's hand.* loose 4. crowded, packed, cramped, close, restricted *Space in the small room was tight with so many people.* 5. ungenerous, stingy, penny-pinching *Dad tells me he's not tight, just frugal, when I ask him for money.* generous

tighten *verb* constrict, contract, stiffen, tense, shorten, make tighter *He tightened his belt a notch.* loosen

till 1. *verb* cultivate, plow, work, turn *The farmers are tilling and planting their fields.* 2. *conjunction and preposition* until, before, earlier than, prior to, up to *We won't go outside till it stops raining. We stayed outside till dark.*

tilt 1. *verb* tip, slope, slant, incline, lean, list *The old shed is tilting and should be torn down.* 2. *noun* slant, slope, incline, angle *The architect can control the height and tilt of her drafting table.*

time 1. *noun* period, while, spell, interval, duration, term *He's worked at the same place for a long time.* 2. age, era, epoch, period, generation *We are living in a time of great change in technology and science.* 3. occasion, opportunity, chance, opening *This would be a good time to call Grandma.* 4. *verb* schedule, arrange, plan, set, fix, organize *We timed our departure so we'd arrive in the afternoon.* 5. measure, calculate, clock *We timed him at 4.4 seconds in the 40-yard run.*

timid *adjective* meek, fearful, afraid, restrained, reserved, retiring, shy, bashful *He was too timid to raise his hand and speak when he knew the answer.* bold

tingle *verb* sting, prickle *My foot is tingling because it fell asleep.*

tint 1. *noun* color, tinge, hue, tone, shade, highlight *That gray has a bluish tint.* 2. *verb* color, dye, stain, tinge, shade, highlight *She tinted her hair red.*

tiny *adjective* small, minute, little, slight, wee, diminutive, microscopic *You have a tiny speck of food on your tie.* large, big

tip 1. *noun* point, end, top, peak *I cut the tip of my finger while chopping celery.* 2. gratuity, bonus, gift, present, reward, premium *Dad left the server a tip.* 3. advice, warning, information, pointer *The website gives tips on how to use the software.* 4. *verb* knock over, overturn, upset, tilt, topple *He tipped the tray and the dishes slid to the floor and broke.*

tired *adjective* 1. weary, exhausted, fatigued, worn-out, sleepy *I was tired after running all the way home.* rested 2. bored, weary, annoyed, irritated, fed up *I'm tired of playing cards—let's do something else.*

title 1. *noun* name, label, designation, caption, heading *What's the title of the book you're reading?* 2. ownership, right, claim, possession *When we sold our house, we gave title to the buyer.* 3. championship, crown, first place *Muhammad Ali held the heavyweight title in boxing for many years.* 4. *verb* name, call, designate, entitle *A famous poem by Robert Frost is titled "The Road Not Taken."*

toast *verb* heat, warm, brown, grill, cook *We toasted marshmallows over the campfire.*

together *adverb* collectively, jointly, mutually, cooperatively *If we work together, we'll finish more quickly.* alone

toil 1. *verb* work, labor, strive, struggle, slave *Workers toiled for six years laying track to build the transcontinental railroad.* 2. *noun* work, labor, exertion, drudgery, struggle *Homesteading required backbreaking toil.*

token *noun* sign, indication, mark, evidence, memento, remembrance *Dad brought Mom roses as a token of his love.*

tolerant *adjective* accepting, understanding, charitable, broad-minded, open-minded *My parents have taught me to be tolerant of all religious beliefs.* intolerant

tolerate *verb* 1. allow, permit, accept, stand for, put up with *Our teacher will not tolerate any disruption in class.* prohibit, forbid 2. stand, abide, endure, bear, suffer *My grandparents moved to Arizona because they can't tolerate northern winters.*

toll 1. *noun* charge, fee, fare, tax, duty, tariff *Cars and passengers pay a toll to ride the ferry to the island.* 2. *verb* ring, peal, chime *The bell in the tower tolls at noon.*

tomb *noun* grave, vault, crypt, shrine, mausoleum *The tomb of King Tutankhamen was found in Egypt's Valley of the Kings in 1922.*

tone *noun* 1. sound, pitch, key, note, intonation *His voice has a deep, mellow tone.* 2. color, shade, hue, tint, tinge *The room was decorated in tones of beige and blue.* 3. spirit, nature, attitude, mood, character, quality *His last letter was very optimistic in tone.* 4. heath, vigor, strength, fitness, firmness *He exercises every day to maintain muscle tone.*

tongue *noun* language, dialect, speech *Jacques speaks three languages, but his native tongue is French.*

too *adverb* 1. also, besides, additionally, as well, furthermore *If you're going to the mall, I'd like to come along, too.* 2. very, exceedingly, overly, excessively *It's too hot today.*

tool *noun* implement, utensil, instrument, apparatus, device, gadget, appliance *The personal computer has become an indispensable tool.*

top 1. *noun* peak, crown, tip, apex, zenith *We looked out over the countryside from the top of the hill.* bottom 2. cover, cap, lid, cork, stopper *I lost the top to my pen.* 3. *adjective* highest, uppermost, maximum, best, greatest, chief, leading *He's the top player in the league.* 4. *verb* outdo, beat, better, exceed, surpass, improve on *She topped her previous record time in the race.*

topic *noun* subject, theme, text, issue, point *The main topic of conversation Monday morning was Sunday's football game.*

topple *verb* knock over, overturn, upset, tip over *The high stack of boxes toppled.*

torch *noun* light, flame, lantern *The Statue of Liberty holds a torch, which represents liberty.*

torment 1. *verb* pester, annoy, irritate, bother, torture, plague *Flies tormented us during our picnic.* 2. *noun* agony, anguish, distress, pain, torture *The torment from my toothache was barely endurable.*

torrent *noun* flood, stream, deluge, rush, gush *A torrent of lava flowed from the volcano.*

torture *noun* persecution, torment, punishment, abuse *Torture was used to get the prisoners to talk.*

toss 1. *verb* throw, fling, cast, sling, hurl, pitch *People tossed coins into the fountain for good luck.* 2. roll, pitch, rock, sway, lurch *The ship was tossed around on the waves during the storm.* 3. *noun* throw, pitch, cast, fling, lob *His toss missed the wastepaper basket.*

total 1. *noun* sum, whole, full amount *We each added up the figures but had different totals.* 2. *adjective* whole, entire, complete *Total attendance was 400.* partial 3. *verb* add, sum up, figure, calculate, compute *We totaled our purchases and came up with twenty-five dollars.*

touch 1. *verb* feel, handle, finger, pat, stroke, press, brush, graze *The sign said "Do not touch—wet paint."* 2. contact, reach, meet, adjoin, come against *Don't let the wires touch each other.* 3. affect, move, stir, impress *The orphan's story touched him deeply.* 4. *noun* contact, feel, brush, stroke, caress, pressure *I felt the touch of the cat's fur against* *my leg.* 5. small amount, bit, drop, trace, dash, hint *I taste a touch of garlic in the sauce.*

touching *adjective* tender, moving, affecting, poignant *We read a touching story about the adoption of Vietnam orphans.*

touchy *adjective* irritable, sensitive, moody, grumpy, grouchy, quick-tempered *Don't mention his losing the match to James—he's very touchy about it.*

tough *adjective* 1. durable, sturdy, strong, rugged, hardy, firm *His backpack is made of tough weatherproof material.* weak, flimsy 2. difficult, hard, complicated, demanding, challenging, tricky *The reporters asked the candidates tough questions.* easy

tour 1. *noun* journey, trip, voyage, excursion, expedition, visit, outing *The Wagners are going on a tour of Italy next summer.* 2. *verb* travel around, explore, sightsee, visit *I'd like to tour Mammoth Cave.*

tourist *noun* visitor, sightseer, traveler *Millions of tourists visit Las Vegas every year.*

tournament *noun* competition, contest, tourney, event, match, meet *Mom is participating in an amateur golf tournament.*

tow *verb* pull, haul, draw, drag, tug *Most barges on the Mississippi are not self-propelled and need to be towed or pushed by tugboats.*

tower *noun* steeple, spire, belfry, minaret *Forest rangers act as lookouts, watching from observation towers for signs of fire.*

towering *adjective* huge, lofty, high, soaring, immense *Giant redwoods are towering trees.*

town *noun* community, municipality, village, city *We live in a small Midwest town.*

toxic *adjective* poisonous, harmful, noxious, deadly *Automobile exhaust contains toxic chemicals.*

toy 1. *noun* plaything, trinket, bauble *Our cat tosses its catnip-filled toy in the air.* 2. *verb* play, fiddle, mess around, putter *Mom realized I was sick when I just toyed with my food.*

trace 1. *noun* small amount, bit, touch, dash, hint, suggestion *There was a trace of anger in her voice.* 2. evidence, sign, indication, mark *The expedition found traces of an ancient civilization.* 3. *verb* follow, track, trail, seek, pursue *Dogs' keen sense of smell enables them to trace other animals.* 4. copy, reproduce, duplicate, draw, sketch *The thieves traced the map to the hidden treasure.*

track 1. *noun* path, trail, road, footpath, course *We hiked through the woods along a dirt* *track.* 2. footprint, paw prints, mark, sign, trace *We saw rabbit tracks in the snow.* 3. *verb* follow, trail, trace, hunt, pursue *The scientists were able to track the bear by its radio collar.* 4. bring, carry *I took off my boots so I wouldn't track snow into the house.*

tract *noun* area, region, expanse, plot *My uncle farms a large tract of land in Nebraska.*

trade 1. *verb* exchange, swap, switch, barter, negotiate *My sister and I traded nights for doing the dishes.* 2. *noun* business, commerce, industry *U.S. companies engage in trade with foreign companies.* 3. exchange, barter, swap, switch, substitution *The dealer made an even trade with Dad: our older car for a used truck.* 4. occupation, profession, business, career, vocation, line of work *Our neighbor works in the building trade as a carpenter.*

tradition *noun* custom, habit, practice, belief, convention, usage, folklore *According to tradition, the first Thanksgiving took place in 1621 after the Pilgrims' first harvest.*

traditional *adjective* conventional, customary, usual, normal, routine *A fireworks display is the traditional way in which we celebrate the Fourth of July.*

traffic 1. *noun* movement, flow, travel, transport *Traffic is stop-and-go on the expressway this morning.* 2. commerce, trade, business, sale, exchange, dealing *Governments are trying to stop the traffic in illegal drugs.* 3. *verb* buy, sell, exchange, trade, deal *The police arrested the man for trafficking in stolen diamonds.*

tragedy *noun* disaster, catastrophe, misfortune, accident, calamity *It's a tragedy that so many people were left homeless because of the hurricane.*

tragic *adjective* sad, unfortunate, dreadful, disastrous, catastrophic *The earthquake was a tragic event.*

trail 1. *verb* pull, drag, tow, haul, draw *The little boy trailed his toy train behind him.* 2. follow, tag along, straggle, lag, linger *The puppies trailed behind their mother.* 3. pursue, hunt, trace, track, tail, shadow *The dog trailed the rabbit to its den.* 4. *noun* scent, track, signs, marks *The police are on the trail of the burglars.* 5. path, footpath, road, track, route, course *This trail leads to the pond.*

train 1. *verb* teach, coach, instruct, educate, school, tutor, drill, prepare *We took our puppy to a school that trained him to behave.* 2. *noun* procession, row, line, string, column *A train of climbers passed us as we trudged up the mountain.*

trait *noun* characteristic, feature, quality, property, attribute *One of the most endearing traits of a pet is its ability to give its owner unconditional love.*

traitor *noun* betrayer, spy, double-crosser, turncoat, double agent *Benedict Arnold became a traitor to the Revolution by agreeing to turn over the fort at West Point to the British.*

tramp *verb* hike, trudge, march, plod, trek, walk *The explorers tramped through the Amazon jungle in search of the lost city.*

trample *verb* crush, flatten, squash, walk on, tread on *The deer trampled Mom's flower garden.*

tranquil *adjective* calm, peaceful, quiet, serene, untroubled *We enjoyed a tranquil evening without television.* noisy

transfer 1. *verb* move, convey, carry, shift, transport, transmit, pass on *Our luggage was transferred to the wrong plane. He transferred his property to his son.* 2. *noun* relocation, move, change, shift *The transfer of Sandy's father to the Denver office meant that they had to move.*

transform *verb* change, convert, alter, turn *In science class we watched as a tadpole transformed into a frog.*

transition *noun* change, conversion, transformation, alteration *The transition from ugly caterpillar to beautiful butterfly is a miracle of Mother Nature.*

translate *verb* interpret, convert, render *Ms. Cortes asked me to translate a passage from English into Spanish.*

transmission *noun* 1. broadcast, communication, dispatch *The spy sent a coded transmission to headquarters.* 2. spread, conveyance, transfer *Washing your hands frequently helps to prevent the transmission of germs.*

transmit *verb* send, pass along, dispatch, forward, transfer, relay *Satellites transmit information around the world.*

transparent *adjective* 1. clear, see-through, translucent *A greenhouse built of transparent plastic lets in the sunlight.* 2. evident, obvious, apparent, plain, undisguised, recognizable *Her transparent excuse fooled no one.*

transplant *verb* transfer, move, relocate *We transplanted the tomatoes from pots to the garden when they were six inches tall.*

transport 1. *verb* carry, convey, move, haul, transfer, ship *Trucks transport goods across the country on interstate highways.* 2. *noun* transportation, shipment, conveyance, shipping *The railroad is used for the transport of coal.*

transportation *noun* conveyance, transport, carriage *Our city has good public transportation for getting across town.*

trap 1. *verb* catch, capture, snare, hook, net *We only buy tuna that is caught with nets* *that do not trap dolphins.* release, free 2. *noun* ambush, snare, lure, bait, decoy, trick, deception *The police set a trap to catch the thief.*

trash *noun* rubbish, litter, garbage, waste, debris *We separate our trash from our recyclables.*

travel *verb* 1. journey, tour, voyage, visit, sightsee *We traveled to Yellowstone Park and camped for a week.* 2. go, move, progress, proceed, pass, traverse *The police car had its siren on and was traveling at high speed.*

travels *noun* journey, trip, excursion, expedition, tour, sightseeing, visit *He wrote about his travels through Africa.*

treacherous *adjective* 1. dangerous, hazardous, unsafe, perilous, risky *Freezing rain made the roads treacherous.* 2. disloyal, deceitful, untrustworthy, traitorous *Robin Hood returns from the Crusades to restore King Richard's throne that his treacherous brother Prince John has stolen.*

tread *verb* walk, step, trample, stomp *Please don't tread on Mom's flower bed.*

treason *noun* betrayal, disloyalty, treachery *Mary Queen of Scots was found guilty of treason after being involved in a plot to assassinate Queen Elizabeth I.*

treasure 1. *noun* fortune, wealth, riches, jewels, gems, gold, plunder *Pirates roamed the Caribbean Sea and captured ships full of treasure.* 2. *verb* cherish, value, hold dear, adore, love, prize, appreciate *I'll always treasure my old teddy bear.*

treat 1. *verb* deal with, think of, consider, regard, handle, behave toward *Our parents taught us to treat others with courtesy.* 2. care for, take care of, doctor, attend to, minister to *Chinese doctors have long used herbal remedies to treat disease.* 3. *noun* delight, pleasure, thrill, joy, enjoyment *It was a treat to see my cousins at the family reunion.*

treatment *noun* 1. cure, medicine, remedy, therapy, care *A massage is great treatment for stiff muscles.* 2. conduct, behavior, handling, management *We complained to the manager about the clerk's discourteous treatment.*

treaty *noun* agreement, compact, alliance, settlement, arrangement *The treaty that ended World War II was signed on September 2, 1945.*

trek *verb* walk, hike, trudge, tramp, journey, travel *We trekked through the snow to the cabin.*

tremble *verb* shake, quake, vibrate, shiver, quiver, quaver, shudder *Her clothes were soaked through, and she was trembling from the cold.*

tremendous *adjective* 1. enormous, huge, immense, gigantic *A tremendous whale breached beside our boat.* small, minute 2. magnificent, marvelous, terrific, sensational *We had a tremendous time at Martha's party.*

tremor *noun* quake, shudder, shaking, tremble, vibration, earthquake *Scientists detected a tremor moments before the volcano erupted.*

trench *noun* ditch, channel, furrow, trough, moat, excavation *The machine dug the trench, laid the electrical cable, and filled in the trench.*

trend *noun* tendency, direction, course, current, movement, drift, inclination *The trend is for computer chips to get smaller and smaller.*

trial *noun* 1. court case, hearing, lawsuit, suit *The defendant has requested a jury trial.* 2. test, tryout, assessment, experiment *The seed company is conducting trials to see what plant varieties grow best in this area.* 3. trouble, hardship, misfortune, ordeal, tribulation *Immigrants have endured trials such as poverty and discrimination after arriving in this country.*

tribe *noun* people, group, family, clan *Native American tribes' status is that of sovereign nations.*

tribute *noun* 1. praise, honor, gratitude, acknowledgment, recognition *Labor Day is celebrated in tribute to working people.* 2. tax, duty, fee, levy, money *After Julius Caesar invaded Britain, its inhabitants paid tribute to Rome.*

trick 1. *verb* deceive, cheat, swindle, dupe, fool, outwit *Internet scams trick people out of their savings.* 2. *noun* deception, ploy, deceit, scheme, fraud, scam, swindle *The wealthy man saw the plan as a trick to take his money.* 3. joke, prank, antic, gag, mischief *April Fool's Day is a day for harmless tricks.* 4. stunt, act, feat, skill, technique *Cats are very smart and can be trained to do tricks.*

trickle 1. *verb* drip, dribble, drop, leak, flow, seep *Tears trickled down the child's cheeks.* 2. *noun* dribble, small amount, drip, drop *The first trickle of lava from the volcano has reached the sea.*

trim 1. *verb* cut, clip, snip, shear, pare, prune, shape *Dad trims his beard regularly so that it looks neat.* 2. decorate, adorn, embroider, embellish, edge *Donna's wedding dress is trimmed with pearls.* 3. *adjective* fit, lean, slender, slim *Regular exercise keep him trim.*

trip 1. *verb* stumble, tumble, topple, fall *I tripped while getting in the boat and landed in the lake.* 2. *noun* journey, voyage, tour, expedition, excursion, outing *We enjoyed our ski trip to Colorado.*

triumph *noun* success, accomplishment, achievement, victory, conquest, win *The Hoover Dam, completed in 1936, was an engineering triumph.* failure, defeat

triumph over *verb* beat, defeat, overcome, conquer, get the better of *Our soccer team triumphed over last year's champion.*

trivial *adjective* unimportant, petty, insignificant, trifling, slight, superficial *There's no sense in getting upset over something so trivial.* important

troop 1. *noun* group, band, unit, company, bunch *Our Girl Scout troop is going on a wilderness camping expedition* 2. *verb* march, trudge, traipse, file *We trooped off to get ice-cream cones.*

trophy *noun* award, medal, prize, laurels, crown *Our bowling team took home the first-place trophy.*

trot *verb* run, jog, bound *My little sister trotted after me to the park.*

trouble 1. *noun* difficulty, problem, predicament, dilemma, trial, snag *Her troubles began when she didn't back up her computer and accidentally deleted her file.* 2. effort, work, bother, care, thought, attention *Mom went to a lot of trouble to find just what I wanted for my birthday.* 3. *verb* distress, worry, disturb, bother, upset *Is something troubling you?* calm, soothe

truce *noun* armistice, ceasefire, lull, stop, pause, break *The armies agreed to a truce while peace talks continue.*

trudge *verb* plod, tramp, hike, march, slog *We trudged through the snow to get to school.*

true *adjective* 1. truthful, accurate, correct, valid, exact, factual *I know what you say is true.* false 2. faithful, dependable, loyal, sincere, trustworthy, devoted *My brother is also my truest friend.* 3. genuine, authentic, real, legitimate, bona fide *She showed true courage when she stood up to the bully.*

truly *adverb* sincerely, honestly, genuinely, really, very, extremely *I'm truly sorry that I hurt your feelings.*

trust 1. *verb* believe in, rely on, depend on, count on *I trust you to always tell me the truth.* 2. believe, hope, expect, assume, presume *I trust I'll see you at school tomorrow.* 3. *noun* faith, belief, confidence, reliance *I have complete trust in my family.* 4. care, custody, protection, charge *I left my wallet and watch in Karen's trust while I went swimming.*

trustworthy *adjective* dependable, reliable, responsible, honest, truthful *We elected*

Jim troop treasurer because he's trustworthy. untrustworthy

truth *noun* truthfulness, honesty, accuracy, fact, validity *There is no truth in what he said about Frank.* dishonesty

try 1. *verb* attempt, endeavor, strive, struggle, aim, seek, make an effort *I'm trying to do better in math.* 2. sample, test, taste, evaluate, check out *Dad bought a new breakfast cereal for me to try.* 3. judge, hear, consider *The case is being tried by a jury.* 4. *noun* attempt, effort, go, shot *Donald passed the bar exam on the first try.*

trying *adjective* annoying, distressing, difficult, troublesome, bothersome, burdensome *It was very trying to have visitors for a week with Mom and Dad both working.*

tug 1. *verb* pull, jerk, tow, haul, draw, yank, wrench *The child kept tugging at his mother's skirt.* 2. *noun* pull, jerk, yank, wrench *Give the kite string a gentle tug.*

tumble 1. *verb* fall, topple, stumble, trip, lose one's balance *I stopped my little sister from tumbling down the stairs.* 2. *noun* fall, spill, dive, stumble *Valerie took a tumble and broke her ankle.*

tune 1. *noun* melody, song, air, refrain *The tune from that commercial keeps running through my head.* 2. agreement, harmony, accord, conformity *His old-fashioned ideas are not in tune with the times.* 3. *verb* adjust, alter, modify, regulate *We waited for the performer to tune his guitar.*

tunnel 1. *noun* underground passage, shaft, channel, subway *The train passed through a tunnel in the mountain.* 2. *verb* excavate, burrow, mine *The groundhog tunneled under our shed.*

turmoil *noun* disorder, tumult, uproar, commotion, disturbance, confusion *Everything was in turmoil on moving day.* quiet, peace

turn 1. *verb* rotate, pivot, swivel, revolve, spin, whirl *My desk chair turns on its base.* 2. shift, veer, curve, angle, bend, circle *Turn right at the next corner.* 3. change, alter, become, transform *Caterpillars turn into butterflies and moths.* 4. spoil, sour, go bad, curdle *The milk has turned.* 5. *noun* bend, angle, veer, curve *The road makes a turn to the left just ahead.* 6. change, alteration, shift *Granddad was sick, but he's taken a turn for the better.* 7. chance, opportunity, time, try, attempt *It's your turn to play.*

tutor 1. *noun* teacher, instructor, coach, educator, trainer *University students act as volunteer tutors for any students who need extra help.* 2. *verb* teach, instruct, coach, educate, train *My older sister is tutoring me in math.*

twilight *noun* dusk, nightfall, sunset, sundown, early evening *The sky sometimes glows pink at twilight.*

twine *noun* string, cord, yarn *She tied the package with twine.*

twinge *noun* pain, pang, ache, stab *I felt a twinge in my side after running.*

twinkle *verb* sparkle, glitter, glisten glimmer, shimmer, shine *The turbulence of the earth's atmosphere makes stars twinkle.*

twirl *verb* spin, rotate, whirl, turn, swirl *The drum majorettes twirled their batons at the head of the parade.*

twist 1. *verb* turn, wind, coil, curl, bend, loop *The vines twisted around the tree trunks.* 2. change, alter, distort, misrepresent, falsify *She twisted the facts to make herself look better.* 3. sprain, hurt, injure, turn *I twisted my ankle playing badminton.* 4. *noun* bend, turn, curve, angle *The mountain road is full of twists.* 5. development, change, turn, variation, alteration *Events in last night's episode took an unexpected twist.*

twitch *verb* jerk, jolt, jump, quiver, move *The doctor hit my leg just below the knee, and my leg twitched.*

type *noun* 1. kind, sort, variety, class, group *We saw many unusual types of plants at the botanical garden.* 2. print, printing, font, lettering, character *Put the heading in bold type.*

typical *adjective* ordinary, usual, average, normal, routine *A typical day in our family starts around 6:00 in the morning.*

tyranny *noun* oppression, repression, despotism, cruelty, unjustness *He escaped the tyranny of the dictator by defecting.*

tyrant *noun* dictator, despot, oppressor *The tyrant was overthrown by the people.*

U

ugly *adjective* 1. unattractive, unsightly, homely, hideous *Mom made me return the ugly purple chair to the neighbor's trash, where I found it.* pretty, attractive 2. disagreeable, unpleasant, bad, offensive, nasty, obnoxious, foul *Skunk cabbage is named for its ugly smell.* pleasant

ultimate *adjective* 1. last, final, conclusive *The ultimate goal in chess is to checkmate your* *opponent.* 2. greatest, highest, supreme *The former palace has been turned into the ultimate luxury hotel.*

umpire *noun* judge, referee, arbitrator, mediator *The umpire called the player out at second base.*

unable *adjective* incapable, powerless, unfit, unqualified *I am unable to get a real job until I'm fourteen.* able

unanimous *adjective* agreed, undivided, united, solid, in complete accord *We made a unanimous decision to order a pizza, rent a movie, and stay home tonight.*

unaware *adjective* ignorant, unconscious, unmindful, oblivious, unsuspecting *I was totally unaware that my friends were planning the surprise party for me.*

unbelievable *adjective* 1. incredible, doubtful, questionable, unconvincing, suspicious *Scott's story about seeing a UFO was a bit unbelievable.* believable 2. amazing, astonishing, impressive, extraordinary *The northern lights are an unbelievable sight.* unimpressive

uncanny *adjective* strange, mysterious, unusual, astonishing, incredible, remarkable *The comedian is known for his uncanny imitations of famous people.*

uncertain *adjective* 1. unsure, unclear, hazy, vague, undecided, doubtful *I'm uncertain about what I should do next.* certain 2. changeable, unpredictable, unsettled, insecure, precarious *The victims of the earthquake face an uncertain future.* secure

uncomfortable *adjective* 1. uneasy, awkward, self-conscious, nervous, anxious *I feel uncomfortable in a group of people I don't know.* comfortable, at ease 2. ill-fitting, tight, scratchy, painful *I can't wait to take off these uncomfortable shoes.* comfortable

uncommon *adjective* rare, unusual, unique, novel, different, infrequent *Snow is uncommon in Florida.*

unconcerned *adjective* uninterested, indifferent, apathetic, unworried, blasé, nonchalant, easygoing *The soldier appeared unconcerned about his own safety when he saved his comrade.* concerned, interested

unconscious *adjective* 1. senseless, out cold, knocked out *He was unconscious from a blow on the head.* conscious 2. unaware, oblivious, heedless, ignorant *She was concentrating so hard on her work that she was unconscious of the activity around her.* aware

uncover *verb* reveal, expose, disclose, turn up, discover *The police uncovered a plot to steal the diamonds.* cover, conceal

undecided *adjective* uncertain, unsettled, indefinite, undetermined *I'm still undecided about what to get Dad for his birthday.* certain, settled

under *preposition* 1. below, beneath *The cat hides under the bed when it thunders.* above 2. lower than, less than, smaller than, below *I paid under $5.00 for this.* above, more than 3. according to, subject to, because of *Under the dress code, we can't wear shorts to school.*

undergo *verb* experience, go through, have, endure, meet with, encounter *Our community is undergoing a lot of growth.*

underground *adjective* buried, belowground, subterranean, sunken *Before you dig where there may be underground cables, you must call the utility company.* aboveground

underneath *preposition and adverb* below, beneath, under *Let's sit in the shade underneath the tree. He seems grouchy; but underneath, he's really very nice.*

understand *verb* 1. comprehend, follow, grasp, realize, know, appreciate *You need to understand the importance of washing your hands after handling your pets.* 2. learn, gather, hear, believe *I understand she will be a few minutes late.*

understanding 1. *noun* knowledge, comprehension, appreciation, grasp, awareness *Today you need some understanding of how to use a computer.* 2. agreement, arrangement, deal, bargain *My brother's and my understanding is that if our doors are closed, we don't want to be bothered.* 3. *adjective* sympathetic, compassionate, kind, sensitive, forgiving *Dad is understanding about giving an employee with a sick child time off.*

undertake *verb* take on, assume, tackle, shoulder, attempt, try, begin *I undertook the responsibility of caring for our hamsters.*

undo *verb* 1. unfasten, untie, take apart, disassemble, dismantle *I undid the knots in my little sister's shoelaces.* assemble, fasten 2. cancel, wipe out, reverse, nullify *Once you've lied, you can't undo the damage you've done to your credibility.*

uneasy *adjective* anxious, nervous, distressed, worried, agitated *I felt uneasy the first time I flew in an airplane.* calm, comfortable

unemployed *adjective* jobless, out of work, unoccupied, idle *If Mom or Dad become unemployed, we may have to cut back on our spending.* employed

unequal *adjective* 1. unfair, unbalanced, one-sided, unjust *It would be an unequal match if the sixth-graders played the fourth-graders.* equal, fair 2. lopsided, uneven, unbalanced, asymmetrical *Do those chair legs look to be of unequal length to you?* equal

uneven *adjective* 1. rough, bumpy, irregular, jagged *We bounced along the uneven road surface.* even 2. unequal, unbalanced, lopsided, mismatched, unfair *The teams are uneven because our team is short one player.* even

unexpected *adjective* unforeseen, unanticipated, surprising, sudden *We really enjoyed Aunt Flo's unexpected visit.* expected

unfair *adjective* unjust, biased, prejudiced, unreasonable, inequitable, unjustified *Their complaint of having received unfair treatment will be investigated.* fair

unfamiliar *adjective* 1. unusual, strange, uncommon, rare, unique, novel, new, different *The first settlers encountered plants and animals that were unfamiliar to them.* familiar 2. unacquainted, uninformed, inexperienced, unaccustomed, ignorant *She can use a computer but is unfamiliar with how it works.* familiar

unfortunate *adjective* unlucky, ill-fated, unhappy, unfavorable, regrettable *It was unfortunate that it rained the whole week we were on vacation.* fortunate

unfriendly *adjective* unsociable, aloof, standoffish, distant, cool, inhospitable *Our new neighbors seemed unfriendly at first, but we found out they just didn't want to intrude.* friendly

unhappy *adjective* sad, sorrowful, downcast, discontented, dejected, depressed, blue *It makes me unhappy when I hear that people abandon their pets.* happy

unhealthy *adjective* 1. sick, ill, weak, unwell, frail, sickly, run-down *Mom says my vitamins will keep me from being unhealthy.* healthy 2. unwholesome, harmful, dangerous, damaging *Secondhand cigarette smoke is unhealthy.* healthy

uniform *adjective* 1. even, constant, steady, unvaried, regular *The temperature on the island is relatively uniform year-round.* uneven 2. like, same, similar, equal, identical *Potatoes of uniform size are packaged together.* irregular

unify *verb* combine, unite, consolidate, join, merge, blend *In 1990 East and West Germany became unified into the Federal Republic of Germany.*

union *noun* 1. joining, merger, combination, blending, unification *The United States began as the union of thirteen British colonies.* 2. association, alliance, federation, coalition, league *The labor union has a large membership.*

unique *adjective* single, sole, only, distinctive, different, rare, unusual *Each humpback whale has a unique pattern of black and white on the underside of its tail.*

unit *noun* 1. part, component, section, division, element, constituent *The apartment* *building has twenty-four units.* 2. amount, quantity, measurement *The inch is a unit of length.*

unite *verb* combine, merge, join, unify, link *Our community united to raise money for a library.* separate

universal *adjective* general, widespread, unanimous, common, worldwide *At the end of the nineteenth century, L. L. Zamenhof proposed a universal language called Esperanto.* local

unkind *adjective* mean, cruel, heartless, harsh, inconsiderate *She apologized for her unkind remark.* kind

unknown *adjective* anonymous, unnamed, unidentified *Folktales have unknown authors because they have been passed down orally through the generations.* known

unlike *adjective* different, dissimilar, distinct, contrasting *My brother and I are unlike in appearance—he looks like Mom, and I look like Dad.* like, alike

unlikely *adjective* doubtful, improbable, remote, questionable *Its unlikely that I'll win the race.* likely

unnatural *adjective* unusual, strange, odd, bizarre, weird, abnormal *Her hair was dyed an unnatural shade of red.* natural

unpack *verb* unload, empty, take out, discharge, dump *I unpacked my suitcase completely without finding my toothbrush.* pack

unpopular *adjective* unwanted, disliked, unappreciated, undesirable, unwelcome *She lost the election because of her unpopular opinions.* popular

unreasonable *adjective* 1. irrational, illogical, senseless *It's unreasonable to expect Mom to do all the housework.* reasonable, rational 2. extreme, excessive, outrageous, extravagant *We don't shop at that store because of its unreasonable prices.* reasonable

unreliable *adjective* undependable, unpredictable, untrustworthy, questionable, uncertain *Don't expect them to help—they're unreliable. Our washer is unreliable and keeps breaking down.* reliable

unrest *noun* agitation, disorder, commotion, turmoil, disturbance, trouble *Opposition to the Vietnam War caused unrest across the country.* calm, peace

unruly *adjective* disorderly, wild, uncontrollable, unmanageable, rowdy *What started out as a peaceful protest turned into an unruly mob.* orderly

unsatisfactory *adjective* inadequate, insufficient, inferior, second-rate *The roofer did an unsatisfactory job of repairing the roof—it still leaks.* satisfactory

unskilled *adjective* untrained, inexperienced, amateurish, untalented *The company says it is willing to hire unskilled workers and train them.* skilled

unsteady *adjective* unstable, unsound, weak, wobbly, unsafe *Don't use that ladder—it's unsteady.* steady, stable

untie *verb* undo, loosen, unfasten, unknot *She quickly untied the package.* tie

unused *adjective* new, fresh, firsthand, original, untouched *Some of my parents' wedding presents are still in their boxes, unused.* used, secondhand

unusual *adjective* uncommon, rare, unique, out of the ordinary, novel, odd, different *It's unusual to have an insect for a pet.* common

uphold *verb* support, sustain, maintain, defend *The city council voted to uphold the mayor's decision.*

upkeep *noun* maintenance, repair, preservation, support *Upkeep on an old house costs a lot.*

upper *adjective* higher, top, superior, greater *The book you're looking for is on the upper shelf.*

upright *adjective* 1. standing, erect, vertical *Dad bought an upright vacuum cleaner.* horizontal 2. honorable, upstanding, reputable, respectable, moral *The judge is an upright member of the community.* dishonorable, immoral

uproar *noun* noise, disturbance, commotion, racket, tumult, turmoil, hubbub *There was an uproar from the stands when the home team scored the winning goal.*

upset 1. *verb* overturn, tip over, capsize, topple *Kenneth upset the canoe when he stood up.* 2. disturb, agitate, trouble, bother, shake, fluster *Bev's rude remark upset Nora.* calm, comfort 3. disrupt, change, spoil, mess up *The stormy weather has upset our plans for a bike trip.* 4. *noun* defeat, loss, rout *The team suffered an upset.* win 5. *adjective* disturbed, agitated, troubled, bothered *I'm not upset by anything you've done.* calm

up-to-date *adjective* modern, contemporary, current, advanced, fashionable *We just bought a new, up-to-date computer.* old-fashioned

urban *adjective* metropolitan, city, municipal, civic *The urban area has expanded into what used to be farmland.* rural

urge 1. *verb* drive, press, goad, prod, force *The cowboy urged his horse on with his spurs.*

2. coax, prompt, plead, encourage, beg, recommend *Dad urged his friend to see a lawyer about the contract.* 3. *noun* desire, wish, impulse, longing *I had a sudden urge to call my friend in California.*

urgent *adjective* pressing, important, crucial, vital, essential *The victims of the hurricane have an urgent need for help.* trivial, unimportant

usage *noun* treatment, handling, use *The washer finally quit after many years of hard usage.*

use 1. *verb* utilize, employ, exercise, apply, make use of *Dad uses a chain saw to cut dead trees for wood for our fireplace.* 2. finish, consume, exhaust, use up, go through *Did you use all the butter?* 3. *noun* purpose, function, application *Anything we can't find a use for, we can donate to the rummage sale.*

useful *adjective* helpful, beneficial, practical, handy, valuable *A can opener is a useful gadget.* useless

useless *adjective* worthless, ineffective, inadequate *My old computer is so slow, it's useless.* useful

usher 1. *noun* escort, guide, attendant, leader, conductor *The usher showed us to our seats.* 2. *verb* escort, conduct, guide, lead, accompany *Our names were called, and we were ushered to our table.*

usual *adjective* customary, ordinary, normal, common, typical *I went to bed at my usual time.* unusual

utensil *noun* implement, tool, instrument, apparatus, device, gadget *The dishes and utensils are still in the dishwasher.*

utter 1. *verb* voice, say, speak, pronounce, vocalize *Shh, don't utter a sound.* 2. *adjective* complete, absolute, total, thorough, downright *That's utter nonsense!*

V

vacant *adjective* empty, unoccupied, uninhabited, deserted *Someone bought the vacant lot next door and is building a house on it.* occupied, filled

vacation *noun* holiday, rest, leave, break, furlough *Each year, Dad gets three weeks of vacation from his job.*

vacuum 1. *noun* void, empty space, nothingness *Outer space is a vacuum with nothing to see.* 2. *verb* clean, sweep *Part of cleaning my room each week is vacuuming the floor.*

vague *adjective* unclear, indefinite, indistinct, dim, faint, obscure, blurred, fuzzy, hazy *She saw the vague shape of a building ahead in the fog. I had only a vague idea of what he was talking about.* clear, definite

vain *adjective* 1. unsuccessful, futile, ineffectual, fruitless *I've made several vain attempts to reach her by cell phone.* 2. conceited, haughty, self-centered, egotistical, proud *He's very vain about his appearance and wears only custom-made suits.* humble

valiant *adjective* brave, courageous, bold, gallant, heroic, chivalrous *The firefighters' valiant efforts saved everyone from the burning building.* cowardly

valid *adjective* 1. sound, true, good, convincing, credible *Oversleeping is not a valid excuse for being late for school.* invalid 2. legal, lawful, legitimate, effective, authentic *You need to show a valid ID when you check in with the airline.* invalid, false

valley *noun* hollow, glen, vale, dale *The river valley wound through the hills.*

value 1. *noun* worth, merit, weight, quality, importance, significance *Sugar has no nutritional value.* 2. price, cost *The jeweler placed a value of $350 on the ring.* 3. *verb* appreciate, admire, respect *She values her mother's opinion.* 4. appraise, price, evaluate, assess *The appraiser valued our house at $160,000.*

vanish *verb* disappear, fade, go away, perish, cease to be *Dinosaurs suddenly vanished from the earth 65 million years ago.* appear

vapor *noun* gas, mist, steam, fog, fume, smoke *Trails of water vapor from an airplane's exhaust can be seen high in the sky.*

variable *adjective* changing, fluctuating, unpredictable, unsteady, uncertain *The forecast today is for clear skies and light, variable winds.* constant, unchanging

variety *noun* 1. collection, assortment, selection, mix, array *The museum has a variety of interesting exhibits.* 2. change, diversity, variation *Mom makes certain we have variety in our meals.* 3. kind, type, sort, class, brand, category *The university's agriculture department conducts experiments to see what varieties of plants grow best in our state.*

various *adjective* different, diverse, assorted, several, many *The class discussed various ideas for a fund-raising project.*

vary *verb* change, differ, alter, fluctuate, modify *The weather varies from season to season.*

~~~~~~

vast *adjective* large, immense, great, huge, enormous *The pioneers were brave to venture into the vast, unknown wilderness.* tiny

vault 1. *noun* strong room, treasury, safe, storeroom *The bank vault has heavy steel doors and an alarm.* 2. *verb* jump, leap, spring, bound, hurdle *The horse vaulted over the fence.*

vegetation *noun* plant life, plants, flora, growth, greenery *Deserts have little vegetation.*

vehicle *noun* conveyance, means of transportation *Which vehicle did Dad take, the car or the truck?*

veil 1. *noun* cover, cloak, mask, screen *In some Muslim countries, women are required to wear veils.* 2. *verb* cover, hide, conceal, cloak, obscure *Fog veiled the far shore.* reveal

vein *noun* streak, line, stripe, mark, thread *The marble had veins of green in it.*

velocity *noun* speed, swiftness, quickness *The wind velocity is ten miles per hour.*

vendor *noun* seller, peddler, salesperson, dealer, merchant *She purchased a magazine from the vendor on the corner.* buyer

venom *noun* poison, toxin *It is believed that only 1/14,000 of an ounce of venom from the Australian brown snake is enough to kill a person.*

vent *noun* hole, opening, outlet, duct, passage *I made sure the container I put my caterpillar in had plenty of air vents.*

venture *noun* adventure, project, enterprise, undertaking, experiment, attempt *Mountain climbing is among the riskiest of ventures.*

verbal *adjective* spoken, oral, uttered, voiced, articulated *Gloria gave the class an oral account of her trip to Chile.* written

verdict *noun* decision, judgment, finding, ruling *The jury brought in a verdict of not guilty.*

verify *verb* confirm, prove, validate, support *I checked an encyclopedia to verify the facts in my report.*

versatile *adjective* adaptable, all-around, flexible, many-sided *He's a versatile actor, able to play serious and comedy roles.*

verse *noun* section, passage, part, division, measure *We sang the first verse of the hymn.*

version *noun* account, interpretation, story, understanding, impression *Each witness gave a different version of what happened.*

vertical *adjective* standing, upright, perpendicular, erect *That post isn't vertical—it leans toward the left.* horizontal

very 1. *adverb* extremely, much, exceedingly, greatly *The teacher said she was very impressed with my progress.* 2. *adjective* exact, precise, same, right, identical *That's the very CD I was looking for.*

vessel *noun* 1. container, receptacle, barrel *Wine fermentation is carried out in large, stainless-steel vessels.* 2. boat, ship, craft, liner, freighter, tanker *Many pirate vessels sank in the Caribbean.*

veteran *adjective* experienced, practiced, skilled, professional, expert *The veteran quarterback guided the team to seven consecutive winning seasons.* inexperienced

veto *verb* refuse, deny, block, stop, reject *The president vetoed the legislation and prevented it from becoming law.* accept

vibrate *verb* quiver, shake, tremble, quaver *When a string on a guitar vibrates, it makes a sound.*

vicinity *noun* surrounding area, region, locality, neighborhood *Do you know of a restaurant in the vicinity?*

vicious *adjective* 1. cruel, mean, spiteful, malicious *Why would someone spread such a vicious rumor?* kind 2. ferocious, savage, fierce, dangerous *No one should keep a vicious animal as a pet.* gentle 3. evil, wicked, ruthless, brutal *The dictator was punished for his vicious crimes.* good

victim *noun* casualty, sufferer, injured party, fatality *There were fewer victims of highway accidents this year than last.*

victorious *adjective* successful, winning, triumphant, champion, conquering *The victorious team arrived home to a celebration.* defeated

victory *noun* success, triumph, conquest, win *Alexander the Great won some of the most impressive military victories in history.* defeat

view 1. *noun* look, sight, peek, glimpse, glance, observation *We moved closer to the stage to get a better view.* 2. opinion, idea, belief, attitude, feeling, impression *What's your view of television violence?* 3. outlook, scene, panorama, scenery, vista, picture *The view from our hotel room balcony was great.* 4. *verb* see, look at, observe, behold, watch, regard *We viewed the birds through binoculars.*

vigorous *adjective* strong, healthy, energetic, hearty, robust, active *Our eighty-eight-*

~~~~~~

year-old neighbor is still vigorous enough to work in her garden all afternoon. weak

village *noun* hamlet, small town, rural community *The village has a population of under one thousand.*

villain *noun* scoundrel, rogue, rascal, bad guy, crook, criminal *The villain tied the heroine to the railroad tracks*

violate *verb* break, disobey, disregard, ignore *The driver violated the law by going through a red light.* obey

violence *noun* 1. fury, force, intensity, strength, severity *The hurricane's violence was felt for miles inland.* 2. brutality, savagery, force, cruelty *We are not allowed to watch TV shows that depict violence.*

violent *adjective* 1. intense, strong, severe, powerful *The violent winds knocked down power lines and left thousands without power.* 2. fierce, uncontrolled, unrestrained, raging *Tracy needs to learn to control her violent temper.*

virgin *adjective* pure, spotless, unspoiled, unused, fresh, original *Virgin redwood forests once covered 3,000 square miles of land.*

virtual *adjective* effective, near, essential, practical *Traffic is moving so slowly, it is at a virtual standstill.*

virtue *noun* goodness, decency, morality, integrity, honesty *Voters will respect a candidate of great virtue.* wickedness, dishonesty

visible *adjective* noticeable, perceptible, observable, evident, apparent, obvious *The moon is only visible when it is on your side of the earth. The patient is making visible progress.* concealed

vision *noun* 1. eyesight, sight *She wears contacts to improve her vision.* 2. perception, imagination, insight, farsightedness, forethought *The drafters of the U.S. Constitution had real vision.* 3. dream, idea, image, illusion *She had visions of fame and fortune.*

visit 1. *verb* call on, drop in on, look in on, stay with *Mom invited Aunt Sylvia to visit us.* 2. *noun* call, stay, stopover, trip *Our friends are coming for a visit next week.*

visitor *noun* caller, guest, tourist, sightseer *Yellowstone Park has more than 4 million visitors a year.*

vital *adjective* necessary, essential, fundamental, required, needed, important *Good nutrition is vital to your health.* unimportant

vivid *adjective* 1. bright, brilliant, rich, dazzling, colorful *My walls are painted a vivid blue.* dull 2. clear, distinct, strong, powerful *Dad say seeing the old neighborhood brought back vivid memories of his childhood.* unclear

vocal *adjective* spoken, oral, uttered, voiced, sounded, choral *He prefers vocal music to instrumental music.*

voice 1. *noun* sound, speech, singing, expression *I really like that singer's voice.* 2. *verb* express, verbalize, declare, tell, communicate *You will all have an opportunity to voice your opinions.*

volume *noun* 1. amount, quantity, capacity, content, measure *A cup has a liquid volume of eight ounces.* 2. book, publication, work, writing *Robert Frost's first volume of poetry was published in 1913.* 3. loudness, intensity, sound *Please turn down the volume on the TV.*

voluntary *adjective* elective, discretionary, optional, of one's own free will *There are envelopes at the museum desk for voluntary donations.*

volunteer 1. *noun* unpaid worker *She works as a volunteer at the nursing home.* 2. *adjective* unpaid, voluntary *The village has a volunteer fire department.* 3. *verb* offer, come forward, donate, contribute *Dad has volunteered to help with the library book sale.*

vote 1. *noun* ballot, election, referendum, choice, selection *The vote for class secretary was close.* 2. *verb* cast a ballot, choose, select, elect *Don't forget to vote in the election.*

vow 1. *verb* promise, pledge, guarantee, swear *Knights vowed loyalty to their king.* 2. *noun* promise, pledge, guarantee, oath *Grandma and Grandpa took their wedding vows forty years ago.*

voyage *noun* journey, trip, expedition, tour, cruise, sail *The first voyage around the globe took almost exactly three years.*

vulgar *adjective* coarse, crude, offensive, obscene *No vulgar language is permitted in our house.*

W

wad *noun* lump, mass, hunk, chunk *I got rid of my wad of gum before I got to class.*

 wag *verb* wave, flutter, sway, swing *My dog wagged its tail when it saw me.*

~~~~~~

wage 1. *noun* pay, payment, salary, compensation, fee *He receives a wage of $15 per hour for his work* 2. *verb* conduct, carry on, engage in, pursue *The governor waged a successful campaign against her challenger.*

wail 1. *verb* cry, howl, bawl, weep, moan *My baby brother wails when he's hungry.* 2. *noun* howl, holler, cry, sob, moan *The child let out a wail when she got her shot.*

wait 1. *verb* stay, linger, remain, delay *I had to wait a long time for the bus.* 2. *noun* delay, postponement, pause, interval, break, rest *There is a ten-minute wait for a table.*

wake 1. *verb* awake, get up, rise, stir *I woke when the sun came streaming through my window.* 2. *noun* path, trail, aftermath *The tornado left a wake of destruction.*

walk 1. *verb* step, tread, stroll, amble, hike, march, trek *Doug and I walked home from school together today.* 2. *noun* hike, stroll, amble, trek *Dad took the dog for a walk after dinner.* 3. path, trail, footpath, sidewalk *The walk down to the river is steep.*

wallet *noun* billfold, purse *I never carry much money in my wallet.*

wand *noun* baton, rod, stick, staff *With a flick of her magic wand, she turned the pumpkin into a coach.*

wander *verb* 1. meander, roam, ramble, amble *We wandered through the woods searching for edible mushrooms.* 2. stray, drift, depart, swerve, digress *He wandered off the point and never finished his story.*

want 1. *verb* desire, wish for, long for, hope for, yearn for, crave *What do you want for your birthday?* 2. *noun* need, requirement, desire, wish *Grandma and Grandpa say they have few wants.*

war *noun* conflict, battle, combat, fight, warfare, strife, struggle *Governments say their countries are engaged in a war against terror.* peace

wares *noun* goods, merchandise, products, produce, crafts *Local farmers and craftspeople sell their wares on the town square.*

warm 1. *adjective* balmy, tepid, lukewarm, heated *The cat curled up by the warm fire.* cool, cold 2. friendly, cordial, enthusiastic, affectionate, loving *We received a warm greeting.* cool 3. *verb* heat, warm up, heat up, cook, thaw, thaw out *We warmed some soup for lunch.* cool, cool off

warn *verb* caution, inform, alert, notify, advise *The sign warned us of a detour ahead.*

warning *noun* caution, notice, admonition, advice *Medicines contain warnings of side effects.*

warrior *noun* soldier, fighter, combatant, trooper *Many brave warriors have died in battle.*

wary *adjective* careful, cautious, guarded, suspicious, distrustful *My parents have advised me to be wary of strangers.*

wash 1. *verb* clean, scrub, launder, bathe, rinse, scour *Dad washed his and Mom's cars.* 2. erode, wash away, carry, sweep, transport *The floodwaters washed the topsoil down the river.* 3. *noun* washing, cleaning, scrubbing, shower, shampoo, bath *The curtains are in need of a wash.* 4. laundry, washing, clothes *We took our wash to the Laundromat when our washer broke down.*

waste 1. *verb* squander, use up, throw away, misuse, misspend, exhaust *I wasted time watching TV when I should have been studying.* save 2. wither, weaken, shrivel *Grandma always tells me I should eat more so I don't waste away.* 3. *noun* misuse, squandering, extravagance *The report said that bottled water is a waste of money.* 4. garbage, refuse, rubbish, trash, litter, dregs *The city picks up our waste every Wednesday.*

wasteful *adjective* extravagant, lavish, uneconomical, careless *My sister was wasteful with her allowance this week and asked me for a loan.* frugal

watch 1. *verb* look at, view, observe, regard, gaze at *We watched the game on TV.* 2. guard, protect, mind, tend, care for *I watched my little sister while Mom went to the grocery store.* 3. *noun* clock, timepiece, wristwatch *I forgot to adjust my watch for daylight saving time and thought it was an hour earlier than it was.* 4. guard, lookout *Jan kept watch while the rest of us hid so we could surprise Karen on her birthday.*

watchful *adjective* alert, attentive, vigilant, sharp, close *Be sure to keep a watchful eye on your sister when you cross the street.* inattentive

water *verb* soak, spray, wet, dampen *The houseplants need watering once a week.*

wave 1. *verb* sway, flap, flutter, move, swing *The tall prairie grasses waved in the breeze.* 2. signal, gesture, beckon *I waved good-bye to my brother.* 3. *noun* breaker, surge, swell, roller *Children played in the waves near shore.* 4. gesture, signal, sign *I returned my friend's wave as her train pulled away.*

way *noun* 1. manner, style, fashion, mode *I like the way in which she wears her hair.* 2. means, method, procedure, process *Scientists are looking for new ways to treat disease.* 3. direction, course, route, road, path *Can you tell us the way to Sherman Avenue?* 4. distance, reach, length, stretch *It's a long way between here and the West Coast.* 5. will, wish, desire, choice *My parents don't always let me have my way.*

~~~~~~

weak *adjective* frail, fragile, feeble, powerless, helpless *I felt weak after being sick in bed for three days.* strong

wealth *noun* 1. riches, fortune, money, assets, treasure, prosperity, affluence *He inherited his wealth from his father.* poverty 2. abundance, quantity, profusion, store *The World Wide Web has a wealth of information on nearly any subject.* scarcity

wealthy *adjective* rich, affluent, prosperous, well-off, well-to-do *Many wealthy people donate millions to charity.* poor

wear 1. *verb* dress in, have on, put on, don *I can't decide what to wear today.* 2. deteriorate, corrode, erode, wear away, fray, rub, scuff *I wore holes in the knees of my jeans.* 3. *noun* clothing, apparel, attire, clothes, garments *There's a sale on summer wear at the department store.*

weary 1. *adjective* tired, fatigued, exhausted, worn-out, listless, drained *Mom says she's weary and plans to take it easy this weekend.* lively, energetic 2. *verb* tire, fatigue, wear out, exhaust *The daylong hike wearied us.*

weather 1. *noun* climate, temperature, the elements *Hawaii is known for its mild weather throughout the year.* 2. *verb* erode, corrode, wear, dry, bleach *The driftwood had weathered to a silvery color.* 3. withstand, survive, endure, overcome *The ship weathered the storm.*

weave *verb* 1. braid, intertwine, lace *She is weaving a rug from scraps of cloth.* 2. wind, zigzag, wander *Mom and I wove through the crowd looking for Dad.*

web *noun* cobweb, net, mesh, network *The spider caught a fly in its web.*

wed *verb* marry, join, unite *My parents wed fifteen years ago.*

wedge *verb* jam, force, push, squeeze *She couldn't wedge another thing into her suitcase.*

weep *verb* cry, shed tears, sob, bawl, blubber *My little sister wept when she fell and hurt herself.*

weigh *verb* consider, balance, compare, evaluate, assess *We weighed the features of the two cameras and decided the less expensive one would be fine.*

weight *noun* heaviness, poundage *I've grown taller and gained weight.*

weird *adjective* strange, unusual, odd, bizarre, eerie, spooky *He says he saw weird lights in the sky last night.* normal, ordinary

welcome 1. *verb* greet, receive, meet *They welcomed their guests at the door.* 2. *noun* greeting, reception *We always receive a warm welcome when we visit Grandma and Grandpa.* 3. *adjective* pleasant, appreciated, pleasing, agreeable *Spring flowers are a welcome sight after a long winter.*

welfare *noun* well-being, good, happiness, comfort, interests, prosperity *Uncle Henry called, concerned about our welfare after hearing about the storm we had.*

well 1. *adverb* satisfactorily, nicely, happily, agreeably, fine *Everyone is doing well.* 2. thoroughly, completely, fully *I know the subject well enough to get a good grade.* 3. considerably, substantially *The bake sale brought in well over two hundred dollars.* 4. *adjective* healthy, fit, strong, hale *The patient is well enough to go home.*

wharf *noun* pier, dock, mooring *The ship is unloading at the wharf.*

whim *noun* notion, fancy, impulse, urge *I had a sudden whim to buy presents for my brother and sister.*

whine *verb* cry, whimper, complain, moan *When my brother is sleepy, he begins to whine.*

whip 1. *noun* lash, strap, switch, crop *The wagon driver cracked his whip in the air to get the horses going.* 2. *verb* strike, hit, lash, beat, thrash, flog *The cruel captain whipped his men for the least offense.* 3. defeat, beat, overcome, overwhelm, crush, rout *We whipped the other team in football.*

whirl *verb* spin, turn, wheel, twirl, rotate, pivot *The dancers whirled faster and faster.*

whisk *verb* 1. sweep, brush, flick *He whisked the crumbs from the table.* 2. rush, speed, hurry, hasten, dash, race *The star was whisked away in a limousine.*

whisper 1. *verb* murmur, mumble, mutter, speak softly *The librarian said that if we must talk, please whisper.* 2. *noun* soft voice, murmur, mumble *We spoke in a whisper.*

whole 1. *adjective* complete, total, entire, all, full *We didn't stay for the whole movie—it was terrible.* partial 2. *noun* total, entirety, sum total, aggregate *I've already spent the whole of my allowance.*

wholesome *adjective* healthful, beneficial, nutritious, healthy *Fresh fruits and vegetables are wholesome food.*

wicked *adjective* bad, evil, nasty, vicious, sinful *The wicked witch cast a spell on the princess.* good, kind

wide *adjective* broad, extensive, expansive, roomy, ample, spacious *The highways are wide and relatively straight. Prairie grasses once covered a wide area of the United States.* narrow, cramped

width *noun* breadth, wideness, size, span *The room has a width of twelve feet.*

wife *noun* spouse, mate, married woman *Jerry introduced us to his wife, Sarah.*

wig *noun* hairpiece, toupee *I have to wear a wig to play George Washington in the school play.*

wiggle *verb* squirm, fidget, wriggle, twist, twitch *Our puppy was wiggling so much, I couldn't hold him.*

wild *adjective* 1. untamed, undomesticated, uncultivated, natural, native *The wild carrot is known as Queen Anne's lace.* domesticated, tame 2. unruly, rowdy, undisciplined, disorderly, uncontrollable, violent *Someone called the police after the party next door became wild.* calm

wilderness *noun* undisturbed land, wilds, forest, jungle, desert, wasteland *Millions of acres of wilderness have been preserved in Alaska.*

will 1. *noun* wish, desire, hope, inclination, determination, resolve *The team is doing well because of the players' will to win.* 2. testament, last wishes, legacy, bequest *His will left everything to charity.* 3. *verb* want, wish, desire, determine, resolve *I willed myself to stay awake during the boring lecture.* 4. leave, bequeath, pass down *He willed everything to his children.*

willing *adjective* ready, agreeable, eager, happy *Dana says she's willing to help.* unwilling

wilt *verb* wither, droop, fade, shrivel, dry up *You need to water the plants before they wilt.*

win 1. *verb* triumph, be victorious, prevail, succeed *I know Dad sometimes lets me win at tennis.* lose 2. gain, earn, acquire, obtain, capture *My sister's calf won a blue ribbon at the county fair.* 3. *noun* victory, triumph, success *The team had its first win of the season.* loss

wind 1. *noun* breeze, draft, gust, gale *A strong wind blew down a tree in our yard.* 2. air, breath, respiration *The heavy blow knocked the wind out of him.* 3. *verb* turn, twist, roll, coil *She wound the yarn into a ball.* 4. meander, wander, bend, snake, twist *The stream winds through the hills.*

wipe *verb* rub, clean, mop, wash, brush, dust, scrub, dry *He wiped up the spilled milk.*

wire 1. *noun* cable, filament, cord, line *The electric company is burying its wires along the highway.* 2. *verb* connect, hook up *Our house is wired for cable TV.*

wisdom *noun* common sense, good judgment, knowledge, reason, understanding *Native Americans appreciate the wisdom of their elders.*

wise *adjective* sensible, smart, shrewd, rational, intelligent, bright, knowledgeable, knowing *It was wise to not drive home in this blizzard. She's a wise judge of character.*

wish 1. *noun* desire, longing, hope, fancy, need *She has a wish to travel.* 2. *verb* want, desire, long, yearn *I wish to go home now.*

wit *noun* 1. humor, wittiness, fun, comedy *Her wit made what otherwise might be a dull subject enjoyable.* 2. mind, sense, intelligence *People with quick wits will understand.*

witch *noun* sorceress, magician, enchantress *The good witch Glinda made the ruby slippers appear on Dorothy's feet.*

withdraw *verb* 1. retreat, leave, go, depart, pull back, fall back, retire *The troops have begun to withdraw from the region.* advance 2. remove, take away, deduct, extract *He withdrew money from his checking account.* deposit

wither *verb* shrivel, dry up, wilt, droop, die *The tomato plants withered after the first frost.*

within *preposition* inside, in *Keep the dog within the fenced area.* outside

without *preposition* lacking, missing, short of, needing *Don't leave without your jacket.* with

withstand *verb* endure, bear, resist, oppose, put up with *The settlers withstood the hardship of their first winter.* succumb, give in

witness 1. *noun* observer, onlooker, eyewitness, bystander *The witness gave a statement to the police officer.* 2. *verb* see, observe, view, perceive, watch *Several people claimed to have witnessed a strange, glowing, saucer-shaped object in the sky.*

witty *adjective* clever, funny, humorous, amusing *Mr. Lyons made me laugh with his witty remark.* dull

wizard *noun* sorcerer, magician, enchanter *With a snap of his fingers, the wizard turned the lump of coal into a diamond.*

wobbly *adjective* unsteady, shaky, rickety *Don't sit on that chair—it's wobbly.* steady

woman *noun* female, lady *Do you know the name of the woman in the green dress?*

wonder 1. *noun* marvel, sensation, spectacle, miracle, phenomenon *Of the Seven Wonders of the ancient world, only one, the Great Pyramid, is still standing.* 2. awe, amazement, astonishment, fascination *We gazed in wonder at the spectacular northern lights.* 3. *verb* question, speculate, ponder, think *I wonder what we should do next.*

wonderful *adjective* marvelous, remarkable, astonishing, amazing, incredible *We had a wonderful view of the ocean from our window.* ordinary, plain

wood *noun* lumber, planks, firewood, logs *My brother is splitting wood for our fireplace.*

woods *noun* forest, woodland, bush, grove *Let's take a walk in the woods.*

word 1. *noun* term, expression, name *What's the French word for "hat"?* 2. talk, chat, conversation, discussion *I need to have a word with you.* 3. promise, pledge, assurance, vow *She gave me her word she wouldn't tell anyone.* 4. information, news, notice, report *Do you have any word yet of when they'll be arriving?* 5. *verb* phrase, say, express, state, put into words *She worded her answer very carefully.*

work 1. *verb* labor, toil, endeavor, make an effort, exert oneself *She worked hard as a single mom to care for her family.* 2. function, operate, run, go *My computer isn't working.* 3. be employed, earn a living, do business *He works as a nurse at the hospital.* 4. *noun* labor, toil, drudgery, effort, exertion *Moving all this furniture is work.* 5. employment, job, occupation, profession, career, business, trade *She is looking for work as a chef.* 6. chore, task, duty, responsibility, project *I had makeup work to do when I returned to school after being sick.* 7. creation, composition, artwork, piece, product *Her work will be on display at the gallery.*

workout *noun* exercise, training, weight training, fitness program *He goes to the gym every day for a workout.*

world *noun* 1. earth, globe, planet *Francis Chichester in* Gypsy Moth IV *sailed around the world alone in his fifty-three-foot ketch.* 2. humanity, humankind, the human race *Renewable sources of energy would benefit the world.* 3. great deal, large amount *A world of information is available on the Internet.*

worn *adjective* damaged, tattered, ragged, threadbare, shabby *My favorite jacket is getting a bit worn.*

worry 1. *verb* bother, trouble, distress, upset, concern, agitate, vex *It worries my parents if I stay out late without calling.* soothe, console 2. *noun* anxiety, distress, concern, care, uneasiness *She doesn't want to cause her parents any worry.*

worship 1. *verb* praise, honor, adore, glorify, deify *The Romans worshipped many gods until the Emperor Constantine made Christianity the official religion.* 2. *noun* praise, adoration, glorification, honor *Muhammad forbade the worship of idols.*

worth *noun* merit, value, benefit, importance, usefulness, significance *The lawn mower we bought ten years ago still runs and has proved its worth.*

worthless *adjective* useless, valueless, insignificant, of no use *Our encyclopedia is so out-of-date, it's worthless.* useful

worthy *adjective* deserving, meriting, creditable, commendable, worthwhile *His plan is worthy of further consideration.* unworthy, undeserving

wound 1. *noun* injury, hurt, damage, sore *A doctor should look at that wound.* 2. *verb* hurt, harm, injure, damage, offend *By ignoring her, he wounded her pride.*

wrap *verb* bind, bundle, gift wrap, wrap up, tie up, package *When you've wrapped the package, I'll take it to the post office.* unwrap, open

wreck 1. *verb* destroy, ruin, demolish, break, smash *A hailstorm wrecked many farmers' crops.* 2. *noun* accident, crash, collision, ruin, destruction, devastation *It was fortunate that no one was hurt in the wreck.*

wrench *verb* 1. pull, twist, jerk, tear from, wrest, yank *The wind wrenched the door right out of my hand.* 2. sprain, strain, injure, hurt *She wrenched her ankle when she missed the bottom stair.*

wrestle *verb* struggle, fight, tussle *The puppies have fun wrestling with one another.*

wretched *adjective* miserable, rotten, lousy, bad *Don't go to that restaurant—the food is wretched.*

wring *verb* twist, squeeze, force, press *Wring the water out of the sponge so it'll dry.*

wrinkle 1. *noun* fold, crease, pucker, crinkle *Dad ironed the wrinkles out of his shirt.* 2. *verb* crease, pucker, crinkle, crumple *Linen fabric wrinkles easily.*

write *verb* 1. record, inscribe, mark down, note, jot down *Write your name, address, and phone number in the blanks.* 2. compose, author, create, produce *He writes a daily column for the newspaper.*

wrong 1. *adjective* incorrect, inaccurate, mistaken, untrue, false *I think I picked the wrong answer for the second question on the test.* right, correct 2. bad, evil, wicked, nasty *It is wrong to mistreat animals.* good 3. inappropriate, unsuitable, unacceptable, unfit, improper *It's wrong to interrupt people when they're talking.* proper 4. defective, faulty, damaged, amiss *There's something wrong with the gears on my bike.* 5. *adverb* incorrectly, inaccurately, improperly *I guessed wrong on the second question.* correctly 6. *noun* bad, evil, harm, injury, offense, crime *Some people don't know right from wrong.* right, good 7. *verb* harm, injure, hurt, mistreat, insult *You wronged him when you talked about him behind his back.*

X

X-ray 1. *noun* image, photograph, picture *The doctor says the X-ray shows that my wrist is broken.* 2. *verb* photograph, film *The dentist X-rayed my teeth for cavities.*

Y

yacht *noun* boat, ship, cabin cruiser, sailboat, sailing yacht *Mr. Pearson invited us aboard his yacht.*

yank 1. *verb* jerk, pull, wrench, tug *The puppy yanked at my pants leg.* 2. *noun* pull, tug, wrench, jerk, heave *When I gave the rope a yank, it came loose and I fell over backward.*

yard *noun* backyard, lawn, grounds, courtyard *The kids are in the yard playing.*

yarn *noun* 1. wool, fiber, thread, strand *She bought yarn to knit a scarf.* 2. story, tale, fable, anecdote *The elderly sea captain liked to tell yarns about his adventures at sea.*

yearn *verb* desire, long, pine, wish, want *Grandma yearns to see the mountain village in Italy that her family came from.*

yell 1. *verb* shout, cry out, call, holler *Mom yelled up the stairs that Danny was here to see me.* 2. *noun* shout, cry, call, holler *A passerby heard her yells for help and saved her from drowning.*

yet 1. *adverb* until now, so far, up to now *He hasn't phoned yet.* 2. *conjunction* but, however, still *I'm doing all right in school, yet I could do better.*

yield *verb* 1. produce, bear, provide, supply, furnish *The orchard yields more fruit than we can eat.* 2. surrender, give in, submit, succumb *I yielded to my parents' wishes and stayed in tonight.*

yoke *verb* harness, join, hitch, tie *The farmer yoked the oxen to the plow.*

young 1. *adjective* youthful, immature, adolescent, juvenile *I'm too young to drive.* 2. *noun* offspring, children, babies, brood *Our mother cat takes good care of her young.*

youngster *noun* child, youth, boy, girl, adolescent, juvenile *Ms. Arnold has ten youngsters in her preschool.*

youth *noun* 1. childhood, boyhood, girlhood, adolescence *Dad claims Mom had lots of boyfriends in her youth.* 2. adolescent, teenager, juvenile, minor, child *As a youth, Dad spent summers working on his parents' farm.*

youthful *adjective* young, juvenile, childish, boyish, girlish *My parents say I sometimes have too much youthful energy.*

yowl 1. *verb* cry, howl, yell, wail, shriek, scream *He yowled in pain when he bumped his elbow.* 2. *noun* howl, yell, wail, screech, shriek, scream *The cats' yowls outside my window woke me up.*

Z

zenith *noun* peak, summit, pinnacle, top, apex *At its zenith, the Roman Empire extended from Persia across Europe to Britain.* bottom, base

zero *noun* nothing, naught, nil, none *Ten minus ten is zero.*

zest *noun* spice, flavor, tang, taste *Hot peppers on pizza give it extra zest.*

zone *noun* region, area, territory, district, vicinity, neighborhood *The city received funds to renovate the downtown business zone.*

zoom *verb* speed, race, shoot, zip, whiz, fly *The police car zoomed past us.*